HUMAN RESOURCE MANAGEMENT

for

Higher Awards

HUMAN RESOURCE MANAGEMENT

for

Higher Awards

Rob Dransfield • Steph Howkins
Frank Hudson • Wendy Davies

Heinemann Educational Publishers
Halley Court, Jordan Hill, Oxford OX2 8EJ
a division of Reed Educational & Professional Publishing Ltd

OXFORD MELBOURNE AUCKLAND
JOHANNESBURG BLANTYRE GABORONE
IBADAN PORTSMOUTH (NH) USA CHICAGO

© Rob Dransfield, Steph Howkins, Wendy Davies,
Frank Hudson 1996

First published 1996
99 98   10 9 8 7 6 5 4 3 2
A catalogue record for this book is available from the British
Library on request.

ISBN 0 435 455281
Designed by Roger Denning
Typeset by TechType, Abingdon, Oxon
Printed and bound at The Bath Press, Bath

Acknowledgements

We would particularly like to thank Ken Onion, Malcolm Plant,
Alan Morris, Connie Marsh and Mike O'Neill, who created the
course at Nottingham Trent University out of which this book
developed – and of course the students themselves.

We are also appreciative of the encouragement, support and skill
of the editorial team at Heinemann – Margaret Berriman, Jan
Nikolic and Ros Bass.

Also our thanks go to Caroline Liddel, Anne Lyons, Paula Clay,
Andrea Harmer, John Barnes, Alan Field, Derek Smith, Dave
Needham, Laura Schuster, Bryan Oakes and the library staff at
the Nottingham Trent University.

Frank Hudson would like to thank his wife and family for their
support and patience.

Wendy Davies would especially like to thank Simon for his
support and expert guidance throughout, and her family and
friends for their valuable contributions and continuous
encouragement.

The authors and publishers would like to thank the following for
their permission to reproduce photographs:

Allsport (Stu Forster)
Camerapress
Trevor J. Hill
Chris Honeywell
Science Photo Library
Andrew Wiard
ZEFA (M. A. Keller and S. Javelberg)

Crown copyright material reproduced with the permission of the
Controller of HMSO.

Preface

There can be no doubt that human resource management is the most important aspect of business decision-making today. In this text we have set out to illuminate the key features of HRM and the main points in the debate that surrounds it.

In particular, we have placed very strong emphasis on the fact that the world of work is changing and will continue to change in the foreseeable future, to reflect technological, political, economic and social conditions.

This book provides comprehensive coverage of HRM issues for managers and university students alike. Our text is focused on the requirements of HND and HNC courses in Business, and professional qualifications in Personnel Management including IPM Higher courses. The book systematically and comprehensively covers the BTEC HND/C Human Resource core and option units.

Many of the approaches to learning used in this book were developed as part of a B.A. course at Nottingham Trent University, in which we were preparing students for work in broad vocational areas involving the development of the skills, knowledge and attitudes appropriate to human resource management. We are confident that the resulting text will prove highly relevant and useful to all students and managers in the human resource field.

Rob Dransfield
Steph Howkins
Wendy Davies
Frank Hudson

October 1996

Contents

Introduction

1 The changing world of work

In this opening chapter we provide an introduction to some of the key issues which dominate the human resource management debate. Today we live in a world of rapid and unpredictable change. Human resource management helps to shape and is shaped by this environment of change. It is essential to take stock of this changing world of work before examining the detail of human resource management.

An environment of change

'A lot of fellows nowadays have a BA, MD or PhD. Unfortunately they don't have a JOB.'

    – Fats Domino.

Any text which purports to explore human resource management today must start by examining the changing world of work. Today, more than ever, organisations operate in an environment of change. These environmental changes necessarily shape the way in which organisations manage their resources. As we move into the twenty-first century, organisations stand or fall on the relationship they are able to build with their people – i.e. their human resources.

Like it or not, the world of work in this and many other developed countries has changed and will continue to change. Many people do not like it. We hear frequent complaints about the loss of manufacturing, the loss of job security, the erosion of craft skills, the replacement of full-time jobs by part-time ones, etc. We all need to face the reality that the future is uncertain and therefore it is necessary to develop the skills, knowledge and attitudes to cope with this period of change.

Figure 1.1   The changing world of work

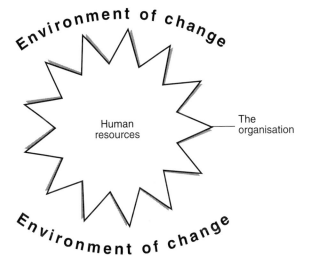

The authors would like to thank Cecilia McNicholas for her work on this chapter

One of the major issues facing us all is the extent to which preparing for and coping with these changes is the responsibility of individuals, organisations, or society as a whole. In recent years the responsibility for preparing for the future has increasingly been placed on individuals. In their paper *Flexible Labour Markets: Who Pays for Training?*, the CBI argued that:

> 'By the year 2000 it is possible that only half the UK's workforce will be in full-time, permanent positions. Flexible workers may lose out by getting trapped in a cycle of low-skill, low-pay and low-security jobs. The government has put the ball firmly in the individual's court.'

At the launch of the CBI paper, the employment minister, James Paice, stated:

> 'People are at the heart of our competitiveness and future prosperity, but for too long many have seen education and training as something which just happens to them. That attitude needs to change. People are responsible for their own futures.'

Clearly, this perspective is one which is at odds with the social democracies which lie at the core of the European Union and with that of our own Labour Party. Social democratic governments favour a partnership approach in which international and national government bodies, organisations, trade unions, and individual employees manage change through co-operation and shared initiatives.

Causes of change in the world of work

The days of jobs for life (if they ever existed) are now behind us. Instead, we find ourselves in a situation in which those who are most able and skilled are able to command high-paying jobs, with relative security, while those who are less able or less skilled are left to fend for themselves. Clearly a major causal factor, in this country at least, has been the creation of a way of thinking which stresses the importance of the free market and one's ability to sell labour services in this market, i.e. employability. However, it would be foolish to argue that this is simply a problem in the UK.

Today, unemployment in Europe is an everyday reality for many people. In late June 1996, there were about 18.1 million jobless people or close to 11 per cent of the active population in Europe.

In an incisive analysis of Europe's labour problems, Jean-Paul Fitoussi, one of France's best known economists,

wrote recently that 'Work was a project for the future, matched by career prospects.' Today this possibility has moved further and further into the mists of time. Increasingly organisations are looking to be leaner and fitter and this means that the notion of 'jobs for life' is disappearing. The concept of **job security** has increasingly been replaced by that of **employability.** Individuals have to continually prove their worth to an organisation.

Thierry Naudin, the Economics Editor of *The European*, places the blame for the increasing numbers of jobless people on the breakdown of established patterns. In February 1996 he argued that:

> 'The culprit is, once again, the breakdown of the old model that stood Europeans in such good stead for the three decades that followed the end of the Second World War. The model consisted of a series of tacit compromises between governments, entrepreneurs, trade unions and the public at large. These kept every participant secure in the knowledge that the benefits of this unprecedented period of high growth on the back of post-war reconstruction would be fairly shared among them.'

One of these compromises was that as young people began their professional lives they were offered wages that did not match their productivity, but they were looked after and received training from a benevolent employer. The difference between the young person's pay slip and what it should have been was put towards two good uses. The short-term benefit was training, which helped to give firms a competitive edge as well as to create a sense of social stability for those employees requiring employment in new fields such as office work or on the shop floor. The longer-term benefit was that young people knew at the end of their working lives they would benefit from a secure pension.

Unfortunately this **consensual model** has been abandoned as firms and governments have increasingly sought to adjust staff levels to their short-term needs and have tended to resort more and more to temporary work. Employees are all too aware of the shortness of short-term contracts. Young people in the workplace are no longer prepared to work for 'peanuts' when they know that their jobs are no longer for life, and firms have cut back on training. The young have therefore become too expensive, and the old also look overpriced. The only security is for those who have today's skills coupled with a willingness to work hours which sap health and destroy the quality of family life.

The name of the game for most (if not all) large organisations in the 1990s has been that of **delayering.** Stripping out layers from organisational structures inevitably involves getting rid of people and also requires the development of new skills for those that remain working in the organisations.

Jobs that are needed in delayered organisations require increasing skill levels such as the ability to work with **information technology**, the ability to **communicate** clearly, and the ability to **work well with others**. Today, there are fewer and fewer secure jobs, and people with jobs have to change what they do throughout their working lives. As Charles Handy has written in his key work *The Empty Raincoat*:

> *'Businesses prefer half as many people, paid twice as well and producing three times as much.'*

There are a number of interrelated factors leading to this delayering process: decline of manufacturing; development of the global marketplace; increased competition from developing economies; the influence of information technology; and demographic changes. We look at these in more detail below.

Decline of manufacturing

The proportion of those employed in industry fell from 36 per cent to 28 per cent of the workforce between 1981 and 1991. In manufacturing, employment fell faster still and is now well below 20 per cent of the workforce. Work carried out by the Institute for Employment Research (1995) has led them to forecast that, over the 1994–2001 period as a whole, manufacturing is expected to lose 200 000 jobs from its total. This implies a significant slow down in the loss of jobs from manufacturing. Between 1994 and 2001 the projected fall is 4 per cent; this is only around one-quarter of the rate of decline seen during most of the 1970s, 1980s and the first part of the 1990s. This situation of decline is typical of all modern industrial economies. In January 1994, Richard Brown and DeAnne Julius argued in the *Amex Bank Review* that employment in manufacturing could drop to 10 per cent of the total workforce or below in modern industrial countries during the next 30 years. Fortunately, this country is well in advance of some of its rivals such as Germany in the restructuring process. However, it is important to remember that many of the organisations that have restructured are the tall industrial companies which for decades offered secure employment to people and provide the lifeblood of many 'regional economies'.

The development of the global market place

Today business organisations increasingly operate in global markets. For example, the Coca-Cola trademark is recognised by 94 per cent of the earth's population and Coca-Cola is the second most universally understood phrase after OK.

Companies like Coca-Cola, Shell, Mars, Peugeot, etc. operate in global markets and are able to produce vast quantities of products at very low prices. Only the most successful can be sure of their long-term future. In recent times they have seen the need to be lean and fit with highly flexible people if they are to prevent rivals from stealing a march on them. Global corporations seek to reduce uncertainty in an age of uncertainty. The global economy has a potential for chaos; as Paul Hurst and Grahame Thompson have argued, 'the populations of even successful and advanced states and regions [are] at the mercy of autonomous and uncontrollable … global forces'.

The lifespan of industries and organisations is constantly decreasing as they struggle to change quickly enough to survive. Corporate restructuring has become intense, driven by more competitive global markets, privatisation and technology which have all conspired to create both less and differently shaped work. Many of the more aggressive companies now employ significantly fewer people and more younger people than older, thus creating an early exit culture with limited career expectancy.

The growth of the new economic powerhouses

The Japanese economy has been one of the great success stories of the post-war world. Today most of the fastest growing economies are in the Pacific Rim area and include countries such as South Korea, Malaysia and Thailand which are increasingly taking an important share of world trade.

The Pacific Rim is made up of millions of people whose incomes are increasing (particularly for people living in urban areas). Here, markets are developing for branded goods such as Johnny Walker whisky, Chanel No. 5 perfume etc. However, these countries are also manufacturing and exporting their own high-quality branded products, such as motor vehicles. Increasingly these economies are coming to develop a competitive edge in consumer product markets.

The key role of information technology

Information technology (IT) lies at the heart of modern organisations and also provides a driving force for change. Information technology makes it possible to empower project teams, thus seeing off the tall bureaucratic company of the past. IT applications are able to replace millions of routine tasks, so that many non-skilled and partly skilled employees are no longer required.

There are two economic views on technology. One approach is that advanced technology makes it possible to do more tasks with fewer people, i.e. a drive towards greater efficiency. This leads to falling costs and prices, releasing increased spending power which helps to create new jobs in new growth sectors. An alternative view is what is known as the '**lump of labour theory**', which assumes that there is a fixed amount of work to be done and, if fewer people are required to do it, this will lead to more unemployment.

Demographic changes

One of the most significant demographic changes today is the ageing of the population. This has many implications for business. On the one hand it means that there is a bigger demand for the products that older people buy.

On the other, it means that there are fewer people available to work, and that those people who are in work have to support an increasingly large dependent population. It is forecast that from 1995–2010 there will be a 28 per cent rise in 55–64-year-olds and a 22 per cent fall in 25–34-year-olds. The growth in part-time work means that conventional retirement as we understand it will also disappear. The over-50s will find they are being courted for their experience and expertise.

A flexible response

In response to these changes, businesses are increasingly adopting more flexible working patterns. The flexible firm model has been put into practice by many large organisations in the public and private sectors. The flexible firm distinguishes between:

- *Core workers.* These are employees who are multi-skilled, work full-time and who receive good pay, conditions and benefits.
- *Peripheral workers.* These are short-term, temporary and part-time workers, who receive less favourable pay, conditions and benefits.
- *External workers.* These are not employees of the firm, e.g. agency temps, workers in contracted-out services and the self-employed.

The flexible firm cuts its labour costs to a minimum by limiting core workers relative to peripheral and external workers (see Figure 1.2).

Figure 1.2 The shrinking core of a flexible firm

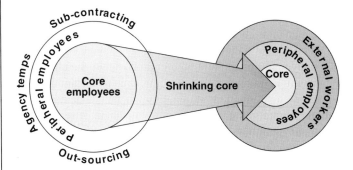

The core worker of the past was someone with considerable job security who operated within a consensual model in which firm and employee showed a good measure of loyalty to each other (although there were many exceptions). Today, the core worker is someone that is privileged in terms of status, pay and conditions, but may work extremely long hours, in very tense and stressful conditions.

The flexible firm **contracts out** non-core work whenever possible. For example, there is no need for a large business organisation to take responsibility for transporting all of its inputs and outputs, to produce all of its own advertising materials and to undertake many other functions which can be delegated to outside agencies. Contracting out can help to reduce the size of an organisation, reduce central costs and increase operational efficiency.

Shell UK typifies this process as it has gone through a period of **downsizing** during the 1990s. For example, in its public relations department, instead of employing large numbers of graphic designers, artists, photographers, etc., it has increasingly turned towards buying in these services as and when required, often from former Shell public relations department employees. In the North Sea drilling operations it began to contract out operations to private firms who would, for example, provide crews to man drilling operations.

In the public sector, contracting out has been the order of the day. For example, in the BBC many programmes are now produced and made by outside contractors who sell their products to the BBC (which is thus able to reduce its operating costs and the size of the organisation to a manageable core).

This practice has become commonplace in all types of organisation. In an obituary for the musician Frank Zappa, I remember reading that Zappa abandoned his policy of employing a large number of musicians on full-time contracts when he saw a celebrated American jazz band leader having to empty his pockets to pay the wages of his large group of hungry full-time musicians who were on an ongoing contract, leaving nothing for their employer and 'star performer'.

The growth of female employment

In analysing the response of organisations to the changing environment in which they operate, it is important to highlight the spread of female employment. The move by organisations to employ increasing numbers of females in the workplace has been one of the most significant changes in the world of work.

In 1985 the number of men in employment (full-time and part-time) exceeded the number of women by more than 45 per cent – 13.1 million compared with 9.4 million. In May 1993 the figure was 10.7 million men compared with 10.1 million women.

Recent research by the Institute for Employment Research (1995) indicates that women will increasingly come to dominate employment, as will the proportion of employees working part-time (see Figure 1.3).

Between 1994 and 2001 male employment is likely to see only a slight rise (around 3 per cent), while female

Figure 1.3   Trends in employment 1994–2001 (UK)

	1994 %	2001 %
Increased involvement of women		
Female share of total employment	45.8	47.6
Female share of employees in employment	48.9	51.2
More working part-time		
Part-time share of employees in employment	28	32.4

employment will increase more quickly (an extra 11 per cent). The rise in male employment, largely due to the faster growth in overall employment, is a reversal of recent trends of falling male employment. Part-time employment is projected to increase by 22 per cent at the same time as full-time employees decrease in number by 1 per cent. Self-employment will also increase considerably, by 13 per cent.

Current evidence shows that women are less likely to be core workers, more of them being part-time peripheral workers. Almost half the women are in part-time jobs. Large numbers of these, and a large percentage of their colleagues in full-time work, are, by any standards, low paid.

The expansion of part-time and short contract work

Part-time and short contract work have become an increasingly common feature of many different types of employment, such as fast food restaurants, supermarket work, and even teaching. Flexible contracts of employment may only be for a short period of time.

For example, in July 1994 *The Times Educational Supplement* reported that 51 000 teachers in England and Wales were on fixed-term contracts. Many of these contracts were limited to one year, while others were for less than a term's work. This figure accounted for 8.6 per cent of the teaching force, compared with 4.6 per cent in 1983. This trend has continued in the second half of the 1990s.

The principal cause of this huge growth is the local management of schools, coupled with less money being available for education. Head teachers and governors, worried by the prospect of not being able to balance their books if pupil numbers fall, are hedging their bets and creating what they consider to be an easily disposable category of teacher.

In May 1996 the research organisation Mintel reported that Britain will move to a **24-hour culture** in the next century, with the familiar nine-to-five routine disappearing. We have already moved in this direction with, for example, the success of First Direct's 24-hour telephone banking and branches of Tesco opening 12 hours a day, coupled with the 24-hour approach of continuous process manufacturing, e.g. in food processing. There will be more work in early evenings and early mornings as the economy shifts towards a 24-hour day. In the next century there will be an increase in jobs for managers and administrators – particularly in service industries and retailing. Those on the way out are clerical and secretarial jobs, as workers increasingly use their own computers.

Types of flexibility

In the first half of the 1990s **flexibility** became management's new mantra, with many companies taking what they saw as a creative approach to their staffing needs – dismissing all but the core members of their staff and, instead, making use of agency workers and the self-employed. A number of approaches to flexibility were employed, including:

■ *Numerical flexibility.* This is where a firm is able to adjust the number of workers or number of hours worked depending on the demand for goods and services. Typically employees in such a system are part-time and temporary workers. For example, large supermarket chains often vary the number of hours for which employees are employed each week depending on the profit figures in the previous week.

■ *Hours flexibility.* Time flexibility is a variation of numerical flexibility, involving changing the number of hours worked from day to day or from week to week.
■ *Job flexibility.* Employees are increasingly expected to be multi-skilled. Instead of just doing one routine task at work, employees are expected to be able to switch quickly to doing something else. For example, a supermarket till operator could be expected to change to shelf stacking or cleaning up a spillage on the floor as and when required.
■ *Hot desking.* Today many employees share the same desk, with information technology providing a key link in the hot-desking process. Staff are able to work from home or other out-of-office locations so that they only require their desk for a small part of the working week.

Case Study

Zero-hours contracts

In 1995 the national newspapers widely reported a story about a 17-year-old Glasgow student who was told to clock off during slack periods and hang around, unpaid, until custom picked up. As part of the payment system, he often received £1 for a five-hour shift. He was working the notorious zero-hours contract in which pay depends directly on demand in a place of work.

Questions for discussion

1   *What do you think of the zero-hours contract?*
2   *Why do you think the firm used such a system?*
3   *Should firms be allowed to use such systems?*

Responses and attitudes to flexible conditions

The first half of the 1990s was characterised by the acceptance of conventional wisdom that flexibility was a good thing. It seems likely that the second half of the 1990s will be characterised by a reaction against these ideas. While a Mintel survey in May 1996 revealed that 70 per cent of employees prefer being part of a flexible workforce and managing their own timetable, depression and insecurity continue to dog the worker in the 'nervous nineties'. Four out of five workers believe that a job for life no longer exists and a growing number now believe job security is more important than money.

Some commentators argue that job insecurity has gained increasing media attention in the mid 1990s as it has begun to take an increasing toll on 'M people', i.e. middle-class, middle-aged men. Women have always had a higher rate of job turnover, as have the young and the old. During the mid-1990s there have been substantial redundancies for all sectors of the workforce.

A number of commentators have also pointed out that administrative jobs are likely to disappear as part of the information technology revolution, just as manufacturing jobs have disappeared before them. What is not clear is the extent to which new jobs will be created in the early part of the next century.

What *is* clear is that people who keep jobs in big organisations often have to work harder. In his book *The Empty Raincoat*, Charles Handy quotes the case of a young friend whose company expects him to work until

9 p.m. every evening and most Saturdays. His neglected partner complains:

> *'It's a crazy system … Why don't they employ twice as many people at half the salary and work them half as hard? That way they could live a normal life.'*

However, Handy goes on to say that this is not the way in which companies work. He quotes the chairperson of a pharmaceuticals company who told him that his policy was the other way round – 'half $\times 2 \times 3 = P$' – half as many people at the core of the business, paid twice as well and producing three times as much, that is what equals **productivity** and **profit**.

Case Study
The dangers of long hours

A report in 1995 entitled *The Family Friendly Workplace* criticised long hours in Britain. It stated that family life is under threat from increased stress at work, with women coming off worse. Nearly three times as many women as men in office jobs are divorced or separated. The report, which examined the lives of 1350 office employees, stated that long hours are becoming typical. Two-thirds worked 40 hours or more per week and a quarter worked 50 hours or more.

More than half of all white-collar workers felt that long hours were a firm feature of their workplace, while many said they felt under pressure from bosses to work longer hours than contracted. People are working in delayered organisations and they are insecure about job prospects. There is a lot more job insecurity and employees need to be seen to be doing whatever hours are necessary. More than three-quarters of the people in the survey said

that continually working long hours affected them physically. In 1994 almost eight working days per worker were lost due to sick leave.

Questions for discussion

1 *Why do you think that people are working longer hours in many organisations today?*
2 *Do you think this is good for*
   a *the organization*
   b *the employees*
   c *family life?*

Changing perspectives

Too late for many of those that lost their jobs in the early 1990s the conventional wisdom is now moving against the stripped-down corporation.

In May 1996 Stephen S. Roach, Wall Street's leading guru of 'downsizing' declared that he had changed his mind and that relentless cost-cutting was bad for business. His new perspective is that

> *'If you compete by building, you have a future … the pendulum will swing from capital back to labour'. Companies will have to hire more workers, pay them better, and treat them better.'*

In saying this he was merely echoing what a lot of people in business had come to realise for a long time. Findings from research initiated by Roffey Park Management Institute have shown that as few as 1 per cent of employees within a flatter structure are showing the behaviours and characteristics that will make that structure work. The old habits, work patterns, people and bureaucracy remain. The solution for a number of organisations may be to put back in some of the layers of management that they have removed.

The changing workplace

A contrast is often made between organisations that behave like **machines** and those that behave like **people.**

A 'machine company' aims at the maximisation of profit through the most efficient conversion of raw materials into sellable products and services. Its assets – property, equipment and personnel – are deployed in the way that best meets this aim. When it appears that the aim is not being met, the company liquidates itself, converts what assets it can into cash and returns the value to the owners.

However, it is a fact that companies rarely behave like machines. They tend to behave like people. They want to be liked. They develop a personality which transcends the particular products and services they produce and sell. Above all, they want to survive.

The need to be liked and the urge to survive sometimes clash, as when, in order to survive, a company finds it necessary to shed staff. In such circumstances, the need to be liked may encourage the company to treat the employees it proposes to discard with even greater consideration.

A family business is the most obvious example of a 'people company'. What counts is the family who runs it. For their continuing success, family companies require a succession of talented sons and daughters, followed by talented grandsons and granddaughters and so on. But heredity cannot be trusted and family companies tend to be taken over by talented outsiders.

Nonetheless, the ideal of the family company, with staff treated as **members,** lives on, even if the levels of qualifications necessary for continued membership is constantly rising. Such a company will be more likely to enjoy employee loyalty.

Loyalty in a sense can be bought. The 'machine company' that pays the best wages and salaries can expect its employees to continue working for its best interests. But in times of difficulty when the wages and salaries fall, so does the loyalty, and the company suffers. The 'person company' is better placed. Even in prosperity, it will tend to do better than the 'machine' company. People are people, they are not machines. They will generally prefer to work in a company which genuinely cares for its staff.

In this book we set out to show that **human resource management** (HRM) is an essential approach for successful organisations today. HRM is concerned with developing individuals within an organisation so that their needs are met and their interests are reflected in the way the organisation operates and functions. As we shall see in later chapters, HRM has led to the development of a variety of new working practices such as the creation of self-managing teams, total quality management, appraisal, and many other practices which reflect the philosophy of the 'people company'. Many successful organisations have had to transform the way in which they are structured in order to create customer-focused teams – a process which is frequently referred to as **business process redesign** (BPR). Typical features of BPR are:

- The organisation focuses on satisfying consumers or other stakeholders. Process teams work to this end.
- The organisation is redesigned so that teams of people from different specialisations work together on shared projects which are customer focused.
- BPR involves continuous improvement and change rather than standing still.

- Information technology plays a crucial part in **enabling** the process of redesign and the operation of teams.
- Human resources are at the heart of 'people organisations' based on BPR.
- BPR will only be successful if managements are committed to it.

New ways of working

Gone are the days of the 'top-down' hierarchical company in which information flowed down through various layers of the organisation. Today organisations are structured around groups of employees focusing on complete processes which are designed to meet the needs of consumers.

Figure 1.4a Traditional hierarchical structure – the old way

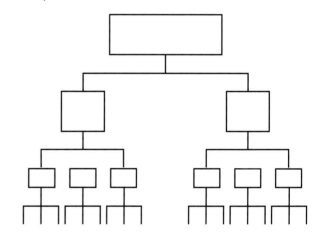

Figure 1.4b Group structure – the new way to view an organisation

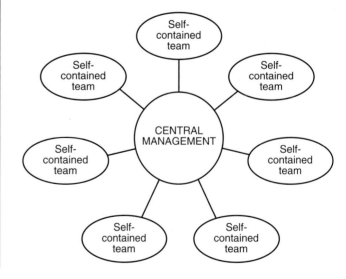

In this new way of viewing an organisation, self-contained teams are responsible for a specific part of the business or a particular project. They work to targets set by central management. They take advice and assistance, as necessary, from specialist departments such as Research and Development, Finance, Personnel and Public Relations – although sometimes they have their own specialists. They also take goods and services from outside suppliers when these are judged to be more cost-effective. Occasionally, central management, or one of its teams, may decide to subcontract an entire project to an outside supplier.

Employability

If the fashion today is to have human-resource-focused organisations based on teamwork, it is worth asking: what sort of people will inhabit these new organisations? That is, what sort of person will be employed by them?

In the new workplace of today, employees require different skills to those that were important in the past. 'People companies' require people with 'people skills' in addition to other job-related skills.

The idea of employability is central to the future prospects of individual employees. Individuals need to have the kinds of skills which are required by modern organisations, where an increasing emphasis is placed on individual initiative.

While there is a consistent call from employers that employees should have the abilities required of a modern workforce, it is by no means clear what these requirements are. For example, Graham Hoyle, the Chair of the TEC National Council Foundation Learning Group, has recently suggested that young people should be **work-ready.** He used this term in preference to the more commonly used 'core skills', a term which he feels has come to mean everything to everyone with little testing for common understanding. However, while the term 'work-ready' is a useful concept, it lacks any definition.

In contrast, there have been more sophisticated attempts to define the sorts of skills that are required. For example, the Skills and Enterprise Network in their 1996–7 report have set out a three-way classification of skills:

- *Core skills.* These are very general skills needed in almost any job. They include basic literacy and numeracy and a range of personal transferable skills such as the ability to work well with others, communication skills, self-motivation, the ability to organise one's own work and, often, a basic capability to use information technology.
- *Vocational skills.* These are needed in particular occupations or groups of occupations but are less

useful outside these areas. They are highly transferable. An example is a basic ability to use common computer packages.
- *Job specific skills.* These are skills whose usefulness is limited to a much narrower field of employment.

Quite clearly, we have seen a shift in the pattern of demand for employees. Today we require fewer people with basic manual skills and more people with the ability to work with others, to communicate with others, to show independence and to work with new forms of technology (in particular information technology). It is therefore important to examine briefly the current occupational trends, in order to get a clearer picture of employment demands.

Important occupational trends

Key occupational trends in recent times have been the move towards higher-level occupations and away from manual jobs, particularly lower-skilled ones. The fastest growing areas will continue to be in managerial and professional jobs, despite the recent trend for many middle management posts to disappear in delayering processes. The Institute for Employment Research has recently forecast that, by the year 2001, managerial and administrative, professional and associate professional, and technical occupations will account for 39 per cent of all employment. Women are expected to take 63 per cent of the additional higher-level jobs.

In most areas of the economy, newly qualified trainees will be required to replace those leaving the workforce. At the same time work itself is now requiring increased skills – a process referred to as **upskilling.** The Employment in Britain Survey identified that between 1986 and 1992 individuals saying their jobs required no or low-level qualifications declined by one-fifth, while those requiring Advanced Level or Higher qualifications had risen by a quarter. Evidence suggests that even in traditional jobs there is a shift away from skills associated with manual dexterity towards those associated with the understanding and monitoring of complex systems.

Skill needs

In recent years employers have increasingly identified communication, interpersonal (including teamworking) and personal (including taking responsibility) skills, as well as literacy and numeracy, as being essential elements of 'work-readiness'. The growth of personal services and customer-focused selling have led to an increase in the importance of interpersonal skills.

Recent years have seen some signs of progress in the growth of educational and vocational qualifications in the labour force. For example, in the Summer of 1994, 40 per cent of employed workers in the UK were qualified to NVQ level 3 or its academic equivalent (two A Levels or a GNVQ Advanced Full Award).

The increasing and changing demand for skills means that most workers should be updating and upgrading their skills regularly. In the late 1980s there was a major increase in job-related training. This trend has again increased in the mid-1990s after falling off during the recession. Commitment to training appears to be a cyclical process depending on the fortunes of the economy.

Many commentators in the United Kingdom feel that if we can improve our education and training then the output of goods and services will be increased because employees will become more productive.

The benefits of flexible solutions

In the increasingly competitive environment in which we operate today, it seems inevitable that we are going to have to look increasingly to flexible solutions in the labour market. In order to see how this situation has arisen, it is helpful to make a brief study of employment patterns in this country.

For approximately 20 years prior to the Second World War, unemployment had averaged at least 10 per cent. The war effort fully employed all our resources and in 1944 the government published a White Paper pledging the maintenance of full employment after the war. The will to provide this was matched by the means, as stated in the White Paper:

'The government accepts as one of their primary aims and responsibilities the maintenance of a high and stable level of employment after the war … total expenditure must be prevented from falling to a level where general unemployment appears.'

For the next 25 years, unemployment averaged only 1.8 per cent. However, a major concern over the policy of maintaining full employment was that it was accompanied by inflation.

In recent years we have seen the resurgence of high unemployment. In the UK, the 1990s have been characterised by unemployment at well over 2 million people. Today unemployment is a problem confronting most industrialised countries.

There are many explanations of how unemployment is caused. One cause of unemployment may be downswings in the trade cycle, i.e. periods of **recession.** In a period of recession, spending, income, outputs and thus employment will all fall. Another explanation of widescale unemployment refers to **structural unemployment.** Structural unemployment arises from longer-term changes in the economy, affecting specific industries, regions and occupations. For example, the coal industry in regions such as Central Scotland, South Yorkshire and the East Midlands has been in decline for a number of years because of the development of substitute fuels such as gas, oil and electricity and the import of cheap coal from Australia, Nigeria, Russia and other places. Changes in demand for products like coal, steel, shipbuilding, textiles, shoes and fish lead to structural unemployment. The effects of structural unemployment can be reduced if:

- people move away from the declining industries and areas and into the new expanding areas and new jobs which are being created
- people are increasingly flexible – able to employ new skills that are required, to replace the old skills which are less in demand
- there are fewer obstructions to flexibility in labour markets.

These changes tend not to occur smoothly, however, so the economy suffers from structural problems and hence, structural unemployment is a major cause of unemployment.

Some commentators argue that the UK has benefited in recent times from adopting increasingly flexible labour markets. For example, people are often surprised that we are not further behind in our productivity compared with rival economies. In 1990 our national output per head was 87 per cent of that in the former West Germany and 92 per cent of that in France. One explanation of the relatively small gap is that workers in this country work longer hours. There is evidence that, because Britain is increasingly employing flexible approaches to work and because of an increased emphasis on training, our productivity increases are greater than those of rival economies.

Recent results from a two-year jobs study by the Organisation for Economic Co-operation and Development (published in May 1996) suggest that flexible solutions are an imperative. The study indicated that almost all the unemployment in the industrial world has structural causes. Structural unemployment has increased due to the effect of existing industrial relations practices and benefit structures in a world economy that has suffered from a series of shocks ranging from higher oil prices in the 1970s to the introduction of new information technologies. The OECD's prescription for dealing with unemployment is summarised below:

- increase the flexibility of working patterns – encourage short contracts and part-time work
- remove restrictions on businesses to encourage enterprise
- make wages and labour costs more flexible by removing restrictions on wage-setting
- reform social security systems which make it expensive to hire workers
- reinforce active labour market policies (e.g. the employment service, and training schemes)
- improve education and training with an emphasis on learning throughout life
- reform unemployment benefits to reduce the poverty trap which makes it too expensive to take a job because of lost benefits
- increase competition in the economy to encourage growth
- encourage the creation and spread of technical know-how

Clearly, the emphasis is very much on creating increased flexibility in the labour market. For many governments, particularly those of a Social Democratic nature, the solutions will be unpalatable. At the end of the day, a trade-off between unemployment and inequality may be necessary. In recent years we have seen economies like the UK and the USA move towards solutions based on low unemployment and high inequality, and countries like Sweden and France taking the position of higher unemployment and less inequality. It seems inevitable that a UK Labour government would want to be seen to be moving in the direction of Sweden and France, although the creation of more unemployment is unlikely to be a recipe for success.

Further reading

- *The Coming of the New Organisation* by Peter Drucker. Harvard Business Review, 1988.
- *Economics in a Changing World* by Jean-Paul Fitoussi. Macmillan Press, 1995.
- *The Empty Raincoat* by Charles Handy. Hutchinson, 1994.
- *The Future of Work* by Charles Handy. Martin Robertson, 1994.
- *Unemployment in Western Countries* by Edmond Malinvaud and Jean-Paul Fitoussi. Macmillan Press, 1980.
- *The Pursuit of WOW!, Every Person's Guide to Topsy-Turvy Times* by Tom Peters. Macmillan Press, 1995.
- *Flexible Working* by Stephen Simmons. Kogan Page, 1996.
- *If You Mean Business* by Bryan Oakes and Rob Dransfield. Shell Education, 1996.

2

Managing people

2 Management styles

On completion of this chapter, students should be able to:

- define the term management style

- set out a simple typology of management styles

- analyse and evaluate different styles of management

- describe the major categories of styles and evaluate them

- compare positive and negative management

- explain trait theories of leadership and the strengths and weaknesses of this approach

- explain contingency theories of management and the strengths and weaknesses of these approaches

- identify changes in working patterns and the implications for managers

What is management?

A popular definition of management is *getting things done through or with people.* Of course, experience tells us that some managers are able to get things done in this way and others are not. Many different factors determine whether the manager will be successful or not, including the personality of the manager, the approach employed by the manager, the personality of those being managed, the expectations and values of those involved in the interaction, the type of setting, and so on. The implication is that there is no one best way of managing which will be effective whatever the setting and group of individuals involved.

Mary Follett proposed an alternative definition of management as *getting things done by other people.* The suggestion is that managers can create systems and procedures which will enable management decisions to be carried out within an organisation. The traditional view of management sees managers as having a number of responsibilities: planning, organising, staffing, decision-making, co-ordinating activities, tasks and resources, and budgeting. All of this gives the impression of the manager as someone who operates in a very tight and organised way. However, research into what managers do in practice has revealed a rather different picture. Managers in the real world operate in a whirl of activity, rushing from meeting to meeting and handling a range of projects and activities at the same time. What is required is the ability to juggle several schemes and ideas while managing and motivating people to create the best results.

Managers should not get trapped in an existing order or accepted way of going about things. Today, we work in an environment of change and effective managers need to be able to help organisations to move forward in a creative way. As managers accept ever more responsibility in an organisation, they will take on roles requiring planning, innovation and leadership. As we move beyond the millennium, managers will increasingly be involved in the management of change. As we shall see in this chapter, this requires the ability to live with new styles of management. Gone are the days when managers dictated most decisions downwards. Increasingly management is having to develop the skills to empower others within an organisation to take decisions for themselves. **Leadership** is an important part of management. It is the process of motivating other people to act in particular ways in order to meet an organisation's objectives. The word leader is derived from words meaning a path or road, and identifies the role of leader as giving direction to others and enabling them to follow the chosen path.

Management behaviour

A person's management style is the pattern of behaviour he or she exhibits in carrying out a management role over a period of time. An assumption can be made that employees will work harder and perhaps better for managers who employ certain styles rather than others.

One simple way of categorising management style is according to whether it is **dominant** or **submissive**, and **warm** or **hostile.**

Figure 2.1 Management styles

Dominant

The dominant style involves making things happen by exercising control and influence. In order to be dominant, managers need to be forceful and dynamic. They therefore need to be assertive and push forward their ideas in order to get people to follow their lead. This type of

manager is in charge, guiding and leading others into action.

Submissive

Submissive managers let things happen rather than taking control of events. They take a back seat and follow the lead of others rather than standing up for their own ideas. They give in easily, and quickly accept the superiority of other people's ideas.

Warm

Warm managers are sensitive to the needs of others and responsive to those needs. They show open and caring behaviour with a high regard for other people's ideas and feelings. This does not mean that they are affectionate or gushing, but that they have a genuine and caring approach.

Hostile

Hostile managers, in contrast, are insensitive to the needs of others and are therefore unresponsive to human needs at work. They have a selfish approach in which they place their own needs and requirements above those of everyone else. They can be hostile without letting this spill over into open anger.

Case Study

The ASDA way of working

The UK-based ASDA chain of supermarkets has carried out some detailed research into management styles in order to outline a better way of working for its managers. The company argues that management style can be placed on a grid depending on whether the manager leans towards:

- *a dominant and hostile position* – 'tell and do', typical of British retailing until very recently
- *a dominant and warm position* – 'challenge and involve', what ASDA characterise as the ASDA way of Working (AWW)
- *a submissive and hostile position* – 'avoid and abdicate'
- *a submissive and warm position* – 'pacify and socialise'.

These four positions are set out in Figure 2.2, with the ASDA way of working appearing in the top right-hand cell. ASDA recognises that nobody ever behaves in just one of the four ways all of the time. However, the

Figure 2.2 The four main management approaches

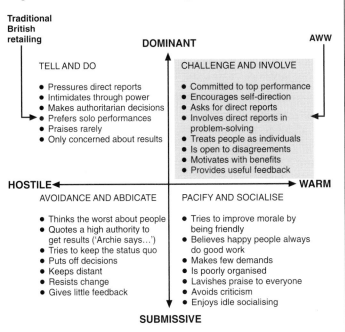

company would like to feel that its managers take up the **challenge and involve** position most of the time.

Figure 2.3 illustrates the aims and attributes of a manager using the ASDA way of working.

Figure 2.3 The ASDA way of working

Questions for discussion

1 *What do you see as being the main merits of the ASDA way of working:*
   a. *to the managers involved*
   b. *to subordinates working with these managers*
   c. *to the ASDA organisation as a whole?*
2 *To what extent do you think that it would be practical and appropriate to employ this style of supermarket management all the time?*
3 *In what situations might it be more appropriate to employ an alternative form of management style?*
4 *Consider one other form of organisation that is not involved in retailing (perhaps the organisation that you work for). Which of the four management styles would be most appropriate as the dominant style for this type of organisation? Why?*

Major categories of styles

In this next section we will look at some of the work carried out by researchers and analysts which explores major categories of styles and the effectiveness and appropriateness of each in different situations.

Autocratic versus democratic styles

An **autocrat** is someone who possesses absolute and unrestricted power. The term is generally used to refer to a domineering or dictatorial person. In contrast, a **democrat** is someone who enjoys sharing powers and decision making. While the autocratic approach may be necessary in some circumstances, it has become less appropriate in modern organisations which need to draw on the abilities, skills and knowledge of a diverse human resource.

In the autocratic style power tends to be vested with the leader/manager and during this century has been characteristic of a number of media tycoons, e.g. Lord Beaverbrook, Rupert Murdoch and Robert Maxwell.

Rensis Likert, in his book *New Patterns of Management*, outlined a continuum of management styles ranging from authoritarian to democratic. Four types of leadership style were highlighted:

System 1: exploitive authoritarian. This approach to management is based on exploitation and a concentration of authority as typified by Fordism. In such a system the emphasis is very much on negative sanctions. The use of threats and punishments are used as a driving force to maintain control; for example, employees may lose pay as a result of errors and mistakes. Communication is predominantly in a downward direction and teamwork is not encouraged.

System 2: benevolent authoritarian. This management style is based on a paternalistic approach. The emphasis is very much on downward communication, but managers are seen as having a benevolent interest in employees. The employers have a genuine concern for the welfare of their employees, but decisions are still imposed from above, although there may be some opportunities for consultation and delegation.

System 3: consultative. This approach to management involves consulting employees about decisions that are to be made. This makes it possible to draw on the knowledge and skills of employees so that they feel part of the decision-making process. However, management is still responsible for making the decisions after the initial process of consultation.

System 4: participating groups. This approach to management is based on democracy in the workplace. An organisation in which everyone is seen as a decision-maker is one in which there should be the greatest commitment to shared ideals and goals.

A continuum of leadership styles

Good management alone will not ensure the success of organisations or the people that run them. Good management needs to be complemented by good leadership. Leadership involves drawing together the various parts of an organisation in order to help them to work together to achieve the objectives of the organisation. It goes beyond the creation of systems and procedures; it must also involve the creation of a drive and momentum for change and a dynamism within the organisation.

However, there is not necessarily one best style of leadership. What is best for a particular situation depends on many factors such as cultural climate, time available for decision-making, context, and the personality of the individuals involved.

Tannenbaum and Schmidt (1973) described the factors which influence a manager's choice of leadership style. Their research led them to argue that there are three main forces influencing the style adopted:

- *personal forces* including the manager's own background, personality, confidence, and preference for leadership style
- *characteristics of others involved in the decision-making process (e.g. subordinates)* – including the subordinate's background, personality, confidence and preferred

style of leadership, and the willingness of subordinates to take responsibility
- *the situation* including the existing culture of the organisation, the nature of the decision that needs to be made, the time available to make the decision, and the existing way of working in the organisation.

Tannenbaum and Schmidt set out a continuum of management styles which is shown in Figure 2.4.

Figure 2.4   Continuum of leadership styles

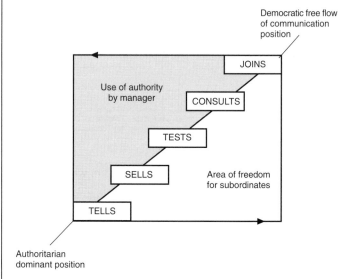

In the diagram, as we move upwards to the right the manager is using less authority and is instead allowing a greater amount of democratic decision-making.

The 'best' style of management depends on the situation and the people involved. In an emergency situation you will certainly need a manager that tells people what to do rather than one who tries to set up a committee. In contrast, when a group of people come together to share ideas they may resent someone who takes on the role of manager and tries to tell everyone else what to do.

A **telling style** is best when subordinates are not prepared to take responsibility themselves. They may be unable and/or unwilling to take responsibility and therefore need direction.

A **selling style** is best when subordinates are only moderately ready to take responsibility themselves. This approach offers both direction about what to do and support to those who are unwilling or unable to take responsibility. The manager will direct subordinates but also explain to them what they need to do and give them feedback on their performance in order to maintain motivation.

A **testing style** involves allowing subordinates to try out decision-making processes for themselves. The manager may test out new ideas on subordinates, encouraging them to start to take some responsibility for decision-making themselves. They can then begin to take on more responsibility themselves, knowing that if things do not work out there is still scope for managers to take back this responsibility.

A **consulting style** involves giving more freedom to subordinates to make decisions. This style is best when there is a fair amount of readiness among subordinates to carry out and make decisions for themselves. By enabling others to make decisions, the manager is able to motivate them by giving them a sense of ownership – although not the complete control of the decision-making process. Subordinates are in a position to consult managers about decisions that they want to make. This gives them the sense of security that their ideas have been screened by someone with more responsibility than themselves.

A **joins style** is at the democratic end of the continuum. The manager does not use authority over others. This would be the case in a self-managing team in which each individual has a key contribution to make to the decision-making process. Everyone is broadly at the same level and therefore takes an equal share of responsibility.

Supportive styles

A supportive manager is one who actively seeks to encourage others to develop their own roles within an organisation. This involves identifying individual needs and how they can best be met.

A supportive style involves a manager looking beyond his or her own individual needs to recognise the needs of others in the organisation. The supportive manager will use appraisal as an ongoing process to find out what aspirations and ambitions others have and will regularly coach people in order to help them develop within the organisation. This management style leads to greater job satisfaction, higher returns, and much lower rates of staff turnover and absenteeism. The organisation is likely to be based on shared values with far fewer disputes between individuals and cliques within the organisation.

Research has shown that most employees prefer a supportive style of management. With such an approach they feel that they are part of the organisation, rather than simply as subordinate employees within it.

Task orientation and people orientation

The task of a group within an organisation or the organisation as a whole is to ensure that certain targets or outputs are met. Some leaders become wrapped up in the task and forget about the people that are involved in carrying out the tasks. The problem with this approach is that the leaders may find that they fail to meet targets and objectives because they have not been able to carry the people with them. Employees may feel demotivated by working with leaders who just focus on meeting targets. For example, in recent years schools and colleges have been subject to external inspections. This has meant that the managers within the schools have sometimes become obsessed with meeting the requirements of the inspection, e.g. are we working within our budget; are we attracting enough pupils, are our examination results up to standard? The task-orientated manager may forget that it is the people within the organisation who make it possible for these standards to be achieved. People need nurturing and support. If you keep beating them over the head with performance indicators they may become disenchanted and feel that they are not valued. The effective leader therefore needs to balance task orientation and people orientation.

Some leaders who are purely task orientated employ what others see as a pedantic approach which, in extreme cases, may lead to a loss of focus on what the real task is. This type of failure is highlighted again and again in Joseph Heller's classic account of the failure of the American military in Vietnam, *Catch 22*, illustrated by the following extract:

> *The U.S.O. troops were sent by General P.P. Peckem, who had moved his headquarters up to Rome and had nothing better to do while he schemed against General Dreedle. General Peckem was a general with whom neatness definitely counted. He was a spry, suave, and very precise general who knew the circumference of the equator and always wrote 'enhanced' when he meant 'increased'. He was a prick, and no one knew this better than General Dreedle, who was incensed by General Peckem's recent directive requiring all tents in the Mediterranean theatre of operations to be pitched along parallel lines with entrances facing back proudly toward the Washington Monument. To General Dreedle, who ran a fighting outfit, it seemed a lot of crap. Furthermore, it was none of General Peckem's goddam business how the tents in General Dreedle's wing were pitched. There then followed a hectic jurisdictional dispute between these overlords that was decided in General Dreedle's favor by ex-P.F.C. Wintergreen, mail clerk at Twenty-seventh Air Force Headquarters. Wintergreen determined the outcome by throwing all communications from General Peckem into the wastebasket. He found them too prolix. General Dreedle's views, expressed in less pretentious literary style, pleased ex-P.F.C. Wintergreen and were sped along by him in zealous observance of regulations. General Dreedle was victorious by default.*

In contrast, a person-orientated style will show itself in a strong concern for employees. This type of manager sets out to boost morale and encourage employees to work together to get tasks completed.

The management grid

Blake and Mouton devised a matrix model comparing these aspects of management style; they set out a contrast between concern for production and concern for people within an organisation.

This is easier to understand by looking at a diagram (see Figure 2.5).

Figure 2.5   The management grid

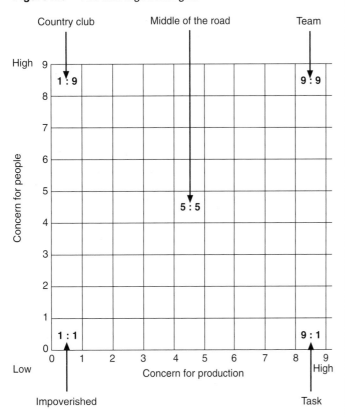

The management grid is made up of 81 squares representing different combinations of emphasis on production orientation and people orientation. Referring to Figure 2.5:

- [1 : 1] shows a very low emphasis on both production in the workplace and looking after people. It seems unlikely that such a situation would exist in the real world. Blake and Mouton refer to such a situation as **impoverished.**

- [1 : 9] shows a situation in which there is a maximum emphasis on looking after the needs of people in the workplace but only a very little emphasis on production. Clearly such a situation would be unsuitable because very little would get done. The researchers call this the **country club** position.
- [9 : 1] shows a strong emphasis on production with very little emphasis on people. This is referred to as a **task** position. This approach could lead to considerable job dissatisfaction and tension among the workforce.
- [9 : 9] is the ideal position and shows a strong emphasis on both people and output. This situation is typified by the 'high-performance team' in which everyone works flat out to meet shared goals and objectives. There is considerable satisfaction for all concerned in such a situation. The researchers call it the **team** position.

Clearly there are also many other intermediate positions, such as positions [5 : 5] which is referred to as **middle of the road.** Unfortunately, there are too many middle-of-the-road organisations in the UK today. Perhaps, as a group, you can identify a number of positions which exist in organisations that you have worked for.

Task

Where would you place the following managers against the management grid?

1   John runs a small plant producing components for 'classic cars'. In recent times the company has found it increasingly difficult to win orders and has to 'make do with what it can get'. This means that it is forever having to chop and change what it produces, and goes through periods of extremely intense production in which large outputs need to be produced quickly. At these times John has to take his employees 'beyond their endurance levels'. This results in extreme tension and difficult working relations.

2   Jane is a line manager in a food-processing factory. She has worked there for a number of years, but feels that she has no loyalty to the organisation as they have shown little loyalty to her. She has decided to finish working for the company in three months' time. She has let working standards fall and recently has taken little interest in the problems of her subordinates. She feels that she 'couldn't care less' whether her production line is a success or not.

3 Nina has recently started working as a section head in the underwriting department of a large insurance company. The company encourages managers to develop working groups in which ideas and achievements can be shared in the workplace. Nina is very keen on this approach and has gone out of her way to consult employees working in her section at every opportunity. In fact, she feels that she may have been overdoing it a bit.

Positive and negative management

Managers may adopt a positive or negative style. A positive manager will emphasise rewards, for example in the form of money, benefits, or better working relationships. Negative leadership, in contrast, places more emphasis on punishments and sanctions. Negative leaders stress their superiority and domination over others – they play a boss role, using power as a threat.

Case Study

Bullying at work

In June 1996 the national newspapers reported the case of a librarian who had gone to an industrial tribunal because her supervisor had made her life a misery at the British Library's stores in Boston Spa. She claimed that her boss had made her work late even when her mother died; told her off for sneezing; timed her lavatory breaks; and criticised her for taking less than her full lunch breaks.

A number of commentators have argued that harassment is on the increase and is linked closely to rising job insecurity. Professor Cary Cooper has stated that:

'People's fears over losing their jobs makes a more likely ground for bullying. The growing group are the "situational bullies". When people are under a lot of pressure themselves through job insecurity, they can express this pressure through bullying. The bullying can then cascade down through the system.'

Questions for discussion

1 *What do you understand by the term 'situational bully'?*
2 *What factors do you think might give rise to the 'situational bully' in management positions?*

3 *How might an organisation set about creating a more positive approach to management?*

Power as style

Power is the ability to influence people and events. It is acquired by individuals and groups through their personalities, their activities and the situations in which they operate and can be used in different ways. Davis and Newstrom, in their book *Human Behaviour at Work*, identify three major styles:

1 *Autocratic leaders* centralise power and take all decisions themselves. They specify what subordinates will do, when and how. Their power tends to be based on threats and punishments.
2 *Participative leaders* delegate authority. Decisions are made after consultation with a number of individuals. The power is shared as the leader and group work as a social unit. This style of management is becoming increasingly popular.
3 *Free-rein leaders* avoid power and responsibility. They expect groups to establish their own objectives and to sort out their own problems.

It is rare for managers to use only one of these styles – they will tend to use all three over a period of time and in different situations. However, one style may dominate, as illustrated in the following case study.

Case Study

Robert Maxwell – media tycoon

A number of aspects of Robert Maxwell's style of management were revealed during the trial of his sons in 1996.

Maxwell operated from the ninth floor of the Mirror Building. It was typical for three meetings to be in progress at the same time: there might be a meeting with trade union officials in the dining room, a foreign print executive in Maxwell's office, and a recruit for a new post in the sitting room. Other people with appointments would be queuing up in the reception area, while senior executives would be pressing the appointments secretary to let them know when RM would be free for just two minutes.

The reason for all the bottlenecks that occurred was that Maxwell rarely delegated his work. Written authority for every new car and every new position on the newspapers, whether for a secretary or a managing director, had to be personally approved by Maxwell.

Senior executives had authority to spend up to set limits without reference, but they used it with care. Nearly all the important negotiations, whether with trade unions, printers or journalists, were handled by Maxwell himself.

Kevin Maxwell said of his father: 'He was driven by power not by money, by the ability to change things, not only in this country but abroad.' He achieved power and wealth by combining personal charm with a bullying nature that frightened his family as well as senior employees. Kevin described his father as:

> 'somebody who dominated any business he was involved in ... he had a commanding presence in a room and, given his weight and bulk, he could dominate, and did dominate, every meeting he attended.'

Arguing with him was a 'gruelling, physically demanding' task. Kevin admitted to having been 'very frightened' of his father as a child.

He went on to explain to the court that his father was a 'spectacular risk taker', who had turned round companies on the brink of bankruptcy and amassed a personal fortune of more than £1 billion by the late 1980s.

> 'He was basically a man possessed by business. He had no interests outside business. It consumed his life. He worked from very early, sometimes 5 in the morning, to 10 at night every day, including weekends. He wasn't motivated by money, but by power, the ability to influence events, the ability to make a difference, to change things, not only in this country but abroad ... he inspired loyalty ... and was a charismatic leader ... he was capable of being extremely charming to

> people, he was capable of winning, but he was also capable of verbal brutality in meetings, public dressing-downs not only of his children but of his senior managers.'

Kevin recalled how he had been sacked by his father while working for him on a defence periodical in Washington in the early 1980s, 'because he objected to my marriage to Pandora!'

Questions for discussion

1 Identify the sources of power that Maxwell made use of.
2 What do you see as being the strengths and weaknesses of Maxwell's leadership style for an organisation?
3 How might Maxwell have made it difficult for other managers to manage?

Trait theories of leadership

A trait is a *characteristic feature or quality distinguishing a particular person or thing.* Many studies have been carried out that purport to identify certain traits which are predominantly found in good leaders or managers. Trait theories may be used, for example, to explain why certain individuals such as Margaret Thatcher, Richard Branson or Anita Roddick have been particularly good leadership material.

The trait approach is based on the assumption that certain individuals are born with or acquire outstanding leadership qualities which enable them to be more effective managers. Desirable traits for strong leadership have traditionally been seen as self-assurance, dominance, intelligence, determination, and a desire to work hard to achieve targets. However, the traits which are appropriate for a modern organisation based on teamwork may be quite different (see Figure 2.6).

Figure 2.6 Leadership traits

Strong leadership	Teamwork
■ Self-assurance ■ Dominance ■ Intelligence ■ Determination ■ Desire to work hard to achieve targets	■ Self-assurance ■ Sensitivity to others ■ Intelligence and interpersonal skills ■ Perseverance ■ Desire to work hard to create team goals, co-operation and team success

It is not too difficult to think of individuals who are intelligent, self-assured and decisive. However, these people may lack the sort of sensitivity and interpersonal consideration that is so essential in modern workplaces.

A number of writers have argued that it is important to identify the traits necessary for leadership in a particular area of work. Management can turn on matters of process and experience, and many people in a profession can become good managers. Leadership requires very special personal qualities which fewer people in a profession have or are able to develop. However, it is possible to enable people to develop more of these qualities, although it is important to first pin down what these qualities are and to set out how they can be developed.

Obviously **imagination, creativity** and **charisma** are important characteristics of leadership. Passion and energy need to complement experience and ability. Leadership training becomes possible once you have identified the sorts of characteristics that are required by leaders in particular types of organisations. Organisations and professions therefore will benefit from making explicit the key characteristics of those most likely to succeed in establishing and maintaining excellence in a leadership role.

Charles Handy has identified a number of general characteristics which tend to be present in good leaders. These traits include:

- *Intelligence.* Leaders should have above average intelligence but not necessarily be geniuses. Often a 'down to earth' sort of intelligence may be required if someone is going to work well with others.
- *Initiative.* Leaders need to be able to take responsibility on themselves and show a certain amount of willingness to follow unexpected paths rather than wait for approval from others. They need to have that spark of creativity which will enable them to identify avenues for opportunity that others may see or not have the courage to pursue.
- *Self-assurance.* Leaders need to have a good self-image which will give them the confidence to take others with them. However, leaders should also show respect for other people with whom they work. It has been suggested that good leaders will adopt an 'I'm OK you're OK' position when dealing with others rather than a rather disdainful 'I'm OK, you're not OK!'

Handy also identified a **helicopter factor** as being important for leaders. In other words, they need the ability to rise above a situation rather than being bogged down in minute details. In addition, good leaders also need to be generalists. They need to be able to build up an understanding of new situations quickly and apply broad-based experience of other fields and organisations.

In general, good leaders tend to be healthy, of above average height or well below it, and from privileged sectors of society.

Of course, there are many criticisms of trait approaches. For example, you may be able to think of leaders that do not have the traits outlined above. Also, the traits which are often identified by researchers are rather general and not clearly outlined. In any case, the traits in themselves are not sufficient to describe the characteristics of effective leaders. Perhaps it would be more helpful to identify the sorts of leadership qualities that are useful in a specific context in order to identify the sorts of people who will best be able to lead in such a context.

As we move towards the year 2000, organisations are beginning to take on new shapes in which the customer outside the organisation and the human resource within the organisation are gaining more and more importance. The modern organisation is increasingly looking for managers with traits which include interpersonal, teamwork and communication skills. The modern manager in a leaner and flatter organisation is quite different from the manager who was so successful in the tall organisation of the past.

Contingency theories of management

In addition to trait and style theories of management, increasing emphasis is now placed on contingency theories. Contingency theories take account of the many different variables involved in a management situation, such as:

- the task
- the work group
- the position of the manager within the work group.

A model of leadership effectiveness

An important early contribution to contingency theory was made by **Fred Fiedler.** Fiedler's approach helped to identify the kinds of characteristics in a situation that would foster group effectiveness. His view was that it depended on creating a suitable match between a leader's style and the demands of the situation. Any given situation allows a leader to have more or less control. Fiedler referred to this as **situational control:** the extent to which a leader can determine what the group is going to do as well as the outcomes of the particular task or situation.

Fiedler studied leadership situations in a variety of organisations before concluding that the effectiveness of a leader depends on:

- the leader's position in terms of power
- the type of relationship between leader and followers
- the extent to which the task is structured.

A structured task is one for which:

- goals are clear
- there are well-defined criteria for success
- there are only a small number of possible successful outcomes for the task
- there are only a limited number of ways of completing the task.

Fiedler identified three main types of conditions in which a leader will be expected to operate:

Condition 1
Highly structured task
Leader has a high position of power
Good relationship between leader and followers

Condition 2
Unstructured task
Leader has a low position of power
Moderate relationships between leader and followers

Condition 3
Unstructured task
Leader has a low position of power
Poor relationships between leader and followers

Condition 1 requires a leader who concentrates on getting tasks carried out. In this situation there is a clear focus on the task, there are clear objectives, work performance can be monitored and progress made quickly. There is no real need for a leader who focuses on human relationships, because working relationships are already good.

Where Condition 2 exists, however, a leader orientated towards human relationships will be more successful. The leader will need to be able to foster good relationships to reduce the likelihood of conflict and ensure that tasks are performed effectively. Because the tasks lack structure, it is necessary for relationships to be good to hold things together.

In Condition 3 there is a lot of uncertainty: there is no clear focus for the task and relationship are poor. Fiedler argued that what is required is a task-orientated leader who can exert pressure on followers to get things done and reduce the ambiguity in the situation. A leader orientated towards human relationships may be seen as being too weak in these circumstances.

Figure 2.7 illustrates the relationship between the most appropriate type of leadership and the situation. According to this model, then, the most effective type of

Figure 2.7 Fitting leadership to the situation

	Employee-centred leader	Task-oriented leader
High control over situation	Poor performance	Good performance
Moderate control over situation	Good performance	Poor performance
Low control over situation	Poor performance	Relatively good performance

leadership will be contingent on the situation. This indicates that a situational analysis should be made before deciding on the best way to lead: looking at the powers vested in the leader, the type of task to be completed and the relationship between leader and followers.

A best-fit approach

This approach explores the idea that there should be a good fit between the main ingredients of a leadership situation. The four main ingredients are:

- *the leader* – his or her preferred style of operating and personal characteristics
- *the subordinates* – their preferred style of leadership in a given context
- *the task* – the job to be performed and the technology involved
- *the environment* – the organisational setting of the leader, group and task.

The best fit will, of course, be contingent on the situation. However, leadership will be most effective when the requirements of the task, the leader, and the followers do not conflict. The concept of 'fit' can be represented on a scale running from **tight** to **flexible.** This is best illustrated by an example. Figure 2.8 represents a situation where the task is relatively unstructured and the leader likes to operate in an unstructured way, yet the employees are looking for structure and organisation. This is likely to lead to conflict and poor performance. Over time the three factors should move closer together. If this does not happen, however, the effectiveness of the group will be

Figure 2.8 'Fit'

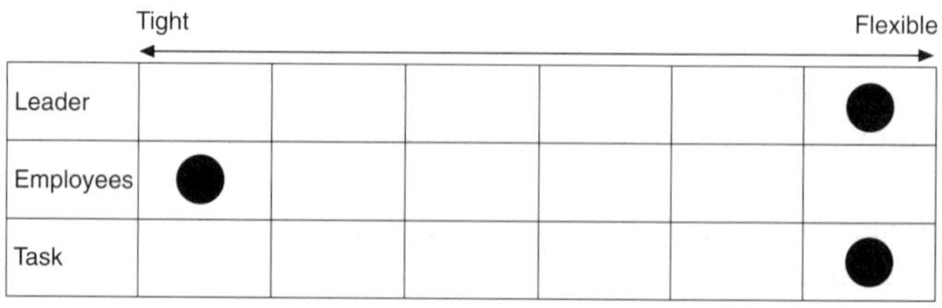

poor and tasks will be handled badly. Leaders need to adjust factors towards the best fit for a given situation. In the short-term it may be easiest to adjust managerial style. However, in the longer-term the most benefit may be achieved by redesigning tasks.

A normative theory of leadership effectiveness

A useful view of leadership effectiveness which is associated with Vroom and Yetton is what is called a 'normative' approach. These researchers argued that it was up to managers to be flexible and change their style according to the situations in which they were operating. This contrasts with Fiedler's view that leadership style was less likely to change than the situation.

Vroom and Yetton identify the quality of a decision and the acceptance of a decision as being the key criteria for decision effectiveness. In simple terms they argued that where managers are involved in decision-making that is felt to be of only limited importance by a work group, it would be appropriate for managers to be autocratic or to consult the group in only a limited way. However, when decisions are seen as having key importance by the working group, e.g. changes to working conditions, contractual arrangements and reward systems, it is necessary to employ a style which involves a far greater element of participation and discussion.

Maturity of subordinates

We have already set out the importance of the relationship between the leaders and others in an organisational setting. Clearly, an important determinant of whether managers are able to give autonomy to subordinates is the readiness of subordinates to take on more powers and responsibilities. Hersey and Blanchard (1982) put forward the view that this depends on the maturity of subordinates where this is defined as *the desire for achievement and willingness to accept responsibility*.

In the course of time, subordinates are likely to develop more mature approaches so that managers are increasingly able to devolve decision-making outwards.

When new employees join an organisation, it will be helpful initially to give them clearly defined tasks and responsibilities. For example, they will need to be inducted into the organisation's rules and requirements. Over time, however, subordinates can take on an increasingly responsible role within an organisation. Clearly some individuals and groups will mature faster than others. It is important for management to create the structures and systems which enable personal development within an organisation and increase the speed of maturation.

Attribution theory

A new line of thought about the effectiveness of management has arisen recently called attribution theory. This theory argues that often we attribute the label of 'good manager' or 'good leader' because it appears to us that these qualities exist in a given situation. For example, if a business organisation is doing particularly well, we may attribute this to good management or an appropriate management style for the time. In a similar way, managers may attribute to situations or groups certain qualities which they think exist. For example, if a unit in a workplace has poor results, managers may make the assumption that this is based on poor teamwork.

Attribution theory, therefore, indicates that the effectiveness of managers in a given situation may lie as much 'in the eyes of the beholder' as in concrete reality. For example, individuals working for an organisation will have particular views about what makes a good leader, that is the required traits and competences. If an individual 'appears' to have these traits then people working alongside them will ascribe to them the 'attributes' of a good leader. If someone does not appear to have these characteristics they may be attributed the position of a poor leader.

This line of thinking can lead us in a number of alternative directions. On the one hand it is possible to argue that the notion of good leadership is really a myth – if you swap one leader for another this may have little impact.

Alternatively it would be possible to argue that leadership can make a major difference – if the person looks the part in a post, people will respond in a dynamic way because of their perception that improvements will follow.

New managers for new organisations

The current emphasis in organisations is on the creation of teamwork, empowerment and self-management. This calls for new approaches to management. Yesterday's good manager may be today's dinosaur. Modern organisations aim to create **high-performance teams** which are managed by people with the skills to make such teams buzz. Clearly, the type of leadership needed depends on the requirements of individuals within the organisation. If employees can move in the direction of self-leadership then it is possible to create **self-managed organisations.** Perhaps the best way of identifying the changes that are taking place in organisations is to look at a case example.

Case Study

ICI

ICI is a major producer of paints, materials, explosives and industrial chemicals. As a multinational corporation, ICI runs and operates these businesses on a global scale. Inevitably, its business is subject to intense competition and to fluctuations in demand caused by cycles in economic activity.

Along with other modern high-technology corporations, it must make best use of the resources available. Failure to do this will inevitably lead to loss of market share. Of course, today the most important resource of any organisation is its human resource, i.e. the people that ICI employs. In order to make best possible use of this resource, ICI has set out to create a structure in which the potential of its people can be unleashed. In a number of areas this has had outstanding results.

The way it has gone about empowering staff is based on a simple yet highly effective formula. ICI has been reorganised to create a simple organisational structure in which everyone is clear about what is expected of them, i.e. individuals understand the objectives of the organisation, the team in which they operate, and their individual objectives. At the same time, ICI employees are given the tools and training necessary to do their jobs. Additionally, they are given recognition for what they and their teams have achieved. All of these changes have come about through a process of training managers to unleash the potential of their employees by creating team structures.

The best way to outline the way in which ICI has been operating human resource policies in recent times is to provide an example which highlights this practice.

In October 1995, the ICI Films plant at Fayetteville, USA, held a press briefing on its programme to devolve more responsibility to staff. To emphasise the point, the managers left the room half way through to give line staff the chance to contribute. Lab technician Deborah Peterson commented:

> *'I was thrilled at being able to talk to the press. It goes to show that everyone's input is valued. It's not like your ideas have to go back to management to be watered down and handed back.'*

One of those on the receiving end was journalist Ian Griffiths of the London *Evening Standard*. 'I've always found it better to talk to staff than managers', he commented. He added that ICI Films' empowerment programme is a structured exercise yielding benefits for employees and company alike.

> *'People talk animatedly about the new sense of pride they have in their jobs. They feel more involved and believe they've had some insight into how the company works.'*

ICI Films' empowerment programme produced tangible results when a shop-floor team at Hopewell, Virginia, chose to make direct contact with a major customer to shorten the lines of communication and offer a better service. The group of employees met directly with buyers from a business to which it was supplying film for packaging purposes. The buyers were able to explain difficulties which they had in using the product. The shop-floor team from ICI were then able to improve the quality of their product because they had a clear understanding of the customer's problems. Being at the sharp end of production, shop-floor employees were the team most likely to be able to come up with effective solutions. The result of the meeting was a leap forward in quality production and the enhancement of morale and motivation on the shop floor. Talking to customers shop-floor to shop-floor saved a lot of money.

The ICI case study provides an excellent example of the way things are changing in many organisations. The new style of manager that is needed today is someone that is able to enthuse and facilitate effective teams and teamwork approaches.

Managers are no longer people who retain power for power's sake and engage in downward communication of decisions that they have made and routines and schedules

Figure 2.9 Staff empowerment at ICI

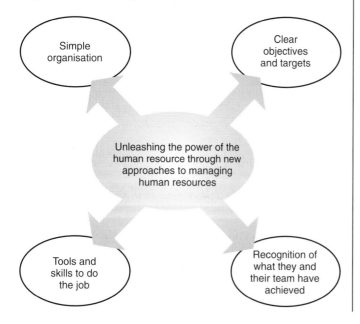

that they have set out. The emphasis is no longer on creating compliance with management decisions. Instead, the new management perspective is concerned with creating an overall vision of the direction that an organisation will take and making sure that everyone is familiar with this vision. Modern managers will need to motivate and inspire others while creating change in the organisation. Empowerment will be the key to involving everyone. Leaders will take a keen interest in people and will coach others so that they can improve their performance.

Levels of leadership

Commentators have argued that leadership will still be needed in organisations at a number of levels. At the top level, leadership will be required to create strategy and systems for the organisation so that there is an overall sense of purpose and direction. At the middle level, leadership will be concerned with creating the organisational structure to ensure that strategy and systems are put into effect. Finally, at the bottom level of the organisation, the production domain will be concerned with the nuts and bolts of getting things done. However, in a modern organisation these levels will be **interconnected** in a number of ways so that there is no rigid division as in the old hierarchical organisations of the past. There will be free flow of communication between all involved in decision-making, and the emphasis will be on **co-operation** in performing tasks and projects which are the mutual concern of all involved. The qualities required of new managers will be team focus, effective communication skills, interpersonal skills, problem-solving skills, information-technology skills, and analytical skills.

Charles Handy has recently argued that modern organisations will need to:

> 'Learn new ways and new habits, to live with more uncertainty, but more trust, less control, and more creativity.'

Changes in working patterns

Large organisations throughout the world have been restructuring and reorganising in order to meet the challenges of a dynamic business environment. In Chapter 1 we explored a number of changes in the world of work and identified some of the consequences for the management of organisations.

Today a lot of emphasis is given to creating the **architecture** for business success. Professor John Kay of the London Business School defines the architecture of an organisation as *the network of relational contracts within or around the firm.* He sees building successful relationships as a key to business success. He cites Marks and Spencer as an example of a company with a strong architecture that depends very little on any individual or group of individuals. All too often, however, businesses are limited because an effective organisational architecture is not in place. In the first part of the 1990s, it was very popular for organisations to strip out layers of managerial and supervisory staff in order to create flatter organisations. However, in the second half of the 1990s, there has been a reaction against this. There is a very real danger that if you strip out layers, you also strip out part of the **wisdom** and **experience** of an organisation, while at the same time breaking down the bonds that link individuals to their organisation. Recently, commentators have come to regard organisations such as BMW and Volkswagen, which have held on to their people, as enlightened human resource managers. These organisations have discussed the need for change with employees and, instead of making widespread redundancies, have introduced a host of flexible measures involving a more **adaptive** use of the human resource.

Flexibility

Increasingly, managers today are introducing flexible arrangements in the workplace. The major driving force behind this has been the requirement to be competitive. Management, therefore, has sought ways of increasing the ability of the organisation to move employees from one task to another (functional flexibility); to change the number of employees according to the cycle of demand for a product (numerical flexibility); and to have the ability to change rates of pay according to sales figures (financial flexibility).

Flexible firms operate a variety of different contractual arrangements for different types of employees. Huczynski and Buchanan have pointed out that:

> 'Workforce contracts differ according to whether the employee is directly employed, full-time; directly employed, part-time; on short-term contract; a public subsidy trainee; on delayed recruitment; job sharing; an agency temp; sub-contracted; or self-employed.'

Clearly such a bewildering array of contractual conditions impacts on the style of management which is required to manage such a diversity of human resources. Different approaches may be required according to the context in which management takes place.

Multi-skilling

Multi-skilling means training people to do a range of tasks in the workplace. For instance, a machine-operator can be trained to perform maintenance work and repairs. Multi-skilling can be a great motivator because it gives job variety as well as opportunities for higher pay. It also makes the factory or office more productive and more competitive, and therefore more able to offer better wages and conditions.

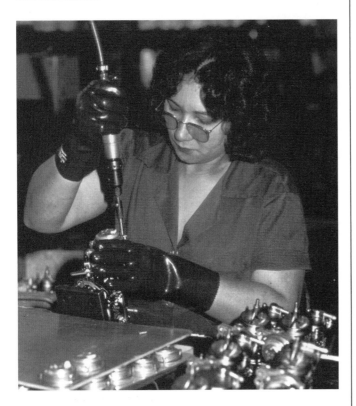

Multi-skilled teams

In place of the specialist departments, large companies have begun to organise themselves into multi-skilled teams responsible for whole projects. Such teams can focus more easily on customer needs and so direct and combine their specialist skills to meet those needs more effectively. They are also better at judging what effort and expenditure are needed to do that. Other important benefits follow. Individuals feel that their worth is valued. They can often make useful suggestions outside their specific areas of expertise. They are no longer required simply to carry out orders, but take responsibility for improving their own work and dovetailing it with the work of other specialists. Above all, they can shape their specialist contribution to the precise needs of their specialist colleagues and so of the project itself because they understand at first hand what those needs are. The idea goes further. People working in teams find it easier to learn new and different skills, perhaps to enable them to take over when a

colleague is absent, to help a colleague when pressures are high, or to provide variety in the course of everyday work. This so-called 'multi-skilling' is the diametrical opposite of the old tradition of demarcation, where skilled workers jealously guarded their preserves and warned off any who were not fully paid-up members of the craft. Today's flexibility works to everyone's advantage.

Empowerment

Who then makes the everyday decisions? A company prospers best when everyone in it believes that success depends on the excellence of his or her contribution. Short-term decisions made many times a day by individuals determine the quality of that day's work. Long-term decisions made by individuals about their own career, training and ambitions also affect the quality of their contribution.

The governing principle, whether recognised or not, is that everybody has a customer – either outside the company (the traditional customer) or inside the company (the internal customer). Both kinds of customer expect to be supplied with the product or service they need, on time and as specified. The principle holds good for everyone in the company, whatever their level of skill and experience, and whether their 'product' is answering a telephone in a helpful way or masterminding a new project. It works to everyone's benefit. It gives the individual genuine responsibility and scope for initiative, and it virtually guarantees that the company's performance will be improved.

For any company, but particularly one with a wide geographical spread and a wide range of product types, **decentralisation** of one kind or another is essential. Most decisions, especially tactical decisions, cannot be taken effectively at the centre, which may be miles – or continents – away. They have to be taken quickly, on the spot, by people who know all the circumstances. There is often no time for referral back to central office, even if central office had complete understanding of that particular problem. The information technology revolution, by putting massive computer power into devices that can be carried around like notebooks and can communicate instantly with other devices and their databases anywhere in the world, has made decentralisation even easier to handle and even more efficient in its effect. One of the major effects of IT is that it liberates employees to make more decisions for themselves based on detailed information.

The term empowerment, in an organisational context, is used to mean the increased participation by employees in their organisation and is being practised today by top companies such as Shell UK, Philips and ICI. It is a powerful tool for encouraging individual initiative and entrepreneurialism among the people that are the human resource of organisations. More recently it has also been seen as a vehicle for enabling women to rise above the invisible barriers (the glass ceiling) that formerly prevented them from progressing in organisations.

Rosabeth Moss Kanter, in her famous study *Men and Women of the Corporation,* argued that organisations need to make substantial changes to improve the quality of working life and to create equal opportunities for all groups, as well as to help members to develop their talents to the benefit of the organisation. This would involve, for example, opening up management positions to individuals by promotion from a wide range of junior positions. Intermediate jobs might need to be created as a stepping stone to senior management. All this would involve developing empowerment strategies such as autonomous work groups with decentralised authority and flatter hierarchies (see ICI case study above). The group would be set up to manage a particular project and would take responsibility for steering this project through to completion.

Empowering others in an organisation involves giving them the responsiblity to use their talents and express themselves. Rosabeth Moss Kanter argues forcibly that:

> *'By empowering others, a leader does not decrease his power; instead, he may increase it – especially if the whole organisation performs better.'*

Managing a modern organisation today, therefore, is a considerably different task from what it was in the past. We have moved away from the old machine organisations of the past to the people organisations of today. Modern organisations require managers with 'people skills' – for example, the ability to work with others, the ability to give responsibility to others, the ability to communicate effectively with people at a number of levels, the ability to use IT and so on. These managers need to be able to operate in new environments, working in team situations with multi-skilled and highly capable colleagues. It seems likely, therefore, that there will be a lot less scope for the autocratic and hostile manager in the modern workplace.

Task

What characteristics do you think organisations will require of managers in the workplaces of the future?

Further reading

- *The Transformation of Management* by M. Davidson. Macmillan, 1995
- *The Empty Raincoat* by Charles Handy. Hutchinson, 1994.
- *Management Concepts and Practices* by Tim Hannaghan. Pitman, 1995.
- *The Pursuit of WOW!, Every Person's Guide to Topsy-Turvy Times* by Tom Peters. Macmillan Press, 1995.
- *The Reality of Organisations, A Guide for Managers* by Rosemary Stewart. Butterworth Heinemann, 1993.
- *Managing People* by Rosemary Thomson. Institute of Management, Butterworth-Heinemann, 1994.
- *In Search of Management* by Tony Watson. Routledge, 1994.
- *If You Mean Business* by Bryan Oakes and Rob Dransfield. Shell Education, 1996.

3 Individual and interpersonal behaviour

On completion of this chapter, students should be able to:

- describe and explain the term motivation

- trace and explain some important historical developments in job design, e.g. Taylorism, Fordism, human relations approaches, etc.

- explain the importance of the hierarchy of needs and its implications for the creation of job satisfaction

- describe and evaluate the approaches of Herzberg and McClelland

- identify factors affecting motivation

- analyse and evaluate approaches to empowerment.

Employees: the primary resource

For the majority of business organisations, people are the most expensive and valuable asset which they have. The wage and salary bill is usually their largest single cost. That is why managing human resources in order to get the best out of them, in terms of the quantity and quality of the work, is so vital.

Many organisations recognise that its employees are the primary resource which they have for gaining a comprehensive advantage in the marketplace. Effective human resource management can lower the costs of production, improve product development and enhance marketing and other activities. People can often provide a distinctive service or product which cannot be matched by the most sophisticated machines. An organisation will need to look after and support the people who give it such a distinctive edge. Therefore, the responsibility for managing human resources is increasingly being seen as part of the role of all managers, not just the personnel department. As people are so important to organisations, the recruitment, motivation, development and appraisal of employees should be of critical concern to any business.

The human resource is in many ways the most complex resource because it concerns people who have thoughts and feelings and express views. They can evaluate and question management actions and their co-operation and commitment have to be won. One of the key issues which human resource management must therefore be concerned with is the complex area of **motivation.**

Motivation theory

Motivation is concerned with the strength of commitment which individuals have towards what they are doing. It is what causes people to act or do something in a particular way. If human resource managers understand why people behave in the ways they do, i.e. what motivates people, they can then affect the working environment in order to improve motivation. For example, managers may improve the design of jobs, rewards and the working environment to meet the needs of their employees more closely. This should improve motivation, raise the quality of work and therefore benefit the organisation by improving efficiency.

There has been extensive research into the behaviour of people at work and their motivation; it is therefore useful to explore some aspects of motivation theory.

The scientific approach

The traditional management approach, prevalent until the early 1990s concentrated on increasing the efficiency of workers by carefully planning workers movements in the most efficient way. This was the scientific management approach pioneered by **Frederick W. Taylor** (1856–1915).

Taylorism

Taylor was appalled by what he regarded as inefficient working practices. He set out to analyse scientifically all the tasks which needed to be done in a job and then to redesign jobs in order to eliminate **time-and-motion** waste. Labour tasks were therefore reduced to machine-like efficiency. He felt that employees would be prepared to work in this way in order to gain greater rewards in the form of higher pay. Taylor therefore assumed that workers would be motivated by money.

Taylor's approach to job design was based on five principles:

- Tasks should be separated into their simplest constituent elements.
- Decisions about how tasks should be done should be taken by management.
- All preparation and servicing of tasks should be removed from the skilled worker and given to an unskilled worker.
- The skill requirements to perform a task should be reduced.
- The machinery should be organised to minimise the movement of people and materials.

Although Taylor's work has been questioned for many years, such is its influence that some writers argue that many modern managers continue to practise Taylorism without really realising it.

Task

Can you give examples of ways in which managers you are familiar with have employed Taylorist approaches. What has been the impact of their using these approaches?

Fordism

Between 1908 and 1929 Henry Ford applied the major principles of Taylorism to car manufacture, but also installed specialised machines and perfected the continuous-flow production line. This kind of job design has come to be called Fordism. Labour productivity could be increased by breaking down jobs into simple tasks and increasing mechanisation. Standardised products meant the use of standardised components which could be mass produced. Detailed time-and-motion studies identified the shortest possible time needed to undertake a task.

Ford's production system was not without its problems. Workers found the repetitive work boring and unchallenging. Job dissatisfaction was expressed in high rates of absenteeism and turnover. To combat this Ford introduced the Five Dollar Day, thus paying his workers more than similar workers in other organisations.

Taylorism and Fordism became the predominant approach to job design in vehicle and electrical engineering firms in USA, Canada and Britain. The problems caused by lack of job satisfaction, however, led to new approaches to job design. The human relations movement began to shift managers' attention to the perceived needs of workers.

The human relations approach

The human relations movement emerged in the 1920s and emphasised the psychological and social aspects of work and the effects that these had on motivation and productivity. The movement grew out of the **Hawthorne experiments,** conducted by Elton Mayo in 1927.

Mayo set up an experiment in the assembly room at the Hawthorne plant of the Western Electric Company in Chicago. The experiment was designed to test the effects on productivity of variations in working conditions; lighting, temperature and ventilation. The research team found no clear relationship between any of these factors and productivity. The experimenters worked with a small group of women in a separate room. They discovered that as the level of lighting decreased, the women's productivity was not affected. What had happened to the surprise of the researchers, was that by showing an interest in what the women were doing, this had raised motivation and increased effort and output.

The conclusion was that workers are motivated by more than economic incentives and the immediate work environment: recognition and social cohesion are important too. The human relations movement therefore advocated various techniques, such as worker participation and non-authoritarian supervision, in order to promote a climate of good human relations.

Motivation and the hierarchy of needs

One of the first comprehensive attempts to classify needs was undertaken by **Abraham Maslow** in 1954. Maslow's study of human behaviour led him to devise a hierarchy of needs, with the most basic needs at the bottom and higher needs at the top. Maslow's hierarchy is usually represented by a pyramid (see Figure 3.1). His general argument was that people would tend to satisfy their lowest level of needs before moving on to higher level needs.

According to Maslow we are motivated to satisfy five sets of needs, but the lower-order needs have to be satisfied before higher-order needs can be considered. So, if a person is hungry and feeling unrecognised, they will seek to address their hunger before worrying about how to get recognition of their worth as an individual. Only when the lower-order needs are well satisfied do people move upwards towards satisfying their higher-order needs. The implication for the motivation of people at work is that, by ensuring the lower-order needs are met, you remove possible demotivators and can then help employees to address their higher-order needs through their work (see Figure 3.2).

Figure 3.1   Maslow's hierarchy of human needs

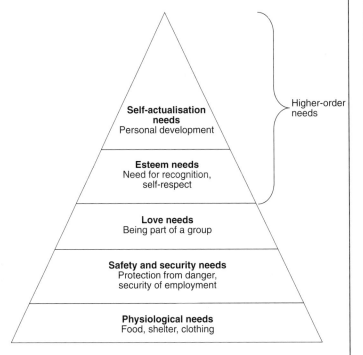

Figure 3.2   Addressing people's needs at work

The hierarchy of needs	Practical examples
Self-actualisation needs These are concerned with individuals' personal development and creativity: their ability to achieve their full potential.	People specialising in what they are good at Project groups which make use of individuals' particular skills Allowing project groups to organise their own work The use of appraisal systems to aid personal professional development
Esteem needs These are based on individuals' desire to have self-respect and the respect of others, leading to self-confidence.	Designation of job titles Use of status symbols, e.g. company cars Recognition of good work, merit pay, commission, promotion Praise from peers, managers
Love needs These are concerned with individuals' needs for love and affection. This involves relationships and a feeling of belonging.	Working in groups or teams Team meetings to discuss work progress Social activities Company sports activities
Safety and security needs These involve protection from danger and a safe environment.	Contract of employment Pension rights Sick pay scheme Safe workplace, e.g. guards on machinery, protective clothing Good employment prospects
Physiological needs These are basic needs necessary for physical survival – food, shelter and clothing.	Living wage Good working environment, heat, light, etc. Canteen facilities Washroom facilities

Maslow's theory has its critics, who suggest that there is little evidence that people tend to satisfy their needs in a relatively systematic way from the bottom of the hierarchy to the top. For example, a creative person like a designer may work non-stop on a project and go without food.

Task

Fill in the table below with ticks to show where you think each of the characteristics in the left-hand column fits into Maslow's hierarchy of needs.

	Physio-logical	Safety and security	Love	Esteem	Self actual-isation
Operating in conditions where there is a comfortable working temperature					
Working in a safety-conscious organisation					
Being respected and looked up to by work mates					
Being given the opportunity to use creative talents to the full					
Working in a high-performance team					
Working in a sweat shop with an income just above the poverty line					

McGregor's Theory X and Theory Y

Douglas McGregor's development of Theory X and Theory Y is a good example of a human relations approach to people management.

In the *Human Side of Enterprise* (1960) McGregor pointed out the different effects which management attitudes can have on the motivation of employees. McGregor suggested that by observing managers' actions it was possible to tell what assumptions they were making about how employees are motivated. McGregor used the term **Theory X** to apply to the types of management assumptions that were being made by 'scientific' managers. These managers see their main function as the direction and control of their employees. **Theory Y** managers, on the other hand, adopt more of a human relations approach. These managers see their function as the creation of suitable conditions to enable workers to achieve their goals. McGregor argued that supervisors and managers' behaviours would reflect their attitudes and assumptions about their employees.

Theory X Managers assume :

- most people dislike work and responsibility and prefer to be directed in their work
- the primary motive that people have for working is financial rather than a desire to do a good job
- most employees need to be closely supervised, controlled and coerced into achieving the organisation's objectives.

Theory Y Managers assume :

- if suitable opportunities are provided, people can enjoy their work and be capable of exercising considerable control over their own performance
- employees are not just concerned with financial rewards, but also seek social contact and wish to do a good job
- employees may work better and more productively if supervision is kept to a minimum and employees are allowed to take responsibility for decisions.

Questions for discussion

How useful do you think Theory X and Theory Y are? Do you think that managers actually fit into these two categories?

Herzberg's motivation – hygiene theory

Herzberg's original study into the good and bad experiences at work of 200 engineers was designed to test the view that human beings have two sets of needs; firstly their need as an animal to avoid pain and secondly their need to grow psychologically. The interviewees were asked initially to recall a time when they felt exceptionally good about their jobs and why this was so. They were then asked to describe events which gave rise to bad feelings about their jobs. Good feelings came from the challenge of tasks and the work itself: achievement, responsibility, recognition. These factors relate to the content of the job and are viewed as motivating factors or satisfiers. Bad feelings came from company policy, working conditions, salary, job security, quality of supervision and interpersonal relations. These factors relate to the context of the job. They are viewed as hygiene or maintenance factors, which could be the source of dissatisfaction (see Figure 3.3).

Herzberg's two-factor theory suggests that satisfiers would motivate employees if present, whereas hygiene factors would give rise to dissatisfaction and demotivate if absent.

For organisations, the implication of this theory is that it is necessary to ensure that negative hygiene factors (e.g. low

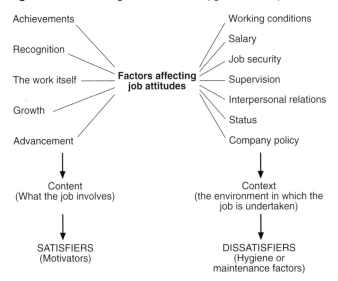

Figure 3.3 Herzberg's motivation–hygiene theory

pay and unsocial hours) are not present and equally that motivational factors (e.g. achievement and recognition) are provided.

As a theory of motivation Herzberg's ideas have been criticised, mainly on the grounds that there is little evidence to support his concept of these two independent sets of factors in motivation. Factors which give rise to one person's job satisfaction may cause dissatisfaction to another person.

Questions for discussion

To what extent do you agree with Herzberg's statement that:

> *'the causes of satisfaction at work lie in the content of the job and the causes of dissatisfaction lie in the working environment.'*

Present clear arguments to support your point of view, and use examples.

McClelland – achievement motivation

David McClelland argues that people have three basic needs; the need for **achievement, affiliation** (belonging) and **power.** He found that individuals with a high achievement factor display a number of characteristics. For example, they enjoy taking on responsibility, they like tasks which present a challenge and seek feedback on their performance. People with high affiliation or power factors will display other characteristics. A business would therefore need to know how these three needs affect individual employees. McClelland's ideas have been used

in the selection of managers, where tests are used to identify attributes associated with achievement, affiliation and power. If particular attributes can be matched to particular jobs, then a person with high affiliation needs, for example, may be identified as being particularly suitable for a particular job.

Putting theory into practice

Having reviewed a range of motivation theories, it may appear that all organisations need to do is to use those views it considers would be effective and to take suitable action to motivate its employees. In practice, the motivation of individual employees is extremely complex. It seems clear that a whole range of factors need to be taken into account when considering the influences of motivation and the appropriate approach of the organisation in order to gain the best performance from employees.

Factors affecting motivation

Motivation is concerned with having an incentive to do something and therefore achieving a certain outcome. Motivation can be seen as originating from two sources: the **needs** which exist within an individual and the **goals** which exist in the environment.

Clearly the extent to which individuals are motivated will be determined by how much they value the goal they are seeking to achieve and how likely they are to be successful in achieving the goal. The more individuals can control

Figure 3.4 The cycle of needs and goals

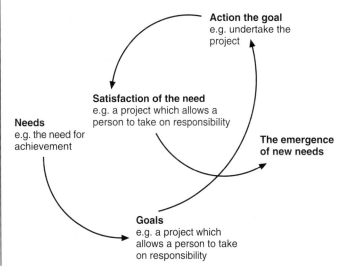

the means to achieve their goals, the more highly motivated they are likely to be.

In terms of work, then, if employees are to be motivated to work, they must expect worthwhile rewards to be the result of their effort.

The question of motivation and job satisfaction is clearly not a simple matter: different people will be motivated to work by different rewards. The various theories of motivation which we have examined suggest that job satisfaction may depend upon a good level of pay opportunities for promotion and recognition, acceptable working conditions, and a certain level of control over working methods. High levels of job satisfaction do not necessarily produce high levels of performance. In some cases it is high levels of performance – doing the job well – which increases job satisfaction.

In terms of motivation, it is important to distinguish between extrinsic and intrinsic forms of motivation. **Extrinsic motivation** is concerned with actions undertaken by those other then the individual, which may affect the motivation of an individual, e.g. pay. This was held to be an important factor in a famous study of car workers, undertaken by Goldthorpe and Lockwood in 1969. The Affluent Worker Study found that workers in a Vauxhall car assembly line saw work as a means to obtain high wages; this would then allow them to do things outside work and with their families which they would otherwise be unable to do. **Intrinsic motivation** is concerned with self-generated factors which influence people to behave in a particular way. These include freedom to use one's skills and abilities, having interesting and challenging work and the level of responsibility. Clearly some employees who are well paid for undertaking routine, unchallenging work may be dissatisfied with the lack of intrinsic rewards.

Because of the differences between individual employees, such as personality and aptitude, and the range of work in which they are involved, it can be difficult to generalise about what motivates employees. Individuals have widely different needs and motivations. Theories of motivation may help to inform possible actions, but do not offer ready-made solutions to the issue of motivation.

Empowerment

Empowerment involves giving people more power to exercise control over and take responsibility for their work. Employees may be given more control over their work in a variety of ways, e.g. teamworking, quality circles and job enrichment. Armstrong (1955) suggests that the concept of empowerment has been around for a long time. He suggests that there is nothing original in enriching people's

Figure 3.5 Armstrong's view of empowerment

jobs, involving people in decision making and avoiding excessive layers of management. He points to the fact that these ideas were present in Herzberg's concept of job enrichment and McGregor's theory X. He does, however, identify that the reason for empowerment emerging as a concept is to do with the recognition of the importance of human resources as essential to the competitive edge of organisations in the current climate.

Case Study
Harvester Restaurants – empowering service workers

Harvester Restaurants are owned by the Bass Group. There are 78 outlets employing approximately 3000 employees of whom 40 per cent are full-time and 60 per cent are part-time. The restaurants are family-orientated restaurant/pubs. The decoration is English country style and menus offer traditional English fare with prices in the mid price range.

The menus offer a reasonable choice of dishes, but preparation techniques are based on simple routine tasks requiring relatively simple skill levels. The service style is through waiters/waitresses taking orders and serving plated meals. All menus are devised and priced centrally; individual restaurants therefore have little discretion. Products, preparation methods and serving instructions are developed at head office and then key personnel from restaurants are trained in the procedures. Product, service and presentation should therefore be largely standard across all restaurants. What cannot be standardised are the actual encounters between staff and customers. It is hoped that empowerment will encourage employees to accept responsibility for the service encounter and to respond appropriately to customer needs.

Organisation and management

Prior to reorganisation, the restaurants were managed in a traditional hierarchical manner (see Figure 3.6).

Figure 3.6 Former hierarchical organisation of Harvester Restaurants

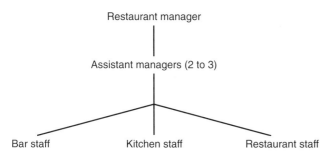

The management team was responsible for the day-to-day running of the unit: ordering stock, maintaining security of materials and money, receiving and checking goods, cashing up and banking takings, locking premises, staffing and the management of staff.

In the early 1990s recession in the British economy, along with a desire to improve customer satisfaction, led to the identification of a number of difficulties which the restaurants faced:

- low-quality commitment
- selective communication
- manager dependent
- under-utilized resources
- lack of ownership
- us and them
- lack of trust
- too much attention to process not values
- tackle one job at a time
- limited accountability
- development lies in other people's hands
- information giving not receiving
- not consistent
- contributions not listened to.

As a result, staff within the restaurants were reorganised into autonomous work teams. Each team has its team responsibilities and some team members take on additional duties as shift co-ordinators and appointed persons. Restaurant management now consists of just two roles: team manager and team coach.

Researchers investigating employee empowerment in the restaurants, identified a number of ways in which

Figure 3.7 Employee empowerment at Harvester Restaurants

Intention	Method
Empowerment through participation	Employees take on some form of decision-making which might traditionally be done by managers at more senior levels, through autonomous work groups or work councils
Empowerment through involvement	Employees are consulted over items of importance to the firm through quality circles or team briefings
Empowerment through commitment	The main focus is to encourage employees to take responsibility for the service encounter through training programmes and quality of working life programmes
Empowerment through delayering	Layers of management are removed, which results in authority being divided out among less senior members of the organisation

senior management were concerned with winning greater employee commitment (see Figure 3.7).

Researchers were keen to investigate the experiences of those involved in working in the restaurants and to identify their experiences of empowerment. The study also aimed to gain some indication of the perceived organisational benefits of empowering employees.

At restaurant level the team manager and coach are responsible for enabling and facilitating staff to be more self-managed and empowered. Each of the three teams in the restaurant has its own responsibilities. For example, one team is responsible for:

- guest service
- guest complaints
- sales targets
- ordering cutlery and glassware
- cashing up
- team member training.

A shift co-ordinator helps to co-ordinate the activities of the team. This person is an ordinary team member who assumes additional responsibilities during the shift, e.g. responsibility for cashing up and ensuring the table layout matches prior bookings. The role of co-ordinator rotates around team members. Shift co-ordinators receive no extra pay.

The team coach organises and co-ordinates training. As employees progressively undergo training and acquire a wider range of skills, their hourly rate of pay increases. Weekly team meetings are held to share information and to identify goals and problems.

Interviews with all team members in the sample confirmed that the communications aspect was a positive outcome of reorganisation. Team members liked knowing how they were doing and seemed to take a personal interest and pride in the unit's performance, quoting figures about sales, growth, profits, average spend per head, etc.

Team members who took on the role of shift co-ordinators seemed to like the additional responsibilities and the feeling of being in charge which the role allowed.

Senior managers believe that overall organisational performance has improved since the introduction of the flat structure. There has been a sales increase of 7 per cent, team member turnover has fallen by 19 per cent and liquor stocks have been reduced by almost £250 000. Wage costs have marginally reduced, from 24 per cent to 23.2 per cent, and administration costs have fallen by 41 per cent.

Empowerment, then, in Harvester Restaurants appears to involve a degree of responsible autonomy. However, discretion is limited to the intangibles in the guest encounter. Brand values allow little scope for product variation. Work teams do have some discretion over task allocation and organisation. The organisation appears to be moving from a control to a more trust-orientated culture, although trust is exercised within boundaries of control set by management.

Questions for discussion

1 *Why did Harvester Restaurants make the decision to restructure the organisation?*
2 *What were the main features of the restructuring and reorganisation?*
3 *How were employees to be empowered by the reorganisation?*
4 *Why and in what ways should the reorganisation and the resulting empowerment, increase the motivation of employees? Why might it fail to increase motivation in some cases?*

Further reading

- *Empowering Service Workers at Harvester Restaurants* by Diane Ashness and Conrad Lashle. In *Personnel Review,* Vol 24, No 8, 1995.
- *Behavioural Sciences for Managers* by Cowling, Stanworth, Bennet, Curran and Lyons. Edward Arnold, 1990.
- *Human Behaviour at Work* by O. J. Harris and S. Hartman. West Publishing, 1992.
- *The Human Side of Enterprise* by D. McGregor. McGraw-Hill, 1960.
- *Managing People* by Rosemary Thomson. Institute of Management, Heinemann Butterworth, 1990.

4 Teams and teamworking

On completion of this chapter, students should be able to:

- define a team
- describe different types of teams that operate in the workplace
- explain the various ingredients of team processes
- identify and evaluate different types of workplace networks
- evaluate different roles performed by individuals in team situations
- evaluate their own performance as a team member
- analyse the various stages in team development
- identify the features that enable a team to be successful.

Teams

Increasingly it is suggested that **teamwork** and **interpersonal skills** are required by the workforce of the future. More and more employees are finding themselves organised into teams in order to undertake their work. The tendency for organisations to delayer means that responsibility is delegated downwards to teams who need to co-ordinate their work. Often projects are interdisciplinary, drawing on expertise across an organisation, so it is vital that teams work effectively.

A team is a group of people with a common aim or purpose who are committed to using their complementary skills in order to achieve their goals. Dumaine (1994) identifies five common types of team.

- *Management team.* Managers representing various functions, such as production and sales, co-ordinate work among the teams.
- *Problem-solving team.* A group of employees who work together as a team to solve a specific problem and then disband.
- *Work team.* An increasingly popular type of team, undertaking the daily work of the organisation. When they are empowered, they are known as self-managed teams.
- *Quality circle.* A group of workers and supervisors meeting intermittently to discuss workplace problems and suggest solutions.
- *Virtual team.* A characteristic of this new type of teamwork is that members talk and participate by computer.

Dumaine suggests that a common problem with teams is that organisations do not think carefully enough about what sort of team will be most effective for the job. In some cases teams may be over-used. Does the task in hand really require interaction in a team or would it be more effectively undertaken by an individual?

The focus on teams which surfaced in the 1980s was partly influenced by Japanese working methods and also by a need to compete. Quality circles were used to meet to discuss improvements in quality and many reduced the number of rejects and improved quality control.

In recent years downsizing in organisations has meant that many middle-management responsibilities have been shifted down onto teams of employees who have also taken on the authority to make decisions.

The emphasis on teamwork suggests that well-organised teams will outperform the same group of individuals operating in isolation. It is therefore important to identify the processes involved in teamworking and some of the characteristics of an effective team.

Case Study
Creating an integrated working approach at Blue Circle Cement

Like many companies in the UK in the 1980s Blue Circle Cement was desperately in need of change. At that time, the UK cement industry was losing out to its European competitors in terms of sales because its costs were too high relative to output. Employment was characterised by relatively low wages, restrictive practices, and demarcation between crafts and between craft and process workers. There was a 'them and us' adversarial culture within the organisation. It was felt that all of this would need to be swept aside if the organisation was to flourish again.

A programme of change was therefore introduced. It involved a radical overhaul of working practices, reward systems and, not least, company culture. The results included gaining a flexible, multi-skilled workforce working on annualised hours contracts which eliminated overtime. Higher productivity and lower unit costs have been reflected in the bottom line.

It was decided to create a new shared vision of the way forward. To create the vision, best practice in other companies such as Pilkington Glass and Carreras Rothman was studied. Visits were made by groups of management and shop-floor representatives, to encourage growth of a new team spirit.

A shared vision was developed of a highly skilled and flexible workforce, working as an integrated team. Together with the new technology in which the firm was to invest, the team would be able to compete with the best in the world.

At the heart of the new way of working was to be a system known as Integrated Working, which relied on:

- An annual hours contract.
- A reduction in job categories from 14 to 3. Jobs are now defined far more broadly than in the past, and employees have been involved in detailed new skills training to perform these jobs. Employees are required to adopt a much more flexible approach to

work and are given training in the necessary skills. All personnel, whatever their classification, must be prepared to carry out any duty, to work without direct supervision, and to assist other personnel as necessary in any part of the works.
- A new teamworking approach. Working together and having mutual respect were considered essential to the development of the new culture. This has involved considerable resource implications for the development of teamwork skills through training, including the training of team leaders.

These changes have proved to be highly successful and have led to a considerable increase in motivation, commitment and productivity.

Questions for discussion

1 *Why do you think that Blue Circle Cement decided to change the culture within its organisation?*
2 *Why do you think it chose teamworking as a means of driving this change?*
3 *What benefits would you expect them to have reaped from this change process?*
4 *Can you identify other organisations which have adopted a similar approach? What have been the results of their initiatives?*

Team processes

Whenever a team is functioning, there are three strands involved in moving from the start of the decision-making process to the finish: the task, the process, and the action schedule.

Figure 4.1 The decision-making process

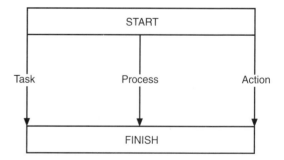

The task is the content of the work. For example, the task of a management meeting of a charity may be to decide how a substantial donation is to be spent. The task of an interview panel may be to select the best candidate for the post. The task therefore is the conversion of information, opinions and evaluations into decisions or recommendations. Depending upon the type of team involved, tasks may be routine or highly specialised.

The process relates to the interaction which takes place between members of a team. It is about people working together and their behaviour within the team. Interpersonal skills, such as listening, encouraging, clarifying and compromising, will to some extent determine how effective the group is. In general it covers who does what and when. Groups often pay insufficient attention to the process.

The action schedule is concerned with how the team will be organised to undertake a particular task. It covers questions such as: What roles will team members fulfil? How will progress be checked and monitored? How will the team ensure they keep to their timetable and meet deadlines? It also deals with the procedures for decision-making.

In trying to develop effective group decision-making, it is important to give attention to all three aspects of team working. Concentration purely on the task, for example, may well expose disagreements about how things should be organised and lack of monitoring of progress.

Communication

In groups, communication and the exchange of information are influenced by the way in which the group is organised and the means of communication employed. It is possible to identify four basic types of communication network. These types of communication network can be identified as being centralised, where information is channelled through one person, or decentralised, where members of the group share in the process.

Centralised communication

The wheel and chain networks rely on a centralised flow of information. In these networks one position is more central than the others. The quality of decision-making thus depends on those in key central positions and the quality of the communication channels to them.

Centralised networks have the following characteristics:

- The group is dependent on those with access to relevant information.
- The leadership position is strengthened as information tends to pass to the leader.

Figure 4.2 Centralised communication networks

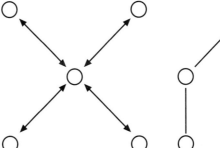

a The wheel network   b The chain network

- Well-structured and straightforward activities can be carried out effectively and quickly.
- Levels of satisfaction for group members tend to be lower than in decentralised groups.

Decentralised communication

The circle and completely connected networks lend themselves to a more open decentralised way of working. No one position in the network is more central than the others. Members of these groups are mutually interdependent and share information and the decision-making process.

Figure 4.3 Decentralised communication networks

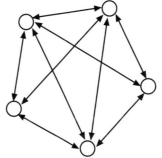
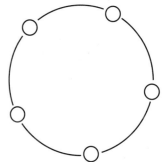

a The completely connected network   b The circle network

Decentralised networks have the following characteristics:

- The group is not so dependent on key individuals.
- Information is shared between group members.
- There is greater participation by all members in discussion and decisions.
- Levels of satisfaction are usually greater than in centralised networks.

The effectiveness of a group will be influenced by the appropriateness of its structure and communication network, for the type of task to be completed. If the task requires quick action and a swift decision then the wheel network may be most effective: here one individual gathers information from four contacts and executes a quick decision. The decentralised networks may be more appropriate for periodic control and strategic decisions where all members' contributions and discussions are essential in order to produce high quality decisions.

Roles within teams

When people work together in a team, the members of the team usually adopt particular roles. For example, one person may have the role of monitoring progress, checking the time-keeping or acting as leader. There is a tendency for one member of a group to take on the task functions and for others to adopt the maintenance role.

Task functions are those which will help the group to get the task done as effectively and efficiently as possible, including:

- proposing objectives, clarifying goals
- seeking information and opinions
- keeping the group on track
- summarising ideas
- suggesting ways forward
- evaluating contributions.

Team members who take on the **maintenance role** offer support and encouragement to the group. This involves:

- supporting other group members
- ensuring all members of the group are included
- reconciling disagreements and reducing tension
- making suggestions for compromise
- monitoring the group.

The effectiveness of a team will, to some extent, depend upon the mix of roles which team members take on. Successful teams will tend to have a range of appropriate personalities and qualities.

Belbin (1981) identified eight roles required within a well-functioning team:

1 *The chairperson* co-ordinates the efforts of the group and ensures the team makes best use of its resources in achieving its goals.
2 *The shaper* sets objectives and priorities and drives the team towards successful completion of the task.
3 *The plant* comes up with new ideas and strategies.
4 *The monitor evaluator* is able to analyse problems and evaluate progress.
5 *The resource investigator* is outgoing and will explore and report on ideas and developments from outside the group.

6 *The company worker* is an administrator rather than a leader and good at carrying out agreed plans.
7 *The team worker* supports the team, helps to keep it together and tries to improve communication between members.
8 *The finisher* maintains momentum in the team and plays an important part in getting the task finished.

Belbin suggested that, although team members may tend towards one of these roles, most people would also be able to undertake a second role.

If people have particular attributes and ways of working which suggest that they will tend to take up particular roles within teams, then it is obviously important that there is a balance of roles in order to produce an effective team.

Questions for discussion

Reflect on your own experience of working in teams. To what extent do you feel that the roles outlined above are necessary in effective team working? Which of the roles do you see as the most important?

Team-mapping

Research has shown that individuals do have different ways in which they like to organise their work. This involves the way in which they plan, organise and communicate. Management consultants have attempted to

Figure 4.4 The Margerison McCann Team Management Indicator

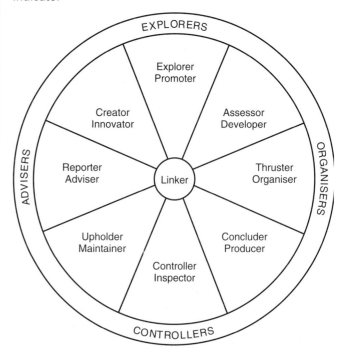

devise techniques for identifying people's work preferences in order to be able to identify the sort of roles which people are likely to take on in a team situation.

For example, the Margerison McCann Team Management Index can be used to elicit information about people's work preferences. These preferences are then used to place individuals on a Team Management Indicator (see Figure 4.4).

The Margerison McCann index identifies nine key team roles:

Reporter-Advisers are good at generating information and gathering it together in such a way that it can be understood. Such people are usually patient, and prepared to delay making a decision until they know as much as they can about the work to be done. Some people feel that they procrastinate and put things off. However, for the Reporter-Adviser it is better to be accurate than to put forward advice which later might be seen to be in error. Such people are invaluable as 'support' members of the team, but they are not likely to be the ones who will get things organised. Indeed, their concern is to make sure that the job is done correctly.

Creator-Innovators are people who have a number of ideas which may well contradict and upset the existing way of doing things. Such people can be very independent and wish to experiment and pursue their ideas regardless of the present systems and methods. They need to be allowed to pursue their ideas without disrupting the present way of working until their new approaches have been proved. Many organisations therefore set up research and development units (often separated from the production units) to allow such people to develop their ideas and see if they come to fruition. On *every* team it is important to have people who are idea-orientated and to give them an opportunity to talk through their views, even though it may seem at the time to be disturbing the existing way of operating.

Explorer-Promoters are usually excellent at taking up an idea and making people enthusiastic about it. They will find out what is happening outside the organisation and compare new ideas with what is being done by other people. They are also good at bringing back contacts and information and resources which can help the innovation move forward. They may not necessarily be good at controlling details, but they are excellent at seeing the wide picture. They are very capable of pushing an idea forward, even if they are not always the best people to organise and control it.

Assessor-Developers look for ways and means in which an idea can work in a practical way. Their concern is to see if the market wants the innovation and they will therefore test it against some practical criteria. Very often they will produce a prototype or do a market research study. Their whole interest is in developing an innovation to the point where it can work. However, once they have done this, they will probably not be interested in producing it on a regular basis. Instead, they prefer to move off and look at another project which they can assess and develop.

Thruster-Organisers are the people who get things done. Once they have been convinced that the idea is of interest, they will set up procedures and systems and make the task into a work reality. They push people and systems to ensure that deadlines can be met. They can be extremely impatient but they get things done, even if it does mean that on the way certain 'feathers are ruffled'.

Concluder-Producers take great pride in producing a product or service to a standard. They will do this on a regular basis and feel that their work is fulfilled if their quotas and plans are met. Indeed, they like working to set procedures and doing things in a regular way. The fact that they produced something yesterday does not mean that they will be bored with producing it tomorrow. This is in contrast to the Creator-Innovators who dislike doing similar things day after day and want the variety and challenge of doing things differently. For the Concluder-Producer the important thing is to use existing skills rather than to continually change and learn new ways of doing things. They therefore enjoy reproducing things and achieving the plans that they set.

Controller-Inspectors are people who enjoy doing detailed work and making sure that the facts and figures are correct. They are careful and meticulous. Indeed, one of their great strengths is that they concentrate for long periods of time upon a particular task. This contrasts with the Explorer-Promoter who continually needs a wide variety of tasks. The Controller-Inspector likes to pursue something in depth and to make sure that the work is done according to plan in an accurate way. They are extremely valuable in financial and quality issues.

Upholder-Maintainers are very good at making sure the team has a sound basis for operations. They take pride in maintaining both the physical and social side of work. Such people can very well become the 'conscience' of the team and provide a lot of support and help to team members. They usually have strong views on the way the team should be run based on their convictions and beliefs. If these are upset, such people can become rather obstinate and difficult. However, when they believe in what the team is doing, they can become a tremendous source of strength and energy and often make excellent negotiators.

In the middle of all these work functions are the **Linkers**. These are people who map close to the centre of the team and therefore have considerable co-ordinating abilities. All of the other roles that we have mentioned also involve some aspect of Linking, but the people closer to the 'hub' of the team are more able to co-ordinate and integrate the work of others. Essentially, all managers should look towards developing linking skills, whatever other key strengths they have. However, not all managers are good at linking. They therefore need to have someone on their team who can perform this role. On many occasions the manager needs to make a conscious effort, otherwise the team will begin to disintegrate.

If an organisation is aware of the preferences and strengths of individuals, it should be possible to select and develop more effective teams.

Group decision-making

It is generally accepted that the quality of decision-making in a group is likely to be higher because of the quantity and quality of input. It is also clear that the cost to organisations of teams instead of individuals undertaking tasks is high. It is important, therefore, that teams operate effectively and make quality decisions and that their work is more effective than that which an individual could produce.

Various training exercises can be used to show the effectiveness of team decisions. For example, a team of people can be asked to assume that their aircraft has crash landed in the desert. They have a range of things which have been saved from the aircraft and must prioritise these in order of importance for their survival. Participants first undertake the task individually and then as a group. The most common outcome of exercises like this is that the group is more successful than the individual.

Vroom and Yetton (1973) identified three criteria essential for measuring good decision-making:

- the objective quality of the decision reached
- the time it takes to reach the decision
- the extent to which the decision is accepted by those whom it affects and who have to work with it.

It is obviously important that, once a decision has been taken, it is implemented effectively. One of the advantages of team decisions is that there should be a higher commitment to the decision and its implementation if people have shared in the decision.

Gilligan, Neale and Murray identified the following features that should lead to effective group performance.

1 The structure of the group and the status of group members should be stable and well formed.
2 The group should be large enough to fulfil the tasks, but not so large as to encourage the formation of sub-groups.
3 The group members should have the appropriate skills for the task.
4 The atmosphere should be informal and relaxed.
5 Objectives should be understood and accepted by group members.
6 Discussion should be encouraged and members should be willing to listen to each other.
7 Decisions should be reached by consensus.
8 The leader of the group should not dominate, nor should there be evidence of a struggle for power.
9 The group should operate with mild or moderate levels of stress.
10 Disagreements should not be overridden; instead, the reasons for disagreements should be examined and an attempt made to resolve them.
11 The allocation of tasks to members should be clear and accepted.
12 The group should act in a cohesive way.

Phases of team development

Tuckman and Jensen identified four phases of team development: forming, storming, norming and performing.

Figure 4.5 The phases of team development

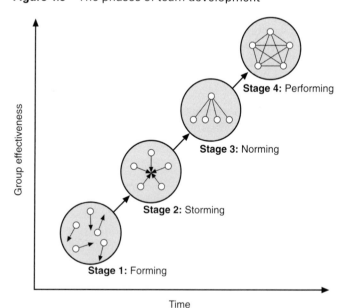

Stage 4: Performing

Stage 3: Norming

Stage 2: Storming

Stage 1: Forming

Group effectiveness

Time

Phase 1: Forming
A number of individuals come together. They start to exchange ideas and gather information about the nature of the task: what needs to be done and by when? They also

explore how other members of the group operate and what behaviour is acceptable.

Phase 2: Storming

The group begins to exchange ideas as they try to reach agreement on objectives and strategy. There is often conflict and disagreement.

Phase 3: Norming

The group begins to share ideas. Group cohesion starts to develop and members start to act collaboratively.

Phase 4: Performing

The group is able to turn its attention to the task. A pattern of working is established. Members may assume particular roles or functions. Every member of the group is therefore able to make the best possible contribution to the team.

Different groups will obviously go through this cycle at different rates and may face different problems at each stage. The early stage of group formation, when there is no leader, may be dominated by particular individuals. At this point quieter members of the group may not be heard. If a group is very task-focused then, while in the short-term progress may be rapid, the group may face long-term difficulties. Social relationships in the group may be so poor that no clear team spirit is evident. On the other hand an over-emphasis on team processes may mean that the task is never completed.

Groups may well go through these phases in a non-linear way, repeating earlier phases in the cycles. A change in group membership, for example, may cause the group to revert to an earlier phase.

Creating a well-functioning team

Characteristics

McGregor (1960) identified the main characteristics of a creative, well-functioning team.

1 The atmosphere of the group is comfortable, informal and relaxed.
2 Discussion is open and extensive; everyone participates but remains focused on the task.
3 The task or goal of the team is clearly understood by team members and is accepted. Full and free discussion of the task or goal will have taken place before it was formulated in such a way that members of the team could be committed to it.
4 Team members listen to each other's contributions and discuss things openly and freely. They are not afraid of feeling foolish in each other's eyes.

5 Disagreements are open and not suppressed by the team. The team seeks to resolve any disagreements.
6 Decisions are reached by consensus, through discussion and persuasive argument. The team does not accept a majority vote as a proper basis for action.
7 Criticism is frank and frequent and is related to the task rather than personalities.
8 Team members can express their feelings and ideas about the task and how the team operates.
9 When the team takes action, assignments are clear and accepted by the team members. There is an understanding of what has been agreed and who will do it.
10 The team leader does not dominate and team members do not defer to the leader.

Question for discussion

To what extent do you agree that the points outlined above are features of a high performance team? Support your argument by well chosen examples.

Team-building

Most organisations introduce teamwork in order to gain from the benefits in terms of motivation of personnel and reduced costs due to more effective working practices or decisions. If teams go wrong, however, they can be very costly.

Armstrong (1992) identified seven stages involved in introducing and developing teams (see Figure 4.6).

The plan suggests that teamwork is most likely to be successful when it operates in a supportive environment. The culture of an organisation should therefore be one which supports **co-operation**, **trust** and **compatibility**.

The development of teamworking skills may include exercises and sessions which seek to explore and develop relevant skills. Tasks may be devised for groups to help them develop consensus decision-making or listening skills.

Case Study
Introducing a teamworking approach at Blue Circle Cement

When Blue Circle Cement decided to introduce teamworking, team training was an important part of the change package. Team training involved everyone in the workplace and was given active support by management and trade unions. The training involved four elements:

1. Senior managers' workshops

These workshops looked at all aspects of team-building, leadership and teamwork. For example, they were concerned with procedures involved in building high-performance teams, and ways of ensuring that suitable resources were provided for team-building. Managers needed an in-depth understanding of the training to be given to the rest of the workforce.

2. Staff team training

Staff team training was given to all middle managers and supervisors. Attendance at each session was organised so that all managers were accompanied by their supervisors. The focus was very much on putting teamwork into operation and ways of organising the team-building workshops.

3. Team leader briefings

The role of the team leader was seen as crucial. The purpose of the team leader briefings was to prepare the leaders for the workshop sessions with their teams and to ensure as far as possible that they assumed a leadership role in team-building.

4. Team-building workshops

The workshop was the key element of the change process. During the workshop, an important part of the leader's job was to relax the team and ensure that they became involved in the training experience. Because many employees were unused to the processes of teamwork, it was necessary to encourage and develop participatory and co-operative approaches. Team members were asked to list all their concerns, e.g. problems about flexibility, the need for job training, the prospect of not being able to earn more than a stable income, etc. All the concerns were listed and displayed until the end of the workshops. Team-building sessions included syndicate exercises, identification of roles within a team, and discussion of leadership styles. Practice in working as a team was provided by problem-solving syndicates. The workshops concluded in an open forum with the managers in attendance, responding to concerns and answering any unresolved questions.

Questions for discussion

1 *How effective do you think the above approach to team-building would be in securing the support of all members of an organisation?*

2 *Why do you think that team members were encouraged to highlight their concerns at the start of team-building workshops?*

3 *To what extent do you think it was necessary for the teams to have team leaders?*

Figure 4.6 Developing teamwork: a seven-stage plan

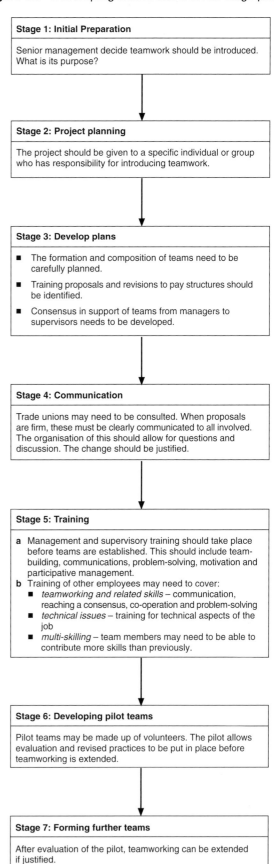

Teams in action and their problems

Dumaine (1994) suggests that one of the most common problems with teams is that organisations rush into forming them and end up with the wrong kind of team for the job. Another problem is that organisations move into team-working with little or no training or support. Downsizing, where an organisation cuts out layers of middle management, may allow teamwork to be introduced, but there is a paradox here. The very thing which often gives rise to teams can also have a devastating effect on morale and team spirit. He also suggests that it is essential that organisations are clear about what the different types of teams can be expected to produce. For example, quality circles might help an organisation to cut defects and reduce rework, but, because they do not accompany more fundamental changes in the way in which the work is done, they can not produce leaps in productivity. It is the self-managed teams or project teams which can raise productivity radically, because these teams can substantially change work processes.

Dumaine suggests that teams may not be as simple to introduce into organisations as many would like to think. However, many organisations will make the investment in teams because in a competitive environment it may be harder to operate without teams than with them.

Case Study

Team working at Land Rover

In the mid 1990s Land Rover, the Midlands-based specialist vehicle company, introduced teamworking for the production of its latest Range Rover; 650 workers were selected from Land Rover's other production lines. The workers, or **associates** as they are called, were only accepted for the project after passing interviews for their attitude and compatibility. They also underwent a range of psychometric tests. The new team's high productivity and quality rates were to be used as examples for the rest of the organisation.

Under the acronym CONQUER – Commitment, One team open minded, No second best, Quality image, Utmost honesty, Effective communication, and Respect

– the team is supposed to be loyal, uncompromising in its drive for quality, have a sense of humour, consider others' opinions, lead by example, be friendly, share knowledge, accept there is no demarcation, and give praise and reward where due.

The move is part of an overall employment policy at Rover, which is the owner of Land Rover, of job security. Employees are guaranteed a job at the company, although in what role and where is subject to change.

Team managers lead the workforce in the assembly of the car. Productivity is up by 50 per cent and the new Range Rover takes just half the time to build compared with the previous model.

Questions for discussion

1 *Why have Land Rover moved towards teamworking for the production of the Range Rover?*
2 *Why should teamworking have a positive effect on quality and productivity?*

Further reading

- *Managing Human Resources* by Michael Armstrong. Kogan Page, 1992.
- *Management Teams: Why they Succeed or Fail* by R. M. Belbin. Heinemann, 1981.
- *Total Quality and Human Resources* by B. Dale and C. Cooper. Kogan Page, 1992.
- *The Trouble with Teams* by B. Dumaine. In *Fortune*, September, 1994.
- *Business Decision Making* by C. Gilligan, B. Neale, and D. Murray. Philip Alan, 1994.
- *Team Work* by C. Larson and F. Lafarsto. Sage Publications, 1990.
- *Margerison McCann Team Management Index*, Prado Systems Ltd, 1990.
- *The Human Side of Enterprise* by D. McGregor. McGraw-Hill, 1960.
- *States of Small Group Development Revisited* by B. Tuckman and N. Jensen. In *Group and Organisational Studies*, Vol 2, 1977.

5 Performance at work

On completion of this chapter, students should be able to:

- define performance
- identify the features that lead to high performance in an organisation
- explain and evaluate the ingredients of effective coaching
- outline and evaluate coaching methods
- define, explain and analyse different methods of training
- explain the importance of lifelong learning
- identify initiatives to support lifelong learning in the UK
- explain the importance of Learning Targets
- analyse approaches to counselling
- identify major forms of disciplinary procedures.

Performance

High performance is desirable in business. A high-performance team or individual makes good use of time, skills, abilities and knowledge, as well as making effective use of an organisation's resources. A high-performance organisation will have high-performance teams and individuals working for it.

However, high performance does not just rise out of the blue. High performance is the product of clear thinking and careful planning to make sure that organisational members are fully motivated and provided with the means to make the most of themselves within an organisation. Oliver and Lowe (*The High Commitment Workplace*, 1991), have put forward a Commitment Model that lends itself to high performance in the workplace. This model comprises a number of features:

Job design:

- multi-skilling and flexible job definitions
- work teams as the unit of accountability
- emphasis on complete tasks (i.e. employees work together to complete a whole task, e.g. producing a major section of a car rather than a disembodied part such as a wheel nut).

Structure, systems and culture:

- flatter structures
- co-ordination is based on shared goals and values
- communication flows are flatter rather than downwards
- task culture.

Employee–organisation relationships:

- security of employment
- company-based systems of employee involvement
- emphasis on mutual benefits of all in the workplace
- pay linked to skills and performance
- high levels of trust.

In this chapter, therefore, we want to introduce some of the ways in which organisations can encourage high levels of performance at work by looking at:

- coaching skills
- training and development

- counselling
- discipline
- monitoring and reporting individual and group performance.

The learning organisation

Case Study
The Body Shop

'You have got to have energy to work with us and you have got to have a sense of curiosity, but what I particularly like is to find people who are bright enough to want more, who can see that there are ways of getting more within the company, who can learn and grow and be somebody, who take all the information and education we give them and run with it and challenge the management. We have always believed in widening the windows of opportunity for everyone who works for us, whether they are making paper in Nepal or packing in the Littlehampton warehouse. Self-empowerment is the aim.' (From *Body and Soul* by Anita Roddick, founder of The Body Shop.)

Questions for discussion

1 *What does the above extract tell us about Anita Roddick's approach to empowering employees at the Body Shop?*
2 *What do you think will be the resultant effects on performance in the organisation?*

Learning is the act of gaining knowledge. By gaining knowledge an individual or organisation is able to move forward and make improvements. Organisations operate in dynamic environments. Not only do they need to adapt and adjust on account of external changes, they also need to adapt as a result of internal changes such as the creation of new strategies and policies and because of the development of new human resources within an organisation.

A learning organisation is one that sets out to understand the changes that are taking place within its environment and within itself. It is an organisation that moves forward and takes steps to develop its human resources in order to accommodate for these changes. Today, all organisations need to be learning organisations, flexible and adaptable. Organisations cannot afford to get stuck in an existing state of order, however attractive and appealing that might be.

In his book *The Empty Raincoat*, Charles Handy has pointed out the importance of the **Sigmoid curve** to the

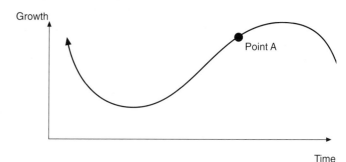

Figure 5.1   The Sigmoid curve

intelligent organisation. The Sigmoid curve is an S shape on its side (see Figure 5.1). As shown in this curve, all activity goes through a period of growth and development followed by maturity and decline. The important thing for an organisation is to recognise when it is nearing the top section of the Sigmoid curve: the best time for change is at Point A.

At this point it looks as if everything is going well. However, just round the corner is a period of decline. It is when organisations appear to be most successful that they need to make changes. The learning organisation therefore seeks to understand its environment and itself in order to make changes at this point, so that it can go through a new period of growth (see Figure 5.2).

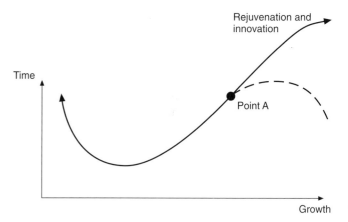

Figure 5.2   Intelligently extending the period of growth

Coaching skills

The intelligent organisation will place a strong emphasis on the **development** of its people in order to make best possible use of them and to motivate them. A key part of this development process is that of coaching. Coaching is an ongoing process in which one person works closely with another – the coach – to develop skills and abilities.

We are particularly familiar with the term 'coach' from the fields of athletics, boxing, football and other sports. In these areas the coach plays a number of roles in enabling an individual sportsplayer to achieve a high standard of performance. The coach is someone who has had a lot of experience in a particular field and is able to focus time and effort in helping the person he or she is coaching to improve performance, e.g. by developing schedules of activities, training regimes and diet. Coaches do more than simply provide technical support, although this is a key part of their role. In addition they give moral and mental support and play a key psychological supporting role. Top swimmers and tennis players will want their coach to accompany them to key sporting events and to discuss their progress on a regular basis. Coaches are often said to play the parts of surrogate parents. Many coaches have become almost as famous as their proteges, e.g. Terry Venables who coached the English football team in the mid-1990's and the legendary boxing coach Cuss Damato.

Coaching can be seen as someone with more expertise supporting and mentoring someone with less expertise. It is an essential ingredient of effective management and managers need to learn to be good coaches. It is by building one-to-one relationships with the people with whom you work that you are most likely to win their loyalty and support as well as to unleash their potential. At the end of the day, coaching is not a costly business, and yet the benefits can be enormous both for individuals, teams and ultimately the whole organisation. Good coaching is an express route to high performance and results.

In developing a coaching role, it is important that the coach picks up on aspects of performance that need improving rather than aspects of personality. For example, a coach may notice that an individual is spending more time dealing with some people than with others in a situation where this is not appropriate. The coach might then suggest: 'Each of your clients needs to be given an equal amount of time and attention. Perhaps you could record the amount of time you spend with each, just to check that you are doing this.' Clearly this would be a better approach then stating: 'You are clearly showing favouritism here. You obviously like some of your clients better than others. Cut it out.' In a similar vein it may not be productive to tell individuals they are lazy, aggressive or rude. Instead you should help them to identify strategies which will enable them use more positive behaviours.

What the good coach does

The good coach is what the good coach *does*. The following are key ingredients of good coaching.

Ongoing

Coaching is not something which is piecemeal or haphazard. Instead it is organised and ongoing. Managers should develop a coaching role as a natural part of the way in which they operate. Managers should therefore see themselves as providing regular coaching sessions to subordinates which are both of a formal and informal nature. This mentoring role should be something that is a constant part of the relationship between manager and subordinate. It is not something that just happens at planned meetings. The mentor will regularly say the right word, make the right suggestion, and provide helpful support.

Accepted

Because the good coach provides useful help and support, this comes to be accepted by the person being coached. The guidance and support should become such a regular and natural part of the relationship that the subordinate will have no qualms about asking for further guidance. He or she should be able to say things like 'What advice would you give me about…?', 'Do you think I handled that right?', 'I'm not sure what to do about … What would you suggest?' Of course, this relationship will only develop if the coach has been able to inspire **confidence.**

Based on trust

The coach will therefore have to win the support and confidence of the person that he or she is coaching. This will only come about if the coach is seen to listen and provide helpful and authoritative advice. Trust and confidence will come about when it is felt that the coach has the best interest of the other person in mind at all times, rather than using that person for his or her own ends.

Offered as advice and support

The feedback that the coach gives will be based on ideas and suggestions from his or her own experience. It is important, however, that the feedback is given in such a way that it is seen as advice rather than a prescription – 'Do it my way because this is the best way.' If the subordinate chooses not to accept the advice given every time, this should not lead to recriminations.

About long-term development

Coaching advice is concerned more with long-term than short-term development. Clearly it is helpful to be given advice and help that supports short-term decision-making and ways to deal with immediate problems. However, coaching should be seen as a way of enabling someone to develop over a long period of time, e.g. five years rather than five minutes.

Systematic and planned

It is important that coaching should be systematic and planned rather than a random exercise. The plan should outline when meetings will take place and define what will be discussed in meetings. Once this framework has been agreed, coaching can then take place in an informal rather than a highly formalised way.

Case Study

Ron Roddan

Linford Christie is one of the most famous UK athletes of all time. However, less is known about his coach Ron Roddan.

Roddan is a former civil service laboratory assistant, who was a county sprinter in the 1950s and 1960s. Since the early 1960s he has worked as a coach with the Thames Valley Harriers and it is in this capacity that he has had the greatest success. Over the years more than 30 of his athletes have been picked for British teams, but Linford Christie has been the greatest success as an Olympic and world champion who has set the standard for 100-metre runners for a number of years.

Christie first went along to what was then called the West London Stadium as a 17-year-old. At first he went unnoticed. Roddan soon recognised Christie's talent but

waited until he was prepared to do something about it. He did not put any pressure on Christie, just the occasional word suggesting that it would be a waste if he failed to use his ability to the full. When Christie was ready and willing to take advice, Roddan was there to give it, and over the years Christie has been willing to listen to every word of advice.

The great thing about Roddan is that he is able to give Christie advice without threatening the athlete's morale. Criticism and praise are made and accepted without emotional scenes. 'If I say "Ron that was rubbish",' Christie says, 'He will say, "That's what I thought. Never mind, we can do this …".' Christie says that whatever medals he wins or money he earns, the thing he prizes is 'seeing the smile on Ron's face'.

Question for discussion

What aspects of good coaching are apparent in the relationship between Linford Christie and his coach Ron Roddan?

Self-discovery

Coaching requires a good measure of modesty. In helping someone to develop within an organisation or to develop personal confidence and ability, it is important to remember who the emphasis for development is on. If the coach is forever saying 'look what I've taught you', or 'he or she learned that from me' then the coaching process may well be deficient. For learners to gain the maximum amount of motivation they need to take on new ideas and initiatives for themselves. They need to feel that it is through their own efforts that much of the learning and development has taken place. Self-discovery is therefore a key element in the development process.

When taking on a coaching role, a manager should not always provide answers to the development issues that subordinates raise. Instead, the manager should try to suggest options or alternatives so that subordinates will actually make the choice for themselves. This is the process of 'self-discovery' whereby subordinates are able to make personal choices, supported by guidance from the coach, and become independent learners.

Christopher Orpen, in his book *Behaviour in Organisations*, outlined a number of characteristics which subordinates see as being the features of a good coach. This is a manager who:

■ treats me as a person in my own right, uniquely different from other employees with whom he or she works

- sets a good example; is an appropriate person on whom to model oneself
- encourages and supports me, especially when things are not going well
- praises me when I do well, but still lets me know when I do poorly, in a straightforward and understanding manner
- supports me to his or her superiors, wherever it is appropriate to do so
- performs his or her own job conscientiously and competently and enjoys a high reputation throughout the organisation as a result
- does not try to pull rank on me; does not make me aware that he or she holds a higher position than me and should be listened to for that reason
- keeps me fully informed about everything I need to know to perform well, including aspects of the organisation not immediately related to my current job
- takes time out from his or her normal duties and tasks regularly to coach me in my job, without forcing him or herself on me or requiring me always to do things his or her way
- never underestimates what I am capable of doing; leads me forward and upward, often stretching me to perform even better than I thought I could.

Orpen also produced a number of tips for coaching which can be summarised as follows:

1 *Coach on a regular (not annual) basis.* Formal and informal coaching sessions need to be regular and continuous.
2 *Recognise your contribution as the manager.* As a manager you may form part of the problem for individuals working with you. You need to recognise this and jointly consider with subordinates ways of improving the work situation.
3 *Provide alternative examples when coaching.* Do not rely on verbal suggestions as to how improvements can be made. Wherever possible provide concrete examples, e.g. by modelling appropriate actions through your own behaviour. When subordinates try out new ways of operating, give them feedback on how you think they are doing.
4 *Focus on behaviours, not attributes.* It is much easier to change the behaviour of individuals than their personality traits and attributes. The coach should therefore focus on altering the way in which subordinates carry out particular actions rather than their underlying personality.
5 *Use positive reinforcement.* Wherever possible, give rewards and positive feedback.
6 *Don't coach too closely.* There is a danger of overcoaching. Individuals need to learn from their own mistakes if they are to become independent learners.

Task

Explain whether the following situations reflect good coaching or not.

1 Terry has recently started working in a bank. She has been allocated a mentor – Sally. Sally says to Terry on the first day: 'Because you are new to this job I want you to copy everything I do. There is no need to ask questions because everything will be self-explanatory. That's the way I learned and look where it's got me!'
2 Steve has been acting as a coach to Graham for several years. Graham regularly asks Steve for advice about a wide range of work issues and feels confident that Steve will come up with useful answers. However, in recent times Steve has been more reluctant to give advice because he feels that Graham should become more independent.
3 Hamid coaches John. Initially they had planned to have a formal discussion every two weeks and to discuss work issues more regularly on an informal basis. However, John missed a couple of the planned sessions in the early days. Hamid has therefore decided to miss out on the informal coaching in order to make sure that John attends the planned sessions on a regular basis.

Training and development

Training and development are two complementary strands of the process of enabling people to become more effective employees and better members of organisations, as well as serving to meet the needs of individuals.

Training should be designed to fill the gap between what a person can do at a particular moment in time and what he or she should be able to do when given appropriate training.

Development involves changing behaviour in the light of learning. In helping individuals to develop it is therefore necessary to provide them with a range of experiences which will enable them to improve themselves. It should be seen as a lifetime process, i.e. **lifetime learning.**

Training helps those being trained and also benefits the organisation they work for. Benefits to individuals include greater skills, more knowledge, more confidence and better career prospects. Benefits to the organisation include more productive employees, better quality work,

Figure 5.3 Enabling a person through training

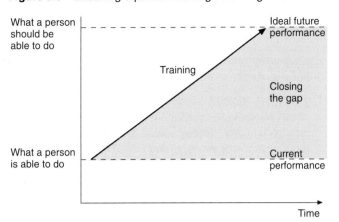

more job satisfaction leading to lower absenteeism and staff turnover, and greater ability to use the latest technology.

Case Study

Training opportunities in a biscuit factory

The following is a short extract from an employee's handbook in a biscuit factory:

'This company values training and development for all our employees, in order to widen your experience and to help you to gain promotion. Your most important contact is your line supervisor or manager (the person directly above you). This person will help you to deal with any immediate problems. In your first six months there will be opportunities to discuss your training needs with your immediate superior. The training needs of all employees are constantly examined. Together with your supervisor, line leader and training instructors, we will teach you the skills you require, including the importance of safety at work. The company also encourages you to continue with education courses in your spare time. If you choose an appropriate course we will refund your tuition and exam fees.'

Questions for discussion

1 *Why do you think this company stresses the importance of training?*
2 *Who will benefit from this training process?*
3 *Give examples of the way in which this company encourages:*
   a *on-the-job training*
   b *off-the-job training*

Employers are increasingly seeing training as an essential part of their activities. The Employers' Manpower and Skills Practices Survey in 1994 indicated that the most important reasons given by employers for training were to:

- improve quality
- improve health and safety
- maintain and update job skills
- better meet customer requirements
- facilitate the introduction of new products and services
- introduce new technology
- bring about organisational change
- enhance employee loyalty
- attract recruits.

'To improve quality standards' was the most highly rated reason for training, with 85 per cent of employers saying it was very important. **Quality** is frequently the key issue on which employers compete and through which they aim to distinguish themselves in the marketplace. In 84 per cent of workplaces, management had introduced measures to raise the standard of customer service, and training was the most frequently mentioned measure to achieve this.

Employers and training

Before looking at ways in which employers can identify and meet training needs, it is helpful to look first at some of the research.

In 1994 the Policy Studies Institute carried out a survey of 600 employees. The survey showed that 95 per cent of employers provided at least some of their employees with some kind of training. In most cases, employees higher up in an organisation were more likely to receive training. A

Figure 5.4 Training by occupation

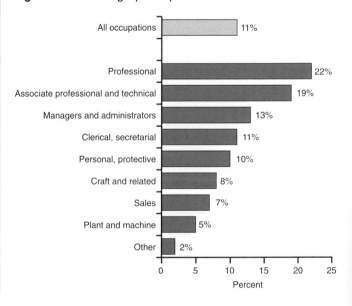

large majority (70–80 per cent) of employers said that managerial, professional and technical staff were 'likely' to receive training, but only 30 per cent said they provided training for unskilled manual workers (see Figure 5.4).

Most of this training was job-specific and relevant to the current skill requirements of job holders. The report of the survey expressed doubts as to whether this was enough to constitute lifelong learning. 'The crux for lifetime learning is not whether employers are training, but whether they provide continuous and progressive training for employees', says the report, which defines three types of training:

- *job-specific training* – to improve performance in tasks in the employee's current job
- *training for promotion* – to enable the employee to be promoted to a higher position
- *other* – training for some other reason defined by the employer.

Around 80 per cent of employers gave skilled craft and clerical employees job-related training, but fewer than 40 per cent gave them training aimed at preparing them for promotion. Managers, technical and other professionals were much more likely than employees in lower-level occupations to receive training for promotion and other types of training. Nearly half the employers who provided other training restricted it to certain occupations, mainly managerial and other professional staff.

Larger organisations were more likely to provide training than smaller ones, and public-sector organisations were more likely to provide training than those in the private sector. Employees in the service sector were more likely to receive training than those in manufacturing.

Identification of training needs

Companies who took part in the Policy Studies Institute Survey used one of four ways to identify their training needs:

- *joint assessment* – where discussions take place between employees and their managers (or supervisors)
- *managerial identification* – where managers identify training needs with little employee input
- *employee identification* – where employees identify their needs with little managerial input
- *standardised training* – where training is automatically provided for certain jobs.

Service-sector organisations, and larger employers in all sectors, were more varied in their use of these methods and more likely to use methods involving consultation with employees. A large majority of public-service organisations allowed employees to identify their own

training needs, but the number of employers in the distribution, hotels and retail industries doing so was much lower.

Individual training plans

Individual training plans can help to motivate employees. They also ensure that the training for which a need has been identified will be given. Individual training plans are most common in large organisations – in 1994, 91 per cent of organisations with 500 or more employees had such plans, compared with 25 per cent of organisations employing only 10–20 people.

Job analysis

A useful starting point for identifying training needs is a job analysis, which describes the tasks involved in performing a specific job. A **training specification** may be outlined from the results of a job analysis. Every job consists of a series of tasks and these need to be analysed for training purposes. The following aspects of the job will be identified:

- *skills* – the necessary manual, social, intellectual and perceptual skills
- *knowledge* – what the employee needs to know to do the job well
- *attitudes* – what attitudes the employee needs to perform well in the job.

Performance appraisal

In a performance appraisal, a comparison is made between what an employee currently does and what he or she is *expected* to do. By giving a clear indication of the present position, it gives a good starting point from which to improve performance. The manager or supervisor meets the employee in order to discuss and agree on:

- the job's overall purpose
- the tasks that must be carried out to achieve this purpose
- targets and standards appropriate to each task
- a timescale specifying when these targets and standards will be reviewed and when the possibility of setting new targets and standards will be discussed.

The performance appraisal programme should identify where an employee is not meeting required targets and standards, and will also indicate an individual's training needs.

Training methods

On-the-job training

The most common form of training is on-the-job training, in which the employee becomes more knowledgeable and skilled in the tasks of his or her job by working with and alongside others. This type of training has the advantage of permitting the trainee to learn in the real environment of the job, while experiencing the work at first-hand.

To be effective, this type of training must be carefully planned and supervised. The trainee will require a **mentor** who oversees and takes responsibility for day-to-day training.

The mentor will need instruction in training methods. Training may involve the mentor in demonstrating tasks that need to be performed and then coaching the trainee as he or she attempts similar processes. On-the-job training is most successful where individual tasks can be learned quickly, and where one-to-one learning situations are appropriate.

One disadvantage of on-the-job training is that the trainee may acquire too narrow a view of the tasks involved in the job and may be unable to generalise the skills. The trainee may focus on skills and knowledge that are appropriate only in one or a limited number of work environments and may imitate the working style of the mentor rather than using the style most appropriate to the circumstances. On-the-job training, therefore, should always be complemented by **off-the-job training** (described below) because, in the longer-term, organisations need people with flexible skills rather than those who can perform well in only one context or on one set of tasks.

Vestibule training

Vestibule training is the term used where one skilled instructor trains a number of employees at the same time, usually in semi-skilled clerical and production jobs. Trainees are given the opportunity to simulate work processes using similar materials and equipment to those used in the workplace. Vestibule training is often used to train bank clerks, secretaries, machine operators and quality control inspectors.

Classroom training

Many types of training can take place in more formal settings in the classroom.

- **Lectures** are an efficient way of communicating a lot of information to a large audience. To be effective in training employees, lectures should use interactive methods wherever possible and encourage audience participation.
- **Seminars** are meetings of a more open format between trainees and training staff or employers. The leader of the seminar will seek to move trainees through learning experiences towards certain outcomes.
- **Programmed learning** involves the learner working through a particular learning package at his or her own pace. Learning may be based on manuals or books, or it may use computers or videos. Computer-assisted learning is becoming cheaper and more widely used, particularly with the development of CD-ROMs. Working through a sequence of instructions, the trainee is able to check his or her answers at regular intervals. This form of training is cheap and easy to run, and can focus on specific learning outcomes. However, it lacks the essential motivating ingredient of human contact.
- **Learner-controlled instruction** gives learners considerable choice in determining the pace at which they learn and their preferred sequence of learning steps. A variety of media and instructions can be provided.
- **Case studies** are another useful learning tool, where learners are invited to tackle problems and issues which replicate real work challenges. Cases may be based on a real or fictitious situation. Often the tasks will be open-ended and will aim to stimulate discussion and encourage initiative.
- **Role plays** involve asking trainees to act out assigned roles. There are no scripts or rehearsals. The players are provided with a description of a situation and after being given time to plan and perhaps discuss their action, they act out their roles as spontaneously as possible. Role-playing is a form of learning by doing and is particularly good for developing interpersonal skills and flexible attitudes.

- **Simulations and games** can be used to replicate real activities and situations. Trainees participating in simulated activities learn in an experiential way. There is an increasing trend towards the use of 'virtual reality' simulations, particularly for applications such as learning to carry out a medical operation, or learning to fly an aeroplane. Mistakes can be made in the virtual world without great risk to the trainee or to others.

Types of training

Induction

Induction training is given to new employees. It familiarises them with the organisation and its rules. It can also be used to show a new employee particular skills, e.g. a supermarket cashier being trained to use electronic scanning equipment and checkout procedures.

Upgrading skills

Work changes all the time. This is particularly true considering the pace at which new technology is introduced. It is therefore essential for businesses to upgrade the skills of their employees. Employees working in insurance and banking, for example, need to regularly update their skills to deal with the latest developments such as on-line databases and networked information systems.

Retraining

As time moves on, jobs change or disappear. As a result, the employees who previously did these jobs need to retrain to do something else. Computer systems and other forms of new technology have altered many jobs out of all recognition. In the currently changing world of work, we all need regular periods of retraining. The phrase **lifelong learning** is used to describe this need for ongoing education and training. The days are long gone when someone could leave school and expect to work for the same organisation doing a similar job throughout his or her life.

Multi-skilling

Multi-skilling is the process of training employees to do a number of different tasks. Today's employees need to have a range of skills and to be able to turn their hand to a variety of tasks. We also call this **flexibility**. Work flexibility can be developed through training. Many modern organisations want flexible employees. These employees need to have new attitudes, including a 'can do' approach to problem-solving. The Japanese have been a major force behind moves to flexibility. Workers in Japanese car factories, for example, are expected to both work on the production line and fix it when things go wrong.

Training schemes

There are a number of government and company-run training schemes for different groups of employees, e.g. school leavers, graduates and the long-term unemployed. Other training schemes include apprenticeships with companies. The aim of these schemes is to provide relevant training in a useful field.

Staff training

This form of training is run by an organisation for all members of staff to enable them to develop new skills, e.g. school staff training in information technology skills such as a database package. Many organisations have set up training rooms in which they stock a range of training packages, often enabling staff to employ a self-managed distance-learning approach to training.

Staff development

In many businesses, training courses are run for employees who are seeking promotion. They are able to increase their knowledge and skills in areas such as management.

The importance of education and training

Education and training lie at the heart of creating a successful human resource base for an economy and for organisations, as well as helping individuals to compete effectively in the labour market. There is a clear link between creating an effective system for education and training and the resultant competitiveness of the UK labour force. Britain's workforce will become more skilled, if:

- employers' investment in people increases
- more employers across a broader range invest in training
- more people, including the young, are in jobs with training
- individual motivation to undertake vocational education and training increases
- more people across a broader range participate actively in training and development
- more people, including the young, and those seeking work, acquire relevant skills and vocational qualifications

- more people, including the young, achieve higher-level vocational qualifications
- more people, including the young, develop enterprising attitudes.

Clearly, the resultant effect of all the above would be a more skilful and competent workforce leading to higher productivity, competitiveness and profits for business, coupled with higher pay, prospects and job security for employees.

In June 1996, the government published a White Paper including a skills audit of the UK economy. The report highlighted a number of areas for optimism, coupled with others leading to a more pessimistic approach. On the positive side, the report indicated that the UK was better than its competitors in higher education; it had a stronger system for lifetime learning than either France or Germany; and employers thought young people were particularly strong in information technology skills. The report also highlighted recent moves to create a major programme of education and training reforms to tackle more than a century's neglect of this country's training needs.

However, the report went on to highlight a number of weaknesses. For example, at Level 2 (GCSE and equivalent) there are fewer people qualified in the UK than France or Germany. Although the studies of particular sectors found few differences in actual skills between the three countries, multinational employers perceived relative weaknesses in key work-related skills and the basic skills of literacy and numeracy in the UK. When 40 multinationals were asked to rate the basic skills of recruits (40 points for good, 20 for adequate and 10 for poor), the UK came bottom along with the US, mustering only between 21 and 23 points for all assessments. France was next, hitting the mid-20s; Germany and Singapore hit the high 20s to mid 30s; and Japan came top with ratings between 34 and 40 points.

In recent times the UK has shown healthy progress in education and training at Level 3 (A Level or equivalent). Between 1990 and 1995 the proportion of people completing Level 3 courses rose from 30 to 44 per cent. The figures for 18-year-olds taking part in education and training also rose from 45 to 60 per cent.

However, this trend is not only true for the UK. In fact, France, Germany, Singapore and the US are improving more quickly.

At Level 2 the UK is still substantially behind its European neighbours. Some 58 per cent of 19–21-year-olds have reached the grade, compared with 66 per cent in Germany and 78 per cent in France. Among 25–28-year-olds the difference is more striking, with the UK lagging behind France and Germany which had traditionally had more

impressive apprenticeship systems. The spread of qualifications is shown in Figure 5.5.

The UK figures indicate that anyone who reaches Level 3 has excellent access to higher education, while those who fail or drop out have poor prospects for improvement and skills upgrading compared with their peers overseas.

While there is an apparent UK lead in lifetime learning systems, there is little evidence in the skills audit report that this compensates for earlier failures to give the UK a competitive edge. The message coming through from the skills audit is fairly clear. The UK needs to invest more resources in helping young people to acquire basic literacy and numeracy in the early years of schooling. More resources are required at Level 2 to ensure that performance catches up with those of competitors. Greater provision is required at Level 3 to help those students who are slipping through the net. Effective avenues need to be created to put all citizens on the ladder of lifetime learning. Many are still slipping off the lower rungs.

The importance of lifelong learning

The increasing and changing demand for skills means that regular training to update or upskill those already in the workforce is essential. Individuals, like employers, seldom need persuading of the desirability of training in principle. The task is to convince them that there is provision suitable for them.

It is difficult to establish a precise picture of adults' participation in learning after 16 because of the wide range of definitions in use. In 1993, the National Institute of Adult Continuing Education estimated that there were 6 million adult learners in Britain, some 3.4 million of whom were in formal education. More recent research indicates that about 10 per cent of the population over 16 are current learners. However, when

Figure 5.5 Spread of qualifications (population percentages, 1994)

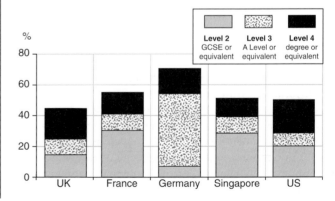

older age groups are excluded (i.e. those over 55), the rate of participation is nearer 20 per cent. By far the highest proportion of adult learners, apart from full-time students, are in their 20s.

The idea of lifelong learning is that individuals and organisations (as well as the government) appreciate the importance of developing individuals as lifelong learners so that they continually develop new skills, knowledge and competence. Individuals need to prepare themselves for change and variety in their working lives. They need to continually **update** and **refocus** their capabilities. However, data on participation rates and characteristics of learners suggest there are still significant **barriers** to overcome to encourage lifetime learning among the whole population. At present it would appear that those who have had the greatest exposure to learning, and who may therefore be considered to have gained greatest benefit or reward from the system, are also those who continue to be exposed to the system.

Funding is a significant influence on the nature of the learning carried out. Employers appear to continue to want to fund short-term training, of immediate relevance to the job, and to be less concerned with qualifications. Individuals, however, have an increasing need for skills which they can take with them from employer to employer. The signs are that individuals who fund their own learning are investing in longer duration courses, aimed at future jobs and at qualifications. This suggests that individual funding has an important part to play in supporting lifetime learning of relevance to the changing world of work. To foster lifetime learning, the government could perhaps subsidise training courses or give out training vouchers to individuals.

National standards in education and training

In recent years there has been a major overhaul of national standards for qualifications. A lot of the pressure for these changes came from employers and from those involved in working in education and training. Prior to this there was a wide variety of qualifications on offer which made it difficult for employers and others to compare and assess the qualifications achieved. **The National Council for Vocational Qualifications** rationalised the range of qualification on offer. They must now conform to certain standards, and qualifications are pitched at various levels. One of the main thrusts of the rationalisation of qualifications was to provide a 'parity of esteem' of vocational and academic qualifications which are 'at the same level'.

In 1996 Sir Ron Dearing carried out a review of 14–18 qualifications in the UK. As a result of his findings, national standards and 'National Certificates' were created for students who are now able to follow three pathways – an academic pathway, an applied pathway, or a vocational pathway of qualifications.

Following on from Dearing's review of qualifications, the new framework of qualifications is made up of four common, national levels: Advanced, Intermediate, Foundation and Entry. These are referred to as national awards (see Figure 5.6).

Dearing's review highlighted the extent to which the existing post-16 educational structure had failed to address the needs of lower attainers, underachievers and young people with learning difficulties – as well as gifted students. In 1996, around one-fifth of school leavers did not attain GCSE grade G in English and mathematics, a level expected to be reached by an average 12-year-old.

To unlock the potential of these students, a new Entry Level award was introduced to provide a common route to the higher rungs of the new national framework of qualifications. To develop and recognise the abilities of gifted students, Dearing called for a greater use of special papers and for specially developed courses and assignments.

The idea is that students will move upwards from the first rung of the new qualifications ladder, taking one of a series of routes: vocational, applied or academic. For example, at the National Advanced Level, students could focus on traditional A Levels, Applied A Levels or a vocational National Vocational Qualification (NVQ) at Level 3. The new framework will enable students to build up a portfolio of vocational and academic awards, reflecting their own individual needs and aspirations.

Figure 5.6 Dearing's proposed framework of national awards

National Award: Advanced Level		
AS and A Level	GNVQ Advanced Level	NVQ Level 3
National Award: Intermediate Level		
GCSE grades A–C	GNVQ Intermediate Level	NVQ Level 2
National Award: Foundation Level		
GCSE grades D–G	GNVQ Foundation Level	NVQ Level 1
National Award: Entry Level		
Common to all pathways: three grades A/B/C		

One of the key objectives behind Dearing's use of the term 'national' is to reinforce the credibility of this new body of qualifications. This immediately tells employers and other organisations that students have gained a nationally recognised qualification at a specific level. In addition, it is geared towards creating a common currency for qualifications as well as a clearly understood system of levels.

National Vocational Qualifications (NVQs)

A National Vocational Qualification is a statement of competence, clearly relevant to work, that is intended to facilitate entry into or progression in employment, further education and training. It is issued by a recognised body to an individual. The statement of competence should incorporate specific standards – the ability to perform a range of work-related activities and skills, knowledge and understanding which underpin performance in employment.

For example, an NVQ in hairdressing has been designed by the lead body in the field which has the clearest understanding of what standards are required in hairdressing today. Employees working in hairdressing will build up their skills in this field and will progress through successively higher levels of competence as they develop the ability to wash hair, dry hair, cut hair, apply dyes and other substances etc. Clearly, it is in everyone's interest that these standards are applied rigorously so that employers, employees and customers can feel confident in the quality of the service.

By gaining higher levels of qualification, employees are able to demonstrate their potential for promotion and for taking on increasing levels of responsibility. Employers who encourage their employees to take NVQs will reap the benefits of more productive and more highly motivated employees.

NVQs do not indicate simply that a person possesses the required skills and knowledge for an occupation. They also show that a person can apply those skills and knowledge in the workplace to the standards demanded by employers – in other words that the holder of an NVQ is occupationally competent. After all, there would be very little point in having a qualification that was only valid on paper. When I visit my hairdresser who has an NVQ Advanced Level Certificate, I can be assured of a good cut, a pleasant conversation, and an accurate calculation of my bill.

There are five levels of competence currently recognised :

- *Level 1:* competence in the performance of work activities which are, in the main, routine and predictable or provide a broad foundation for progression to a higher level.
- *Level 2:* competence in a broader and more demanding range of work activities, involving greater individual responsibility and autonomy than at Level 1.
- *Level 3:* competence in skill areas that involve performance of a broad range of work activities, including many that are complex and non-routine. In some areas, supervisory competence may be a requirement at this level.
- *Level 4:* competence in the performance of complex, technical, specialised and professional work activities, including those involving design, planning and problem-solving, with a significant degree of personal accountability. In many areas supervision or management will be a requirement at this level.
- *Level 5:* competence which involves the application of a significant range of fundamental principles and complex techniques across a wide and often unpredictable variety of contexts. Personal accountability and autonomy feature strongly, as well as significant responsibility for the work of others and for the allocation of substantial resources.

General National Vocational Qualifications (GNVQs)

NVQs prepare people for specific jobs; GNVQs are designed to prepare students for a broad range of employment opportunities.

A GNVQ course is a preparation for work and/or further education and training. For example, a GNVQ Advanced (Applied A Level) qualification is recognised as being the equivalent of two traditional A levels. Most universities recognise the GNVQ Advanced qualification to be an appropriate qualification for entry to relevant university courses.

General means that a student is provided with the knowledge, skills and attitudes that will be required in a variety of occupations in a particular field, e.g. business or travel and tourism.

National means that the GNVQ qualification that students attain is recognised nationally.

Vocational means that a GNVQ qualification prepares students for the world of work. It provides real opportunities for students to develop understanding and skills that can be applied in many work situations.

Qualification means that a GNVQ provides students with a nationally recognised qualification. It should tell employers and universities that these students can work well with others, can express their ideas with confidence, have a good understanding of a relevant subject area, can use information technology to a good standard, will listen to others, can make informed decisions, and many other things.

One of the main criticisms of qualifications prior to the Dearing review of 1996 was the high drop-out rate. Around one-third of A Level students either abandoned their courses or failed exams, while the figure rose to 40 per cent for GNVQs. One of the main reasons for this high wastage was that students realised too late that they had chosen the wrong course for them. To address this problem, Dearing proposed alternatives to the 'all or nothing' approach of traditional qualifications. Instead, students are now able to take staged or part awards. For example, the GNVQ at Advanced Level is now structured as follows:

- full GNVQ of 12 units, plus three NCVQ units in communication, application of number and information technology = Applied A Level (Double Award)
- six units, plus three NCVQ units in communication, application of number and information technology = Applied A Level.

National Education and Training Targets (NETTs)

A five-year project called the 'Campaign for Learning' was launched in July 1995. Its declared aim was 'to change the culture of a nation'. The campaign set out to identify what educational opportunities already exist and what kinds of opportunities are required for the future. It addresses the question of training needs at national, organisational and individual levels.

Today it is widely recognised that flexible and lifelong learning opportunities are necessary if training and development are to keep pace with society's changing needs. The National Education and Training Targets are eight specific targets for the education and training of young people and working adults. The **foundation** learning targets aim to raise attainment at school and at the start of working life, while the **lifetime** targets set benchmarks for improving both employers' investment in people, and employees' investment in training and education for themselves.

Figure 5.7 National Education and Training Targets

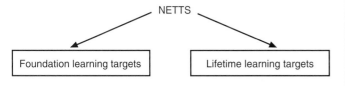

Foundation learning targets

- By age 19, 85 per cent of young people to achieve five GCSEs (grades A–C), Intermediate GNVQ or Level 2 NVQ.
- By age 19, 75 per cent of young people to achieve Level 2 competence in communication, numeracy and IT and 35 per cent to achieve Level 3 by age 21.
- By age 21, 60 per cent of young people to achieve two A Levels, Advanced GNVQ or NVQ Level 3.

Lifetime learning targets

- 60 per cent of the workforce to have a Level 3 NVQ, Advanced GNVQ or two A Levels.
- 30 per cent of the workforce to have a degree, a Level 4 NVQ, or a professional, management or other academic qualification.
- 70 per cent of all organisations employing 200 or more employees, and 35 per cent of those employing 50 or more, to be recognised as Investors in People.

These targets clearly set the framework for training and development within organisations. Critics argue that the government cannot just expect firms to provide training; it must also back initiatives to the hilt with finance for training.

Recent figures on progress were published in July 1995 by the National Advisory Council for Education and Training Targets (NACETT); 63 per cent of under 19-year-olds had achieved NVQ Level 2 or equivalent and 41 per cent of under 21-year-olds had reached NVQ Level 3 or equivalent. The lifetime target, relating to employed adults, showed that 40 per cent of the workforce were qualified to NVQ Level 3, its vocational equivalent or a higher qualification, compared with 31 per cent in spring 1991. Although progress has been made there is clearly still some way to go.

Case Study

Missing the targets

The government's strategies to raise the standard of Britain's workforce are failing, a leaked government report indicated in late November 1995. The report stated that 'The scale of current lifetime learning remains well below the levels required.'

The report provided the first admission of failure by the government in the light of figures indicating the dramatic gap between targets for the year 2000 and the existing level of education and training. Only 40 per cent of the British workforce – two-thirds of the target – had reached NVQ Level 3 standard. Only 8 per cent of large organisations have been recognised as Investors in People against a target of 70 per cent. The document added that only 7 per cent of people over 25 were pursuing qualifications, while 30-40 per cent of people of working age expected never to undertake any further education or training.

The report acknowledged a risk that growth in training spending by employers could 'plateau' as firms which are reorganising their structures are expected to need fewer permanent workers in future. There will also be a greater proportion of small and medium-sized firms who are less likely to invest in training.

Questions for discussion

1   *Why do you think we have been falling short of the targets?*
2   *What sorts of positive actions are required to bring training back towards the required targets?*
3   *Why are employers unlikely to create the required level of training if simply left to their own devices?*

Counselling

Counselling is the process of giving systematic guidance to help other people with the problems and issues with which they are faced.

Support counselling involves allowing employees to 'talk through' their feelings and experiences. An experienced counsellor will play the part of supportive listener rather than someone who imposes ideas on the person being counselled. Employees require counselling about all sorts of matters including stress and health, financial worries, bereavement, legal problems, redundancy, difficulties with colleagues at work and other work-related matters. By carefully listening and prompting, a counsellor can help the person he or she is counselling to identify the root causes of problems and strategies for dealing with them. In this way the person being counselled can keep the ownership of a problem and also **take responsibility** for sorting out the problem. Very often people simply want someone to act as a sounding board for their problems and to help them to structure an appropriate way forward.

Counselling in the workplace

Penny Swinburne has suggested the following model for counselling in the workplace. She argues that it is

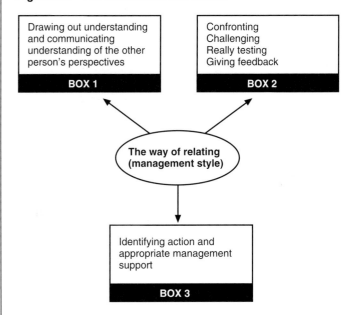

Figure 5.8   The three skills sets model

important to listen carefully to people's problems and to listen to 'feelings' just as much as to 'facts'. She puts forward what she calls a **three skills sets model** for helping people to solve difficult situations and problems at work. The three basic 'sets' of skills, as outlined in Figure 5.8, will determine how managers relate to their employees. Swinburne identifies the 'way of relating' as the essential nature of the manager–employee relationship.

When you ask a group of managers how they want to be treated by senior managers, they tend to give similar answers: 'with respect', 'non-judgementally', 'with understanding', 'openly', 'fairly' 'as equals'. She argues that these are not terms typically associated with old-fashioned management styles and that they show a distinct preference for democratic approaches.

Managers are often concerned when they have to handle difficult interpersonal situations, and may fear causing offence, leading to a worsening of the situation. Swinburne suggests that trying to ignore personal issues such as anger and frustration is a mistake. Often managers try to focus on pushing a task through rather than focusing on the feelings surrounding change, but it is far more helpful to deal with the feelings first.

An important step to empowerment is to allow employees to take more responsibility for issues and for managers to take on a supporting role. This is the key to the effective use of Swinburne's model. Unfortunately, it is often the part which many managers find difficult to adopt.

The model can be used to cover many interpersonal situations. Managers who want to use the model need to identify the box that they should be in at a particular moment in time. Once they have identified the appropriate box, they can identify the appropriate sets of skills to employ.

If, for example, a manager needs to talk to an employee about poor performance, which box should he or she start in? Managers often think that in wanting to act supportively they should start in Box 1, asking generally about the job, how things are going, etc. However, the employee is likely to be thinking 'When are you going to get to the point?'. Perhaps, therefore, the manager should start in Box 2 and give a statement of how he or she sees the performance problem, and then move back to Box 1 in order to understand the employee's perspective.

To take a contrasting example, what should a manager do if an employee asks to discuss a difficulty he or she is having doing a job? In this case it would make sense to start in Box 1 to understand the employee's perspective before moving on to Boxes 2 and 3.

A common mistake made by managers is that they want to rush into Box 3 – action – because of time constraints and because they want to move on to other management duties. If instead, managers are prepared to listen more, they will find that a lot of time and trouble is saved in the long-term. By doing this they are starting to focus on the **feelings**, rather than just on the **facts**. By taking this approach the manager gives greater emphasis to:

- *Box 1* – Drawing out, listening and understanding to get a view of the other's perspective.
- *Box 2* – Confronting, challenging and testing in order to build up an agreement or at least a shared understanding of perspectives.

From this position of strength, the effective manager can then move on to action.

This model can be used for discipline and grievance situations, annual reviews or appraisals and other difficult announcements such as redundancy and a whole range of day-to-day interpersonal situations. It can also be used as a model for coaching.

Practical steps to support counselling

You will find the following outline helpful when acting as a counsellor.

- Remember that your key role is as a **listener.** Try to get the person being counselled to talk through his or her problems. In particular, you need to encourage him or her to identify what the real problem is. You can prompt by saying things like 'go on', 'I think we are getting somewhere now' and probe by saying things like 'What do you see as being the heart of the

problem?', 'Do you think you have defined the problem clearly?'
- Try to get the other person to come up with a clear definition of what his or her problem is.
- Once the person being counselled has identified the problem, encourage him or her to come up with a list of alternative ways of dealing with it.
- Help him or her to identify what the best way of solving the problem will be from the range of alternatives.
- Help him or her to create a constructive route to solve the problem based on short term action steps and long term objectives.
- From time to time you will need to focus the discussion, perhaps by making a summary of what has been said.
- Make sure that the person being counselled has set down an agreed plan of action.
- Outline how and when this plan of action will be reviewed, i.e. in order to check that appropriate actions have been taken, as well as to evaluate the steps that have been taken.

Discipline

It is unrealistic to assume that 'good performance' can be created in every organisation simply by treating employees in an open way and by empowering them to make decisions for themselves. Every organisation will sometimes have to deal with disciplinary issues, which may range from poor time-keeping and unsatisfactory work to gross misconduct. The level of response should be graded according to the severity and frequency of the indiscipline. For example, for persistent bad time-keeping it will be necessary to establish a series of warnings – somewhat like a football referee's use of yellow and red cards. Employees should be made aware of the consequences of breaking codes and rules, and be given a clear indication of the types of conduct that will lead to punishment.

Key ingredients of a disciplinary procedure

- The procedure should be in writing and specify to whom it applies.
- It should show the disciplinary actions that can be taken, and specify who will be responsible for carrying out the actions.
- It should specify that individuals will be informed of the charge of indiscipline and given an opportunity to put their side of the story.
- It should allow for representation by a trade union official or chosen representative.

- It should ensure that disciplinary action is not carried out until a case has been thoroughly investigated; there should be the right of appeal.
- No employee should be dismissed for a first offence, except for gross misconduct.

A typical pattern of warnings leading to eventual discipline as as follows:

1 informal verbal warning
2 formal verbal or written warning
3 final written warning
4 disciplinary transfer, suspension or dismissal.

Each warning should set out the nature of the offence, and the next likely step in the disciplinary procedure:

Gross misconduct

Summary dismissal (dismissal without notice) can occur within the law only if the employee does something that cancels the contract of employment. Examples of such actions include dishonesty, assault on the employer, damaging the employer's property, refusal to obey a reasonable and lawful instruction, revealing trade secrets to competitors, or revealing the employer's business records to others. The disciplinary procedure should specify what will be regarded as gross misconduct.

Monitoring performance

Most large organisations have well-established procedures for monitoring and reporting the performance of both groups and individuals. In individual **personnel evaluation**, these procedures often include appraisal schemes. They are used mainly for white-collar staff, managers and technical staff, although large modern organisations may have an organisation-wide policy.In any organisation, it is vital that managers are clear about the key objectives they have to attain, and how these relate to the work of others. Appraisal is a systematic way of finding out this information. It also provides:

- an opportunity for the appraisee to know what performance is expected of his or her now and in the future
- an opportunity for the appraisee to receive high-quality, specific feedback on his or her performance
- a chance to develop a common organisational culture, improve overall performance and achieve organisational objectives.

The appraisal scheme usually requires individual post holders to collect and record, in a set way, the impressions they have gained of each subordinate in their charge.

Figure 5.9 An appraisal system gives employees an opportunity to receive high-quality, specific feedback

Appraisal interviews

An appraisal interview should set out to provide appraisees with an opportunity to discover what they need to know to do their jobs more effectively and motivate them to do the job effectively. There are many ways of carrying out appraisal interviews. However, it is important to remember that they are conversations with a purpose. General rules for appraisal are as follows

- *Purpose.* Identify the nature of the appraisal; for example, is it a performance review, counselling session, coaching session, etc?
- *Objectives.* One objective is to move the appraisee forward by creating a development step. What does the appraisee need to know or be able to do to move forward? Another objective is to achieve motivation growth. What does the appraisor need to know or do to help to increase the motivation of the appraisee?
- *Preparation.* Having done the groundwork outlined above, the appraisor should prepare relevant questions, background information and facts required for the interview, and organise a suitable location for the interview. Make sure that there are no interruptions, and that the interview can go on as long as is necessary.
- *Flexibility.* The appraisor needs to be flexible. There is no 'best' approach; you need to adapt to the situation.
- *Structure.* Establish the nature of the meeting (a beginning); establish the facts of the situation (a middle); and agree future action (an end).
- *Timing.* Use an appropriate amount of time. Do not drag out the interview or cut it short.

■ *Learning*. After an ineffective appraisal, always ask the question: 'What did I do wrong; how can I improve?' After an effective appraisal ask: 'How much help did I get? Did I deserve it? Could I have done even better?'

Appraisal is dealt with in greater depth in Chapter 14.

Further reading

■ *Personnel Management*, 3rd edition, by G. A. Cole. DPP, 1993.

■ *Personnel Management: A New Approach*, 2nd edition, by Derek Torrington. Prentice Hall, 1991.
■ *In Search of Management* by Tony Watson. Routledge, 1994.
■ *Competence, Education and NVQ's* by Terry Hyland. Cassell, 1995.
■ *Human Resource Development* by J. Stewart and J. McGoldrick. Pitman, 1996.
■ *Managing Change Through Training and Development* by J. Stewart. Kogan Page, 1996.
■ *Face to Face in Management* by D. Torrington. Gower Press, 1993.
■ *Motivation* by I. Robertson, M. Smith and D. Cooper. Institute of Personnel Development, 1995.

3

Personnel management in the organisation

6 Personnel/human resource management policy

O n completion of this chapter, students should be able to:

- identify and evaluate appropriate frameworks for effective personnel policy

- describe and explain the nature of control within personnel practices

- show why some personnel decisions are centralised while others are decentralised, and evaluate these alternative approaches

- critically evaluate the human resource management/personnel debate

- identify the relationship between corporate business objectives and human resource management planning/policy

- discuss the importance of developing a cosmopolitan approach to international labour markets

- describe and explain the importance of health and safety legislation

- identify the main statutory health and safety requirements for organisations

- describe and explain the importance of the European Social Chapter.

Human resource management

In the late 1990s we talk of human resource management as if it presents a model of how managers should approach their relationships with people at work. However, the concept of HRM is a very slippery one. It shares common characteristics with words like fairness, equality and progress, which prove to mean different things to different people. In this chapter, therefore, we will look at different approaches to human resource management, as well as drawing a distinction between HRM and personnel management.

What do human resource managers manage?

HRM management is concerned with taking responsibility for others in the workplace. Clearly, in any workplace this will cover a wide variety of people. Indeed it could be argued that everyone at work is a human resource manager, although levels of responsibility will clearly vary, for instance when we compare a line operative with his or her supervisor or section manager.

Once we accept that HRM is the responsibility of everyone within an organisation, it becomes obvious that every organisation must have clear guidelines for human resource management and that everyone in an organisation must be prepared for this responsibility. In particular, HRM should be a key part of the training and development of every manager.

Policy frameworks for effective HRM/personnel management

Strategic decisions are the major long-term decisions which an organisation takes concerning its aims, purposes and the use of resources. An important area of strategy, therefore, is the way in which the organisation plans to use its human resource.

Figure 6.1   Implementing human resource strategy

Human resource strategy needs to be created at the top level of an organisation, so that it can filter down into every aspect of activity in the organisation that concerns the management and use of people.

This does not mean that the strategy is imposed on people lower down the organisation by those higher up (although this may be the case). Ideally, the creation of a strategy will involve some form of input from everyone in the organisation.

We can look upon the creation and implementation of a strategy within an organisation as providing the engine which determines and drives the way in which the organisation is run and operates.

The starting point is to set out the **values** which permeate organisational activity. These values are set out in a mission (vision) or statement of philosophy which should include a statement about valuing the human resource. Once these values have been determined, it becomes possible to provide more detailed **aims** which provide direction and a means of measuring the success of the organisation. Aims establish generalised targets to work towards. If you want to be more specific, you must break down your aims into **objectives** (objectives are subsets of aims and are more easily measurable). Having established clear aims, the **strategy** of the organisation can then be set out which identifies the broad approach and the major decisions which will enable the organisation to meet its aims, e.g. to create a decentralised teamwork approach throughout the organisation. Strategies are specific plans to achieve the objectives you set after creating the vision. Objectives are the ends, strategies are the means. **Policies** can then be set out in detail, outlining the way in which the organisation and its people will operate. The implementation of all of the above is then set out in the **tactics**, i.e. the operating plans for the organisation.

Figure 6.2   Creating a strategy

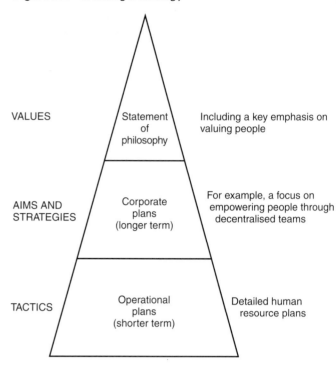

Creating a framework for action

Every organisation should have:

- visions and values
- aims and objectives
- strategies and planning frameworks
- policies
- a means of evaluating its policies and plans.

It is essential that these elements are closely integrated and that they actually operate in practice. For example, the aims and objectives, strategies, plans and policies should all reflect the central vision and values.

These frameworks should not exist only on paper; more importantly, they should exist in practice.

In recent times these aspects of business decision-making having become popular features of 'management speak'. Every chief executive talks about building a vision, developing a strategy, and communicating the core values of the organisation. However, employees at ground level often treat such 'mantras' with a certain amount of cynicism. The real test of the effectiveness of management theory is the way in which it translates down into operational activity. For example, an organisation may have policies for every aspect of its operation from production methods to dealing with suppliers, equal opportunities to training and development, harassment to appraisal.

However, unless these policies actually lead to the required operational activity, they will never be more than bits of paper and 'hot air'. It is essential, therefore, that plans and policies are regularly evaluated and reviewed so that there are checks on how things operate in practice.

The human resources policies will be a key element of overall policy and will reflect organisational values and strategy. Of course, different organisations will have different missions and values depending on their history and culture and what the purpose of the organisation is. However, increasingly organisations – whether in the private or public sector, profit or non-profit making – are placing a central focus on their human resource.

Human resource policies

Policies are concerned with setting out *how* and often *why* an organisation will go about meeting its objectives in a generalised way. In addition, policies may also include a moral element showing a commitment to principles and values.

Figure 6.3   Elements of human resource policy

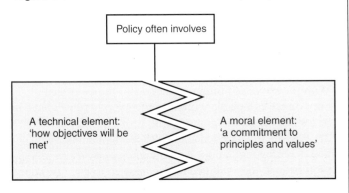

Case Study

Equal opportunities policy statement

Study the following extract which is the opening part of an equal opportunities policy statement in Melton Mowbray College. Explain how the statement contains both a technical and a moral element.

Statement
1   The atmosphere and physical environment of the College will ensure that equal value is given to all members of the institution regardless of gender, race or ability.

2   Every effort will be made to ensure that equal access to the College is available to prospective staff or students and racial or gender stereotyping is avoided.
3   The College categorically condemns the expression of attitudes and dissemination of materials which are discriminatory in nature. Incidents of discriminatory behaviour will be dealt with under the appropriate section of the Code of Practice.
4   All staff and students should accept their individual and collective responsibility for challenging racist and sexist attitudes. Development programmes for staff and students should recognise Equal Opportunities as a high priority area.
5   The content and delivery of the curriculum will be reviewed with the aim of countering discrimination and promoting positive attitudes.

A policy is very important. It can be seen as *A public commitment to a way of acting in the future.* It is vital, therefore, to put a lot of thought into creating policies, because they will be published and made generally available. An organisation may look foolish if it fails to live by the policy framework that it has established. Once it has created a policy, it must therefore communicate the policy framework to everyone within the organisation as quickly as possible and make sure that they are operating these policies.

A classic case of the apparent failure of policy in recent times occurred in Ford's Dagenham plant. An industrial tribunal, in June 1996, was told that four out of ten workers at the company's Dagenham complex are black, yet only a tiny fraction have ever broken through a 'wall of racism' to secure elite jobs in the Ford truck fleet. Truck fleet drivers, who deliver car components from one part of the plant to another and from one factory to another across the UK and Europe at all hours of the day and night, are the company's jugular vein. Ford has had an equal opportunities programme in place for years, but this had gone largely ignored in the fleet department. This case highlights the importance of ensuring that policy frameworks are put into practice and that there is some means of regularly checking policy implementation in action.

There are four key ingredients of effective human resource policies:

1   They should establish commitment to specific objectives by setting out the technical and ethical outlines for achieving these objectives. In other words, the policy should establish the theoretical framework which will underpin practical actions.

2   They should be set out in a written statement of policy. The policies should provide a clear written code of action which guides and governs behaviour in an organisation. Moreover, these policies should be communicated to everyone, e.g. through training and development sessions.

3   The policy frameworks should provide clear guidelines which govern behaviour. However, they should be seen as providing general guidelines rather than specific detail about every action. For example, the policy statement that sets out that all individuals should challenge discriminatory behaviour, does not set out how this should be done. Instead, individuals will be given more guidance to this through codes of practice and training sessions.

4   Policies provide a broad framework for action and behaviour so that individuals have guidelines in which to operate.

Policies therefore provide a structure for actions within an organisation. If policies are clearly communicated, people know what is expected of them and can take the required actions. A standard is therefore established against which actions and performance can be judged.

Policies are concerned with providing people with **guidance** as to how they should operate now and in the future. They give them direction and a clear focus for action. They also give them a way of judging their own performance, and a means for others to judge their performance. An individual within the organisation has the security of knowing that he or she operated within the framework of the company's policies and guidelines.

Examples of policies

We have already seen that the policies which an organisation has should reflect the mission or guiding principles of that organisation. For example, the Levi Strauss Company has the following mission statement:

> 'We all want a company that our people are proud of and committed to, where all employees have an opportunity to contribute, learn, grow and advance based on merit, not politics or background. We want our people to feel respected, treated fairly, listened to and involved. Above all, we want satisfaction from accomplishments and friendships, balanced personal and professional lives, and to have fun in our endeavours . . .'

Quite clearly, such a mission will translate down into policies concerned with equal opportunities, teamwork, personal development, appraisal and personal development.

A policy dealing with **equal opportunities** will be concerned with the maximising of opportunities for everyone, the avoidance of discriminatory behaviours, equal opportunities in recruitment and selection, etc.

A policy dealing with **working relationships** will be concerned with developing a climate for teamwork, the sharing of ideas, and person-centred appraisal, etc.

Other policies will be concerned with providing a framework that minimises or eliminates harassment at work, sets out terms and conditions for those at work, and provides a framework for industrial relations, etc.

The problem with policies

Care needs to be taken not to create a 'dead hand' of policy-making. For example, in recent years, with the development of a professional managerial class in education, hospitals, the police, local government and many other organisational areas, we have seen the growth of an obsession in some quarters with the creation of 'policies on paper'. There is considerable evidence that the creation of these policies is wasteful in resources and can have a negative effect on employee motivation. Ground-level employees may find themselves submerged under a mountain of paperwork. In time it becomes impossible to keep up with all the changes that are taking place in an organisation and employees move into a state of inertia. Because they do not have time to come to terms with all of the new paperwork, and because the new policies concern so many aspects of decision-making, employees become reluctant to make decisions in case they make a mistake.

With the move to human relations and the increased importance of flexible working practices, there will have to be less emphasis on 'going by the book', as people need to develop the independence to work freely without being tied down by regulation. As workers become more professional, they will need to be allowed to exercise more personal discretion.

Task

You are a personnel manager in a medium-sized insurance company. The company has established guidelines whereby departments wishing to recruit new staff have to establish criteria for selecting candidates to interview, and an equal opportunities procedure whereby all candidates being interviewed should be asked the same set of questions in an interview situation.

It has come to your notice that one of the department heads has been setting criteria for choosing candidates to interview. However, she has not been applying these criteria when sifting through application forms. In addition, the department head has been asking a range of different questions to different candidates. The head of department's view is that 'equal opportunities is all very well in theory, but you need to choose the best people to work with your existing team.'

1 *How would you deal with this situation?*
2 *How would you go about making sure that the equal opportunities policy is adhered to throughout your organisation?*

Monitoring policies

At the end of the day, policies will only be as effective as the way they operate in practice. It is therefore essential to monitor and evaluate the way in which these policies are implemented. As a result of this monitoring process, it is possible to take stock of performance, to evaluate the success of individual policies, and to make adjustments and improvements where necessary.

For example, an organisation may have a policy of creating equal opportunities in order to make best possible use of the available talent which exists in recruiting from its local community. However, the reality may be that the organisation recruits very few people from minority groups. This would come to light as a result of an analysis of the make-up of its workforce. It therefore becomes necessary to find out what it is about the organisation's recruitment policies that prevents or discourages suitable candidates from minority groups from applying for jobs.

Figure 6.4 Ensuring effective policies

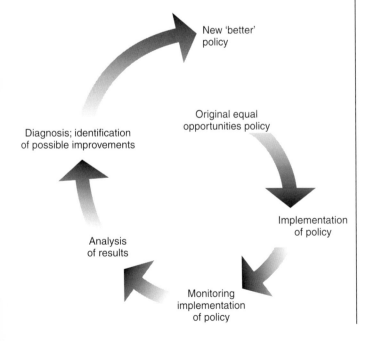

- Diagnosis; identification of possible improvements
- New 'better' policy
- Original equal opportunities policy
- Implementation of policy
- Monitoring implementation of policy
- Analysis of results

As a result of this process, the organisation may see ways in which it can modify its policies, in order to create equal opportunities more effectively.

Control within personnel and human resource practice

To ensure that human resource and personnel policies are implemented correctly and effectively, it is necessary to develop some means of control. A useful way of doing this is to create a clear control framework, by establishing:

- *systems*, e.g. a system for recruiting and selecting new employees
- *plans*, e.g. a plan for managed redundancies over a period of time
- *rules*, e.g. clear disciplinary or health and safety rules and regulations
- *codes of conduct*, e.g. a code of conduct covering equal opportunities and harassment at work.

By establishing such a framework, it becomes possible to take appropriate measures when something moves out of line. For example, if there is a case of harassment at work, there are clear steps to follow and appropriate actions to be taken (e.g. verbal warnings, suspension from work, etc.).

In other organisations there is more of an emphasis on self-regulation of working practice – reflected in the creation of self-managed teams and quality circles. The literal Japanese translation of the term quality circle is 'the gathering of the wisdom of the people'. Using a quality circle approach, small groups of people meet to identify problems and find solutions to all sorts of problems, from health and safety to training needs and product improvement. For quality circles to be effective, it is essential for companies to have a culture which encourages participatory management. However, while self-regulation of relationships and practices is important because it allows maximum possible input by employees, it is also important that such freedom exists within a structure of guidelines and policies that provide an overall framework for relationships within an organisation.

Ongoing control

Management control is the process of monitoring and adjusting activities in order to achieve the greatest efficiency. An important aspect of human resource control is therefore that of monitoring and adjusting your strategies, policies and practices.

The starting point is to have effective monitoring procedures. For example, in monitoring recruitment policies, you would want to check the extent to which you were recruiting the right sort of personnel to perform required jobs and how long they stayed with the organisation. In monitoring health and safety training, you would need to monitor the impact on accidents. In monitoring a harassment policy, you would want to note the impact on numbers of complaints. Once you have established a policy, you need to check on the impact of the policy in action.

Quantitative techniques are essential for measuring the effectiveness of a particular policy. For example, an organisation may set out a policy of recruiting individuals regardless of their gender, ethnic origin or sexual orientation. They may then set out a monitoring device to check on the breakdown of their new recruits according to whether they are male or female, etc. At the end of the day, the results of their monitoring may show that their policies are not working and need to be taken back to the drawing board.

Qualitative techniques should be used to support quantitative methods. For example, it is possible to carry out in-depth interviews with individuals who work for an organisation to find out their views about the company's equal opportunities policy, harassment policy, etc. These qualitative approaches can be very useful. For example, an employee from a minority group may be able to supply information about why the company is not attracting other minority applicants.

Monitoring how policies actually operate is therefore a very important practice. The problem is that many policies are created by those at the higher levels within an organisation who may have little experience of working for an organisation at ground level. A lot of their thinking may be influenced by what they have read in books of management theory. They may not understand some of the obstacles that stand in the way of making policies work in a specific organisation. Managers may be inclined to judge their own performance by the amount of paper they produce. However, the real success of the organisation lies in the relationships and motivation that exist at its heart. To understand the organisation in action, it is essential to find out in depth how it works in practice. Some of the most effective managers are those who actually track the implications of their policy-making in detail. This involves getting out of the office and talking to people who are putting policies into practice – finding out what they think of the policy, any misunderstandings they may have, what they see as being the strengths and weaknesses of the policy, and any modifications they would make. We can return to our Ford example to highlight what might happen when policies are not effectively monitored.

Case Study

Trouble at Ford

In recent years Ford has been put forward as a model of equal opportunities practices. However, in 1996 it ran into some difficulties which highlight the importance of ensuring that policy is turned into practice in every aspect of what you do.

The first problem occurred with a poster which was being used for national advertising. This presented a group of Ford workers, a number of whom had been altered so that black people were replaced with white ones. The change had originally been carried out by an artist for a promotional campaign in Scandinavia, but when the pictures were used for advertising in the UK this led to a storm of protest.

In the summer of 1996, Ford was faced with fresh criticism. A group of Ford employees claimed that black workers were being overlooked in promotion opportunities to truck-driving responsibilities in one of Ford's plants. Opportunities for promotion to these posts, which were highly rewarded, were passing down from father to son within the plant. Almost all the jobs in this area had been taken by white employees. Protesting employees argued that high-minded policy was not translating into actual practice.

Questions for discussion

1 *Why do you think that in the cases outlined above there may have been a mismatch between policy and practice?*
2 *How can organisations go about ensuring that a match between policy and practice always exists?*

The control process

The control process in personnel practice is illustrated in Figure 6.5.

This control process can either be carried out in a top-down way or by using a more democratic approach. In the West, business leaders have been used to operating through old-style command and control structures, although gradually they are trying to make themselves more responsive by giving employees greater responsibility for the way business is conducted. Carried to its logical conclusion, the process could lead to the 'virtual organisation', in which flexible teams are brought together for specific purposes and manage relationships within the team for the duration of the project.

Figure 6.5 The control process in personnel practice

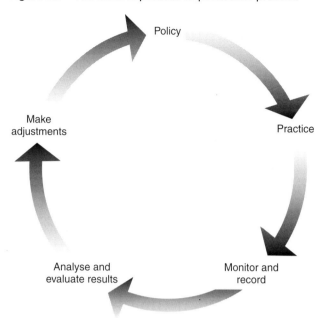

The governing principle in such a situation is that everybody has a customer – either outside the company (the traditional customer) or inside the company (the internal customer). Both kinds of customer expect to be supplied with the product or service they need, on time and as specified. The principle holds good for everyone in the company, whatever their level of skill and experience, whether their 'product' is answering a telephone in a helpful way or masterminding a major new project. It works to everyone's benefit. It gives the individual genuine responsibility and scope for initiative, and it virtually guarantees that the company's performance will improve.

Centralisation and decentralisation of personnel tasks

The technologies and techniques needed to run a successful company developed rapidly in the years that followed the ending of the Second World War. At the time it was believed that no person could possibly be expert in more than one of them. It seemed obvious that they should be developed separately – otherwise it would be impossible to develop them effectively.

So, in every large company, specialist departments flourished, each with their own direction, each with their own hierarchy and each, often, with their own separate office buildings – product research, manufacturing, procurement of raw materials, marketing, advertising, customer service, complaints, distribution, accounts, personnel and others. The system worked for over 30

years. However, as the years passed, the system's inherent tendency to duplication and inertia became dominant. The era of the small company, or at least the big company organised as a group of small companies, had begun. In place of the specialist departments, large companies have begun to organise themselves into multi-skilled teams responsible for a whole project. Such teams can more easily focus on customer needs, and so direct and combine their specialist skills to meet those needs more effectively. They are also better at judging what effort and expenditure are needed to do that.

In the human resources field, we have seen substantial changes which reflect this wider change in thinking. In particular, we have seen a movement away from the centralised personnel department which took upon itself the responsiblity for all aspects of personnel within an organisation.

Decentralisation involves devolving planning and control. Nowadays, the human resource function within many large organisations has been passed along to individual operating units and managers within the organisation (see Figure 6.6). Of course there is still a key role for the human resources director, but this role is now a strategic one – creating strategies for the organisation as to how best to nurture and develop the human resource to its maximum potential by creating aims, strategies, plans, policies and ways of monitoring performance at an organisation-wide level. Today's human resource manager plays a key role in preparing others within an organisation to take on responsibility for human resource management.

Figure 6.6 Decentralisation of personnel tasks

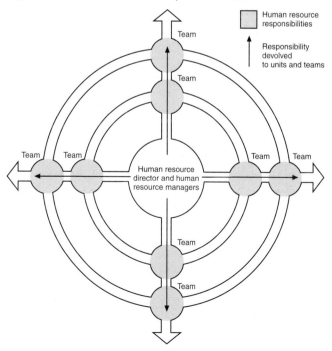

Figure 6.7 Developing a customer-focused approach to human resource management

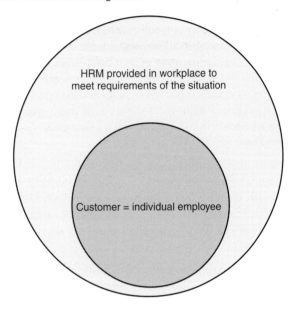

The purpose of decentralising human resource management is to meet the individual needs of employees in the situations in which they work. Human resource management is concerned with meeting the requirements of its customers, i.e. the individual employees that make up the organisation. By making all managers responsible for human resource decisions, HRM effectively gets closer to the customer. Because individual managers are empowered to make human resources decisions, they are able to respond quickly and appropriately to employees' requirements 'on the ground'.

By making HRM more **customer-focused,** it is possible to make sure that it reflects the needs and requirements of employees in the contexts within which they operate, rather than from hundreds of miles away at head office. All of this can lead to improved employee satisfaction.

Decentralisation is not just about splitting up personnel into smaller divisional personnel units. More importantly, it is concerned with spreading the human resource message to self-managing teams and units within the overall organisation. It is about asking managers and other employees to see themselves as having a role in human resource management, rather than leaving it to the 'experts'.

Inevitably, the ability to cope with this new type of human resource management, and the new type of 'millennium organisation', requires new management skills. *Fortune* magazine (22 February 1993) suggested that the new manager can be distinguished from the old manager in the following ways:

Old manager	New manager
Thinks of self as manager or boss	Thinks of self as sponsor, team leader or internal consultant
Follows chain of command	Deals with anyone necessary to get the job done
Works within a set of organisational structures	Changes organisational structures in response to customer
Makes most decisions alone	Invites others to join in decision making
Hoards information	Shares information
Tries to master one major discipline, e.g. personnel	Tries to understand a broad array of managerial disciplines
Demands long hours	Demands satisfied customers

Human resource management and personnel management

During the late 1980s and 1990s, an increasing emphasis was placed on creating a distinction between HRM and personnel management. Perhaps the most important reason for this change was that organisations were increasingly coming to depend on people to give them a competitive edge. Business writers began to write about the 'intelligent organisation', in which the knowledge and personal skills of people in industries as diverse as computing and insurance were more important than the physical plant and equipment which the company owned. It therefore became important to create new ways of thinking which gave more importance to 'the human resource'.

Personnel management

For many years, responsibility for people at work was seen to be the province of 'personnel'. Personnel management in organisations deals with the practical aspects of recruitment, induction, training, staff appraisal, and other specialised aspects of people at work. In this respect, personnel work is a specialist function within an organisation which is practical in nature and largely concerned with the administration and implementation of policies.

We will look at personnel management in detail later on. However, the important point to bear in mind is that until fairly recently 'people' work was seen as being the responsibility of the personnel director and personnel department.

Human resource management

Human resource management works on a larger scale. It is concerned with:

- making commitments to people in terms of defining the mission and goals of the whole organisation
- considering the implications for human resources of any major decision made by the organisation
- designing the structure of the organisation in such a way as to meet the needs of the employees
- having the director of human resources working at board level in an organisation
- ensuring that management actions and decisions within an organisation continually focus on human resource considerations.

The human resource as an asset

Human resource management recognises the key stake that people have in an organisation and acknowledges that this stake provides employees with an entitlement to recognition, training and fulfilment.

Case Study

Human resource approaches

John works for a medium-sized company in the human resources department. His view is that: 'The human resource is the chief asset of the company. It is also the major cost, taking up over 70 per cent of the business's costs in any one time period. It is therefore essential to gain the maximum possible return from this expenditure. People need to be motivated if they are to be made best use of. Anything which adds to the productivity of individual employees should be seen as an essential ingredient of human resource policy.

Jane also works for a medium-sized company in the human resources department. She agrees with John that the Human Resource is the key resource. She says: 'Human resources should be seen as an asset by the organisation. The organisation needs to look at how it can best meet the needs of this asset in order to help people to develop themselves to the full. By involving people in decision-making, it is possible to enable them to help the organisation to develop while meeting their own development needs.'

Questions for discussion

1 *Are John and Jane saying the same thing or can you see a difference in their approach?*

2 *How might the views of these two individuals influence the sorts of actions they would take in human resource management?*
3 *Can you give any specific examples of actions that John might take which would be different to the actions that Jane would take?*

In many organisations today, human resource management has become a natural part of the way in which a manager will operate. For example, a manager working as part of a project team in product development might see him or herself as having a responsibility to help to create effective working relations between team members and to help individuals to identify development opportunities.

Perhaps a more important shift has been that concerning views on the value of people at work. Instead of seeing people as a **cost** they are now seen as an **asset**. This is probably the biggest single difference between the thinking of John and Jane in the above case study.

People as costs
- Employees are a key cost of production.
- Employees are just one of a number of resources that need managing.

People as assets
- People create the added value that makes the organisation successful.
- People are the key resource of the organisation and therefore a prime management responsibility for everyone.

This provides a useful starting point in an exploration of a distinction between personnel management and human resource management that has been made in recent human resource literature. Many writers have said that the move from personnel management to human resource management represents a step forward for a successful organisation.

Personnel management was the old specialist function within an organisation. It was a centralised function, which was the specific responsibility of personnel

Figure 6.8 A staircase to progress

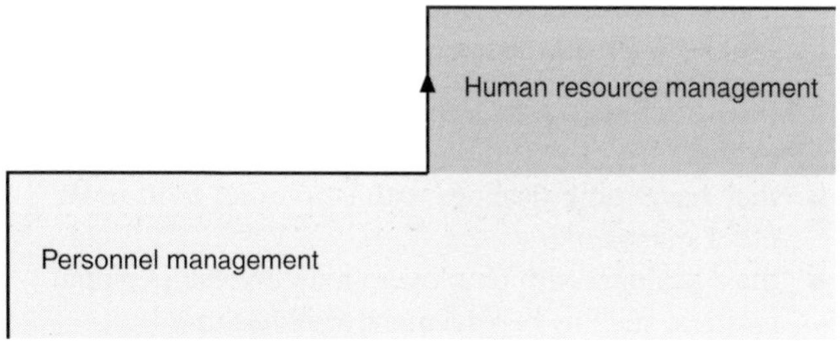

managers, in a scheme of things in which resources needed managing in a top-down way.

Human resource management, in contrast, is a strategic discipline in which human resource responsibilities have been spread out to all managers. It involves a greater emphasis on self-management and empowerment.

The new term is suitable for the current business climate in which decentralisation and empowerment have become a key to competitive advantage. Human resource managers today are in many ways more influential and powerful than their predecessors and HRM is now seen as a key strategic function in most large and many smaller organisations.

At the same time, most organisations in the UK still use the term 'personnel' to describe the workforce-centred discipline which deals with employees from the moment they first consider applying for a post within an organisation.

Personnel management plays a key intermediary role in the workplace. While personnel is a management function, it is also an 'employee-based' function. Research has shown that many employees see personnel as being qualitatively different from other management functions – 'they are not clearly "them" and not clearly "us", but they are nearer to us than the rest of them are!' Because of this privileged position, personnel can play a key mediating role within an organisation.

Figure 6.9 Crossing the divide

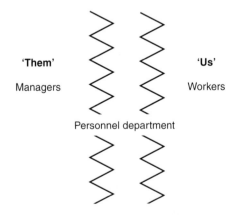

Personnel managers are often perceived by employees to be approachable because:

■ their prime concern seems to be people rather than profits
■ they have more dealings with employees than most other managers
■ their dealings with employees may involve personal matters, such as bereavement or ill health

■ they may have better interpersonal skills than other managers.

The main areas of responsibility for personnel have been termed 'the employment procession'. They include:

■ recruitment
■ selection
■ induction
■ training
■ transfers
■ termination of employment.

However, in modern organisations there are several other important aspects of work including appraisal and personal development programmes for employees; health and safety for employees at work; equal opportunities programmes and policies; administration of disciplinary procedures, and handling of industrial relations issues.

As we have seen earlier, personnel managers and staff are likely to take on board a number of the cultural assumptions and values of ordinary people at work as well as those of managers. Personnel managers are therefore particularly privileged in that they inhabit an ill defined area between management and employees.

A summary of the major distinctions between a human resource management and a personnel management approach is provided in Figure 6.10.

Figure 6.10 Distinctions between the human resource management and personnel management approaches

Personnel management	Human resource management
■ People have a right to proper treatment as human beings at work ■ People will only be effective if their job-related personal needs are met ■ Because other line managers do not see themselves as people specialists, they may neglect personnel work. This necessitates specialist personnel input	■ Management of human resources is like any other form of resource management ■ Human resource management should be shared by people across the organisation rather than being split up artificially into work for specialists ■ People have a right to proper treatment as human beings at work ■ Efficient management with a focus on human needs is required across the organisation ■ Human resource managers are needed to support other managers in their human resource work and to make sure that the organisation is directed at a strategic level to human resource management ■ At the same time, human resource managers are concerned with making sure that there are enough people working in the right places at the right time

At the start of this chapter, we made the point that the concept of human resource management is a somewhat slippery one. The discussion above should bring this point home to the student of HRM. Most managers who work with people will be able to argue that they use an HRM approach and, at times, the distinction between HRM and personnel management becomes vague and unclear. For example, you will find some managers who clearly have little regard for people nevertheless arguing that 'people are the greatest asset'.

Students therefore need to to draw their own conclusions and not become too bogged down in semantics. However, in forming judgements about good and bad practice, you need to ask yourself the following questions:

- To what extent does this organisation really care about the individuals that work for it?
- Is concern for people a function of all managers in the organisation or just a few specialists?
- Are people seen as a cost or an asset?

Task

Draw up a list of criteria which you think would be appropriate for determining whether or not an organisation is employing an effective human resource management approach.

Hard and soft approaches to HRM

When you scratch beneath the surface of HRM you will find that different organisations employ HRM for different reasons, and this will influence the nature of people management within these organisations. At a simple level, it is possible to identify two main schools of thought about HRM: the hard approach and the soft approach.

The hard approach

The hard approach is concerned with treating people as a vital resource, but in a calculating sort of way as you might do with other resources. For example, HRM would be concerned with trying to maximise outputs from given inputs by considering the most cost-effective way of doing things. Employees are encouraged to see their interests as being tied up with those of the organisation. Recruitment is concerned with taking on those employees who best fit in with existing styles and practices in the organisation and are thus likely to be most productive. People are vital but they must fit in with the organisation's needs.

The soft approach

The soft approach is also people-centred, but it recognises that people are different from other resources: people need to be nurtured, motivated and made to feel important. It recognises that people have feelings and that these need to be the focus for HRM. A soft approach therefore emphasises involving employees in the management of work – for example, by creating self-managing teams – and is concerned to build commitment to the organisation by informing employees about the organisation's purposes and values.

Figure 6.11 Contrasting the hard and soft approach to human resource management

Hard approach	Soft approach
People most important resource	People most important resource
People need to be used in a cost-effective way	People's feelings should be considered
People should be used in a productive way	Ways of motivating people and involving them in decision-making and shaping work need to be found
People help the organisation to meet its goals	People need to be involved in helping the organisation to shape its goals

Some people argue that human resource management approaches are more often talked about than practised. Often organisations just treat people as they do any other resource. We have witnessed this recently in the way in which organisations hire and fire large numbers of people at very short notice.

Corporate objectives and HRM

A number of specialists in the field argue that HRM only exists when there is an integrated system of policies and practices for managing the human resource (e.g. for recruitment, selection, bargaining and employee development) which are at the same time integrated with the wider business strategy (corporate objectives). This is the **strategic** view of human resource management. When we look at current practice, however, we can see that organisations use a variety of approaches. At one end of the continuum there are organisations that are genuinely working towards strategic HRM, where human resource considerations are a central part of organisational policy-making. At the other end of the continuum there are organisations that may use the term HRM but in reality operate a fire-fighting approach in which personnel activities respond to problems and difficulties in the workplace.

At the strategic end of the continuum there are two varieties of HRM that we have examined earlier in the chapter: the hard and soft approaches. The hard approach puts an important emphasis on the human resource, but the overall intention is to maximise other organisational returns such as profits and sales. This is a business-orientated approach to strategic management. The softer approach also recognises people as a key organisational resource, but the emphasis is on nurturing and developing them as human beings. Believers in the soft approach would also argue that this will lead to higher business returns.

Strategic approaches to human resource management enable positive and planned steps in the right direction. Unfortunately, however, many organisations view personnel planning and policy-making as less important than other organisational planning. Personnel is frequently seen as a servicing function that responds to company objectives over which it has little influence. In a dynamic business environment, human resource managers need to focus on long-term strategies, rather than responding to the many varied issues and problems as and when they arise.

Moving towards a strategic approach

Increasingly, organisations are seeking to develop a strategic approach which integrates human resource management. Clearly, this involves a shift from past practice but it is an essential change in the current environment where intelligence and flexibility give organisations a competitive edge.

John Storey, in his book *Management of Human Resources*, identifies five types of managed change processes which can move an organisation towards HRM.

- *Type 1: the top-down approach.* Management recognises the need for a strategic approach and sets out to impose HRM solutions on an organisation. There is a clear vision from above and a carefully planned approach to the management of change. If the vision is not communicated clearly to the whole of the organisation, however, it may be ignored or rejected at grass-roots level, resulting in a lack of commitment to the new approach.
- *Type 2: the top-down piecemeal approach.* Rather than creating an integrated view of HRM, new initiatives are

developed in the organisation in a piecemeal way. This may be the chosen way of operating for managers who take the view 'We'll try this first, see how it works, and then bring in the next bit!'. Unfortunately this creates contrasting practices within an organisation and may lead to a lack of commitment to change. Too many people will point out contradictions in policies and practices.
- *Type 3: the group piecemeal approach.* This is where various groups in an organisation will bargain over piecemeal changes. It has the advantage of greater participation, but it is riddled with the disadvantages of the piecemeal approach.
- *Type 4: systemic-jointism.* This involves transforming the whole system to incorporate the HRM approach. It has the advantage of being a participative process based on shared understanding of change. This should lead to wholesale commitment to the new HRM approach. Unfortunately, in the real world this approach has rarely been used.
- *Type 5:* is a mixture of the other 4 types.

National and international labour markets

A key ingredient of personnel policy involves making sure that you have the right people, with the right skills, aptitudes and training, working for you. Large organisations therefore need to be familiar with national and international labour markets and trends in these markets.

All of the human resource management issues discussed in this book are relevant in the international context. However, it is important for managers operating in this context to develop a cosmopolitan approach. Managers who are unable to appreciate cultural differences are ethnocentric. They tend to believe in the superiority of their own particular way of doing things rather than valuing other cultures. In contrast, cosmopolitan managers are sensitive to cultural differences and value the practices, attitudes and values of people with other approaches to doing business. Organisations therefore need to develop policies which both outline what their human resource requirements are in international markets and, importantly, how they will operate their human resource policies in different situations.

It would be possible for organisations to offer the same terms and conditions to their employees throughout the world, and to create the same organisational culture. However, it would seem more appropriate to accommodate and adjust to local conditions. For example,

Japanese companies in the UK have introduced many new approaches in recent years, e.g. quality circles, teamworking, etc, but they have typically modified some of their approaches to accommodate the different cultural perceptions in this country. For example, in some factories employees are encouraged to take physical exercise together with management at the start of the day – but this is done on a voluntary basis.

In creating policy, however, companies often develop a **baseline** of policies on a global level which set minimum standards, e.g. in terms of a baseline rate of pay, a baseline of equal opportunity policy, a baseline of ethical practice, etc.

In Chapter 7 we look at national and local labour market planning in greater detail.

UK employment legislation and European influences

UK employment legislation is wide-ranging and covers the rights and obligations of employees in the workplace. In this section we have chosen to focus on health and safety at work to exemplify one specific area. Chapter 13 looks in depth at issues related to contracts of employment and contractual changes.

Health and safety

The employer has a duty to create a safe and healthy workplace. Health and safety affects all key aspects of human resource work, for example:

- in the *recruitment process,* employees are more likely to want to work for organisations which operate in a safe way; employers are most likely to select employees who have the characteristics and traits which indicate that they will operate in a safe way
- *appraisal* of employees' work takes into consideration aspects of the way in which they work, e.g. in a safe way
- *training and development* has a fundamental concern with each individual employee's understanding of and ability to work in a safe and healthy way.

The way in which health and safety is managed in an organisation is influenced by a variety of factors such as:

- economic costs
- government legislation and regulations (locally, nationally and European-wide)
- trade union pressure
- public opinion and media pressure.

Health and safety legislation

In this section we will look at the specific Acts and regulations which affect health and safety, at work in the UK.

The Health and Safety at Work Act 1974

This Act covers all workers except domestic servants in private households. Sets of regulations under the Act deal with different kinds of work in various places. All those receiving training or work experience in the workplace are covered by the Act.

Under this Act, both employers and employees are responsible for providing safe conditions at work. Employers or employees who do not abide by the rules can be punished in a court of law. The employer's duty is to ensure, as far as is reasonably practicable, 'the health, safety, and welfare at work of all employees'. This general responsibility includes:

- the provision and maintenance of plant and systems of work
- arrangements for use, handling, storage and transport of articles and substances
- maintenance of the place of work and access to and egress from it
- the working environment.

It includes the duty to provide:

- adequate welfare facilities
- necessary information, instruction, training and supervision.

In addition, the employer must consult with union safety representatives if there are any, and a notice containing the requirements of the Act must be displayed.

An example of an area covered by the Act is the use of protective guards on machines and industrial presses. Accidents can occur if the guards are faulty or if they are removed. The Act lays down training standards for workers in potentially hazardous occupations. Generally the workplace must be designed in such a way as to minimise the risk of accidents.

An employer must prepare a written statement of policy with respect to the health and safety at work of employees and show it to an inspector if required. An employer must show similar responsibilities to non-employees, such as visitors in a school or college party, who need to be given information and instruction about health and safety requirements.

The employee's duty is to take reasonable care to ensure both his or her own safety and the safety of others who may be affected by what he or she does or does not do.

The Act is backed up by a **Health and Safety Executive** which includes representatives of employers, employees and local authorities. Health and safety inspectors are appointed with responsibility for making sure that the law is being observed.

There are also laws and codes applying to specific industries. For example, there are laws relating to miners, workers in the explosives industry and in textiles. Many industries also set their own additional safety regulations. A firm's personnel officer will normally attend conferences and refresher courses on safety as a regular feature of his or her duties.

The Factories Act 1961

Until it is fully replaced by regulations under the Health and Safety at Work Act, the Factories Act remains important. It covers most businesses that use mechanical machinery and therefore includes a wide range of premises including garages, printing works, building sites and engineering works. A factory is defined as a place where people are employed in manual labour (work done mainly by hand) in any process for, or incidental to, the making, repairing, altering, cleaning, adapting for sale or demolition of any article. The following are some stipulations of the Factories Act:

- Adequate toilet and washing facilities must be provided.
- The inside of buildings must be properly heated and ventilated.
- Floors must not have slippery surfaces.
- Machinery such as presses must have fenced screens to prevent serious injury.
- Fire escapes must be provided and kept in good order. Fire doors should not be locked or obstructed.

The Offices, Shops and Railway Premises Act 1963

This Act has now been fully subsumed into the Health and Safety at Work Act. Most of its provisions are similar to those covered by the Factories Act, but are applied in office and shop conditions. The following are examples of requirements:

- Temperatures must not fall below 16 degrees centigrade in places where people work for any length of time.
- There must be adequate supplies of fresh or purified air.
- Toilet and washing facilities must be adequate for the number of employees and kept in a clean state. There must be running hot and cold water with soap and clean towels.
- Suitable lighting must be provided wherever people walk or work.
- The minimum amount of space for each person is 12 square metres of floor space.

Reporting of Injuries, Diseases and Dangerous Occurrences Regulations 1985

Injuries that result from accidents at work where an employee is incapacitated for three or more days must be reported to the authorities within seven days. Injuries involving fatalities must be notified immediately by the most practical means (e.g. by telephone). Listed diseases must also be reported.

Control of Substances Hazardous to Health (COSHH) Regulations 1988

Employers must carry out an assessment of work tasks that are likely to create risks for the health and safety of employees. Following on from the assessment, decisions need to be made on how to prevent or limit risks of exposure to such substances. Workers dealing with dangerous substances should be given appropriate information and training. Measures taken to meet the regulations need to be continually monitored. All substances that are potentially harmful to health are covered by the Act, whether in solid or liquid form or in the form of a gas or vapour.

Noise at Work Regulations 1989

Employers have an obligation to reduce the risk of hearing damage to employees to the lowest practical level. The employer has an obligation to make sure that, when the sound reaches or exceeds a set level, ear protectors are worn.

Other regulations

Other regulations cover the use of electricity in the workplace, the provision of first-aid facilities, fire precautions, and other important areas.

Enforcement of the laws and regulations is principally by the Health and Safety Executive backed up by local authority inspections. Inspectors have substantial powers, including the right to enter premises, to obtain information and to take possession of articles and substances. Offending organisations can be taken to court to face substantial fines as well as prison sentences.

Negligence at common law

An employee can claim for damages arising from an employer's negligence if the employer fails 'to abide by the duty of care to the employee so that the employee suffers injury or damage to health'. The employer has a duty of reasonable care for the safety of employees, and this responsibility extends to when he or she sends employees to the premises of third parties. Negligence occurs when there is a breach in the duty of care which applies to:

- safe premises
- a safe system of work

- safe plant, equipment and tools
- safe fellow workers.

The European dimension of health and safety

Today, EU directives under Article 189 of the **Treaty of Rome** and more recently under the **Maastricht Treaty** are an important part of health and safety laws. Directives are binding, although member states can decide upon the means of giving them legal and administrative effect. In the UK this is usually in the form of regulations. For example, the Noise at Work Regulations mentioned earlier are an example of a European directive that has been enacted in the UK.

Health and safety is an important part of the Single European Act, which lays emphasis on providing safe working conditions in all member states. The emphasis is on harmonising working conditions.

In addition, new directives have been established about the technical requirements and safety standards of products. The **working time directive**, which has implications for health and safety, was adopted in 1994. The main provisions of this directive are:

- a minimum daily rest period of eleven consecutive hours
- at least one day off a week
- mandatory daily rest breaks after six hours
- four weeks' annual paid holiday
- no more than eight hours per shift for night work averaged over a period to be determined by each member state.

Clearly, the impact of this directive would have been felt most in Britain, which has the longest working hours and the most shift work. The UK abstained from voting on the directive. All member states except Britain are expected to enforce the directive by 1997. Britain, in contrast, will need only to guarantee three weeks' holiday for a further six years and has ten years before it has to implement the directive fully.

European social policy

It is important for all of those concerned with human relations and personnel work to have an understanding of European social policy.

We need to look back to the first principles established in the Articles of the Treaty of Rome before moving forward to the current European Social Chapter. These principles went well beyond purely employment-related issues, although these lie at the heart of them. The main principles set out in the Treaty of Rome were:

- *Equal treatment for men and women*, in particular regarding equal pay for work of equal value. 'Pay', as defined within the Treaty, includes indirect as well as direct remuneration in cash or kind (Article 119).
- *The free movement of workers throughout the Community*, outlawing discrimination based on nationality regarding selection for employment, remuneration and terms and conditions of work (Article 48).
- *The social security of migrants*, by the provision of benefits to migrant workers and their families based on accrued service across the Community (Article 51).
- *Closer co-operation between member states in a wide variety of areas, mainly concerning employment law and practice*, including vocational training, occupational hygiene, rights of association and collective bargaining (Article 118).
- *Measures to encourage improvements in the working environment*, particularly regarding health and safety (Article 118a).
- *A commitment to develop dialogue between the two sides of industry* (Article 118b).
- *The creation of a social fund* to reimburse member states in part for the costs of retraining and resettling the unemployed.

Many of these issues were not addressed by the European Community in the 1970s and hence remained dormant. It is only in recent times that they have been given greater attention and enshrined in the Maastricht Treaty in the form of the Social Chapter.

The Social Chapter

At the Maastricht Conference, many governments wanted to expand the range of social policy covered by the EU laws. The UK government would not agree to the acceptance of new laws that would increase regulation of the labour market and therefore opted out of the Social Chapter.

The treaty's Social Chapter gives legal force to the social charter signed by 11 EC leaders in December 1989. This gave the European Commission powers to develop social legislation without facing a national veto. For the first time, ministers from the 11 countries are able to agree, on the basis of qualified majority voting, directives on:

- health and safety
- working conditions
- information and consultation of workers
- sex equality in treatment at work and in applying for jobs.

If they are unanimous, the 11 can agree to directives on:

- social security and social protection of workers
- protection of workers where the employment contract is terminated
- representation and collective defence of the interests of workers and employers
- conditions of employment for third-country nationals living in the community.

Before the Maastricht Treaty was signed, the only area of employment law enforceable by qualified majority voting was health and safety. The reforms therefore involve a big increase in union powers. It should also be noted that the previous 11 signatories of the Maastricht Social Charter – France, Germany, Belgium, The Netherlands, Luxembourg, Greece, Denmark, Spain, Portugal, Ireland and Italy have now been joined by three new members, Sweden, Finland and Austria.

The Social Chapter from which Britain has opted out includes the following 12 rights:

1 *The right to work and to fair remuneration for work carried out.* The Chapter makes no reference to an EU-wide minimum wage, only to the desirability of an 'equitable wage' allowing a 'decent standard of living', neither of which are defined. This also includes the fostering of the growth of flexible, temporary and part-time working arrangements drawn up by individual employers, sectors and member states. Measures proposed include equal treatment with full-time workers for such employees.

2 *The right to freedom of movement in the community, equal treatment between community workers and recognition of professional qualifications.* It also proposes equal treatment in Europe in terms of social security and tax entitlements. This includes provision for migrant workers.

3 *The right to improvement of living and working* conditions, including contractual rights such as minimum periods of paid annual leave and a maximum level of working hours.

4 *The right to social protection,* particularly for those excluded from the labour market (including migrant workers). An action programme has been established for 'reinforcing economic and social cohesion', including the provision of funds and resources to redevelop declining industries, combat long-term unemployment and develop employment demand generally.

5 *The right to freedom of association and collective bargaining,* including the right to strike as well as encouraging measures to enhance dialogue between 'social partners', i.e. employers and employees at all levels.

6 *The right to vocational training.* This is seen as helping individual workers in making the transition to work within the wider market. In particular, it relates to new technology training, language learning programmes and increased links between firms and training providers such as colleges and professional institutions.

7 *The right to protection of children and young people,* notably a minimum working age and the protection against physical and moral dangers.

8 *The right to consumer protection,* including the right to information and to protection from environmental risks.

9 *Rights for the disabled,* including integration into working life.

10 *The right to protection of the elderly,* through the provision of adequate social security.

11 *The right to equal treatment for men and women* in all aspects of employment, including pay, access to work, training and career opportunity.

12 *Rights for employees* by the establishment of a standard form of work contract and revised company law procedures to provide increased information, consultation and involvement mechanisms.

Of course, many of these principles are enshrined in existing UK law, e.g. equal opportunities legislation. However, the UK government (Conservative) did not want to be bound by regulations on such things as minimum wages. The fear was that having workplace legislation dictated by directives from Brussels would reduce the ability of the UK to create competitive labour market conditions that would enable it to sell its products in competitive world markets.

The UK labour market is characterised by a lot more flexibility than, for example, Germany or France. This has meant that the UK has had lower unemployment and, by comparison, less of a social security burden. However, it does mean that the UK is out of step with its European partners on a substantial area of policy – although there is increasing recognition at the 'centre' of the European Union that flexibility may be an essential component of competitiveness in the next century. The Labour Party currently has increasing influence in the UK and may well be the government that sees out the twentieth century. It seems inevitable that a Labour government would steer the UK into the Social Chapter and increased regulation from the European Union.

Further reading

- *A Handbook of Human Resource Management* by E. Towers. Blackwell, 1995
- *A Handbook of Personnel Management* by Michael Armstrong. Blackwell, 1995.
- *Human Resource Development* by Jim McGoldrick and Jim Stewart. Pitman, 1996.
- *Human Resource Management* by David Goss. Routledge, 1995.
- *Human Resource Management* by Graham Hollingshead and Mike Leat. Pitman, 1995.
- *Human Resource Vision* by Stephen Connock. Institute of Personnel Management, 1995.

7 Role of the personnel function

On completion of this chapter, students should be able to:

- identify the responsibilities for personnel management within the management team

- explain and analyse the importance of human resource management planning, including:

  - analysis of current resources
  - forecasting future needs
  - the economic climate
  - skills analysis
  - skills available
  - sources of external information
  - demographic trends
  - labour market statistics
  - government incentives
  - financial implications.

Responsiblities for personnel within the management team

Different organisations organise their personnel or human resource functions in different ways. In some organisations personnel work is highly centralised and other managers take little responsibility for human resource management. However, as HRM becomes more of a strategic function, specialists in HRM are seen as experts who are there to support other managers as they take on greater responsibility for the management of human resources.

Figure 7.1 Centralised and decentralised human resource management

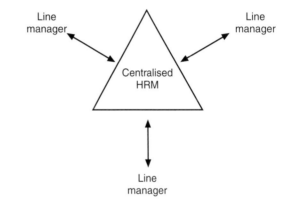

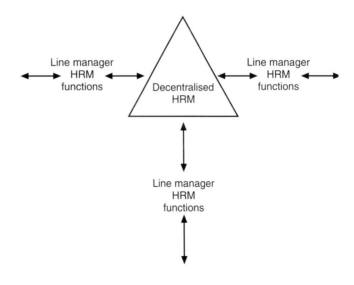

Task

What do you see as being the benefits of having a decentralised human resource system? What might be the drawbacks? Do some organisations lend themselves more to a decentralised approach than others? Give examples.

As we have seen, the place of personnel management in organisations has changed substantially over recent years. The move has been towards a human resource management approach and away from the view that personnel is a separate function with responsibility for 'hiring and firing'. The emergence of a new-style theory of personnel management sees personnel as a human resource concern which works across the organisation in a strategic way. It is therefore the more decentralised approach, referred to above, which has been developing.

According to Krulis-Randa, a writer on personnel management, the new HRM has the following characteristics:

■ *A reduction in hierarchy and a blurring of the distinction between management and non-management.* An example of this is the use of quality circles, where employees form part of a team and are responsible for their own self-management and regulation. For example, health and safety would be a shared concern of the team.
■ *Responsibility for people management is devolved to line managers. Personnel professionals support and facilitate.* For example, line managers are responsible for the appraisal of staff and staff development. Personnel professionals may offer support through appraisal training for staff and managers.
■ *Planning of human resources is part of overall corporate planning.* The mission statements of many modern organisations include references to the place of human resources, e.g. to secure the optimum personal development of company members.
■ *Employees are viewed as individuals with the potential for development, in line with the needs of the organisation.* For example, many organisations have appraisal systems which focus on the continuing professional development of staff.
■ *Management and non-management are committed to common goals and have an interest in the success of the organisation.* The increased emphasis on teams in organisations means that more people are involved in identifying goals and should therefore be more committed to them.

In a large organisation which has a decentralised structure for HRM, the organisation may include a **personnel**

Figure 7.2 A decentralised structure for human resource management

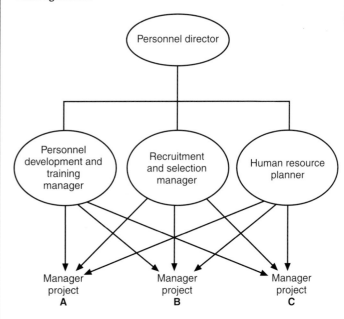

director leading the organisation. A **personnel development and training manager,** who is responsible for staff training and development, will have staff who will liaise with line managers in different areas. The structure may also include a **human resource planner,** responsible for planning the recruitment of the organisation at a national level. The work of this team will include the identification and monitoring of labour market trends. In addition, there may be a **recruitment and selection manager** who has overall responsibility for planning systems for recruitment and selection for the organisation.

In reality this structure combines centralisation of some of the HRM functions and decentralisation via the project managers. Wherever possible, personnel matters and decisions are handled on the ground, and the HRM specialists concentrate on strategic issues and supporting the project teams.

Decentralisation, then, is not just about splitting up the personnel function into smaller divisions. Most importantly, it is concerned with spreading the human resource message to self-managing teams and units within the organisation. The implication is that all managers and staff should have a role in human resource management rather than leaving personnel issues to the experts.

Case Study

Managing human resources in National Westminster Bank

The banking industry in the 1990s has changed dramatically. Levels of competition in banking services have increased. The application of information technology is widespread, and the numbers employed in banking have declined with all banks undertaking a shake-out of employees. This has meant that the banks have switched from tall organisations with many layers to flatter organisations.

This delayering is nowhere more apparent than in the area of human resource management. In the past, nearly all training at the National Westminster Bank was carried out centrally by a large training department. Recruitment, selection and the development of individuals were the responsibility of a centralised human resources department. Now that has changed. There is still some training undertaken by the head office, but the organisation now has human resource directors with a team of field managers.

The emphasis is now on encouraging bank managers and bank staff to take responsibility for human resource management concerns, such as recruitment, selection, appraisal, training and development. The field managers work from home covering a geographical area. Their main job is to support bank managers in the branches in order to assist them in carrying out their human resource functions.

In recent years there has been very little recruitment in the banking sector. The emphasis therefore is on the development of current employees. There is much less movement than in the past. Employees are expected to train to be multi-skilled. Today training and development of the individual is emphasised.

Questions for discussion

1   *Why do you think National Westminster Bank has adopted a new approach to human resource management?*
2   *What advantages are there in the new approach, and what disadvantages might there be?*

Task

Study a relatively large organisation that you are familiar with, e.g. the one that you or a friend work for. How is the human resource function organised? How is it similar or different to the one outlined at National Westminster Bank? Set out a short report outlining its organisation.

HRM planning

People represent the most flexible resource available to an organisation and, therefore, ensuring that they are in the right place at the right time with the right skills is essential to the success of any organisation. Human resource planning, then, is concerned with the acquisition,

Figure 7.3   The human resources planning process

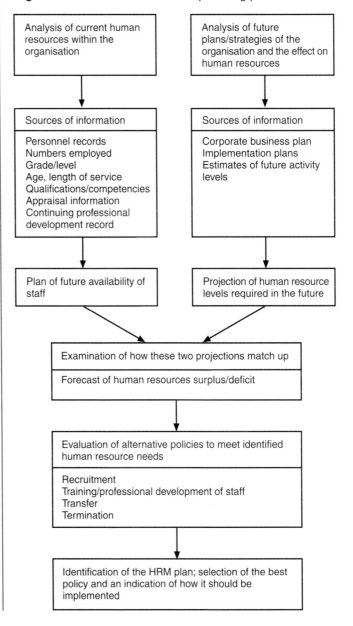

utilisation and development of human resources in order to meet an organisation's goals.

HRM contributes to the formulation of business strategy by identifying opportunities for the more effective use of staff and by analysing how human resource constraints may affect the implementation of a proposed strategy. The human resource planning process attempts to analyse the factors affecting the supply of and demand for human resources with a view to maximising the organisation's future performance.

For example, a transport organisation may make a decision to expand into the European market. It will then need to consider what sorts of skills and competencies will be needed by staff: how many current staff have those skills (e.g. fluency in key European languages); what new staff may have to be recruited; and what training will be needed for current staff.

Figure 7.3 identifies, in general terms, the various stages of the human resources planning process.

The basis of human resource strategies

As we have seen, the basis for determining the human resource strategy for an organisation is its long-term business plans and available financial resources. The development plans of the business will obviously respond to the demand for its products or services. The demand for human resources will therefore be derived from the level of demand for the product or service. Any HRM strategy must also deal with the supply side from both within and outside the organisation.

Forecasting demand for human resources

An organisation's demand for human resources must be estimated by analysing its corporate and future plans and by estimating future areas and levels of activity. In an insurance company, for example, forecasts of new business opportunities would be translated into the number of proposals that would have to be dealt with by the underwriting department. Any substantial increase would obviously require either greater productivity by the department or increased numbers of staff. A hotel complex may have a corporate plan which includes substantial expansion to include a leisure complex. Clearly these long-term plans will affect the numbers of people which the hotel group employs and the sorts of skills and experience required.

There are two main methods of forecasting demand: managerial estimates and work study techniques.

Managerial estimates

Many small companies estimate their demand for human resources by asking managers to estimate their needs on the basis of future workloads, and past resourcing levels. Managerial estimates can also utilise a range of information, including work study, to forecast future requirements.

Work study techniques

These techniques can be used where it is possible to calculate how long operations should take and the amount of labour required. In a manufacturing organisation it would be possible to forecast the volume of output and identify the time per unit which it takes to produce the product. By taking into account the average hours of work per member of staff per week, it would then be possible to calculate staff requirements for annual production.

The supply of human resources

If an organisation is to assess the supply of labour available to it, it must examine not only how many people are available to do particular jobs but also a range of other factors which determine total supply, including hours of work available for the job to be done, the capacity of employees to do the work and their productivity.

An organisation will need to consider both **internal** employee supply (the existing labour force) and **external** employee supply (the external labour market) – see Figure 7.4.

The existing labour force

In analysing the existing labour force, statistics and information need to be gathered on a range of factors to do with employees currently working in the organisation.

Figure 7.4   Analysing current supply

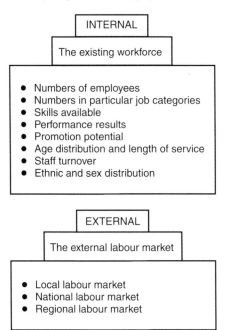

Numbers of employees in particular job categories

The aim here will be to identify particular groups of staff consisting of people with broadly similar skills for which forecasts of supply can be made. In a hotel, for example, you would want to know the numbers of reception staff, kitchen staff, front-house staff, etc.

Skills available

It may be necessary to identify the specific skills available across the current labour force and the extent to which those skills are transferable.

Skills analysis

An organisation needs to be sure that it has the right number of people available at the right time, but also with the right skills. Organisations therefore need to assess their present supply of skills across their workforce and to identify the sorts of skills they will require in the future. A skills inventory of current employees will indicate those who have received recent training and those who will require training. It may be possible to meet the human resource requirements of an organisation by training and developing current staff rather than recruiting externally.

Performance results

An organisation will want to gather information regarding the level of performance that it is getting from the various categories of employees. This sort of information may be **quantitative,** e.g. numbers of items produced of acceptable quality or numbers of items produced rejected

due to quality. Alternatively, it may comprise **qualitative** data, e.g. analysis of appraisal information.

Promotion potential

Internal promotions will change the availability of existing resources. It is therefore useful to an organisation to know how many employees have the skills and aptitude for promotion to more demanding roles. In addition, they might want to know how many employees have the potential, with suitable training, to achieve promotion.

Age distribution and length of service

Analysis of staff by age helps to identify possible problem areas. For example, is there an imbalance between experienced and inexperienced staff? Are promotion prospects blocked because of the age distribution? What planning can be done with regard to retirements?

Staff turnover

Staff turnover should be analysed in order to help an organisation to forecast future losses and to identify the reasons why people leave the organisation. A degree of staff turnover may be advantageous to an organisation as fresh staff can be recruited, promotion channels may be opened up, and it may allow natural wastage when an organisation is trying to reduce its workforce. Too high a level of staff turnover, however, will mean high additional costs of replacement recruitment, additional training costs, and disruption to the quality of service or to production.

Techniques for forecasting internal employee supply

In forecasting internal employee supply, techniques are used to establish labour turnover and stability.

It is possible to calculate the number of staff who leave an organisation as a percentage of the total workforce.

Labour turnover index

$$\frac{\text{Number of staff leaving over a specified period (e.g. 1 year)} \times 100}{\text{Average number of staff employed over the period}}$$

For example, if a Hospital employed a nursing staff of 458 but found that 132 nurses left during the year, the labour turnover index would be:

$$\frac{\text{No. of staff leaving}}{\text{Average number employed}} \times 100 = \frac{132}{458} \times 100 = 28.8\%$$

Task

A book publishing company had a staff of 3000 in 1994, 2806 in 1995 and 2712 in 1996. In 1994, 300 people left the firm; in 1995, 350 left the firm; and in 1996, 380 left the firm. Calculate the labour turnover index for each of these years. What trend can you see in the figures?

Such information is used to predict likely turnover in the future, to establish the need to examine in detail reasons for high turnover, and to establish the need to recruit new staff to replace those leaving. While the labour turnover index is useful, as with most statistics it needs to be considered alongside other factors. For example, are there particular areas of the organisation where the rate of leavers is high? It would also be useful to identify the leavers' length of service: are the most experienced people leaving or are they people with relatively little experience?

Labour stability index

As well as the labour turnover index, some organisations make use of a labour stability index. This provides an indication of the tendency for employees with long service to remain with the organisation, thus linking the leaving rate with the length of service.

$$\frac{\text{Number of staff leaving with 1 year's service or more} \times 100}{\text{Number employed 1 year ago}}$$

If we take the example of nursing staff in a hospital where the number employed was 458, and of the 132 leavers over the course of the year only 28 had 1 year's service or more, the index would look like this:

$$\frac{\text{No. of staff leaving with 1 year's service}}{\text{Average number employed}} \times 100 = \frac{28}{458} \times 100 = 6.1\%$$

Knowing about the existing labour force enables an organisation to make the most of the skill and potential which is already present within the organisation. However, consideration of the availability of people from the local and national labour markets is also vital.

The external labour market

The external labour market for any particular organisation comprises potential employees, locally regionally or nationally who possess the skills and experience required at a particular time. There are a range of factors which affect the size and nature of these labour markets (see Figure 7.5).

Figure 7.5 Factors affecting external labour markets

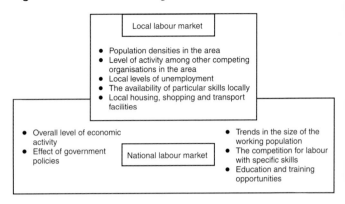

The national labour market

The following factors should be taken into account when assessing the national labour market.

Trends in the size/characteristics of the working population

Changes in age distribution of the population will affect the human resource planning of most organisations. The UK has an ageing population, with fewer school leavers and young workers available for employment. This means that businesses may need to look to other sectors of the population to meet their human resource requirements. For example, they may need to attract women back into the workforce or to employ more older workers. Some employers are already actively recruiting older workers, e.g. Sainsbury's and the John Lewis Partnership.

Competition for labour

Where the demand for people with specific skills is high, there will be competition between employers to attract people with those skills. Currently, universities receive part of their funding for research. The funding available to an individual university is based upon an assessment of each department's research output. There is therefore competition between institutions to attract proven researchers and, accordingly, Universities are having to offer higher levels of remuneration in order to attract researchers to their departments.

Overall level of economic activity

The economic climate will determine whether the general level of demand for goods and services is growing or declining.

In a recession, people generally have less to spend and the demand for goods and services will therefore fall. This, in turn, will lead firms to reduce output and therefore reduce their demand for labour. This may mean increasing levels of redundancies in firms and a general reluctance to take on permanent staff.

In the mid 1990s we have high levels of unemployment and forecasts indicate that unemployment of over 2 million people is likely to remain throughout the decade. However, although there is a large pool of unemployed labour, those people will not necessarily have the particular skills and abilities required in the right place at the right time. It used to be the case that businesses only tended to reduce their labour force during recession. However, many organisations have been going through the process of downsizing: in order to reduce costs, they reorganise and remove a tier of management. It is suggested that a company's financial standing is now measured by the stock market in terms of its most recent redundancy announcement. In October 1995, Lloyds Bank merged with the Trustee Savings Bank and analysts predicted 20 000 job losses. The typical reaction of share prices at the announcement of job losses is for shares to rise. Lloyds shares leapt by almost 5 per cent.

Education and training opportunities

The Education and training opportunities available to people will affect both the numbers of people coming into the labour market and their overall skill level. In Britain over recent years there has been an increasing number of young people participating in both further and higher education. The reasons for this have included more opportunities to stay in education as well as a lack of job opportunities. Young people also appreciate the need for higher levels of skill in order to compete in the job market.

In the early 1990s almost two-thirds of 16-year-olds in Great Britain entered post-compulsory education. The numbers of 18- and 19-year-olds progressing to higher education also rose steadily up to 1991/92. This means that the numbers of graduates entering the labour market has continued to rise.

The effect of government policies

Government legislation can affect the labour market in a number of ways. The government provides incentives to organisations to employ and train people. Where such incentives are available, they will reduce the costs of labour and therefore have implications for human resource planning.

Many of the policies pursued by the Conservative government in recent years have been aimed at removing restrictions on businesses and providing incentives in order to allow them to develop more easily. Some of the incentives have been directly linked to employment, while others are associated with investment. Forms of aid available include:

- *The creation of enterprise zones in inner city areas.* In these relatively small areas, financial incentives are available to firms. There are also tax incentives which can reduce costs and the possibility of locating in subsidised premises.
- *Selective Regional Assistance.* This is available to firms who both create jobs and protect jobs in particular localities.
- *Regional Enterprise Grants.* These are available to small firms in development areas. They take the form of an investment grant or a grant towards a new process or product innovation.

These forms of assistance from government are available only to businesses located or locating in specific geographical areas which have been designated as development areas or intermediate areas. Development areas are those regions which are suffering most in terms of industrial decline.

Local authorities have also become increasingly involved in the economic development of their area. They often provide a range of incentives and assistance to businesses. This includes job creation grants, grants for business start-up, assistance with finding industrial units, and general business and financial advice.

Central government has also been responsible for a number of measures designed to encourage education, training and the development of skills

- The government has identified National Education and Training Targets (NETTs) which it monitors on a regular basis. Through these targets, the government is seeking to raise the numbers of people with qualifications and skills in the population.
- Modern Apprenticeships are an initiative designed to treble the number of young people on government-supported training achieving higher-level skills.
- Investors in People is an initiative which results in an award and the title 'Investor in People' being given to employers who meet certain criteria regarding their training and development of employees.

The local labour market

It is important for any organisation to have information about the local labour market in order to be able to identify whether people with the right skills will be available locally or whether the organisation will need to look regionally or nationally in order to recruit.

Population

The organisation needs to know the population densities which are within reach of its location. What expansion of population might there be in the area?

Level of activity among competing organisations

An organisation will be interested to know whether its competitors are expanding and therefore increasing the demand for labour, or whether local redundancies mean labour is more readily available.

Local levels of unemployment

Local unemployment levels give an indication of the general availability of labour and suggest whether it will be easy or difficult to recruit. This, coupled with information about skills availability, will determine whether an organisation can obtain the human resources it requires from the local area.

Local housing, shopping and transport

All these factors will affect the attractiveness of a particular locality as a place to work. If local housing is readily available at reasonable cost, it may be possible to attract new employees to the area.

Labour market statistics

Human resource planners need to be aware of trends in both the national and local labour markets. They therefore require access to a range of both national and local labour market statistics.

The national perspective

Information charting national employment trends is published on a regular basis by government departments.

Labour Market Trends

This is published by the Central Statistical Office and includes statistical and research features on employment-related subjects, alongside labour market data pages.

The following data (Figures 7.6 and 7.7), published in *Labour Market Trends*, February 1996, are taken from an article, 'Redundancies in Great Britain: Results from the Labour Force Survey'. The article looks at redundancy levels and the likelihood of being made redundant in Great Britain in Spring 1995, as well as redundancy trends over the past few years. These trends are discussed in relation to industry, occupation, region of residence, age, gender and employment status.

The number of redundancies in the three months prior to spring 1995 was 220 000 – a slight increase compared with a year ago (7 percent). Between the peak of spring 1991 and spring 1994, the total number of redundancies has gradually decreased. The data above provide information regarding the characteristics of those made redundant and analyse this trend in more detail for men and women and whether, by the time of interview, the respondent had found a new job.

Employment News

This is a newspaper published by the Department for Education and Employment eight times a year. Its coverage includes a range of employment issues, training initiatives, news from Training Enterprise Councils, government departments and professional bodies. It is available from Central Despatch (Employment News/G), Room W125, Moorfoot, Sheffield S14 PQ.

Labour Force Survey Quarterly Bulletin

This bulletin presents the main results of the

Figure 7.6   Redundancies by sex and current employment status, Great Britain; Spring 1989 to 1995

	1989	1990	1991	1992	1993	1994	Thousands 1995
In paid employment							
Men	30	42	69	54	36	36	56
Women	19	21	31	25	23	14	30
All	49	63	99	79	59	50	87
Not in paid employment							
Men	65	76	200	164	134	107	81
Women	29	42	92	81	70	49	52
All	95	119	292	245	204	156	133
All							
Men	95	118	269	218	170	142	137
Women	49	63	122	106	92	63	82
All	144	181	391	324	262	205	220

Note: Figures show the numbers of people who were made redundant in the three months prior to their interview.

Source: Labour Force Survey

Figure 7.7 Redundancies by current employment status, Great Britain; Spring 1992 to 1995

Thousands

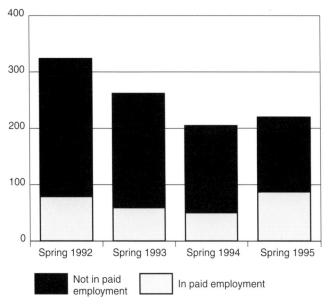

Note: Employment status of respondent at the time of interview.

Source: Labour Force Survey

Government's Labour Force Survey for Great Britain. A survey of around 60000 households is carried out each quarter and provides a wide range of information about the labour force.

Labour Market Quarterly Report
This report is published by the Department for Education and Employment and provides a range of information on national and regional labour market trends and training.

The local perspective
Organisations may also be interested in some of the local labour market data which are available.

Labour Market Review
This is produced by the Employment Service. Figures 7.8a and b are two examples of local data provided by the *Labour Market Review*.

Task

Produce a report setting out changes in the national and local labour market. Identify how they will affect a particular business organisation in your locality.

Local economic bulletins

Many County Council Planning and Economic Development Departments publish economic data which relate to their particular area.

Figure 7.8 Unemployment in the East Midlands and Eastern region
  a Change in unemployment (unadjusted) October 1993–October 1994 by county
  b Change in vacancies notified to Jobcentres (unadjusted) in East Midlands and Eastern counties, October 1993–October 1994

a

County	Oct 1993	Rate	Oct 1994	Rate	Change	% change
Derbyshire	40 632	9.3	37 947	8.7	−2 685	−6.6
Leicestershire	34 843	7.7	30 730	6.8	−4 113	−11.8
Lincolnshire	22 259	8.4	19 880	7.5	−2 379	−10.7
Northamptonshire	22 501	7.9	18 374	6.4	−4 127	−18.3
Nottinghamshire	53 721	11.0	49 394	10.1	−4 327	−8.1

b

County	Oct 1993	Oct 1994	Change	% change
Derbyshire	3 650	4 050	400	10.96
Leicestershire	3 709	5 514	1 805	48 67
Lincolnshire	3 414	3 444	30	0.88
Northamptonshire	2 792	2 835	43	1.54
Nottinghamshire	3 442	3 705	308	8.95
Cambridgeshire	2 671	3 140	469	17.56
Norfolk	3 322	3 412	90	2.71
Suffolk	2 963	3 197	234	7.90

Note: the differences apparent between counties are not necessarily a full reflection of labour market trends in that other factors can influence vacancy notification to Jobcentres. Furthermore, vacancies notified to Jobcentres do not represent the total number of vacancies in the economy. Latest estimates suggest that about a third of all vacancies nationally are notified to Jobcentres.

Financial implications

Human resource planning, as with any other area of organisational planning, involves financial implications. Pay, for example, is usually the largest item of an organisation's costs, amounting to 70 per cent or more of the total budget. It is important to think out the cost implications of all activities within an organisation and to allocate these costs to appropriate headings. It is only by having a detailed understanding of costs that you are able to see which parts of an organisation's activities are efficient and which are not. Of course, it is easier to allocate costs to some activities than to others.

Budgeting and costs

Budgeting is an important management skill for everyone involved in business decision-making processes. A budget is an itemised summary of expected expenditures and incomes, or uses of resources over a particular period of time. Budgeting is a very useful process because it provides a control tool for checking on actual performance compared with anticipated performance, making it possible to take remedial action.

Budgets are typically presented as financial estimates, but they do not have to be expressed in money terms. The key requirement is that you have some form of unit of account or measurement. For example, you may use the measure pounds and pence, but just as easily you could use labour hours, number of employees, etc. In estimating the time taken to do a job, you could for instance allocate 12 hours to the job based on previous performance. You may then find that you have overestimated the number of hours required to do the job because labour has become more efficient.

Projects can often be broken down into **milestone budgets,** i.e. discrete segments. Time and costs are allocated to each segment. Creating a milestone budget makes it possible for a manager to divide a complex project into a number of simpler parts and to maintain control over each of these parts.

Budget planners use a spreadsheet to set out budgets for particular jobs, series of activities and longer-term plans. The budget is prepared on the spreadsheet well in advance. Performance is then compared to budgeted performance on an ongoing basis. Any variances are then noted so that corrective actions can be taken. For example, an organisation may build figures for staff absences, sicknesses and illnesses into its budget calculations. Once certain tolerance levels are exceeded, it is necessary to review what is going wrong.

The size of the global human resource budget will depend on the size of the organisation and the priority given to human resources. Sub-budgets will exist for such things as training and development, recruitment and selection, appraisal, etc. The size of the sub-budget for each heading will be a reflection on the priority that it is given in the organisation.

Where a personnel department is responsible for recruitment, selection and training as a functional responsibility, a budget will be allocated directly to that department. However, when line managers take on human resource tasks, part of the budget will be allocated to them.

When a personnel department introduces its own cost centres, these should be consistent with the cost allocation and reporting systems which exist as part of the organisation's financial systems. The personnel department should not introduce an independent cost-coding system.

Further reading

- *Developments in the Management of Human Resources* by John Storey. Blackwell, 1995.
- *Personnel Management: A New Approach* by D. Torrington and L. Hall. Prentice Hall, 1995.
- 'Redundancies in Britain: Results from the Labour Force Survey' in *Labour Market Trends*, 1996.
- *The Handbook of Human Resource Planning,* by George McBeath, Blackwell, 1993.

On completion of this chapter, students should be able to:

- distinguish between personnel data and personnel information
- identify the main parts of a personnel information system
- describe the uses of computers in personnel
- evaluate a CPIS for selection and training
- describe the criteria for evaluating personnel information systems
- state the key principles of the Data Protection Act and discuss their implications for personnel.

Information and data

In Chapter 7, we discussed the role of the personnel function within an organisation. One very important role of the personnel department is to provide management with accurate information on how effectively human resources are being utilised in the organisation.

By using information models, this chapter focuses on the different categories of information that the personnel department may be requested to provide. Historically, the data upon which this information is based have been collected manually. This process has, however, become much easier with the introduction of computers. The implications of using computers and the legal consequences of this transition will be discussed, together with some examples of the types of systems which may be used for selection and training. Finally, the application of various packages will be considered as to how they can provide statistical information and data analysis upon which to base management decisions.

The importance of information

Clare Morris, in her book *Quantitative Approaches in Business Studies*, summarises just how important information is to an organisation.

> 'A business concern of any kind, even the smallest, today depends to a very large extent on having ready access to large amounts of information, ranging from details of the potential market for its goods and services to estimates of next year's labour requirements, from the attendance record of each employee to the numbers of breakdowns per week for each piece of equipment it owns. The more accurate and complete this information is, the more effective, all other things being equal, the operation of the business can be.'

She stresses how important it is to have **accurate** and **complete** information. Vague or imprecise information could lead to ineffective decisions being made, which could affect the well-being of an organisation. With businesses now operating in such a competitive environment, they cannot afford for this to happen.

Task

Give examples of situations in which poor or inadequate information has led to poor business decision-making. What have been the results?

Obtaining information

Useful information is based on the collection of reliable **data.** Bartol and Martin (1991), describe **data** and information as follows:

> 'Data are unanalysed facts and figures . . . To be useful, the data needs to be transformed into information. Information is data that has been analysed or processed into a form that is meaningful for the decision maker.'

Figure 8.1 illustrates this process.

Figure 8.1   Transforming data into information

Data → Data processing → Information

Task

Discuss what sort of information would be useful to a personnel department.

Personnel data

The facts and figures used by the personnel department would be generated from the **personnel administrative systems.** These are systems which can be used to monitor, control and develop human resources within the organisation. A typical personnel department may have the following administrative systems:

- recruitment and selection records
- absence records
- employee records
- training and development records
- disciplinary records
- payroll records
- productivity records
- employee resourcing records
- employee organisation records.

The facts and figures generated from these administrative systems can be transformed into **personnel information** to provide a basis for decision-making. Figure 8.2 outlines

the personnel data generated from administrative systems and provides examples of the types of information which may be extracted.

Figure 8.2   Personnel data and information

Personnel data	Personnel information
Recruitment and selection	Breakdown of applicants by age, gender, etc.
Absence	Number of days lost individually, by department
Employee records	Personal details
Training and assessment	Number of employees trained to a particular skill level
Discipline	Number and type of warnings issued, individually, by type, etc.
Payroll	Number of full-time, part-time and payroll costs
Employee resourcing	Labour turnover figures
Employee organisation	Organisation charts
Productivity	Output per employee

How personnel information is used

The information obtained from the data can be interpreted for decision-making purposes at various levels inside and outside the organisation. There are essentially four levels:

- employee level
- departmental level
- organisational level
- external level.

The key question for the personnel department is what information should they be able to provide, and so what data should they collect? The information required should drive the data collected, because the data collected limits the amount of information that can be generated. A good system is therefore driven by information needs, i.e. what do we want to know about the people we employ? With a poor system, the information available is determined by the data collected. Information systems can, however, be continuously improved, as Figure 8.3 suggests.

Now that the reader is familiar with the key terms of data and information and their place within the personnel context, the next section focuses on models of information systems and their application to personnel.

Figure 8.3   A continuous cycle for improving information systems

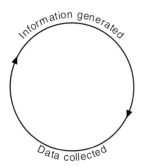

Models of information systems

Bartol and Martin (1991) describe an information system as follows:

> *'An information system can be defined as a set of procedures designed to collect (or retrieve), process, store, and disseminate information to support planning, decision making, co-ordination and control.'*

Figure 8.4 outlines Bartol and Martin's model of an information system.

The effectiveness of the personnel department can be measured by how efficient the department is at providing information. Speed and accuracy become very important factors in a competitive environment. Information systems today are becoming increasingly computerised. This allows greater quantities of data to be transformed into information much faster. The following section describes the concept of a computerised personnel information system and offers the reader a model of how such a system may provide information for the organisation.

Figure 8.4   Basic components of an information system

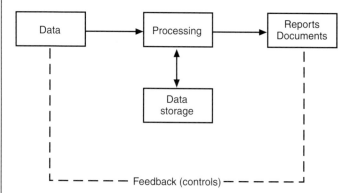

Source: Bartol and Martin (1991)

Computerised personnel information system

A computerised personnel information system (CPIS) has been defined by Gallagher (1991) as:

> *'a computer-based information system which is designed to support the operational, managerial and decision making functions of the personnel division in an organisation.'*

The information provided by the system supports different levels of decision-making in the organisation. Bartol and Martin suggest three information levels within the organisation:

- operational
- tactical
- strategic.

This hierarchy of information levels can be applied to personnel to form a model of an information system – see Figure 8.5. In a personnel context, the sort of information which would required at each level might include the following:

Figure 8.5   Model of an information system

Source: Adapted from Bartol and Martin (1991)

Operational level

- who is at work today?
- who has phoned in sick?
- who is on a training course?

Tactical level

- departmental comparisons – absenteeism, productivity and accidents
- number of employees in a department against the number required
- required skills against the available skills.

Strategic level

- human resource planning – projected skills requirement for the next five years
- pay policy development.

Task

The following is a list of changes that are being considered in areas related to human resourcing in an oil company.

1 Change the company's management structure to increase individual accountability and enhance the speed of decision-making throughout the organisation.
2 Introduce a no-smoking policy for the central office building following a staff survey and consultation with the staff committee.
3 Keep a record of staff absences on a week-by-week basis.
4 Make calculations of overtime pay at the end of the week.
5 Establish a long-term plan setting out labour requirements for the next ten years.
6 Set out ways of increasing empowerment structures within a plant.
7 Transform an organisation from a command and control approach to one based on human resource management.
8 Decide on how many employees will be employed in a specific department over a three-month period.
9 Set up a new health and safety training course for employees.

Which of these are strategic, tactical and operational level decisions? Identify three of each (although it is not always possible to draw hard and fast lines).

Torrington and Hall, in their latest edition of *Personnel Management,* offer an alternative model of a personnel information system which provides information at five

levels:

- individual employee
- personnel systems
- personnel function
- aggregate employee
- organisational.

Potentially, all the manual records kept by the personnel department are capable of being computerised. Alastair Evans, in his book *Computers and Personnel Systems,* categorises the applications of computers into several main areas, including:

- a computerised record system
- a generator of personnel information
- an aid to personnel administration.

The use and implications of computers in personnel

Computers can have an impact on many functions of personnel management. The next section focuses on the use and implications of computers in personnel. The contribution that computers have made in each case is discussed by outlining some of the main human resources areas to be affected (see Figure 8.6).

This is not an exhaustive list of uses or applications, but is designed to give the reader an insight into the flexibility and breadth of the potential uses of computers in personnel.

Task

Identify how an organisation with which you are familiar uses the applications listed in Figure 8.6.

Introducing new technology into any department can have many implications. These can be considered under three headings:

- people
- money
- time.

People

The personnel using the systems must be adequately trained. The organisation must ensure that there is systems support available, for example in the form of a

Figure 8.6 Applications of computers in personnel

Personnel function	Main uses of computerised system
Recruitment and selection	■ Tracking applicant's progress through the recruitment and selection process ■ Skill matching ■ Labour turnover statistics
Absence control and time and attendance	■ Number of days lost by individual, department, organisation ■ Monitoring lateness
Organisation charting	■ Tracking employees, movements, e.g. promotions, lateral moves, secondments. Useful for career development reviews
Equal opportunities monitoring	■ Accurate information regarding age, sex, race, profile of the current and potential workforce. Used for recruitment and selection and for providing details to external agencies
Training and assessment	■ Tracking progress of employees attending courses ■ Monitoring individual skills ■ Organisational skills profile
Performance and appraisal	■ Record of the outcome of appraisals and career development discussions. It can provide useful information for succession planning
Accident records	■ Tracking the frequency of the number and type of accident
Labour scheduling	■ Investigating the most effective way to utilise labour across a multi-departmental organisation throughout the trading day
Modelling	■ For example, pay awards, investigating 'what if' scenarios
Human resource planning	■ Identifying the numbers and skill levels required in the future ■ Human resource budgeting
Measuring productivity	■ Analysing labour efficiencies within the organisation, e.g. output levels, wastage, number of customers served, sales, etc.
Employee database	■ All employees' personal and employment details. Used as the basis for generating information for the other applications.
Diarising	■ Reminders of dates for maternity administration, sickness benefits, disciplinary meetings and reviews, etc.
Generation of memos, letters and reports	■ Various applications across many personnel functions
Payroll	■ Employees paid electronically straight into the bank/building society ■ Activity-based costing – analysing who works where and how much they cost; analysing variances against budgets

help desk. The introduction of computers may lead to job losses in the personnel department. Redeployment and redundancy may need to be considered.

The implications of electronically storing information must also be addressed. An organisation must be fully conversant with the Data Protection Act before commencing any personal electronic data input or transformation. The legal aspects of collection, disclosure and registration are discussed later in the chapter.

Money

Investing in a computerised personnel information system will almost certainly require a significant financial outlay in capital equipment. As with any new investment, careful research should be conducted to ensure that the right system is purchased.

Time

Initially time will be needed to research the most appropriate system and to train all the potential users of the system. Time spent wisely on these initiatives should lead to savings in information-processing time, which may ultimately lead to improved organisational efficiency.

As discussed earlier, the potential uses of computers in personnel are wide and varied. A CPIS will undoubtedly reduce the personnel manager's workload, while minimising the chance of bypassing crucial information, thereby enhancing the effectiveness of human resource management. We will now take a closer look at two areas of human resource management where computers can assist in providing accurate information for decision-making: personnel selection and training and assessment.

Systems for personnel selection

The starting point for any computerised personnel system is to create an employee database from which data can be analysed and information generated. The key information in a database could include the following details about employees:

- personal details
- education
- training
- work experience – prior to and since joining the organisation
- disciplinary record
- appraisal details
- other relevant data.

Recruitment and selection is a fundamental part of any personnel function. As a manual system, the process can be somewhat inefficient due to the high number of stages involved. Alastair Evans, in his book *Computers and Personnel Systems*, highlights some of the potential drawbacks of a manual system:

1 labour intensive
2 fragmented and inefficient
3 slow
4 difficult to co-ordinate
5 poor or non-existent management information.

Dissatisfied with the above drawbacks, organisations are now beginning to computerise their manual selection systems.

To illustrate the sort of system which an organisation may use, a simple model is composed. The model has three functions: planning, routine administration and status reports. Each function forms a separate part of the computerised system, but all are interrelated. Planning can be seen as the driving force of the model. From planning comes objectives. Routine administration provides the data by which to gauge performance against the objectives and thence the plan. This performance is summarised through status reports. Figure 8.7 illustrates the relationship between the functions. By using this model, we can describe how a computerised selection system may work.

Outlined below are the three functions, detailing the sort of data which can be computerised under each heading:

- *Planning* – human resource planning, recruitment and selection budgeting, planning personnel to be involved in the selection process.

Figure 8.7   The relationship between the three functions of a computerised information system

- *Routine administration* – recruitment process, standard letters, applicants, details, vacancy details.
- *Status reports* – analysing information for decision-making.

To illustrate how this model might work, we will look at the process of personnel selection.

Planning

Against forecast production figures for next year, the **human resource plan** has identified a requirement to recruit additional staff. Sufficient funds have been **budgeted** to cover the costs of recruitment and selection. The recruitment activity can be covered within the existing personnel staffing numbers.

Routine administration

The process of recruitment and selection can be viewed as a series of systematic steps, from deciding that a vacancy exists (i.e. job analysis), to conducting interviews to making the final decision. The systematic approach lends itself to computerisation. To facilitate this, the personnel function must be able to formalise the recruitment process into a series of steps which can be used as key inputs into the computer. This can be presented in the form of a flow chart (see Figure 8.8). The process is discussed fully in Chapter 11.

Most parts of the process in Figure 8.8 will require a response from the employer to the applicant informing them of their progress. **Standard letters** can be generated for the relevant section, e.g. acknowledgement of application form, invite for interview, regret, offer etc. A standard letter integrates the applicant's personal details into a pre-formatted letter layout, thus producing a personalised letter in a fraction of the time.

Figure 8.8 A flow chart of the recruitment and selection process

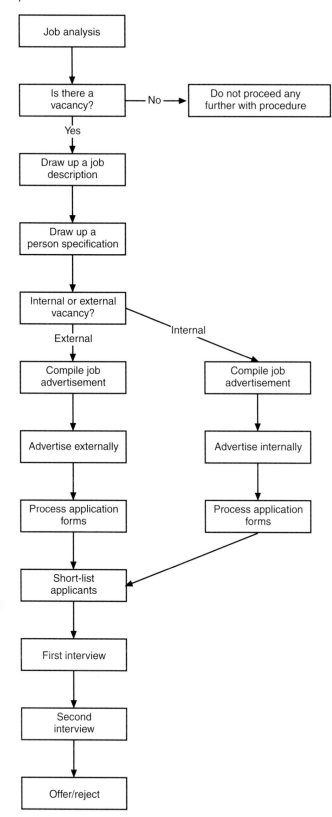

Applicants' details – data regarding each applicant will need to be recorded to form an applicants' database. The sort of information which may be recorded includes:

- name
- address
- age
- sex
- date of birth
- education
- ethnic origin
- previous experience
- skills
- job application route.

In order to match the applicants to a particular job, **vacancy details** will also need to be recorded. This may include:

- job title
- salary
- department
- duties and responsibilities
- qualifications
- previous experience.

Once all the data have been inputted, the user can instruct the computer to sort the data and match the key vacancy criteria against applicants' details, and to provide a list of applicants which match the criteria.

Status reports

The personnel manager will be able to obtain various information about applicants and the selection process very quickly. For example, the system should be able to tell the user at which stage every applicant is during the process, which letters they have been sent, etc. Further analysis could assess the status of the selection process, for example how many people have applied for a vacancy, breakdown of males/females, time taken to fill a post, most effective method of advertising, etc. The system can also be used for identifying internal candidates by matching the vacancy details against the employee database.

Task

1 Discuss the benefits of the computerised selection system for:
   a the job applicant
   b the personnel manager
   c the human resources director.
2 Discuss the potential problems which may arise during the introduction of the new system.

Systems for training and assessment

Training is another key function of the personnel department (see Chapter 5 for a detailed discussion of training and development). Organisations invest in training to ensure that their employees have the required skills and knowledge to be able to do their current jobs effectively, and to prepare them for future organisational challenges. Training can be a huge cost for some organisations. It follows, therefore, that for the training budget to be spent effectively, the personnel department should be able to provide information about who has been trained to a certain level, the cost of training, the effectiveness of external courses, etc. This information can be obtained manually, but again due to the highly administrative nature of the tracking system, it lends itself well to becoming computerised.

By applying the same model as before, we are able to identify the key data which can be computerised within each function.

Planning

The main emphasis here is using the computer system to:

■ plan training needs
■ identify skills gaps
■ assist in succession planning, ensuring employees have the required skills to move up the hierarchy.

Routine administration

Many administrative functions can be computerised, including:

■ booking employees on courses
■ sending out joining instructions
■ maintaining a database of internal and external courses
■ timetabling courses and trainers
■ updating training records.

Status reports

Once the above administrative details have been input, the system can be utilised to produce status reports, for example:

■ number of employees with particular skills
■ number of training days provided individually, by department, etc.
■ cost of training.

Figure 8.9 illustrates the relationship between the key functions of a CPIS for personnel selection and training and assessment.

Figure 8.9 The relationship between the key functions of a CPIS for personnel selection and training and assessment

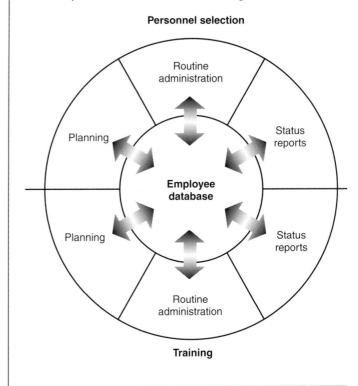

Task

1 Discuss the benefits of the computerised training system for:
  a the employee
  b the personnel manager
  c the human resources director.
2 Discuss the potential problems which may arise during the introduction of the new system.

Statistical information and data analysis

One benefit of the CPIS is to enable the user to extract information based on statistical analysis of the data contained in the database. This statistical output can support management decision-making. It is important to note that it does not replace management decision-making. Stainer (1971) summarises this as follows:

'The aim in employing statistical techniques is to simplify the problem to the extent that the human mind can cope with it efficiently, rather than to eliminate subjective judgement altogether.'

Uses of statistical information

Statistical information can be used to:

- identify past trends
- plan future resources
- provide personnel with key performance indicators
- facilitate modelling and 'what if' type scenarios.

The potential applications of statistical information are highlighted in the following example:

The personnel manager is assessing human resource requirements for the coming year. The sales forecast gives a mix of finished products which can be broken down into skill requirements in terms of hours. To support the decision-making process, the personnel manager will rely on the CPIS to provide statistical information in terms of:

- attendance
- performance levels (productivity)
- staff retention, labour turnover
- seasonality of labour supply
- skills required against skills available (by hour).

From this information, the personnel manager should be able to establish the gross number of employees necessary to achieve production and sales targets after allowances for attendance, performance, etc.

Modelling

Modelling is a statistical tool. It provides the facility to ask 'what if' type questions and to consider many possible scenarios. Continuing the example above, absenteeism may be high due to the boring nature of some of the work. A possible solution to this problem might be a revision of the payment system. Modelling could be used to speculate as to the possible outcomes of introducing several different payment systems.

Transaction processing systems

Transaction processing systems (TPSs) are important for the routine operation of the CPIS. Transactions are events which take place in an organisation. A TPS provides important information involving the following operations:

- *classifying data* – such as new applicants for a job according to their level of qualifications
- *calculating* – such as the number of hours lost due to sickness in a particular week
- *sorting* – arranging data into a sequence, such as listing employees according to the length of time since they last went on a training course
- *summarising* – reducing large amounts of information into a briefer form, such as a summary of the most

important trends in absences
- *storage* – of large quantities of personnel information for future use.

Criteria for evaluating personnel information systems

A significant investment will have been made in the CPIS. It is essential, therefore, that the contribution made by the system is evaluated. The evaluation will ensure that:

- the system is able to provide the information required
- the system represents good value.

This section discusses the criteria for evaluating a CPIS. The criteria are developed around four questions:

- When should evaluation take place?
- Who should be involved?
- How should evaluation be conducted?
- What should be included in the evaluation?

When should evaluation take place?

- *Before implementation.* In order to judge how successful the computerised system is, you need a benchmark upon which to make a comparison. Before the system is implemented, the users of the potential system should have some idea of how long they are spending on the tasks which will be computerised, so that a comparison can be made.
- *After implementation.* Once the system is being used, a detailed evaluation can take place. It is here that the other three questions would be asked: who?, how?, and what?

Who should be involved?

The success of the system very much depends on its users. This does not just apply to the personnel department. The following are all users of a system and as such should all be involved in the evaluation process:

- clerical support, staff responsible for data entry and retrieval
- personnel managers who will be dealing with personal records on a daily basis
- senior managers who will want access to information for management decision-making.

How should evaluation be conducted?

Evaluation can take a variety of forms depending on the time and resources available. The key aim will be to make a comparison between the manual system and the new computerised system and to make recommendations for the future. Evaluation methods which may be used inlcude:

- questionnaires
- group discussions
- interviews.

What should be evaluated?

Several aspects of the CPIS should be evaluated so that an accurate cost-benefit analysis can be undertaken, for example:

- *The work produced.* Is the computerised system having the desired effect on the quality and quantity of work? Is the process of accessing information quicker?
- *The system itself.* How reliable is the hardware and software? How quickly does it respond to requests for information?

Employers will be very keen to assess the costs and benefits of the project as part of the evaluation process.

Costs

These will include:

- equipment costs
- training costs
- inputting the data – the organisation may need to employ extra staff
- support costs, e.g. in the form of a help desk.
- ongoing maintenance costs – hardware and software.

Benefits

An article by Marion Gillie in *Personnel Management* (August 1987) categorised the benefits as 'cost displacement, cost elimination and added value'.

- *Cost displacement* refers to any time or expenditure saved as a result of eliminating routine tasks and removal of the duplication of effort. Cost displacement also refers to achieving the same output for less input.
- *Cost elimination* refers either to the reduction in current costs (e.g. fewer staff needed) or the saving of future expense (no need for additional staff).
- *Added value* refers to benefits such as the ability to respond more quickly to requests for information, or to take on tasks which could not (or would not) have been done without the new computer system.

Legal requirements

Confidentiality, privacy and security of personal information have always been issues of concern for both the personnel department and individual employees. However, with the potential for this data to be computerised, this concern has become heightened. To safeguard employees against the potential misuse of their personal data, employers have to abide by the **Data Protection Act 1984.** This section discusses the main parts of the Act, including the employer's responsibility for registration, recording, collection and disclosure of personal data and records.

Task

Discuss what sorts of personnel records should be open to employee scrutiny. Are there any that should not?

Data Protection Act 1984

The Data Protection Act gives new rights to individuals about whom information is recorded on computer. The Act places obligations on employers who record and use personal data. They must be open about that use and follow sound and proper practices. The Act states eight principles that must be adhered to:

1 The information to be contained in personal data shall be obtained, and personal data shall be processed, fairly and lawfully.
2 Personal data shall be held only for one or more specified and lawful purposes.
3 Personal data held for any purpose or purposes shall not be used or disclosed in any manner incompatible with that purpose or those purposes.
4 Personal data held for any purpose or purposes shall be adequate, relevant and not excessive in relation to that purpose or those purposes.
5 Personal data is accurate and where necessary kept up to date.
6 Personal data held for any purpose or purposes shall not be kept for longer than is necessary for that purpose or those purposes.
7 An individual shall be entitled – at reasonable intervals and without undue delay or expense –
   a to be informed by any data user whether he holds personal data of which that individual is the subject; and
   b to access to any such data held by a data user; where appropriate, to have such data corrected or erased.
8 Appropriate security measures shall be taken against unauthorised access to, or alteration, disclosure or destruction of, personal data and against accidental loss or destruction of personal data.

Data protection registration

Employers who electronically record personal data about their employees must apply for registration to the Data Protection Registrar. The registration must detail what personal data are to be held and the purposes for recording such data. It must also state to whom the data user may disclose the information.

Collection and disclosure

Employers must ensure that data are obtained fairly. Care should be taken not to deceive or mislead employees about the purpose for which the data are to be held or used or disclosed.

Personal data and records

The Act defines personal data as:

'data consisting of information which relates to a living individual who can be identified from that information . . . including any expression of opinion about the individual but not any indication of the intentions of the data user in respect of that individual.'

The Act gives individuals certain legal rights concerning personal data held about them. These rights are outlined briefly below:

- *Compensation.* If damage has been caused by the loss, unauthorised destruction or unauthorised disclosure of personal data, the employee may apply to the courts, for compensation.
- *Correction or deletion.* If personal data are inaccurate, the employee may apply to the courts for correction or deletion of the data.
- *Subject access.* An individual is entitled, upon payment of a small fee, to be supplied with a copy of any personal data held about him or her. The request must be in writing.
- *Complaint to the Registrar.* An employee who feels that there has been a breach of one of the principles, or any other provision of the Act, is entitled to complain to the Data Protection Registrar.

Implications for personnel managers

If using a CPIS, personnel managers must ensure that they are abiding by the principles of the Data Protection Act. Failure to do so may lead to court action.

Bell commented on the 'Practical implications of the Data Protection Act' in an article in *Personnel Management* in 1984. He stated that:

'The most significant part of the legislation for personnel managers concerns the seventh principle – the right to access to personal data by the 'data subject', in this case the employee or the applicant for a job, if details are kept on a computer or a word processor.'

Personnel managers must also consider the implications of recording sensitive information, for example medical records and appraisal documentation. This information is usually kept manually by personnel in a secure place.

A recent *Personnel Review* article summarised the place of a CPIS within the personnel decision-making process as follows:

'. . . completely relying on the computer to make judgements may be hazardous . . . the key insight in the philosophy behind data support systems should be that the tools of management information systems do not replace human beings or the subjective process of human decision making; rather the purpose of a technical system is to support human beings in their decision-making activities . . . . Final judgements ought to be made by personnel managers, not by the computer. After all personnel managers are dealing with the most intangible resources in organisations – human talents.'

Further reading

- *Computers and Human Resource Management,* 2nd edition, by Michael Gallagher. Butterworth Heinemann, 1991.
- *Computers and Personnel Systems* by Alastair Evans. Institute of Personnel Management, 1991.
- *Management* by Kathryn Bartol and David Martin. McGraw Hill, 1991.
- *Manpower Planning* by G. Stainer. Heinemann, 1971.
- *Personnel Management,* 3rd edition, by Derek Torrington and Laura Hall. Prentice Hall, 1995.
- *Principles of Human Resource Management* by David Goss. Routledge, 1994.
- *Quantitative Approaches in Business Studies,* 2nd edition, by Clare Morris. Pitman, 1989.
- *Using Computers in Human Resource Management* by Stephen Forrer and Zandy Leibowitz. Jossey Bass Publishers, 1991.

9 Skills audit and evaluation

On completion of this chapter, students should be able to:

- evaluate the contribution of training and development to improved efficiency

- review and apply methods of analysing training and development needs at the level of a section of staff

- review how and why training needs are analysed at organisational level

- evaluate methods of learning and self-development

- evaluate the prerequisites of effective learning

- review how training programmes are designed

- review the evaluation of training.

Why train?

Organisations provide training for several reasons. New employees need to learn how to do their first jobs correctly, safely and efficiently. Some employees already in post need to improve aspects of current performance, for example their dealings with customers and the quality or pace of their work. Intense competition for business and the pace of change in technology mean that staff must constantly update their skills and knowledge, as new equipment or new processes are introduced.

To reduce costs, many organisations have cut staffing levels. This makes it more difficult to cope with staff absences and fluctuations in workload. One management response is to train staff to handle a wider range of tasks. Their increased flexibility means that staff can be switched to other work as necessary. In addition to these direct benefits of training, there are also indirect advantages. Where there is competition in recruitment for some types of staff, good training schemes attract better applicants to the company. Investment in staff development is a practical demonstration of the value the organisation places on its employees. Together with other enlightened personnel practices, it may increase the loyalty and commitment of the staff.

A reputation for high-quality training enhances the image of the organisation with its customers. Hence companies try to obtain the Investors in People Award explained in Chapter 14. However, staff development is not a welfare activity, and management is likely to give it a low priority unless it believes that its return in increased efficiency and profits is greater than its costs. In practice, the assessment of the financial advantages of training is not easy. It is difficult to separate the contribution of training from all the other variables such as technological and method improvements, marketing initiatives and changes in the economy, all happening at the same time. The view that staff development should contribute to efficiency is emphasised by the following definition: A training need is a shortfall or weakness that hinders the achievement of objectives, now or in the future, and which can be put right by training.

Case Study
Office problems

A local authority office serving members of the public has a staff of sixteen employees. Five of the staff are word-process operators. Each works independently of the other four, word-processing letters and documents for his or her own particular senior member of staff. The other eleven are basic grade administrators. Each of them has learned, through experience, to do a few of the wide range of administrative tasks. The following problems have been identified in this office:

- There are frequent bottlenecks, delays and errors in word-processing.
- Incorrect information is given over the telephone and at the public counter.
- The output of the word-process operators is low. They are frequently interrupted by counter enquiries and by visits to their cramped working area from employees of other departments.
- Staff turnover is high. The average stay is about three years. When staff leave, the error rate increases and the senior staff take a heavier load.

Questions for discussion

1 *What actions, apart from training, might improve the performance of this office?*
2 *What training needs does this office appear to have?*

Possible actions apart from training

To take appropriate action, further investigation would be needed to establish the precise causes of the problems. Some possible actions are:

- reorganise the word-process operators to work as one team
- define quality standards, such as error rates and response times
- change the method of allocating, scheduling and monitoring the day's work against the standards
- revise the office layout
- analyse the reasons for the high labour turnover and take appropriate actions such as improving selection, supervision and salary scales
- measure the workload to see if the staffing level is adequate
- revise the information storage and retrieval system to improve the service on the counter and telephone enquiries.

Possible training needs

Again, management would need to investigate further, using techniques explained later in this chapter. Some possibilities are:

- train new staff in the duties initially assigned to them
- retrain present staff where there are weaknesses in current performance
- train staff to do a wider range of duties so that they are more flexible.

It may not be possible to implement all of these solutions simultaneously. Each needs resources, principally time. Rationally, priority should be given to the solutions that promise the biggest increases in efficiency.

In determining training needs, you should bear in mind the following points.

- Deficiencies in work performance are not attributable solely to poor training. The solution in particular cases may lie with other management action such as better planning, revised methods, better equipment, improved supervision and so on.
- Training costs time and money. Therefore training proposals have to compete for limited resources with other activities in the organisation. These may claim to provide a bigger return on investment than training does. Managers of departments engaged in the main activities of the business – producing and selling, for example – may not necessarily therefore share the enthusiasm of the personnel department for staff development.

How can training needs be identified?

A range of techniques is used to identify training needs. Each can be useful in different circumstances.

Job analysis

The aim is to specify the skills and knowledge needed to perform a given job competently. A comparison can then be made between this specification and the current or new job holder's skills and knowledge. Any deficiencies constitute the training needs of that individual. The starting point is a job description that details the duties and responsibilities of the job (see Figure 9.1). The next stage is to define the skills and knowledge required to perform each duty.

Figure 9.1   Job description

Job title: Office manager

Department: Buying office

Responsible to: Head buyer

Team: Assistant manager
4 supervisors
30 administration staff

Purpose of the job:
To provide an efficient administrative service to:

buyers   warehouses   suppliers
accounts departments   retail branches

so that correct goods are delivered promptly and charged at the correct price.

Responsibilities
1   To ensure that purchase orders are processed and mailed on the same day as the purchase requisitions are received
2   To ensure that urgent orders are telephoned, faxed or sent by electronic mail
3   To maintain the quality and pace of the work in the department
4   To deal with requests for non-stock items
5   To deal with reports of non-delivery
6   To liaise with the three warehouses
7   To maintain morale and discipline in the department
8   To select staff
9   To arrange the training of new staff
10   To assess staff and recommend pay increments
11   To maintain and improve the department's administrative routines
12   To administer the staff purchase scheme for the office

Task

Identify the skills and knowledge needed to discharge responsibilities 7, 8, 9 and 11 in Figure 9.1.

If the typical new starter has few of the required skills and knowledge, the specification provides the syllabus for new entrants' training. For job holders in post, and for partly experienced entrants, training is selective, concentrating on the skills and knowledge deficient in that individual. Figure 9.2 illustrates the sequence of this analytical approach to the analysis of training needs.

While the approach is clearly systematic, there are two main criticisms. Firstly, the analysis is time-consuming. It may be beyond the resources of a personnel department to undertake the analysis of all the jobs. If it is delegated to line managers and supervisors, however, they may give it a low priority in relation to other day-to-day duties.

Figure 9.2   Training analysis procedure

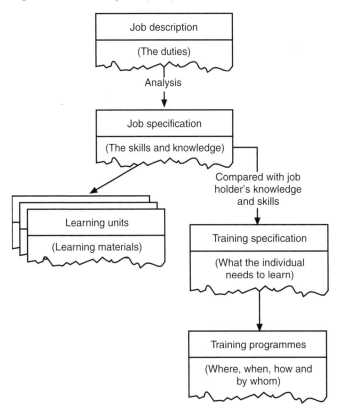

Secondly, the rate of change at work nowadays is so rapid that job descriptions are soon out of date. The time to revise them may not be available. Thus, training may not be sufficiently focused on changes and future skill and knowledge requirements.

For high-volume repetitive work, such as assembly jobs, small increments in individual skill may be significant in total because of the number of times each operation is performed. Thus it may be worthwhile analysing minutely the skills and abilities of the expert worker, so that others may be trained to reach their standard. As production work becomes more technically sophisticated, the method of task analysis needs to change. In the past, such analysis concentrated on the physical movements of the operator. Now it needs to include employees' abilities, such as perceptual skills, and judgements, such as fault-finding.

Consequences of poor initial training

If organisations fail to provide initial training, new entrants learn their jobs either by imitating other employees or by trial and error. The model presented by other workers may be incorrect. They may have inefficient or unsafe work habits. Even where the practices are correct, there are problems for the learner. The pace of performance may be too fast to see clearly what is happening. The newcomer may learn *how* the job is done, but obtain no insight into *why* it is done in that particular way. The effects on quality and safety of doing a task by the approved method may not be self-apparent to the trainee.

Learning by trial and error can be stimulating. The learner is active and uses personal initiative. Success is satisfying and reinforces motivation. There are, however, drawbacks. Progress may be slow since time is spent repeating errors made by previous learners. The individual does not benefit from collective experience. Without guidance, there is no certainty that the best available method or technique will be learned. For example, many people learn to use a keyboard by trial and error. How many can touch type? How many search for the keys and stab with two fingers?

Few of us would like to be treated by a dentist who is learning by trial and error. Yet it is common for job holders, such as supervisors and managers, to receive training well after appointment and in the meantime they learn by trial and error. The consequences are felt by the clients and the staff, as well as the job holder.

Retraining staff already in post

Staff may need retraining for several reasons, for example if their performance is unsatisfactory, or where the organisation has inadequate cover for staff absence or peaks in workloads.

Substandard performance

Where performance is unsatisfactory, the first requirement is that management recognises that a problem exists. If an organisation does not have standards of performance, shortfalls in actual performance will go unnoticed. Substandard performance then becomes the norm. For example, a retail organisation may not recognise it has a problem with the performance of its checkout operators unless, firstly, it has standards for the average throughput rate of customers and, secondly, feedback on the achieved rate. The sequence is: set the standard, monitor actual performance and, where there is shortfall, take corrective action, possibly retraining.

Task

What standards of performance could be set for:
a a hospital cook
b a word-process operator
c the office manager described in Figure 9.1?

Shortfalls in current performance may be revealed in a number of ways. Quality and production control systems provide regular data on the rate of errors and faults, both on individual and overall performance. Computerised equipment, like keyboards, retail checkout tills and telephone exchanges, routinely provide analysed data on employees' performance.

Staff appraisal schemes include formal discussions, at intervals of a year or less, where the individual employee and the immediate senior review performance against targets agreed at the previous meeting. One of the many possible solutions for failure to achieve target is further training for the job holder. If performance in the current job is excellent, training may be agreed for promotion and career development.

Inadequate job cover

Flexibility training, or multi-skilling, is useful where the main problem in a department or section is inadequate cover for staff absence, or for peaks in workload. Staff can then be switched to priority work as the need arises. **Proactive** management will anticipate the need and provide the training. **Reactive** management will wait until the crisis – workload or absence – has occurred and then think of retraining. The worst time to train is when the instructor or coach, probably the supervisor, is under pressure, trying to cope with the work of the absent member of staff. In these circumstances, senior staff often do the work of absent junior staff, since no one else knows how to do it – this is inefficient use of expensive time.

Figure 9.3 The consequences of lack of training

| Little time to train | → | Staff not trained |
| Supervisors busy correcting or doing the work | ← | Correction and close supervision needed |

Management needs to take the initiative in multi-skilling and not assume that staff will learn others' jobs on an informal basis. Expertise is a source of personal power. An employee who has scarce knowledge or skill required by the organisation is more indispensable than an employee who has expertise shared with many others. In the absence of good team spirit, there may be little inclination by staff to help others acquire their particular expertise.

Figure 9.4 Flexibility chart – buying office

Staff	Tasks				
	Quotations	Pricing Requisitions	W/P orders	Invoice queries	Filing
Roberts			N		C
Jones			N		C
Smith	N	N			C
Brown	N	N			C
Clements					N
McGee					N
Adams				N	C
Flint				N	C
Clark				C	C
N = normal duty C = competent in this task					

At the level of the department or section, staff cover on each task can be analysed by constructing a **flexibility chart** (see Figure 9.4).

An initial review of the tasks shows who can do what currently. The next stage is to decide, for each task, the minimum number of trained staff needed to give adequate cover. For example, on the task of pricing requisitions, only Smith and Brown are trained. Although two staff are sufficient normally, if there were sickness during the holiday season, it is conceivable that both of these staff could be absent at the same time. It would be prudent, therefore, to train two of the other staff to cover, should the need arise. The choice of staff would take into account their ability to learn and their availability to switch tasks when required. If the deadlines and peak workloads of pricing requisitions and processing orders coincide, it would not be sensible to train Roberts and Jones as backup on pricing requisitions.

In a larger department, such a review of current cover will probably reveal extensive retraining needs. It is unlikely that time will be available to undertake all of this on-the-job training simultaneously. Therefore it needs to be prioritised and scheduled. Priorities are decided on the importance of the task and its deadlines. If the target is to price and process orders on the same day as the requisitions are received, and if failure means loss of sales, then retraining on these tasks receives higher priority than filing. The review should include any new tasks which arise from reorganisation, new procedures or new equipment.

Case Study

The invoice department

Mathews plc is a retail chain. It has its head office in Leicester and warehouses in London, Manchester and Glasgow.

Depending on the merchandise, the retail outlets receive their supplies from the company's warehouses, direct from the manufacturers or from the local wholesalers. The buying function and accounts are centralised at Leicester. This case study concerns the invoice department. Its purpose is to check incoming suppliers' invoices and pass them to the purchase ledger department for payment.

The invoice department processes an average of 120 000 invoices a month. The procedure consists of reconciling purchase orders, purchase invoices and goods received notes. Inevitably with this volume there are many queries. The terms for settlement are mainly monthly, although there is a significant proportion of accounts with discounts for agreed prompt payment, for example within seven days.

The department is housed on one floor of a four-storey office block and is organised into five sections. Each section has the following grades of staff:

- a supervisor
- invoice assistants who deal with the queries on non-deliveries, shortages and invoice errors; they telephone and dictate letters to suppliers, warehouses and the buying office

- word-process operators, who take dictation and word-process letters
- data-process operators who key in data to the computer
- goods received notes (GRN) assistants who mark off the deliveries of the orders.

The manager, Mrs Adams – a new appointment – has been instructed by the chief accountant to reduce costs. She has spent time with each of the supervisors to familiarise herself with the work. She has identified a number of problems:

- The purchase ledger department complains of invoice department delays in processing invoices, resulting in conflict with suppliers over settlement discounts. There is also a disproportionate number of requests for copies of suppliers' invoices which have gone missing. At present, Mrs Adams learns about bottlenecks and delays in the work flow only when complaints have been received.
- Although the section supervisors are all experienced and hard working, the work rate of the staff does appear uneven. Some sections appear overworked and others slack. There could be some truth in the chief accountant's allegation of overstaffing.
- In previous years, staff holidays were covered by employing temporary staff from a local agency. The chief accountant is anxious to eliminate this cost. Mathews plc does not close for annual holidays.
- New staff work alongside experienced staff to pick up the work. Queries on procedure are referred to the supervisors. Supervisors are promoted largely on the basis of length of service.

Questions for discussion

1 *What approaches, apart from training, could contribute to improving the efficiency of this department?*
2 *Identify the problems which could be helped by training. What would be the appropriate training analysis techniques to use for each of the problems?*

Analysis of organisational training needs

So far we have reviewed training needs at the level of the individual employee and of the section or department. These can be aggregated into a company training plan. An alternative approach is to review the training needs of the organisation from top down. The focus here is the corporate plan. The issues are:

- What are the objectives of the corporate plan?
- What contributions to the corporate plan are expected from each function – marketing, production, finance, etc?

- What problems in each function will hinder the achievement of the objectives?
- What are the solutions to the identified problems?
- Can training contribute to the solutions and, if so, how?

The arguments in favour of this top-down approach are as follows:

- Training needs are identified and assessed in relation to the achievement of corporate plans.
- Training is seen, not as a discrete technique, but as one of a number of related approaches to goal achievement. Others are changes in technology, method improvements and organisational changes. Each of these has implications for training. New technology means new training. A decision to contract work out means less training. A decision to employ fewer core workers, supplemented by part-time workers when orders warrant it, reduces training activity. However, it raises new problems of maintaining quality standards. These examples stress the need for training decisions to be integrated into the corporate plan.
- The cost/benefits of alternative solutions – training or otherwise – can be compared. Training issues are better focused and prioritised. Time will not be wasted on fragmented, detailed training needs analysis when the outcomes do not warrant it.
- Since corporate plans take the longer-term view, analysis of training needs also becomes more forward looking.

Consider the following example:

A group of hospitals has plans to reduce the costs of its separate catering services. The present kitchens will be closed. Food production will be centralised. Meals will be prepared on a flow-line basis, frozen, distributed and reheated at the place of consumption.

The change has radical implications for the skills and attitudes of the staff. Failure to integrate training with the changes in technology and organisation could cause a severe mismatch between the traditional skills and attitudes of the staff, and those required in the future.

Stages of analysis

- *Appoint an individual or team to conduct the training needs survey.* The appointee should report to a senior level in the organisation so that any recommendations are not sidelined.
- *Plan the survey.* The team decides the methods of investigation and sets the timetable for completing each stage of the survey.
- *Collect the data.* Information is collected from each function of the business. The methods are interview, questionnaire and discussion. The questions are directed not at 'what training would you like?', but 'what problems do you face?' The possible range is extensive.

Examples are quality problems, failure on deadlines, customer complaints, low productivity, absenteeism, staff turnover, management succession, system changes, communication failures, and expansion or contraction of business.

- *Analyse the data.* The next stage is to diagnose the causes of the problems. For example, failure to met deadlines could be caused by an inadequate flow of information between departments, a lack of clarity on responsibility for the work, inadequate resources (equipment, space, staff) or inept management or staff. It is important that the solutions address the real prime causes.
- *Find solutions.* Where deficiencies in skill and knowledge are the prime cause, training is the appropriate solution. Otherwise the remedy may be the introduction of new systems, new equipment and changes in job roles. These, in turn, may generate new training needs.
- *Evaluate the solutions.* The solutions are prioritised according to their cost/benefits assessment. There may be other imperatives such as legislation. For example, a revision of hygiene regulations is likely to produce an upsurge of training activity in catering establishments.
- *Report and agree the plans.* A report is written, setting out the proposed solutions. Following discussion and amendments, the training plans and training budgets are agreed for each function or department.
- *Monitor the plans.* Implementation of the training plans and budgets are monitored at regular intervals.

Skills audit

The organisation may want to review the skills available in the workforce compared to the skills required now and in the future. Even in times of recession, there are shortages of particular skills. If the organisation can forecast changes, it creates the necessary lead time to plan, budget and deliver the required staff development. A personnel database which includes a record of each individual's skills can be interrogated, for example, for summaries of employees by types of skill and by age, so that the effects of impending retirements can be assessed. Such analysis from manual records is clumsy and time-consuming. However, the analysis is only as good as the data. It is important to have reliable procedures for updating the individual records as further staff development is completed. Off-the-job training is likely to be recorded, since it has a clear beginning and end. Continuous development on the job is more likely to go unrecorded unless it has a terminal event like a certificate of competence or equivalent.

Methods of managing learning and self-development

Organisations want learning to be both effective and efficient. **Effective** means that the outcome is better job performance. **Efficient** means that this outcome is obtained with no waste of resources. There are many choices in the design of self development and training schemes. Decisions are shaped by beliefs about what influences learning.

Task

Reflect on your past learning in different spheres – school, college, leisure and work.

1 What incentives were there for you to learn?
2 What affected the rate and extent of your learning?
3 What hindered you or turned you off?

Influences on effective learning

Effective learning depends on a number of factors, including the following.

Does the learning meet the individual's needs?

This raises a number of issues. Does the individual recognise and accept that he or she has a development need? Does the individual believe that the training offered will meet that need? If employees have been doing a job for years, they may see training as implied criticism – insulting, demeaning and a waste of time. The more senior the job holder, the more likely is this reaction. The job holder's immediate boss may hold similar views, and scarcely conceal them when reluctantly nominating the employee for training. Training providers are familiar with the problem of dealing with trainees who feel they have been sent for training as a relief from real work, or to make up quotas on training returns. The implications are as follows:

- Individual learning needs analysis should precede nomination for training and self-development.
- The learner should have an input into that needs analysis. The more experienced the employee, the better placed he or she is to contribute. However, the interest of the individual and the manager will not necessarily coincide in all respects. The individual may see self-development as a way of escaping the present job, possibly to a career away from the organisation. Therefore employers may make distinctions, in funding and provision of time, between self-development which is relevant to the job and that which is not.
- Timing is important. Training provided too far in advance of acquiring particular responsibilities may be seen as irrelevant at that stage. On the other hand, development given too late may incur the costs of trial

and error, while the job holder flounders.

- Relevance to the trainee's needs should be made explicit. The employee's senior should brief him or her prior to the learning event, explaining not only its content, but also what the employee will be expected to do with the acquired skill and knowledge. This might involve an agreed action plan, with scheduled completion dates, for the improvement of current practices in the department. After the learning event, the senior should conduct a debriefing, covering both the action plan and the employee's reactions to the training. The employee needs proper support for the action plan by provision of time and ongoing coaching. Otherwise it becomes punishment – yet another imposition of work overload, producing a determination not to be caught again.

- Line managers and the staff development department need to work closely together at all stages: analysis of needs, provision, evaluation and revision of development programmes. There is a debate about the extent to which staff development should be decentralised. This is examined in the section on continuous development.

Are the learner's interests served?

The motives to learn are many and varied. People put effort into learning:

- to gain promotion or a better job
- to earn more money
- to win security by coping with change
- to gain respect and prestige
- to give better service
- to realise their potential
- to experience a sense of accomplishment
- to be stimulated.

Promising tangible benefits, pay increments and promotion, and then not delivering, causes frustration and resentment. Organisations are usually loath to make such promises in relation to training.

Is the learner's motivation sustained?

A learner's motivation can be either reinforced or weakened by the learning process. If the learners feel they are making progress, if they find the process stimulating and interesting, their commitment and effort will be sustained. The variables here are the learning methods and the support of the other learners, the boss, and the instructor or coach.

Is there time and opportunity to absorb and consolidate the learning?

Too often the consideration is how long it will take to deliver, rather than how long it will take to absorb.

Task

If a person wanted to acquire the skills of selection interviewing, what would be the best way of structuring the learning and why?

Does the learner get feedback?

A person could acquire knowledge about selection interviewing from study packs, books, lectures and discussions. Understanding could be tested by questions. Skills such as questioning technique, listening technique, and non-verbal communication, would need practice and guidance. Practice could be provided by role-playing interviews. These could be recorded on video so that the learner and the coach could review the tape and identify areas for further improvement. The consolidation comes from the practice and the feedback. As any amateur golfer will tell you, without feedback and correction, practice may consolidate faults rather than improve performance.

Can the learner use his or her preferred learning style?

Learning follows the cycle illustrated in Figure 9.5. Honey and Mumford have identified that individuals are better at some of the stages of the cycle than others.

Figure 9.5 Learning styles

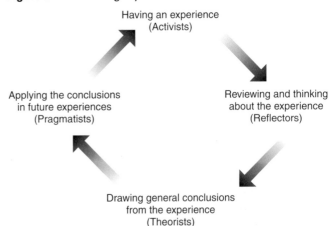

Source: Honey and Mumford (1986)

Activists are outgoing and enjoy new experiences. They thrive on challenge and are enthusiastic about new things. They enjoy experiences like business games, role-playing and competitive team activities. They become quickly bored with passive learning – lectures, reading, watching, writing, repeated practice and detailed analysis of performance.

Reflectors are happiest when they have time to watch, listen, read, probe, research and propose. They least enjoy, and may react against, learning which spotlights them, like role-playing or running a discussion without prior warning.

Theorists learn best when the ideas are part of a coherent model or theory, even when they are not immediately relevant to their job. They enjoy being intellectually stretched, where rationality and logic are employed. They least enjoy unstructured situations which emphasise emotions and feelings, for example sensitivity training and working with lots of activists.

Pragmatists prefer learning which is directed at providing usable techniques, relevant and applicable to their own immediate situations. They respect and work best with coaches/instructors who have had first-hand practical experience. They learn least when they can see no immediate practical benefit, or where the learning event and its organisers have, for them, no practical credibility.

Honey and Mumford have designed a learning style questionnaire. This diagnoses your preferred learning style and suggests which of the other three styles you are under-using. It offers advice on how you might strengthen you under-utilised styles.

Continuous development

The Institute of Personnel Management's publication *Continuous Development,* edited by Sue Wood, argues that changes in society and in organisations require revisions to the way we view and provide staff development. The arguments are as follows:

- The tough economic climate has made the search for efficiency intense and ongoing. In this context, staff development is focused on, and integrated with, efforts to improve work performance.
- The rate and degree of change in the workplace – in technology, in systems, in procedures, in attitudes – mean that the relatively static definition of jobs, on which the traditional systematic analysis of training needs was based, no longer exists.
- Organisations have cut their workforces. The reduction in recruitment has shifted concern from initial training to improving the performance of staff already in post.

- Changes in the values of society place more emphasis on individual responsibility. The argument is that it is inappropriate for the specialist to decide what the individual's development needs are and how they should be met. The individual employee is better placed to identify what he or she needs to learn, in order to cope with the changing work problems. The individual should take responsibility for his or her own development. The individual's boss is an important aid and model in that development.
- For survival in a climate of continuous change, the need to learn is also continuous. Competence in self-managed learning is, therefore, an important basic skill. With it, the learner develops self-confidence and is not dependent on training specialists.
- People learn best from real work situations. A dual purpose is served: the work performance improves and the individual develops. It prevents the problem of transferring skills and knowledge acquired in the training room to the workplace, which is a feature of off-the-job training.

Task

Re-read the section on influences on effective learning.

1 Which of these influences operate under the continuous learning approach and to what extent?
2 What problems are likely to occur in using the continuous development approach?

A review of the experiences of a number of organisations introducing continuous development showed a favourable response. These were some of the criticisms cited:

- Some staff still expected things to be done for them.
- Line managers complained that more time and more help with the techniques were needed.
- More resources were needed, principally time.
- The approach needs to be accompanied by salary and job progression.

The IPM publication suggests that there are certain prerequisites for success with workplace learning and self-development:

- Employees must know how their role is developing and where their work fits into the general plan.
- Development is focused on the key result areas – those aspects of the job which have the greatest impact on overall work results.
- Rewards are given for effectiveness rather than for effort. Staff should know what results they are achieving.

- Learning is principally through experience rather than through unco-ordinated off-the-job training.
- Employees negotiate their learning priorities with the boss and other members of their team.
- The training department is available to provide advice on identifying learning needs and planning to meet them.

Responsibility for training and training budgets

There are different views on whether the responsibility for staff development rests primarily with the individual employee, the line manager or the personnel department. Increasingly line managers have had to take on more of the functions which were formally done on their behalf by the personnel department. This reverses the trend towards centralisation and specialisation of previous decades. The extent to which the reasons are economic, functional or ideological is not clear. Logically, budgets should align with responsibility. Whoever is held accountable for the results of staff development should have that part of the training budget to spend.

The benefits of decentralising the training budget are that:

- it makes the link between business objectives, staff development and performance, ensuring a better return on training investment
- it involves the line managers actively in staff development
- it makes follow-up coaching and on-the-job learning easier to arrange.

The risks are that line managers may:

- underrate the value of training, since the benefits may be difficult to quantify
- give disproportionate attention to technical skills and insufficient attention to longer-term personal development
- be reluctant to contribute some of their budget to cross-company initiatives like training for the introduction of total quality management
- try to transfer some of their training budget to other headings.

Designing training and development programmes

Whoever is planning staff development has to decide the content, timing, place and methods of learning. The results may be summarised for a department, section or individual in the form of a training plan (see Figure 9.6):

Content of training programmes

Training needs will have been identified by one of the approaches discussed earlier. If formal training is to be arranged, job analysis will indicate the skills and knowledge to be learned. The provider of the training will organise the syllabus into learning units. Small modules improve flexibility of choice for the learners. They can choose those which are relevant to their individual needs. For example, instead of attending a three day learning event on supervisory skills, an individual might require only a sub-unit on planning and control techniques. Large organisations may have a menu of learning modules organised by the training department. Line departments nominate staff for these events.

The danger is that a ritual develops. Each department nominates a quota of staff without much thought to suitability and outcome. An alternative approach is to wait until the completion of the annual staff appraisals, or until the annual plan has been decided. Where common needs emerge from these processes, a programme of training modules can be arranged. The provision is then demand led, rather than supplier led.

Learning objectives

Both the provider and the learner should have a clear idea of the purpose of the learning. This requires a precise definition of what the learning outcomes should be.

Figure 9.6 Training plan

Employee/Job title	Development needs	Proposed training	Timing	Action by
J. Blake Supervisor	Staff selection skills	Staff selection course at Trent University	June 199–	K Smith
		Followed by supervised experience with KS	Completed by November 199–	K. Smith (Budget £200)

Task

The objectives for a learning unit are described as 'improving the learner's ability to organise and conduct selection interviews'. Criticise the way the objectives are expressed.

Learning objectives should be expressed in behavioural terms. They should say what the learner should be able to do at the end of the learning unit. In the example given above, there might be a number of component skills:

'After completing the unit, the learner should be able to

- *write an accurate personnel specification for a given job*
- *short-list suitable candidates from applications for a given job*
- *identify what further information is required from a given candidate's application*
- *phrase relevant open questions to solicit the required information.'*

These objectives still have areas of imprecision. What are 'accurate', 'suitable', 'relevant'? However, absolute precision may be pedantic and take excessive time. Clear learning objectives make it easier to design the learning package, easier for the user to decide if it is appropriate to his or her needs, and easier to assess afterwards if the learning has been successful.

Timing

It is useful if we can acquire skills before we have to use them. However, if we have no realistic expectation of using the skills, we may not be very motivated to learn, and training might be a poor investment at that stage. Ideally staff development should progress in line with needs.

Time is a significant cost in both the design of the learning units and their delivery. Providers should examine the cost/benefits of options such as designing their own units of learning or buying them; of delivering the units themselves or using outside agents.

A further consideration is the availability of the learner's time. It is often more difficult to obtain the release of the employee from his or her job to attend a learning event than it is to get the money to pay the fee.

Methods

The choice of learning methods depends on a number of variables:

- *The nature of what is to be learned.* Knowledge can be gained by reading, listening, reviewing experience and discussing. Skills are acquired through practice with guidance and feedback. For example, problem-solving skills might make use of case studies; assertive behaviour skills use role-playing; culinary skills use a demonstration followed by supervised practice. Since learning at work typically covers both knowledge and skills, a combination of methods is appropriate.
- *The learners.* As discussed earlier, individuals have preferences for different methods of learning. Some prefer study packs or programmes of learning which allow them to work at their own pace. Others respond better to the stimulation provided by other learners and by a trainer.
- *The number of learners at any one time and the resources available.* For example, learning social skills such as interviewing requires extended individual practice and feedback. There is a limit to the direct observation one trainer can make. However, the other learners can be trained to use checklists to give structured criticism to each other.

Location

Learning can take place on the job, in a training room or at some outside agency, such as a college. There are advantages and disadvantages to each.

On the job

Managers can give opportunity for employees to learn by temporary changes to their jobs. It can be done by secondment to another department or even to another organisation. Tasks at the same level in an organisation might be rotated in a planned way so that a range of experience is gained. Learners might undertake special projects or assignments serving a dual purpose: solving a work problem and developing the abilities of the learner. Similarly, the employee might become a member of a task group or committee examining a current work problem. The strength of this approach is that learning is practical, applied and relevant.

The main problem is the support for the learner. The extent and quality of support is crucial to obtaining full benefit from the experience. The employee needs a boss or mentor who has the time, inclination and expertise to help the learner review the experience and draw the correct lessons from it.

One way of providing structure to on-the-job development is for the trainee to accumulate a portfolio of evidence of competency in each of the aspects of the job, so that accreditation can be sought for the appropriate National Vocational Qualification.

Off the job

Off-the-job learning – in a company training centre or at an outside agency – may expose the employee to new ideas, fresh approaches and new people. Time to learn is available and the individual is not subject to interruptions and routine work pressures.

The possible disadvantages are that, firstly, the content of the learning may not match the needs or culture of the sponsoring department or organisation and, secondly, the transfer of skills and knowledge from the course to the workplace may be poor.

There are ways of addressing these problems. There should be close consultation between the line management and the providers on the choice and design of the course. The manager should brief the employee on what is expected during and after the course. This should be formalised into an action plan.

Who assists the learner?

Whoever assists learners should have the resources, time, commitment and expertise for the role. Otherwise the employee will have a poor deal, irrespective of whether it is on or off the job. Often supervisors have the responsibility for instructing new staff in the skills of their job. They need to be prepared for the instructor role. Typically they are taught the following approach:

Prepare an instruction plan
- Specify the learning objectives for the session.
- Specify any prior knowledge and skill needed by the trainee to benefit from this session.
- List the materials and equipment needed.
- Analyse the task into stages so that each stage can be consolidated before moving on to the next.
- For each stage, identify the key points which need to be stressed. Typically these will be anything which helps the trainee to do that part of the task safely, correctly, quickly and with understanding.
- Estimate the time needed for this instruction session.

Give the instruction
- Prepare the trainee. Find out what he or she knows about the task. Explain the purpose of the task and its significance. This could include showing the end result of the task, a finished item for example. Put the trainee where he or she has a clear view of the demonstration.
- Demonstrate and explain the first stage, stressing the key points. Keep the stages short to avoid overloading the trainee's short-term memory.
- Get the trainee to do this stage and to give a running commentary, thus testing the pick-up of associated

knowledge as well as the skills. Supplement with open questions where necessary. Use mistakes as an opportunity for learning rather than negative criticism.
- Correct tactfully. There are a number of tactics. Sandwich criticism between praise: 'Excellent up to there; can you see where you went wrong? . . . Apart from that it was excellent.' Acknowledge the difficulty. 'Lots of people have difficulty with that . . .' Share the blame: 'I'm sorry, I didn't explain that properly. What I wanted you to do was . . .'
- When the trainee has successfully completed the first stage, repeat the process with the remaining stages.
- As soon as possible after the instruction session, provide the opportunity to consolidate the learning through extended practice. Arrange suitable support: a training manual or a sympathetic colleague to turn to.

Task

Choose a task from work or a leisure activity. Prepare an instruction plan. Teach a colleague how to do the task. Ask other colleagues to act as observers and give you their comments afterwards. Observers can use the checklist given below.

Observer's check-list

Preparation
- Were all the items of equipment/materials ready?
- Were they clearly laid out?
- Was the job broken down into stages?

Introduction
- Was the learner put at ease?
- Was the learner's prior knowledge known or checked?
- Was interest created?
- Was the purpose of the instruction explained?
- Was the learner in a good position to see?

Demonstration
- Did the instructor tell and show one stage at a time?
- Were the key points stressed?
- Was the instruction clear and at the right pace?
- Was the instructor's attitude helpful and patient?

Trainee's practice
- Did the trainee do the task correctly?
- If not, were the errors corrected tactfully?
- Did the instructor use questions to check understanding?

Follow-up
- Were the learner's questions encouraged?
- Was the trainee told what support was available?

Coaches and mentors

The role of the support staff in the department might be as coaches or mentors rather than as instructors. Managers and supervisors have a responsibility to develop their team members. It is part of their function to give advice and support. Issues of self-development might arise naturally in the course of everyday work or they may be discussed at meetings arranged to review progress on assignments or projects.

A good coach provides a model, commanding respect through his or her performance rather than through rank. He or she treats the employee as a person of individual worth. The coach will discuss and suggest rather than tell, focusing on the learner's behaviour rather than personality. In assigning development tasks, the coach will stretch learners, but within their capabilities. Perhaps the most difficult of all in practice, the manager or supervisor will make regular time available for coaching. Finally, he or she will encourage learners and support them in dealings with seniors. A trainee who has a coach with all these characteristics is extremely fortunate.

Mentors are not necessarily the learners' line supervisors or managers. They will have coaching skills and be experienced in the corporate culture, so they can give advice on who to approach and how to deal with them when tackling cross-department assignments. Mentors are often used as a sympathetic link between an external provider of training and the workplace.

Evaluation

Staff development can be evaluated on different levels.

Validity

The issue here is whether the training objectives are relevant to work performance. Validity should be examined at the stage of the training needs analysis. Outcomes of training are the true test of validity. The validity of an improved training programme for operatives might be measured in terms of reduced learning time to reach trained performance standard, and reduced costs of spoiled work. More typically, the pay-off for staff development is longer term and it becomes difficult to separate the contribution of training to improved performance from other factors.

Reliability

The issue here is whether the particular form of training helps learners to achieve the learning objectives consistently. A scientific approach would be to test the trainees at the beginning of the learning event and then again at the end of the event. The results would show the effect of the learning and whether or not the learning objectives were achieved. This is seldom done, perhaps for a variety of reasons:

- It costs time and money to design, administer and mark tests.
- Learners may find it unpleasantly reminiscent of school, adversely affecting their motivation and attitudes.
- Training providers may find it exposing.

Other methods of evaluation

The organisers may ask those attending a learning event their views on the content and its relevance, the learning methods, the timing, the duration and the facilities. Their views can be collected at the end of the event by open discussion and/or by questionnaire, signed or anonymous. Alternatively, views can be sought by the sponsors at the post-course briefing.

Methods of evaluation should be built into plans for training at the same time as the learning objectives are set. The cycle is shown in Figure 9.7.

Figure 9.7 Managing learning

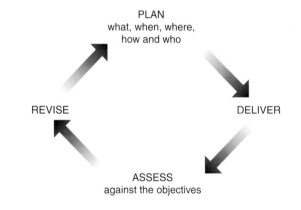

Task

Assess the usefulness of different approaches to the evaluation of training.

Further reading

- *Continuous Development,* edited by Sue Woods. Institute of Personnel Management, 1990.
- *Handbook of Management Development* by A. Mumford. Gower, 1986.
- *Handbook of Training and Development,* edited by Steve Truelove. Blackwell Business, 1992.
- *Human Resource Management* by I. Beardwell and L. Holden. Pitman, 1994.
- *Manual of Learning Styles* by P. Honey and A. Mumford. Maidenhead, 1986.
- *Personnel Management Practice* by Michael Armstrong. Kogan Page, 1995.
- *The Mentor Connection* by M. C. Zey. Don Jones-Irwin, 1984.

4

Employee resourcing

10 Job design

<big>O</big>n completion of this chapter, students should be able to:

- analyse historical approaches to job design and discuss their value in today's working environment

- evaluate the impact that technological change has had on the design of jobs, work patterns and organisational relationships

- describe the process of job analysis and functional analysis and recognise their contribution to managerial decision-making

- identify and explain the key components of a job description and person specification

- comment on the value of the job description and person specification in today's flexible working environment.

Defining job design

This chapter focuses on the issues related to job design. The reader is given an insight into how the approach to job design has changed since the beginning of the century, with particular emphasis on the more recent issues related to the relationship between job design and technological change. The concepts of job and functional analysis are introduced. The chapter focuses on some of the changes in job design that have impacted on organisational relationships. These issues are investigated from both an employer's and an employee's perspective. Finally, the chapter looks at the outcome of job design in the form of the preparation of the job description and the person specification.

What is a job?

All organisations have a purpose for existing; many have a strategy to guide them through the present and to shape their future. This strategy will be supported by a particular organisational structure which will be made up of various types of jobs. *Jobs can therefore be considered as the building blocks of the organisation's structure.* The design of the job will affect an organisation's structure, the overall strategy and ultimately the organisation's mission or purpose. Jobs therefore need to be designed in the most effective way possible to satisfy the needs of the individual and the organisation. Figure 10.1 outlines the

Figure 10.1 Jobs can help an organisation to achieve its purpose

Organisation
Mission /Purpose

Strategy/Plan

Organisation structure

Jobs

structure of how jobs can help the organisation to achieve its purpose.

Figure 10.2   Balancing organisational and behavioural needs

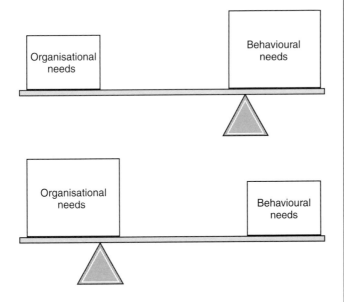

What is job design?

Mullins (1992) defines job design in the following way:

'Job design is concerned with the relationship between workers and the nature of jobs, and their task functions … There are two main reasons for attention to job design: to enhance the personal satisfaction that people derive from their work; to make the best use of people as a valuable resource of the organisation and to help overcome obstacles to their effective performance.'

The challenge facing those responsible for job design is to achieve a balance between **organisational needs** and **individual behavioural needs.** This challenge can be viewed rather like a balancing see-saw (see Figure 10.2). Different organisations will balance at different points along the see-saw, depending where the pivot is placed. Some organisations will balance with a greater emphasis on organisational needs, e.g. efficiency, while others will balance with a greater focus on behavioural needs, e.g. motivation.

Historical approaches to job design

The concept of job design has generated more debate than possibly any other aspect of management. Job design as a

science really began during the eighteeenth century with the work of Adam Smith. Smith developed the concept of specialisation by breaking down jobs into small, highly structured repetitive tasks. Following on from specialisation came the scientific approach to management advocated by F.W. Taylor in the early 1900s. However, at around the same time other management theorists began to suggest that these approaches were counterproductive as they failed to recognise the social need of workers. Elton Mayo advocated that management should organise people into work groups, show an interest in workers' welfare and make them feel that they belong.

The simplification of job design proposed by Smith and Taylor resulted in workers being involved in highly repetitive tasks which quickly led to boredom and demotivation among the workforce. To try to alleviate the monotony, workers were rotated around tasks or jobs. This system became known as the first principle of job design, **job rotation.** Using this system, workers build up a variety of skills as they rotate around different jobs. This concept of multi-skilling should enable each worker to contribute more to the organisation, which may result in higher productivity and greater job satisfaction. The advantages to be gained by rotating workers around short task jobs, however, can be minimal as workers still become bored relatively quickly.

The next development in job design was **job enlargement.** This involves horizontally expanding the number of related tasks within a job, thus adding greater variety. Although an improvement on job rotation, many workers still did not feel stimulated or challenged.

Herzberg presented an alternative approach called **job enrichment.** He argued that, for people to be motivated to do a good job, they should have a sense of doing a whole job and not part of a job. They should also be involved in decisions about the job. Job enrichment increases the variety of tasks vertically, i.e. increases the depth of a job, involving more planning and controlling responsibilities. He argued that by making the work more interesting and challenging, this would lead to an increase in job satisfaction.

Mullins argues that these earlier approaches to job design focused on 'restructuring individual jobs'. He goes on to say that;

'In the context of technological change, the focus of attention has spread from manipulating the tasks of individual jobs to a wider organisational context. Attention needs to be given to improving the effectiveness of the organisation in achieving its goals and objectives; and helping the development of skills and resources to manage successfully changes in the way the organisation functions.'

A more recent approach to job design has therefore been the introduction of **autonomous work groups.** Operators are divided into cohesive teams which integrate the technology and production processes they are using with the social considerations; workers are allowed significant autonomy in organising and monitoring their work. A famous example of how effectively this approach can work is at Volvo's Kalmar plant in Sweden.

Recent debate on job design suggests that there is a tendency towards a more **behavioural focus.** In reality, however, has the debate moved very far? In his book *Job Design and Work Organisation,* John Bailey discusses the impact of a study conducted by J. C. Taylor, which examines whether the criteria used by those responsible for job design has significantly changed from a previous study 20 years earlier. The study examines the approaches of a representative sample of large American firms. Taylor says:

> *'It seems that 20 years of technological progress and innovations have had little corresponding effect on the professional values of design practitioners. The data presented suggests that both production engineers and system analysts select job design criteria remarkably similar to those chosen by their predecessors in the 1950s. They still prefer to minimise the immediate costs of production rather than to emphasise a longer-term approach to job design which recognises the economic costs of worker frustration and acknowledges employee satisfaction and motivation.'*

Task

Discuss to what extent you think the findings of this American survey apply to job-design principles in the UK.

Werther and Davis, in their book *Human Resource and Personnel Management,* summarise the situation facing organisations:

> *'How well jobs are designed will play an increasingly important role in the success, even survival of many organisations during the 1990s and beyond … well designed jobs will become even more important in attracting and retaining a motivated workforce which is capable of producing quality products and services.'*

Balancing organisational and employee job-design needs will become an increasingly important challenge for organisations in the future. Figure 10.3 illustrates this challenge.

Figure 10.3 The job-design challenge – balancing organisational and employee needs

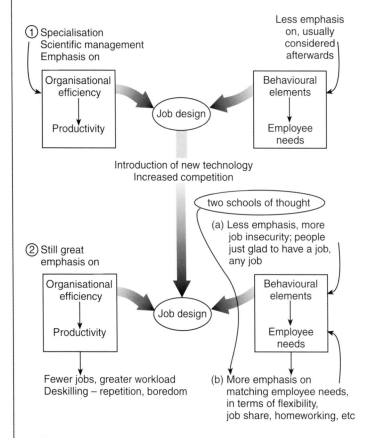

Task

These principles of job design, although historic, may still be found in organisations today. To what extent do you think the principles of scientific management are evident today in the way that jobs are designed? Justify your answer with examples.

The relationship between job design and technological change

Historically, the main technological change in relation to job design was brought about by the industrial revolution with machines taking the place of human labour. This technological change has continued, but now there is a significant increase in the pace of change. Consider the following two scenarios:

- Henry Ford's Model T was built by hand.
- The last two decades have brought us cars built by robots.

Organisations are becoming increasingly reliant on the power of information technology (IT). Computers which were once used to aid people in their jobs are becoming a far more integral part of working life. For example, as decisions have to be made faster and businesses need to be more responsive, computers play a more vital role. Advances in IT have often led to redundancies. For those who are left, IT has meant radical changes in the way that work is organised. For example, there has been an increase in **teleworking** more people working from home using IT. This results in overall cost savings for the employer. Teleworking is not common in all areas of work at the moment, but it is certainly set to be the trend for the late 1990s as employers require employees to be more flexible. In 1992 the National Economic Development Office reported that approximately 1 in 17 of the workforce were involved in teleworking. Teleworking is discussed in more detail later in the chapter. Organisationally, companies have been forced to look at all aspects of their business. The new technology has increased competition not just locally but globally. This has forced some organisations to restructure, which has ultimately had an impact on job design. The main initiatives are listed below:

- *Delayering:* making the organisations leaner, fitter and flatter, thereby making them more responsive and adaptable to change. With the impact of IT, organisations are able to obtain information much faster and in more detail, therefore reducing the need for lots of layers of management. Where information used to be provided by people, it is now in many cases provided by computers.
- *Focusing on 'added value':* eliminating operations which do not add value. This has led to redundancies in some areas, while at the same time other jobs have expanded.
- *Increasing the use of out-sourcing of operations to specialists* in a bid to improve efficiency.
- *Buying in specialist skills for specific projects:* developing a consultancy approach to job design.
- *Introducing a more flexible workforce:* increasing the numbers of part-time, temporary, homeworking and job-sharing opportunities.

In many cases technology has facilitated the growth of these patterns of employment. Figure 10.4 illustrates the changes that have taken place.

Information technology has revolutionised job content. The following are specific examples which illustrate the impact on particular jobs.

The introduction of computer-aided design

In a recent newspaper article, Elizabeth Emanuel, who is best known for designing Princess Diana's wedding

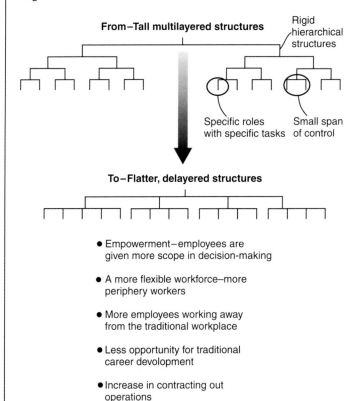

Figure 10.4   Recent changes that have taken place within organisations

From–Tall multilayered structures

Rigid hierarchical structures

Specific roles with specific tasks

Small span of control

To–Flatter, delayered structures

- Empowerment–employees are given more scope in decision-making
- A more flexible workforce–more periphery workers
- More employees working away from the traditional workplace
- Less opportunity for traditional career devolopment
- Increase in contracting out operations

dress, stated 'all the designs are now completed on computer ... five years ago, I hardly used a PC'. The fashion industry is just one example of where jobs have changed with the introduction of computer-aided design.

The introduction of computer-aided manufacturing

In the textile industry, knitting machines were traditionally controlled manually or through basic mechanical devices such as punch cards. They are now controlled by computer disks which are programmed to knit the exact garment specification. The skills a knitter now requires are computer-based rather than traditional mechanical engineering. It has been said that a computer-literate school leaver would be easier to train than a time-served experienced knitter.

Advances in telecommunications technology

Modems, faxes, mobile phones and video-conferencing, for example, allow organisations to communicate very quickly with anyone, anywhere in the world and at any time.

Technology and education

A recent newspaper article discussed the impact of IT on a music teacher. The article makes the point that although 'new technology can never be a substitute for old-fashioned teaching, nonetheless it can fulfil a useful function'. It goes on to say how a flexible learning package is being developed to teach harmony and counterpoint in a way which will enable each student to work independently at his or her own pace. With more demands being put on teachers' time, IT may help ease the burden of the increased workload.

Types of employment

Technological change has had varying degrees of impact depending upon the type of employment being considered. The next section highlights three types of employment:

- jobs which involve contact with the customer, so employees are required to be at the workplace
- jobs which require the employee to be based at the workplace to use specialist equipment, for example an engineer
- jobs which do not require the employee to be stationed at the workplace all of the time.

The impact of technological change on each is illustrated by case studies.

Jobs which involve customer contact

Case Study

The checkout assistant

The primary purpose of the job in this case is to serve the customer. To carry out the job, therefore, the job holder must be present at the workplace. The impact of technology has not been on location, but on technique. Instead of manually keying in the price of the goods, the job holder scans the products using an electronic bar-code reader. This results in a quicker and more accurate service. Technology has also impacted on the way that customers can pay for their goods. The checkout assistant now needs to understand how to process cash, cheques, credit and debit cards and offer cash-back facilities.

The checkout assistant has become a very important person within the store. In some cases this is the only person the customer will come into contact with. The checkout assistant, who in many organisations is now

Figure 10.5 Changes in job design for a checkout assistant as a result of the introduction of new technology

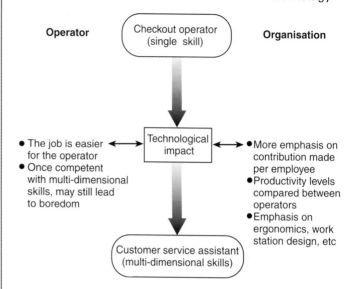

called a 'Customer Services Assistant', is responsible for serving the customer quickly and accurately in a professional manner. He or she is also responsible for processing financial transactions in whichever way the customer prefers, thus adding more responsibility and variety to the job. Technology has enabled the checkout assistant to offer a more professional service to the customer.

The changes in technology have made it easier to monitor the contribution made by individual assistants. There can therefore be a greater pressure to perform against standards and targets. The changes in job design for a checkout assistant are illustrated in Figure 10. 5.

Case Study

The insurance industry

Technology has had a significant impact on the insurance industry in terms of job design and numbers employed. Insurance companies used to be very labour intensive, predominantly paper-based operations. Advances in technology have resulted in significant organisational restructuring and job losses. The design of some of the jobs remaining in the large companies has also changed. Computers have allowed the development of a paperless system where customers' details are stored electronically; they have also increased the speed at which quotes and queries can be dealt with. New companies with alternative approaches, such as Direct Line, have challenged the concept of customer service in the established companies. In a recent television interview the Chairman of Direct Line stated that their costs were up to 30 per cent less than their competitors. All of this has been made possible by advances in technology.

Organisations have undertaken significant restructuring programmes in a bid to become more efficient. As certain operations have been relocated, staff have been given the options of changing their jobs and retraining, travelling to the new offices or leaving. Jobs have been lost at all levels within organisations. Those remaining have been given new responsibilities as a result of the changes. Customer service assistants, who prior to the changes were employed to check customers' details manually on claim forms, may find themselves in a position where they are dealing with the customer direct over the telephone, sorting out queries. Their workload will almost certainly have increased as they are now expected to deal with more and more customers.

Questions for discussion

Consider these questions in relation to the above two case studies: checkout assistant and insurance company.

1 *What impact would the job design changes described in the above case studies have on the following HRM issues:*
   a *recruitment and selection*
   b *human resource planning*
   c *training and development*
   d *remuneration?*
2 *What impact do you think the changes would have on the customer service assistants in terms of:*
   a *morale*
   b *control over their job*
   c *job satisfaction?*

Jobs which involve specialist equipment

Case Study

The changing role of the car mechanic

The traditional role of the car mechanic has been to use his or her experience and training to identify and rectify mechanical faults. Fault-finding might include listening to the sound of the engine; touching engine parts to sense heat or vibration; using sense of smell to analyse fumes, etc. With the advent of technology such as electronic

ignition, fuel injection and engine management systems, fault-finding has become almost impossible without the aid of electronic diagnostic equipment.

Questions for discussion

1 *How has new technology changed the design of the car mechanic's job?*
2 *What impact will this have on the organisation?*
3 *What impact will this have on the customer?*
4 *What problems could occur as a result of introducing this technology?*

Jobs which do not require job holders to be permanently stationed at the workplace

The nature of these jobs can allow the job holders to be flexible about where they work. For example, sales people who cover a large geographical area can travel considerable distances. It may be uneconomical for them to report regularly in person to their head office. Cellular phones, laptops computers and fax machines turn the salesperson's car or hotel room into a mobile office.

According to William Bridges in his highly acclaimed book *Jobshift*, Arthur Anderson, the huge consulting and accounting firm, has already equipped one-third of its professional employees with laptop computers and cut them loose from their offices. This concept is further explained in the next section which looks at patterns of work, for example teleworking.

Case Study

Workplace – home and car

Built-2-Last is a building products supplier which employs several area sales managers. Their role is to visit key customers on a regular basis to discuss new requirements and follow up any problems. They attend national sales meetings once every three months at the head office in Worcester. The purpose of these meetings is to discuss sales performance, trends, new products, competition, etc. The rest of the time they have no physical contact with head office.

Each area sales manager works from an office at home using a telephone and fax. They also have a laptop computer fitted with a modem which allows them to communicate with the head office mainframe computer, sending and receiving electronic information. Each manager has a company car and while on the road they are able to remain in contact using a mobile phone. Both mobile and home phone have answer-machine facilities.

Questions for discussion

1   *How has new technology facilitated the area sales manager's job?*
2   *What impact does this working relationship have on the organisation?*
3   *What impact does this working relationship have on the area sales manager?*
4   *What benefits does this working relationship have for the customer?*

Task

List ten different occupations and discuss how the design of each has been affected by the advance of new technology. What has been the impact on the business, the employees and the customers? Your list must include examples from all three industrial sectors.

Patterns of work

It is not only the content of jobs which has changed with the introduction of new technology; different patterns of work have also emerged in the workplace. The next section discusses three different patterns; homeworking, teleworking and job sharing.

Homeworking

This includes any job which can be carried out at home. Traditionally, the approach to homeworking has been that of the 'cottage industry'. Recently, however, homeworking is often considered by employers as a way of increasing capacity without increasing overheads. Teleworking is one example of this.

Teleworking

Teleworking involves working from home using technical equipment provided by the employer. The benefits for both the employer and the employee have been summarised by Alan Fowler in a recent *People Management* article as follows:

Benefits for the employer:

- a saving in office-based costs
- recruiting people who would not be able to work in an office
- retaining staff who might otherwise leave because of personal circumstances.

Benefits for the employee:

- personal control over flexible working time
- less time and energy spent on commuting to and from work.

Although advances in new technology have facilitated the growth in teleworking, an employer must give very careful consideration to the type of jobs and people most suited to teleworking. Work processes suitable for teleworking:

- require minimal checking
- have no set time for performing tasks
- are driven by the job holder
- produce measurable outputs.

People suited to teleworking are:

- independent
- able to meet deadlines
- self-motivated
- comfortable working on their own and do not require regular personal social interaction
- able to resolve difficulties and correct faults.

As with any employee, teleworkers are making a valuable contribution to the business. It is important that, although they are not working at the normal workplace, that they are not forgotten. Careful consideration must be given to their induction and the continued communication processes once they have started work.

Job sharing

'[Job sharing] involves dividing one established full-time post between two (or possibly more) people. Each sharer does a proportion of the work ... which can be divided by specific duties or areas of responsibility, or merely proportioned as time.' – IDS, 1987

Many people have personal or domestic responsibilities which make full-time employment impracticable. They want, however, to use their skills, training and experience in a job on reduced hours. Job sharing enables people with such responsibilities to continue to contribute and develop, which is of benefit to both the employer and the employee.

The aim of job sharing is to create flexibility. Listed below are various job-sharing patterns; all are based on two people sharing a job:

- daily sharing – morning/afternoon
- part week – two and a half days per week
- split week – two days one week, three days the next.

Benefits for the employer:

- retaining the skill and experience of staff who may otherwise have left if the flexible option was not available
- reduced employee working hours, which leads to less employee fatigue, improved motivation and possibly improved productivity
- less absenteeism – personal commitments arranged around job share.

Benefits for the employee

- a degree of flexibility over working hours, although the sharing pattern must be compatible with the employer
- able to continue with current career while coping with additional personal or domestic responsibilities.

Introducing job sharing into the organisation requires very careful planning, implementing and monitoring. As with homeworking and teleworking, there are three key areas which an organisation would need to focus on:

1 the types of jobs which might be suitable for job sharing, focusing on both employer and employee needs
2 the types of person who might be suitable for the scheme
3 designing and adapting personnel policies and procedures to reflect the contractual changes of job sharing, ensuring that equal opportunity requirements are being adhered to.

Work roles and job analysis

In today's environment of rapid technological change, organisations place increased importance on reviewing job content. This is to ensure that human resources are being used in the most effective way possible, while still meeting the needs of the organisation and the individual. This process is known as job analysis. Job analysis has been described by Cowling and Mailer as, *'the systematic study and analysis of the tasks that together make up a job of work'*.

Collecting job-related information

This section focuses on the two main methods by which job-related information can be collected: observation and interview.

By observation

If a job has a short cycle, for example working on an assembly line where the tasks involved in the job are relatively short and highly repetitive, the job analyst would be able successfully to observe exactly what the job entailed.

By interview

If a job has a longer cycle, or it is not possible to observe the incumbent performing the whole job, then observation is not appropriate. The job analyst would have to take an alternative approach. This could be achieved by interviewing the job holder, finding out exactly what is involved by asking questions. Interviewing job holders about their work, requires skill and judgement. The job analyst must remember that the job is distinct from its holder. The job will probably still exist when the job holder leaves. The style that job holders adopt is personal to them – it is unlikely that two people would do the same job in the same way. What does remain the same, however, is the purpose of the job together with the tasks and duties to be performed. A skilled job analyst needs to extract information regarding the **tasks** and **duties** and be able to distinguish this from the job holder's **style.**

The following is an example of a simple job analysis interview, adapted from Kandola and Pearn (1992).

- What do you understand to be the purpose of this job? What role or roles do you carry out?
- What are the main activities you are involved in and what is your estimate of the percentage of time involved in each one?
- Which of these activities do you consider to be the most important and why?
- What do you consider to be the most difficult things to achieve in your job and why?
- How can you, or others, tell if your role is being satisfactorily carried out?
- What do you consider to be the most important knowledge, skills or other attributes that are required for successful performance of this job?
- What are the main challenges facing you now and in the immediate future (i.e. within the next two years)?
- What are the main challenges facing you in the long-term (i.e. in 3–5 years)?

The uses of job analysis

Job analysis has many useful functions within an organisation. Once the information has been collected and presented in an appropriate format, the results can be used for recruitment and selection, training and development, job evaluation, and organisational/job design.

Recruitment and selection

Job analysis will highlight the skills and attitudes required to successfully carry out a particular job. This information can be used to draw up a realistic but comprehensive job description which will assist in ensuring that the best person is selected for the job.

Training and development

Job analysis provides a framework upon which to develop a job holder's training and development needs. By comparing the skills that a job holder has when he or she takes up a new post with the skills he or she needs to become completely competent, these training needs can then be systematically planned into the incumbent's development plan. Job analysis can also be used during appraisals for career-development discussions. By analysing the content of particular jobs, the appraisor and appraisee can have a realistic discussion about how appropriate particular moves may be for the appraisee.

Job evaluation

Through the analysis of jobs, employers can ensure that jobs of equal value have an equal compensatory award.

Organisational design/job design

Earlier in the chapter, we focused on job design and technological change. In order to find out the real impact of technology on jobs, the organisation may decide to conduct a job-analysis exercise within the departments or areas affected. The results of this should reveal any omissions or duplications of tasks which could lead to restructuring. The main outcomes of such an analysis are considered in Figure 10.6.

Braverman and other researchers have produced evidence that **deskilling** in the 1980s and 1990s in organisations has been accelerated by information technology and automation. Skills have been codified into machines. Other researchers have found the opposite: instead of deskilling, **upskilling** has occurred as a result of advances in information technology, employees requiring increased levels of human judgement to pre-programme machines.

Organisations cannot afford to remain static. As the external influences discussed above place different challenges upon them, their internal structure must be working as effectively and efficiently as possible to enable the organisation to compete. The more closely the design of a job matches the requirements of the individual and the organisation, the more effective will be the use of the human resource. Job analysis is an important management tool used to assist in the process of organisational and job design.

Functional analysis

The purpose and use of job analysis must be clear at the beginning of the process in order to decide on the depth of analysis required. Truelove, in his *Handbook of Training and Development*, describes four levels at which jobs can be analysed:

Figure 10.6 Results of a job analysis excercise conducted to reveal the impact of introducing technology

Job analysis finding	Result	Job-design principle applied
Duplication of tasks	Merging jobs together	Job enlargement
New technology replacing people's jobs	Redundancy	
New technology reducing the skills level required by workers	Deskilling	Job rotation
New technology increasing the skill level required by workers	Increasing responsibility, planning and control	Job enrichment

1 functions
2 tasks
3 skills
4 abilities.

Job analysis can be conducted at each level. The analysis at level four is much deeper than at level one. This section considers analysis at the functional level.

Functional analysis was developed in the 1950s. The structure has been modified by Fine and Wiley and has been defined by them as *'both a conceptual system for defining the dimensions of worker activity and a method of measuring levels of worker activity'*.

This technique splits the job up into three worker functions: **data**, **people** and **things**. The analysis reflects the level of involvement of the worker within the three functions. Each function can be viewed as a hierarchy of levels of involvement which range from simple to complex, with each level incorporating those below it. This process is illustrated in Figure 10.7.

Job description

Once the job analysis process is complete, the next stage is to organise and present the information in a useful format which can then be used to aid managerial decision making. One of the most common formats is a job description.

Ernest J. McCormick in his book *Job Analysis: Methods and Applications*, describes a job description as:

'typically consisting of descriptions of the work activities that are performed in a job. They normally also contain information about other job-related aspects such as working conditions and tools and equipment used. The descriptions can be very detailed or very brief.'

A job description is therefore a record of the key features of a job and would typically include:

- job title
- job grade
- department
- the purpose of the job, why the job exists
- main tasks and duties – detailing the key responsibilities for the post, in terms of staff, finance, planning, etc.
- working conditions – office-based, travelling, working outside, etc.

According to the British Institute of Management (BIM), a job description should be:

'a report which outlines the duties, responsibilities and conditions applicable to the job under review. It is essentially a description of the job itself, and not of the individual who is performing the job.'

How useful is a job description?

In some organisations which are relatively static, so that the nature and function of jobs do not change very often, up-to-date job descriptions can be very useful. However, in more fluid organisations which are constantly changing, job descriptions may be too rigid to use as an effective management tool. They would need to be updated continually to be of any use.

There are probably three levels of job-description implementation within organisations:

- organisations who have never compiled job descriptions and operate without them; producing job descriptions would be a major development
- organisations who have written job descriptions and actively use and update them to reflect the current job structure and profile within the organisation
- organisations who have written and used job descriptions in the past but now view them as too restrictive and rigid.

In their book *Human Resource Management*, Fisher, Schoenfeldt and Shaw comment on the Japanese approach to job descriptions as follows:

'In Japan, large companies have little need for job descriptions ... because of the different philosophy that guides their employment practices. In recruiting white collar employees, traditional Japanese companies do not advertise specific jobs but instead look for new graduates who can contribute in a variety of roles. Employers

Figure 10.7 Worker functions

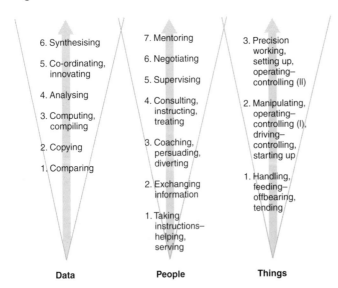

Data	People	Things
6. Synthesising	7. Mentoring	3. Precision working, setting up, operating–controlling (II)
5. Co-ordinating, innovating	6. Negotiating	
4. Analysing	5. Supervising	
3. Computing, compiling	4. Consulting, instructing, treating	2. Manipulating, operating–controlling (I), driving–controlling, starting up
2. Copying	3. Coaching, persuading, diverting	
1. Comparing	2. Exchanging information	1. Handling, feeding–offbearing, tending
	1. Taking instructions–helping, serving	

presume that these individuals will pursue long careers within their organisations and that they will work in many different areas. In evaluating candidates, employers place much more emphasis on personality, attitudes, formal education and family background than on specific job related skills or knowledge.'

Task

The job description is a human resource management tool that has traditionally had a useful role to play in aspects of organisational decision-making. Do you think that the job description will be used as widely in the future? Explain your decision using examples of organisations which do and do not use job descriptions.

Person specifications

Having established a job description, it is then possible to begin considering the type of person that might meet the requirements of the job. Organisations do this through the development of a person specification.

The person specification describes the human attributes required for a particular job. There are two main approaches to designing a person specification: the **seven-point plan** devised by Alex Rodger, and the **five-fold grading system** devised by John Munro Fraser.

The seven-point plan
The following attributes are specified in this plan:

- physique
- attainments
- general intelligence
- special aptitudes
- interests
- disposition
- circumstances.

The five-fold grading system
Attributes are grouped under the following headings:

- first impression
- qualifications
- abilities
- motivation
- adjustment.

Figure 10.8 Translation of job description to person specification

Hospital orderly	
Job description statement on working conditions	Person specification interpretation of working conditions
1 Works in physically comfortable surroundings	1 Must be willing to work hard
2 Deals with physically ill and diseased patients	2 Exposed to unpleasant situations and communicable diseases
3 Deals with mentally ill patients	3 Exposed to verbal and physical abuse

The person specification is designed using the job description; by assessing the key task and duties required, a profile of the ideal type of person can be drawn up. This process is illustrated in Figure 10.8, using the job description for a hospital orderly (from Werther and Davis, 1993).

Person specifications are usually graded, highlighting an **essential** and a **desirable** grade for each attribute.

Task

Discuss whether you think the traditional format of the person specification is still valid in an increasingly flexible workplace. In particular, think about the headings used; do they reflect the dynamism of the workplace today?

Organisational relationships

Having considered the various approaches to job design and the impact that technological change has had on the process, it is important that the reader has an appreciation of how internal organisational relationships can be affected during the changes. This section focuses on the pressure upon the organisation in terms of maintaining and developing effective working relationships, and the impact of this on organisational efficiency.

Job design within an organisation can have a significant impact on organisational relationships, affecting the relationships between the employer and the employee, the relationship between employees, and how these relationships develop over time. The following quote taken from *Learning to Succeed*, the report of the Paul Hamlyn Foundation National Commission on Education, summarises some of the issues:

> '*Rapid change and pressure of competition have made (and will make) it far more difficult for employers to offer secure jobs for their employees. Jobs which are not part of the "core business" are being hived off to contractors who specialise in providing particular services. The sole assumption for people starting work today is generally speaking that they will change employer and sometimes occupation several times in their working careers.*'

An environment of rapid change and competition, as described above, is not conducive to developing and sustaining working relationships.

The traditional employer/employee relationship in some organisations is being eroded in favour of a more flexible disposable arrangement. Although they both still enter into a contract of employment, so there is still a legally binding relationship, the nature of the terms and conditions has changed for certain categories of staff. For example, organisations are now employing more **periphery** workers, part-time, temporary, homeworkers, etc. who are employed to 'flex' around the needs of the employer. Charles Handy in his book *The Empty Raincoat*, cites the Burton Group as one example of a high-street retailer adopting this approach. In 1993 the group announced that it would be cutting 2000 full-time jobs and creating 3000 part-time ones. The nature of the relationship has also changed for the core employees, i.e. those who work full-time in permanent positions. They are generally expected to take on more responsibility and often seem to be doing more than one job.

Periphery workers

Periphery workers can be divided into two general groups. The first group includes part-time, fixed short-term contracts and job share workers who have regular but reduced contact at the workplace (in comparison to full-time staff). The second group focuses on homeworkers and teleworkers, who have very little contact with the workplace in terms of using it as a base due to the fact that they work from home. We look at these two groups in more detail below.

Part-time, fixed short-term contracts and job share

Time
The nature of this category of staff means that they spend less time at work in comparison to full-time, so there is less

opportunity to build up working relationships either between colleagues or with managers. The time of day/year that these people are employed will inevitably be the busiest for the business, and colleagues and superiors may therefore have very little time for employee development issues, this again cuts down on the opportunity to build up relationships. Employees may also be working these hours due to their outside commitments. At the end of a shift, therefore, they are probably more likely to leave work on time instead of socialising with colleagues.

Loyalty
Employees have traditionally been very loyal to their organisation. This loyalty was offered in return for good job prospects and the belief that your position was secure. With increasing competition and rapid environmental change, employers are becoming less able (or willing) to offer such guarantees. This is especially true for employees who work in periphery positions. For employees affected by this loss of job security, loyalty may only make sense until a better offer comes along or until they find a permanent position. Why should they feel loyal when they know that as soon as orders dry up or a particular project or contract is completed they will once again be out of a job? This feeling of insecurity relates back to Maslow's hierarchy of needs (see Chapter 3). Employees have a 'need' to feel secure in order to be motivated to do a good job. Without this security, motivation is reduced and harmonious organisational relationships become threatened, which may lead to a reduction in productivity.

Exclusion
There is a danger that because employees are not working at the organisation full-time, they may be excluded from meetings and training sessions which take place at a time of day when they do not work. These employees feel excluded from the business and undervalued by the employer. Employers can minimise the impact of such a situation with careful planning, ensuring that they treat all employees equally and fairly. It must be remembered that, although periphery workers do not work as many hours as full-time staff, their contribution is usually vital to the continued success of the business.

Homeworkers and teleworkers

The factors influencing organisational relationships for part-time staff will also apply to homeworkers and teleworkers. However, employers must give particular consideration to homeworkers and teleworkers due to the fact that that they are based away from the normal workplace. Exclusion can therefore be a major issue;

employees may have little opportunity to establish organisational relationships. Employers must ensure suitable candidates are chosen for this type of work. Personality questionnaires may be used during the interview process to assess whether an individual has the required personality traits to work alone, for example independence, self-discipline and the ability to meet deadlines. The induction process will also be very important. Homeworkers will have a very limited opportunity to experience the culture of the organisation. It is therefore essential that the induction programme includes office visits and the opportunity to meet staff with whom they will have contact via the telephone and computer.

Core workers

As organisations strive to become leaner and fitter to survive in an increasingly competitive market, controlling costs at every opportunity becomes vitally important. The human resource costs in a business can be sizeable. Employers are increasingly looking at every operation in the business and assessing the contribution that each individual makes to the organisation. The focus is on **added value.** Those operations which do not add value to the business are either restructured or made redundant. In conjunction with this, new technology is changing the shape of jobs and numbers required. Core workers can become the pivotal focus for the organisation's success.

A recent newspaper report, discussing the distribution of jobs, noted that 'you either have one and a half jobs or no job at all'. This emphasises the increased workload and responsibility faced by the core workers.

Core workers are not necessarily protected from redundancy; they may still have a feeling of uncertainty about their jobs which probably means they will work harder to try to safeguard themselves against the risk. Core workers may feel under increased pressure to perform and achieve results, knowing that, if they fail, they could risk losing their job. This pressure can affect organisational relationships as core workers accept more responsibility and work longer hours to ensure they have a job tomorrow.

Other recent trends which have had an impact on organisational relationships include:

- *empowerment* – increased autonomy and contribution to decision-making in the lower ranks of the organisation
- *flatter structures* – less opportunity for career development
- *increasing use of small business units within organisations* – this can lead to a change in the portfolio of skills that an employee requires,

- *increasing emphasis on mergers and takeovers* – employees need to adapt to possible changes in culture and management styles
- *changing role of the trade unions* – trade union relationships between employers and union members have altered as illustrated by the survey results shown in Figure 10.9 from the British Social Attitudes Survey (Social and Community Planning Research).

Figure 10.9 What unionised workers think is the most important role for trade unions

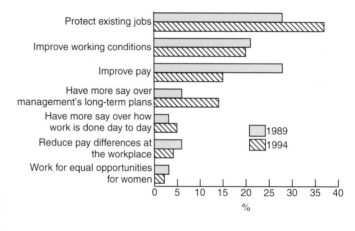

Task

A recent article published in the *People Management* magazine discussed the changing job market. The article began with the following opening statement:

'Workplaces in the UK are characterised by long hours, job insecurity and part time contracts.'

To what extent do you agree/disagree with this statement, justify your answer.

Further reading

- *Human Resource Management: A Strategic Approach to Employment* by C. Hendry. Butterworth Heinemann, 1995.
- *Management and Organisational Behaviour,* 3rd edition, by L. J. Mullins. Pitman, 1993.
- *Job Design and Work Organisation* by J. Bailey. Prentice Hall, 1983.
- *Human Resource and Personnel Management,* 4th editon, by W. B. Werther, J. R. Davis and K. Davis. McGraw Hill International Editions, 1993.
- *Principles of Human Resource Management* by D. Goss. Routledge, 1994.

- *Managing Human Resources*, 2nd edition, edited by A. Cowling and C. Mailer. Edward Arnold, 1990.
- *Jobshift* by W. Bridges. Nicholas Brealey Publishing, 1995.
- *Handbook of Training and Development* by S. Truelove. Blackwell Business, 1992.
- *An Introduction to Functional Job Analysis* by S. A. Fine and W. W. Wiley. W. E. Upjohn Institute for Employment Research, 1971.
- *Jon Analysis: Methods and Applications* by E. J. McCormick. Amacom (a division of American Management Associations), 1979.
- *Human Resource Management* by Fisher, Schoenfeldt and Shaw. Houghton Mifflin Company, 1990.

11 Sources and methods of recruitment

On completion of this chapter, students should be able to:

- specify the different stages of the recruitment process
- explain the roles played by external institutions in assisting organisations in the recruitment and selection process
- describe different methods of internally and externally advertising jobs
- discuss two different selection methods, interviewing and testing, and comment on their contribution to the recruitment and selection process.

Recruitment and selection

Recruitment and selection is the process of filling a vacancy within an organisation by selecting the most appropriate candidate for the job, as this quote from the *Employment Law and Practice* journal 1994 indicates:

> 'In recruitment and selection, what we are trying to achieve is a good prediction of how a person will perform in a given job or role.'

As more and more attention is being placed on the value of the human resources within organisations, decisions about exactly how and when to employ new recruits, let alone who to employ, take on a higher profile. The process of recruitment and selection takes on even greater importance. This chapter analyses the process of recruitment and selection, guiding the reader through various procedures and techniques to ensure that effective decisions are made about potential recruits. The full process, which was introduced in Chapter 8, is summarised again in Figure 11.1.

In order to discuss the concepts related to recruitment and selection successfully, it is important to consider the issues relating to recruitment first, before we move on to focus on selection.

Recruitment procedures

Recruitment procedures relate to the method chosen to recruit a prospective employee into the business. The procedure will vary considerably between organisations; if it is to be effective, however, it must satisfy several criteria. The procedure should be:

- accurate
- appropriate
- convenient
- cost-effective.

The formality of the procedure will also vary between organisations; it is good practice to have a written procedure.

Figure 11.1 A flow chart of the recruitment and selection process

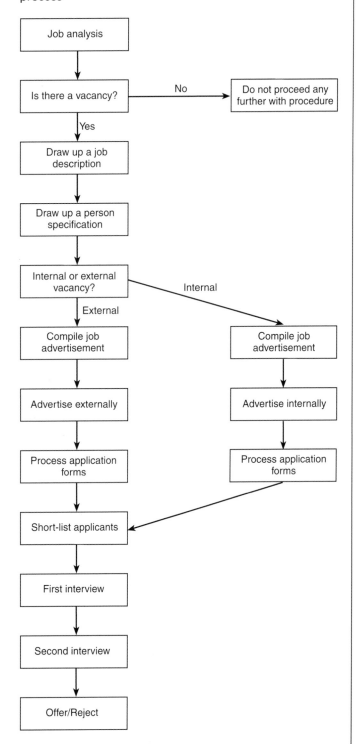

The importance of a written procedure

In order to ensure consistency, fairness and equal opportunities within the recruitment process, many organisations have a written procedure which outlines step by step how to conduct each stage. The procedure may give guidelines for both internal and external recruitment. Some of the issues which may be addressed include:

- Who within the organisation should authorise that a vacancy can be filled?
- What should be included in a job advertisement?
- How long should an internal vacancy be advertised?
- What are the equal opportunity regulations which must be followed?
- What documentation should be completed for each vacancy?
- Where should different jobs be advertised?
- What type of tests should be used for different job categories?

The procedure alone will not guarantee successful recruitment; equally important are the techniques which can be applied throughout the process to ensure that it is a success.

Recruitment techniques

Techniques refer to the way in which the procedure is carried out. Listed below are some of the techniques which support a successful recruitment and selection process:

- planning ahead – filling vacancies can sometimes be a very lengthy process
- being organised – keeping a record of exactly who has applied and the status of their application
- following procedures – to maintain consistency and to ensure that every candidate is treated equally and fairly,
- maintaining a professional approach with candidates at all times, remember they are making a judgement about the organisation as much as the organisation is judging them
- ensuring that all those involved in the recruitment process are well trained and well briefed about the job and the type of person who would ideally fit the vacancy
- keeping up to date with the latest developments in recruitment and selection,
- evaluating the process to ensure that the required outcomes are being achieved.

Choosing the right approach

The starting point for recruiting a member of staff should always be **job analysis** to find out whether a vacancy does exist. If the employer has decided to fill a vacancy and proceed with the recruitment process, the next stage is to draw up a **job description** and a **person specification.** Refer to Chapter 10 for a more detailed explanation of these issues.

At this stage the employer should establish an exact plan of what the job entails, together with a clear picture of the type of person required to fill the vacancy. The next stage is to decide how to recruit; the employer is faced with several options:

- to fill the vacancy internally
- to fill the vacancy externally using the organisation's own resources.
- to place the vacancy with an employment agency or executive search agency.

The approach used will the depend on the following factors:

- *The type of job to be filled* (in terms of skill and experienced required). In most cases, it is advisable for employers to look internally first and to try to develop existing staff. A well-maintained training, development and appraisal system should assist in identifying key people to be considered. If an appropriate person cannot be identified, the organisation will need to draw on its own resources or involve an employment agency.
- *The numbers of recruits required.* If the numbers are small, the organisation may decide to use its own personnel resources. If a large number of people are needed, the organisation may decide to set up a project team to manage the process. This method is often used by large retailers who are expanding and recruiting staff for their new superstores. An organisation may also decide to place the vacancy or vacancies with an employment agency.
- *The level of flexibility required* (whether the job is permanent, full-time, temporary, for a fixed period of time etc). For example, an organisation may decide to handle all permanent vacancies itself and place all temporary, fixed-term contract positions with an agency.
- *The technical nature of the job.* To fill a specific post, the organisation may decide to enlist the expert advice of a specialist employment agency.

The role played by external agencies

There are three main institutions involved in externally assisting organisations with recruitment and selection. These are outlined in Figure 11.2.

Employment agencies

One increasingly popular strategy is to place vacancies in the hands of external employment agencies. An employment agency acts as a **third-party adviser** to organisations in the recruitment and selection process. By assisting in the advertising, short-listing or

Figure 11.2 The main institutions involved in assisting organisations with recruitment and selection

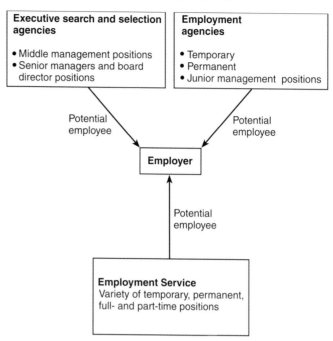

interviewing stage, they operate as consultants offering expert advice.

Employment agencies can provide various recruitment and selection services for different categories of staff (temporary, contract, permanent, etc.) across many industrial and commercial sectors. Agencies often specialise in certain areas of employment, such as office, technical, industrial or educational. The types of positions recruited include customer service assistants, secretarial, driving, data entry, catering, cleaning, nursing and auxiliary staff, industrial temps, and unskilled labourers.

The service provided by employment agencies varies depending on the needs of the employer. Some agencies provide only a screening service for employers, leaving the actual interviewing and selection up to the employer. Other agencies conduct initial interviews, carry out tests and draw up short lists of the recommended candidates for the employer.

Recent trends indicate that the role played by employment agencies in the recruitment process and selection is changing. There is an increasing emphasis on **quality**. Personal training and development for prospective candidates has also become a key issue in ensuring that organisations receive the best possible service and ultimately the most appropriate candidate for the job. A well-known employment agency maintains that it contributes to cost savings within organisations by providing staff who are helping to increase productivity and cut costs dramatically. Some examples of the initiatives being carried out in employment agencies include:

- assessing skills to ensure employees are correctly placed with client organisations
- skill development and training to ensure that employees are kept up to date with technological developments or particular industry-specific developments, for example in driving and customer care training,
- assessing the performance of employees to ensure that the highest possible standard is being delivered to the client organisation.

The relationship which exists between the employer, the employment agency and the employee is illustrated in Figure 11.3 as a **three-way communication process**.

Employment agencies can provide a recruitment and selection service to fill both temporary and permanent vacancies. Examples of situations requiring temporary cover which may arise in an organisation include:

- holiday cover
- maternity leave
- seasonal fluctuations, for example Christmas/holiday times
- a sudden increase in orders
- special projects
- other emergencies
- long-term assignments.

In return for the service provided, the agency receives a fee from the employing organisation. The level of financial reward will depend upon the service provided and the calibre of employee being recruited.

Figure 11.3 The three-way relationship between the employer, employment agency and employee

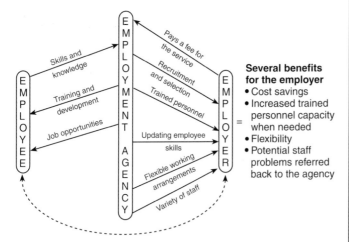

----- Represents the relationship between the employer and the employee which will develop once the agency has recommended the employee

Note
With the increase in demand for human resource services, many firms have entered the industry. The number of employment agencies rose significantly during the 1980s and early 1990s. The *Journal of General Management* (vol. 20, no. 2, winter 1994) stated that 'The number of employment agencies in the UK rose by 198 per cent between 1980 and 1992.'

Task

Research a variety of organisations recruiting temporary employees on a regular basis and use your findings to answer the following questions:

1 *What are the benefits of recruiting temporary employees into an organisation? Relate your answer to a particular organisation.*
2 *What are the costs and benefits to an employer of using an employment agency to recruit temporary, contract or permanent staff?*

Task

Research the role of a temporary employment agency. Compile an employer's awareness package on the benefits of recruiting temporary employees and, in particular, the benefits of using *your* agency.

How would you sell this package to an employer to ensure that your agency secures the contract?

Some organisations who require large numbers of temporary employees throughout the year may consider setting up their own in-house recruitment and selection service/agency. Bear this in mind when you consider the Task below.

Task

Established in the mid 1980s, Vegefast provides quality fast food to supermarkets, restaurants and public houses. Located in Nottingham, the business now employs over 3000 employees. Up to 1000 of these can be temporary; their numbers fluctuate during the year depending upon demand for the products. The temporary staff are mainly employed in packing products and adding the finishing touches to certain lines.

Since starting the business, they have always relied on McIntosh Recruitment (a large temporary recruitment agency) to provide their temporary workers. This has worked well in the past, but with such large numbers of temporary staff now needed it has become a very expensive exercise. Vegefast have also noticed that some of the temps are not meeting the required high standards.

As the human resource director, you decide to look into the feasibility of setting up your own in-house temporary recruitment agency. Construct a cost-benefit analysis of the feasibility of setting up an in-house recruitment service for Vegefast plc.

Executive search and selection agencies

Organisations may also require professional assistance when recruiting a more senior or executive post. In this case they would probably enlist the help of an executive search and selection agency.

As the name suggests, these agencies can provide two types of service. First, they might conduct a **search** for the employing organisation. This identifies candidates who could be suitable to fill a particular vacancy, without the candidate responding to an advertisement. The reason for this level of secrecy is that a company may not want its competitors to know that it is moving into a particular area. This type of search would provide a small number of people with specialist skills.

Second, they might **select** potential candidates. In this case, the candidates reply to an agency through a specific advertisement and are actively seeking to change their job.

This service would produce a larger pool of more managerial personnel. The agency interviews and short-lists suitable candidates, and the employing organisation then interview these and makes the final selection.

The journal of *General Management* (vol. 20, no. 2, winter 1994,) reports that 'Executive agencies accounted for 49 per cent of recruitment advertising in 1993.' At the time of writing the article, there were 300 consultancies offering executive search in the UK. The article goes on to discuss the main reasons why organisations use executive agencies:

> 'Personnel Directors believe they are better able to identify suitable candidates than the internal personnel department. Next in importance is the need for confidentiality, an objective opinion and a perceived failure of the internal personnel department successfully to fill management positions.'

Task

The above quotation is very controversial. Discuss to what extent you agree or disagree with it.

Activities undertaken by executive recruitment agencies include:

- job analysis
- drawing up job descriptions and person specifications
- identifying potential candidates
- initial assessment of candidates
- final assessment of candidates
- job offer.

Figure 11.4 Types of vacancy handled by different employment agencies

Vacancy	Salary range	Method of advertising	Type of agency
Junior management, plus a mixture of permanent and temporary positions	£10 000 – 30 000 for junior management; under £10 000 for some temporary assignments	Local and national press, professional journals	Employment agency
Middle management and some senior management positions	£25 000 – 80 000	National quality press, or professional journals	Executive search and selection consultants
Senior or board-level positions	Above £80 000	Positions may not be advertised, potential candidates may be approached to apply	Head hunting or search consultants

For most of the above activities, there would be considerable liaison between the employing organisation and the agency, with many activities being conducted jointly.

The mix of activities performed by the agency may vary with each vacancy.

Task

Employing someone using an executive agency may mean that the candidates do not meet the employer until the later stages of the recruitment process. Bearing this in mind, discuss the impact that an executive agency can have on the recruitment process.

Figure 11.4, on the previous page, summarises the types of vacancy handled by employment agencies and executive search agencies.

Task

Discuss the factors which you think an organisation should consider when choosing an executive search consultant.

Task

Recruitment and selection has long been one of the major roles performed by the personnel function. Discuss to what extent you think this specialist skill is being eroded by using external agencies.

The Employment Service

A further external service that can be used by employers is the Employment Service (ES), which is an executive agency within the Employment Department Group. The ES was created by the government to provide an effective and high-quality **public employment service.** There are over 1000 Employment Service Jobcentres in England, Scotland and Wales, employing approximately 50 000 staff. The Employment Service Jobcentres are responsible for:

- submitting jobseekers for vacancies
- displaying employer's job vacancies

- taking new claims for benefits
- paying benefits and National Insurance contributions
- giving advice on benefits and finding employment
- providing training schemes and programmes.

The purpose of the ES is to help people into work, thereby filling employers' vacancies, and to pay benefits to those unemployed people entitled to receive them.

The Chief Executive describes the main aim of the ES as follows;

'Our main aim is to help promote a competitive and efficient labour market, by giving positive help to the unemployed. At the same time the ES must be run as a businesslike organisation, so getting value for money and doing our job efficiently and effectively is very important to us.'

Employers can place vacancies with the Jobcentres (usually manual and clerical posts). Interested candidates are sometimes briefly interviewed by the staff at the Jobcentre before referring them to the employer for further consideration. Employers are allowed to use interviewing facilities at the centre to interview prospective candidates if necessary.

The job advertisement

The next stage in the recruitment and selection procedure involves compiling the job advertisement. Job advertisements can be compiled to fill a job internally or externally (see Figure 11.5).

Figure 11.5   Methods of advertising

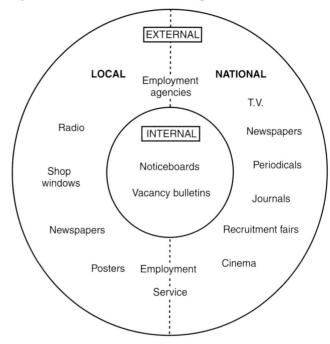

Internally

In a small organisation this may involve displaying the advertisement on a prominent notice board to ensure all staff have the opportunity to see it. In a larger organisation a regular vacancy bulletin may be circulated to all departments to ensure all staff are kept up to date with current opportunities. This method would be particularly relevant in a multi-sited business. Teachers, for example, are kept up to date with a weekly vacancy bulletin advertising all the teaching vacancies across a particular geographical area.

Externally

Advertising externally can take a variety of forms:

- advertisements may be placed in shop windows; we are all familiar with the words 'part-time vacancy, apply within'
- many large supermarkets have vacancy boards located near the checkouts; customers or people enquiring can usually pick up information regarding the vacancies from the customer service desk
- adverts can be placed in the local newspaper or on local radio
- adverts can be placed in the national press; the broadsheets dedicate certain days for particular job categories, e.g. media appointments, law appointments, etc.
- journals and periodicals are used to advertise specialist jobs; for example, *People Management* is a specialist magazine issued to members of the Institute of Personnel and Development, which advertises opportunities in personnel, training and development
- word of mouth.

Job advertisements vary considerably, but many contain common information in order to ensure that employers are successful in attracting the right candidates. Figure 11.6 outlines the key parts of a successful job advertisement.

The style of an advertisement can say a great deal about the employing organisation, so design and presentation are important factors in compiling a successful advertisement. Many companies adopt a **house style** which means they adopt a similar layout for every advertisement.

Advertising can be a very costly exercise; organisations cannot afford for advertisements to fail. In some cases, organisations employ advertising agencies to manage their human resource advertising campaigns.

The main objective of a job advertisement, is to attract suitable candidates for the position; but it should also deter unsuitable candidates from applying. Adverts must therefore be:

Figure 11.6 Key parts of a successful job advertisement

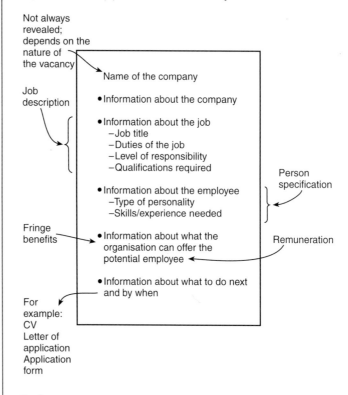

- *honest*
- *legal* – employers must not discriminate in their job advertisements; many will state that they are 'an equal opportunities employer' as part of their advert
- *realistic* – in terms of what they are expecting in relation to the financial reward,
- *eye-catching*.

The procedure for responding to an advertisement must be very clear. Potential candidates will usually be asked to do one of the following:

- send a CV and a covering letter
- telephone the organisation for an initial chat about the job
- send off for an application form.

Task

1   *Monitor the jobs pages of the local and national press over a 1–2 week period. Select an example of what you think is a very effective advertisement, and an example of a poor advertisement.*
2   *How did you decide whether an advertisement was effective or poor? Devise criteria for assessing the quality of advertisements.*

The application form

The application form will aid the selection decision. Potential candidates will be asked for information on their personal details (name, address, etc.), education and training undertaken, work experience, health and interests. Some application forms require candidates to answer job-related questions if appropriate. This information is used to short-list candidates for interview, and will be used during the interview as a basis upon which to find out more about the interviewee.

Task

ICX plc is a major information technology superstore chain providing goods to industry and the public. The business is currently undertaking a major expansion programme. You work in the human resources department at head office. You have just found out that you have been seconded to work with the new store development team as part of the expansion programme. You will be in charge of recruitment and selection for all staff into the stores.

You need to compile a new store opening manual covering all personnel issues. The manual will be used with all future store openings to ensure that each opening is consistent. Each store will employ approximately 150 staff in the following positions:

- 45 management positions (permanent, full- and part-time)
- 50 sales assistants (permanent and temporary, full- and part-time)
- 20 office staff (permanent full- and part-time)
- 10 trainee managers (permanent full-time)
- 5 canteen staff (permanent and temporary, full- and part-time)
- 20 delivery drivers/warehouse people (permanent and temporary, full- and part-time)

1 *Decide a suitable method of advertising for each category of staff.*
2 *Justify your decision, ensuring that you always choose the most cost-effective approach.*
3 *What would be the major headings/areas covered in the manual? Draw up a contents page.*

Short-listing

Having placed the advertisement, the organisation will begin to receive applications from prospective recruits.

The next task is to decide who should be invited for interview. This decision is reached by short-listing.

To decide who should be invited for interview, each candidate's application form details should be evaluated against the job description and the person specification. Those that match the criteria the closest will be short-listed and invited for interview. Those who do not reach this stage will be rejected. Professional organisations will notify candidates of their decision.

Short-listing concludes the recruitment part of filling a vacancy; the next major stage is interviewing, which is part of the selection process.

Task

Employers must ensure that they practise equal opportunities at every stage of the recruitment process. Discuss how they can ensure that all the people involved in the process adopt the policy/code of conduct.

Selection procedures

The interview

The interview is a fundamental part of the selection procedure. It is an opportunity for the employer to meet the prospective candidate and for the candidate to meet the employer.

An interview can be described as an opportunity for the interviewer and the interviewee to find out more about each other by asking questions related to the job, their experience, etc. The main aim of this **information exchange** is for both parties to reach a decision as to whether they would like to take the process any further.

There are four possible outcomes of an interview:

- The interviewer is impressed with the interviewee and makes him or her an offer; the interviewee is impressed with the job and the organisation and accepts the offer.
- The interviewer is impressed with the interviewee and makes him or her an offer; the interviewee is not impressed with the job or organisation and rejects the offer. This decision will obviously depend on how much the interviewee needs the job.
- The interviewee does not suitably match the job criteria and the interviewer rejects him or her; the interviewee is impressed with the job and organisation and feels that he or she does match the criteria. In this case, the interviewer may offer the candidate some feedback.
- Neither party feels they are compatible.

The nature of the vacancy will determine the complexity of the interviewing process. A potential machinist going to work in a textile factory will probably go through quite a different process from an international sales and marketing manager applying for a job with a computer software company.

In the first example, the prospective candidate may have one or two interviews together with some skills tests before a decision is made to offer the job or not. In the second example, the prospective candidate may have several interviews with various parties, such as the personnel manager, senior manager, marketing director and managing director, together with a multitude of tests and assessments before a job offer is made.

Initial interview

An initial interview is the first interview. This is usually conducted by the personnel manager or line manager, or an employment agency. The purpose of this interview is to screen the candidate to find out how closely he or she meets the requirements of the job. The interviewer will try to compare and assess the candidate's experience and training, as detailed on the candidate's application form, to those already determined by the job description and person specification.

Equally during this initial interview, the candidate will ask questions about the job, training and organisation – making an assessment of the employer to decide whether he or she would feel happy working for that particular organisation.

The initial interview may be a one-to-one format, or it may involve more than one interviewer, and take the form of a panel interview.

Case Study
Interviewing a potential teacher

All interviews usually take place on the same day. Candidates are normally invited to spend the day in the school or college and are given opportunities throughout the day to talk to the people with whom they would be working. The interview usually takes the form of a panel interview, with perhaps the Head of Department, Vice Principal and Personnel Manager. Each member of the panel will ask the candidate specific questions about particular aspects of the job. The questions might be structured as follows:

Vice Principal:
- specific questions about the candidate's awareness of educational policies and procedures, including curriculum development
- questions regarding the contribution that the candidate feels he or she could make to the educational institution.

Head of Department:
- specific questions about classroom management
- ideas for lesson planning and writing materials
- experience of teaching various syllabi
- strategies for handling different student ability levels.

Personnel Manager:
- strategies for coping with the job
- development: where does the candidate see him or herself in X years' time
- strengths and weaknesses.

Panel interview

Careful consideration must be given to the preparation stage of a panel interview; because as more people are involved, someone will need to co-ordinate the procedure. It is essential that everyone has a copy of the relevant information. It is also good practice to discuss the format of the interview beforehand, in particular who is going to ask what.

Advantages of a panel interview
More people are involved in the decision-making process; this may result in a more balanced/informed decision being made in a shorter amount of time, although this is

not always the case. The panel interview may have higher validity than a one-to-one interview for predicting job performance because the candidate is put through a more rigorous process. The candidate has a better understanding of the organisation at the end of the interview.

Disadvantages of a panel interview

The experience for the candidate can be somewhat daunting; faced by several senior people, the candidate may be unsure whom to look at or how to respond. It may be more difficult to build up a rapport with the candidate due to the formality of the occasion. This may result in the panel being unable really to find out about the candidate. It is essential in this case that the panel takes time to make the candidate feel as relaxed as possible.

Task

Set up a panel interview for a graduate personnel trainee in an organisation of your choice. There should be three people in the panel.

- Decide on the questions each member of the panel would ask and why.
- Conduct a role play of the interview
- Evaluate the role play; did the panel have enough information to make a decision about the candidate?
- How did the interviewee feel? How did the panel feel?

Questions for discussion

1 *How valuable is the interview as an objective selection tool?*
2 *It has been said that most interviewers make a decision about a candidate within the first few minutes of the interview. Faced with this situation, how would you train a team of interviewers to remain objective throughout the interview? Make a list of the key steps you would take.*
3 *Some organisations use graphology, the study of handwriting, as a method of short-listing candidates. How valid do you think this is as a selection tool?*

Interview techniques

Successful interviewing requires a high degree of skill and judgement. There are also a number of techniques which can be employed throughout the process to ensure that it is a success. These are outlined below.

Before the interview

- have a thorough understanding of the job description/person specification and candidate's application form
- prepare questions based on these documents
- ensure that the interview will be conducted in a professional manner with a well-thought-out structure
- allow enough time and ensure there are no interruptions
- consider the seating arrangements for both the interviewer and the interviewee, to vary the degree of formality.

During the interview:

- **maintain a structure** – the interviewer must keep control of the interview; the predetermined structure will help here (see Figure 11.7)
- **take notes** – if the interviewee has no objections, it is useful for the interviewer to take brief notes during the interview; a checklist approach may be appropriate

Figure 11.7 A simple interview structure

Welcome

- Put the candidate at ease; begin to create a rapport
- Ask friendly questions: Did you have a good journey? Did you have trouble finding our offices?
- Introduce yourself
- Explain the structure of the interview
- Mention note-taking
- Ensure the candidate knows when he or she can ask questions. You may mention how long the interview will take
- Reassure the candidate; smile

Acquire information

- Ask simple questions at first
- Work through the questions and application form in a logical order
- Listen and ask follow-up questions if you do not obtain the required information
- Watch the candidate's body language, facial expressions and eye-contact
- Keep control
- Find out if the candidate is suitable

Supply information

- Provide information about the job, its benefits and the terms and conditions of employment
- Possibly discuss the culture of the organisation
- Give the candidate a chance to ask questions

Part

- Check there are no further questions
- Tell the candidate what happens next
- Thank the candidate
- Shake hands
- Show the candidate to reception

Figure 11.8 The effects of a poor recruitment decision

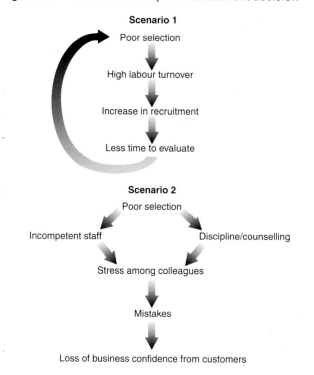

- **use appropriate body language** – it is the interviewer's responsibility to make the interviewee feel at ease; The more relaxed the interviewee feels, the greater chance the interviewer has of finding out more about the candidate.

After the interview

- **record notes** – write up the interview notes straight away; it may be difficult to recall what a candidate said several hours after the meeting, particularly when several people are being interviewed in the same day.

Although the interview is probably the most common assessment method, the *Employment Law and Practice* journal (vol. 1, no. 4, 1994), states:

> *'About 80 per cent of those involved in recruitment always use an interview in spite of the fact that the validity of the method is lower than for most methods.'*

To try to improve the validity of the recruitment process, many employers use more than one method. Psychometric tests and assessment centres are often used to give the assessors a greater opportunity to see the candidate performing in many job-related circumstances and so increase the validity of the process.

Selection tests

A selection test is a method of collecting data about a candidate's abilities, interests or personality under standardised conditions. Tests are used to improve the validity of the recruitment decision by giving the candidate a chance to complete an **objective** test, free from prejudice and bias which may be evident at the interview stage. Selection errors can be very costly to the organisation – testing may help to reduce the errors and so reduce the costs. The two flow charts in Figure 11.8 outline the effects of a poor selection decision.

The main categories of psychometric tests used in selection are:

- ability tests
- personality questionnaires
- interest inventories.

Other types include trainability and diagnostic tests.

Ability tests

Ability tests can be used to look at attainment, intelligence and aptitude.

- *Attainment tests* verify skills already acquired. For example, a secretary may be required to take a typing test in order to demonstrate previously acquired keyboard skills.
- *Intelligence tests* are designed to give an indication of overall mental capacity.
- *Aptitude tests* aim to assess the candidate's potential to acquire further knowledge and skills. There are many aptitude tests which may be used as part of the selection procedure depending upon the nature of the vacancy. Figure 11.9 summarises the main types of tests, their content and target audience.

Personality questionnaires

These questionnaires are designed to give a more objective assessment of personality to supplement the rather subjective interpretation gained during the interview. This would again be conducted under standardised conditions.

There are various questionnaires which employers can use. Examples of personality tests in common use are:

- Cattell's 16 PF
- Myers Briggs Type Indicator
- Occupational Personality Questionnaire (OPQ).

OPQ
The OPQ 'Concept' model has three main sections; each section focuses on a variety of personality dimensions. Candidates are asked various questions which require them to rate themselves honestly as to how they would react in certain situations. The dimensions which are tested are shown in Figure 11.10.

Figure 11.9 Aptitude tests

Type of test	Content	Target audience
Verbal	Spelling, grammar Verbal critical reasoning	Clerical, Managers and graduates
Numerical	Simple arithmetic calculations Numerical critical reasoning	Process workers Managers and graduates
Diagrammatic	Testing logical reasoning, using shapes and diagrams	Data processing jobs
Mechanical	Mechanical problems in pictorial form which need to be solved by the candidate	Apprentice and engineering jobs
Spatial	Assess the ability to imagine the rotation of shapes in space	Design jobs and occupations which require an understanding of how parts fit together
Clerical	Measuring speed and accuracy in checking errors in lists	Payroll and various administrative jobs
Dexterity	Measures hand speed and fine precision skills Co-ordination tests	Assembly line workers Pilots
Sensory	Measures near or far vision, sound or colour discrimination	Military jobs

Figure 11.10 Dimensions tested in the Occupational Personality Questionnaire (OPQ)

Relationships with people	Thinking style	Feelings and emotions
Dimensions assessed: Persuasive Controlling Independent Outgoing Affiliative Socially confident Modest Democratic Caring	*Dimensions assessed:* Practical Data rational Artistic Behavioural Traditional Change-orientated Conceptual Innovative Forward planning Detail conscious Conscientious	*Dimensions tested:* Relaxed Worrying Tough minded Emotional control Optimistic Critical Active Competitive Achieving Decisive

The final dimension is a **social desirability response.** If candidates score a high score on this, they have not been completely honest with their responses. This can reduce the usefulness of the questionnaire.

Once the test is complete, the questionnaire is scored and the results are plotted on a personality profile chart incorporating all the dimensions. This profile is compared against a previously prepared profile chart showing the key personality characteristics identified as being crucial to successful performance in the job. (The previously prepared profile chart would have taken considerable time to develop, administering the questionnaire to people within a particular job who were considered to be successful.) The more closely the profile chart matches the predetermined characteristics, the better match the candidate will be for the job. Some tolerance is built into the process, i.e. the candidate's profile does not have to match exactly.

Interest inventories

Saville and Holdsworth describe interest inventories as 'a wide sample of questions which might cover hobbies, school work or general life experiences which seek to measure the direction in which an individual wants to go'.

Trainability tests

These tests require candidates to perform a practical task which they have not done before after being shown how to do it. The test measures how candidates respond to training and their potential ability to perform the task. This type of test is frequently used in the clothing industry.

Diagnostic tests

This test involves candidates performing a task in which they have to reach a diagnosis of a particular problem. The test may be used in the motor trade when training mechanics, or for medical training.

The value of selection tests

The value of a psychometric test depends on the accuracy of its predicted validity, i.e. how accurately it measures the skills, knowledge or attributes required to successfully carry out the job. Torrington and Hall (1991) emphasise just how important this is:

> 'Tests are chosen on the basis that the test scores relate, or correlate, with subsequent job performance, so that a high test score would predict high job performance and a low test score would predict a low job performance.'

For tests to be a useful tool in the selection process, they must be:

- valid
- reliable
- administered and scored by trained personnel.

The decision-making process

The final stage is for the recruiters to make a decision about who to appoint.

The selection procedure can be a very costly exercise – it is essential that the right candidate is appointed. The decision-making process must therefore be a comprehensive assessment of the candidate. It must also be:

- *fair* – every candidate must have an equal chance in the assessment process
- *legal* – the decision-making process must adhere to employment and equal opportunities legislation
- *honest* – interviewer and assessors must give a true reflection of a candidate's performance
- *objective* – the decision to appoint or not must be made using objective criteria previously determined by the job description, person specification and test selection
- *quick* – the decisions should be made as soon as possible and the outcome communicated to the individuals concerned in a professional way.

Information upon which to base the selection decision

The amount of information available will depend on the position being filled. Four different selection scenarios are

outlined in Figure 11.11; the information which may be available for decision-making is highlighted in each case.

Job category	Decision-making information
1 Checkout operator	Application form, interview, references One or two people involved: personnel manager/line manager
2 Skilled worker/ junior manager	Application form, interview (one or two), aptitude tests, personality questionnaire, assessment centre activities, presentations, role plays, problem-solving exercises, references etc. Several people involved internally: personnel manager, line manager, senior manager. May also require assistance from an employment agency
3 Middle manager	Application form, interview (one-to-one or panel or both), aptitude tests, personality questionnaire, references. Several senior people involved internally. Possible involvement of an external employment agency
4 Senior manager	Similar to above; may use an executive search and selection agency

Figure 11.11 Decision-making information

Making the decision

Each candidate's performance should be judged against the objective criteria outlined above. This may be a relatively quick decision, as in job category 1 above, or it may be a longer process analysing how a candidate has performed in a variety of activities, as in job categories 2 and 3. In the latter example, the decision process may look like this:

- *weight* each element of the recruitment process to reflect its importance: the higher the weight, the higher the correlation with predicted job performance
- *grade* each candidate's performance in each of the activities: for example, 1 = poor performance, 5 = competent performance
- calculate each candidate's *score:* if above a certain value, the candidate is offered a job; if below, the candidate is rejected; if borderline, further discussions would need to take place between the assessors to identify particular strengths and weaknesses before a decision is made.

This decision-making process attempts to turn **qualitative** decisions into more **quantitative** decisions. Every decision must be justified. If a candidate is rejected, there must be a valid reason for this based on the assessment of the job performance criteria. Throughout every stage of the recruitment procedure, notes justifying decisions taken must be made. This is essential for two reasons:

■ a candidate who is rejected may request feedback on his or her performance
■ a candidate may claim that he or she has been unfairly treated or discriminated against.

Notes made during the selection will provide evidence about why a particular decision was made.

Figure 11.12 Possible recruitment procedure for a checkout assistant

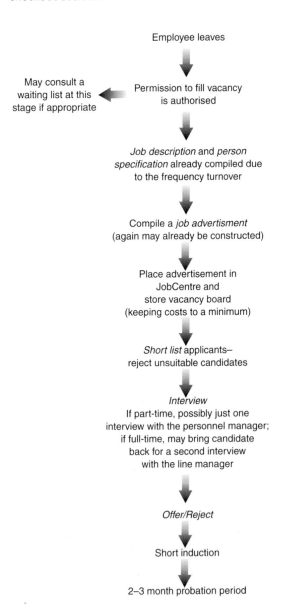

Once the selection decision has been made, it should be communicated to the candidates as soon as possible. This will usually take the form of an offer letter for the successful candidate and a rejection letter for the unsuccessful candidate. Depending upon the position being recruited, an employer may offer the unsuccessful candidate an opportunity to obtain some feedback on his or her performance.

Application of the recruitment and selection process

Now the recruitment and selection process is complete, it is interesting to see how the process might look for different categories of jobs. For example, the procedure for recruiting a checkout assistant in a large retailing organisation would be very different to appointing a senior manager for a computer software company. This can best be illustrated by looking at examples of the types of procedure that these companies might follow to fill their respective vacancies. Figure 11.12 describes a possible recruitment procedure for a checkout assistant and Figure 11.13 gives possible procedure for a senior manager.

Task

1   Suggest the most appropriate recruitment procedure for each of the scenarios outlined below. Present your ideas in the form of a flow chart.
    a   Graduate recruitment, appointing 20 general management graduates
    b   A new store opening, appointing 300 staff – management and non management – to work in a food retailing environment
    c   Appointing a senior executive to a post in a large computer software company
    d   Two vacancies for machinists, working in a textile factory.
2   In order to assist you in the successful recruitment of 20 general management graduates, you need to involve line managers from all areas of the business, e.g. marketing, accounts, production, sales, etc. How are you going to ensure consistency is maintained in the overall process and every candidate receives an equal chance?
3   Outline your plan of how you might implement this.

Figure 11.13 Possible recruitment procedure for a senior manager

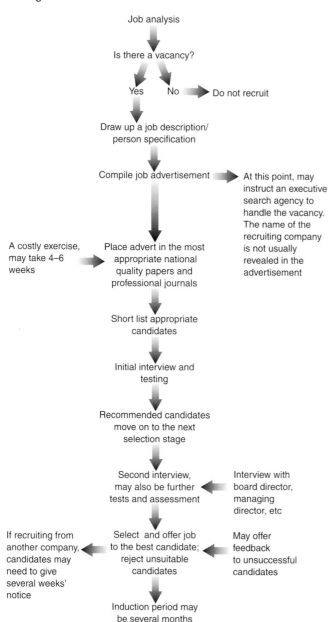

4   *You receive over 1000 application forms for the 20 graduate jobs. How are you going to make objective, fair and consistent decisions about each application to ensure you short-list the best candidates?*

Ethical and procedural issues

Organisations must ensure that their procedures abide by certain criteria. Recruitment procedures must be:

- non-discriminatory
- fair
- valid
- reliable.

Discrimination

In legal terms, discrimination means *treating a person less favourably than you would another person or group of people in the same circumstances.*

Discrimination can take two forms: direct and indirect. **Direct discrimination** can be a direct result of an act or policy, e.g. refusing to employ a woman because she has or might have children.

Indirect discrimination arises where preconditions are set which, although applicable to all groups, are such that only a small proportion of a particular group can comply with them. For example, applying a higher standard of English than is actually needed for the job would be regarded as discriminatory against certain ethnic groups.

Discrimination is discussed in more detail in Chapter 13. From a recruitment and selection point of view, employers must ensure that they do not discriminate during any part of the recruitment procedure. Key areas where discrimination is most likely to arise include:

- drawing up the job description or person specification
- advertising
- short-listing
- interviewing
- decision-making.

Task

Consider the above list of key areas where discrimination can occur in the recruitment and selection process. Discuss how discriminatory practices could occur at each stage. How would you, as an employer, guard against discriminatory practices and ensure that your procedures provide equal opportunities for all?

Fairness

Each stage of the recruitment and selection process must be fair for all candidates. In order to ensure this is the case, the following guidelines should be observed:

- All candidates for a particular appointment should be assessed using the same criteria.

- The procedure must adhere to employment and equal opportunities legislation.
- All personnel involved in the recruitment process must be properly trained to interview, administer/score tests, etc.
- Conditions for assessment must give every candidate the chance to do their best; noise and distractions must be minimised.

It is easier to control fairness where standardised conditions prevail, for example when testing. It is more difficult to monitor fairness in the more subjective areas. For example, how does an employer ensure that each candidate is given fair and equal treatment during an interview? The employer must ensure that all personnel are trained and have competent interviewing skills. Checks may be carried out periodically to ensure procedures are being conducted fairly.

Validity

This is the extent to which the interview/selection process is relevant and measures what it is supposed to measure, i.e. predicting how well a candidate will perform in a particular job. Different parts of the recruitment process are considered to be more valid than others. The validity of various methods of selection, measured by their respective correlation with job performance, was given by Ivan Robertson and Mike Smith in *Advances in Selection and Assessment*. The results can be seen in Figure 11.14.

Figure 11.14 Validity of different selection methods

Method	Validity
Interviews	0.14–0.23
References	0.17–0.26
Personality tests	0.15
Assessment centre	0.41–0.43
Structured interviews	0.54

Four methods of validation have been found to be of particular use in the selection process:

- face validity
- content validity
- concurrent validity
- predictive validity.

Cowling and Mailer, in *Managing Human Resources*, describe these methods as follows:

Face validity asks if there is an apparent relationship between what is being tested at the selection stage and the content of the job. This requires a judgement as to whether the selection device bears a suitable resemblance to the intended work. This is rarely sufficient by itself.

Content validity is a more rigorous version of face validity, involving a detailed examination of the content of the job as well as the content of the selection test.

Concurrent validity can be used with existing employees, where the level of their work performance is already known. Their performance on the test can then be correlated with their performance at work to see if a significant correspondence exists.

Predictive validity requires measurement both during selection and during subsequent work performance. A correlation between the two can then be calculated.

Task

Discuss the factors which could influence the validity of an interview.

Reliability

For the recruitment process to be reliable, it must be consistent in the results it produces each time the process is conducted. The more reliable a particular aspect of the process is, the greater the weight that can be put on that part of the process. It is of no use, however, unless there is also high validity. The following questions need to be addressed to enhance the reliability of the interview:

- Are all candidates being interviewed for the same appointment asked the same questions?
- Are personnel properly trained?
- Was the interview conducted in a professional manner, free from distractions?
- Was the interview consistent for all candidates?
- How many interviews were conducted?
- Was the interviewer tired?
- Do all assessors have the same interpretation of the selection grading criteria?

The three most common methods of testing reliability are:

- test–retest method
- split halves method
- equivalent form method.

Again Cowling and Mailer provide us with a workable definition of these methods.

Test–retest method gives groups of subjects the same test again after a time interval, and the results are compared.

Split halves method divides the test into halves; scores gained in one half are compared with scores gained in the other half.

Equivalent form method administers two different but equivalent forms of the test, and the scores are compared.

Overall, the recruitment and selection procedure should be well researched, workable and regularly updated and evaluated.

The cost of recruitment

As previously discussed, recruitment and selection can be a very costly exercise, especially if the appointed candidate leaves soon after joining the organisation, or proves to be incompetent or not suitable for the job. If this is the outcome, the organisation may have to go through the whole process again.

The cost of recruitment can be broken down into development, human resource, administration and other costs.

Development costs
- drawing up the job description and person specification
- compiling a job advertisement
- designing assessment centres and suitable activities for assessment
- researching appropriate test materials
- developing company recruitment materials.

Human resource costs
- conducting job analysis
- short-listing
- interviewing, assessing and decision-making may require line managers or senior managers to be involved.

Administration costs
- arranging interviews, accommodation, co-ordinating the process
- travelling and accommodation expenses
- cost of test materials.

Other costs
- employment agency fees
- attending recruitment fairs.

All costs involved in the process should be monitored on a regular basis as part of the recruitment and selection evaluation process.

Evaluation of recruitment and selection methods

Many organisations now realise that their human resource is the most valuable resource they possess. It is important, therefore, that the procedure and methods used to introduce people into the organisation are regularly evaluated. The process of evaluation should ensure that:

- the most effective methods are used to select the most appropriate person/people for the job
- financial, time, and human resources invested in the process are justified, i.e. well-motivated recruits are appointed who make long and valuable contributions to the organisation's effectiveness
- the process is accurate, appropriate, cost-effective, convenient, acceptable, up to date, legal and fair.

Task

1 *What questions should an employer address to evaluate the recruitment and selection procedures?*
2 *Compile a cost-benefit analysis of the various stages of the recruitment process for a computer software company facing strong competition for specialist labour.*

Further reading

- *Personnel Management: A New Approach,* 2nd edition, by D. Torrington and L. Hall. Prentice Hall, 1991.
- *Managing Human Resources* by A. Cowling and C. Mailer. Edward Arnold, 1990.
- *Management and Organisational Behaviour,* 3rd edition, by L. J. Mullins. Pitman Publishing, 1993.
- *Principles of Human Resource Management,* by David Goss. Routledge, 1994.
- *Management,* by Kathryn M. Bartol and David C. Martin. McGraw Hill, 1991.
- *Advances in Selection and Assessment,* edited by M. Smith and I. Robertson. John Wiley, 1989.

On completion of this chapter, students should be able to:

- describe the content of an induction programme

- identify various methods of delivering induction programmes and analyse the effectiveness of these methods.

- evaluate different approaches to induction training, commenting on how each approach meets the needs of inductees

- identify the main costs involved in developing, implementing and evaluating induction programmes.

Induction of new staff

Chapter 11 focused on just how important it is to ensure that the right people are recruited into the organisation. Perhaps more fundamentally, having made such an investment it is important that the 'right' recruit does not decide to leave after a few weeks because they are unhappy/dissatisfied with their new role. The higher the turnover of labour, the more recruitment costs will be pushed up. This chapter focuses on these issues and many others related to the induction of new staff. In particular, the chapter analyses the content of induction. A well-thought-out, planned approach to welcoming and developing new employees will enable both the employer and the employee to reap the rewards of an effective working relationship very early on.

Recruiting people into an organisation is an investment for the future. As with any other investment the organisation makes, employers will be keen to ensure that new employees perform and generate the required return on their investment. The induction process can be seen as the first stage of the employees' development, to enable them to contribute to the organisation quickly and remain enthusiastic about their jobs.

What is induction?

Induction is the process of introducing new employees into the workplace, making them feel a valued part of the organisation, ensuring that they are motivated and start making a contribution as soon as possible. It is useful to look at why induction is important from both an employee's perspective and an employer's perspective.

Importance to the employees:

- to make them feel valued and help them settle in
- to give them the information they need about the company
- to give them the information they need to do their jobs
- to enable them to meet colleagues with whom they will be working
- to allay any fears they may have about starting a new job

- to answer any questions they may have about the organisation or the job.

Importance to the employer:

- to integrate new employees successfully into the organisation and so minimise the risk that they will leave
- to ensure new employees perform better in their job as a result of going through a carefully constructed induction programme
- to ensure new employees remain enthusiastic about their jobs.

Induction can be thought of as a process rather than a course or a programme and, as such, it forms part of the employment cycle. This cycle identifies the four key stages that employees might experience during their employment (see Figure 12.1).

As induction is such a fundamental ingredient in the employment cycle, it is important that the objectives are considered carefully.

The objectives of induction

The objectives of induction are:

- to establish a constructive and positive working relationships between the employer and the employee
- to communicate commitment to the new employee
- to produce well-informed, positive and well-motivated employees who are aware of the company's objectives and motivations.

Alan Fowler, in his book *Employee Induction,* summarises the benefits to be gained from a well-planned induction programme:

'Care and attention to induction will secure the same high levels of productivity and efficiency among new

employees as planned installation and preventative maintenance can achieve for new machinery and equipment … The ultimate reward, apart from direct improvements in the organisation's efficiency and competitiveness, is that the contribution that competent and highly motivated employees can make increases as years go by – unlike equipment, which begins to deteriorate from the first day it operates.'

Charles Handy, in his book *The Empty Raincoat,* describes a model he calls the **doughnut principle.** Handy uses a conceptual inside-out American ring doughnut where the hole is on the outside and the dough is in the middle. The dough is the core and the ring that surrounds it is bounded space.

Figure 12.2   Charles Handy's doughnut principle applied to the induction process

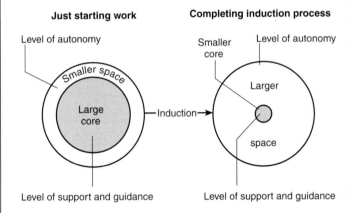

By applying this to the induction process, the level of support and guidance a new recruit needs could be considered to be the core of the doughnut, and the level of autonomy given to the individual would form the space around the core. At the beginning of the induction process, the core would be large and the space around would be small. As the new employee becomes orientated, settled and proficient at the job, the core shrinks and the space (i.e. the level of autonomy) increases. The new employee is now much more confident and can be left to work on his or her own.

This principle, illustrated in Figure 12.2, would best describe the experience of a school leaver or graduate who is experiencing work for the first time. Equally, however, the principle could apply to employees who are changing jobs. In this case the induction process may be quicker, but employees will still go through a similar transition.

Figure 12.1   The employment cycle

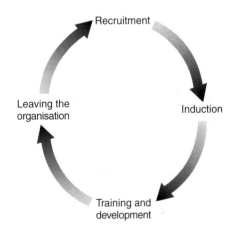

Content and delivery of an induction programme

The main part of this chapter focuses on the content and delivery of the induction process. For each part of the programme, the objectives, content and method of delivery are discussed. The reader must appreciate that the content lists are only examples – they are not definitive. The process and content of induction programmes will vary considerably between organisations depending on time, resources, experience of induction and belief in the effectiveness of the process.

There is a trend for moving away from the more traditional 'chalk and talk' approaches to induction and moving towards more **interactive, employee-centred** approaches. Paul Davis of the Industrial Society recently stated that:

> *'Best practice organisations are characterised by the variety of their induction training methods. Good programmes are challenging and "learner driven", the employees are given real responsibility for their own progress – albeit in a supportive environment.'*

Trainees will probably learn much more if they are involved in the induction process. This must therefore be considered when planning the process. Although it may be more time-consuming to develop a learner-driven programme, the benefits will almost certainly outweigh the costs in the long-term.

Organisational background

Objective
To stimulate an awareness of the history and the culture of the organisation.

Content
- Organisations are very proud of their heritage, proud of how the organisation has grown. It is important for new employees to have an understanding of the company's history so that they can begin to understand the values and beliefs of the organisation. Discussing the historical development will also give new recruits an opportunity to begin to understand and appreciate the culture of the business so that they too can feel proud that they belong to such an organisation.
- It may also be appropriate to introduce and discuss the company's mission statement.
- Many organisations today are experiencing a great deal of change. If appropriate, it may be worthwhile discussing how the organisation is managing this process, to reassure inductees.

Delivery
- company video/slides
- presentation
- facts and figures given to inductees to read for themselves
- Interactive video, where inductees work through a self-study package finding out about the history of the organisation for themselves.

Development/organisational overview

Objective
To provide new recruits with an overview of how the organisation has developed up to the present day, and to discuss the future strategies of the organisation.

Content
- overall structure of the organisation and how this has developed and changed over time
- role of functions and departments across head office, area/regional offices, etc.
- UK structure and international perspective if appropriate
- further discussion of the mission statement and supporting objectives; how the organisation achieves its objectives
- numbers of people employed by the organisation
- annual turnover
- a discussion of important policies and procedures, e.g. health and safety, equal opportunities and customer care
- particular legislation affecting the business
- general information about the business, e.g. competitors and where the organisation fits into its industrial sector

Delivery
- presentation by senior management
- self-study pack: employees read about the company development and answer questions to test their understanding as they go along; their progress can then be checked by a trainer or mentor
- computer-based training if appropriate

Note
Self-study packs and workbooks can be an effective learning medium. To be successful, however, they need to be:

- well produced and readable
- supported by supervisors, mentors or managers
- properly introduced and explained
- acceptable to the users.

Management and activity

Objective

To give new employees an insight into the management structure and style, and to discuss the activities undertaken by the organisation.

Content

- a discussion of the management/supervisory structure: who reports to whom
- an opportunity to meet their immediate supervisor/manager
- an opportunity to spend some time with their supervisor/manager to discuss expectations, targets, etc.
- a discussion about the department and how their job fits into the structure of the department and the organisation
- an overview of the management style adopted by the company
- more in-depth insight into the function of different departments and the activities undertaken; how different departments work together
- the role of the trade union/staff association if appropriate.

Delivery

- This section of the induction programme could be introduced by a senior member of management.
- The best way for new recruits to gain an appreciation of these issues would be for them to spend some time working in different departments, maybe undertaking mini projects. The amount of time spent in each department would obviously be determined by the length of time set aside for the induction programme.
- Computer simulations may be used for inductees to experience the pressures and problems of working in different areas of the business.

Note

If new recruits complete project work as part of the programme, they must be given an opportunity to feed back their findings to their trainer, mentor or senior manager.

Products/service

Objective

To give new employees an overview of the products produced or service provided by the organisation.

Content

The emphasis placed on this section will depend where the employee is working in the organisation. For example, a production operative and a sales person would have different requirements in terms of the information they would need to know about the products/services of the business. These may include:

- production process
- product portfolio
- product development
- product life-cycles
- competition
- buying raw materials
- distribution.

Delivery

- presentation
- factory tour giving an overview of the whole production process
- visiting other organisational sites if appropriate
- spending time in specialist departments, e.g. product development, marketing, buying sales, etc. Work shadowing or undertaking project work

Example

In *Personnel Today*, a recent article focusing on induction training discussed how The Body Shop's induction programme actually gives new entrants an opportunity to experiment with making a new product, which involves time spent in both the marketing department and the research and development laboratories.

Markets

Objective
To give new recruits a useful insight into the market in which the business operates and an opportunity to consider the external pressures facing the organisation.

Content
- an explanation of the organisation's main competitors
- a discussion of the organisation's share of the market: how the market share has changed; where the company is placed in relation to its competitors; strategies to maintain/increase market share; and the potential value of the market
- focus on European and international markets if appropriate.

Delivery
- presentation
- interactive video
- books
- company reports
- project work
- group presentation.

Personnel policies and procedures, and terms and conditions of employment

Objective
To discuss the importance and content of personnel policies and procedures and how they impact on the employee's job, highlighting the responsibility of the employee. To ensure new employees understand all the terms and conditions associated with their job and their working environment.

Content
- equal opportunities policy – discuss the organisation's commitment to equal opportunities and the standards of behaviour expected
- health and safety – an explanation of both the employer's and the employees' responsibilities
- remuneration – an explanation of how the pay policy operates; discuss issues such as performance related-pay, and salary structures
- training and development – a discussion of the organisation's commitment to employees' development, appraisals, training courses, promotion policy, professional development, etc.
- discipline – a discussion of the procedure, highlighting employer's and employees' rights and responsibilities
- grievance – as for discipline
- hours of work

- holiday entitlement
- sickness absence
- uniform/dress code
- pension scheme.

Delivery
- company handbook
- discussion workshops
- study packs
- videos.

Welfare benefits and services

Objective
To ensure new employees have an understanding of all the benefits which the employer can offer and know what they need in order to qualify for these benefits, e.g. length of service.

Content
Depending on the nature of the organisation, this part of the programme could be split into several sections:

Fitness benefits/services:
- gymnasium facilities
- swimming pool
- an explanation of any team sports the organisation may take part in.

Recreational benefits:
- social club
- hairdressing service.

Health and welfare benefits:
- staff canteen – subsidised food and drink
- health checks
- chiropody service
- welfare counselling/stress counselling
- occupational health service.

Financial benefits:
- subsidised travel
- company car schemes
- mortgage assistance
- discount schemes
- share option schemes
- saving schemes.

Educational benefits:
- organisation library
- computer-based training
- provision for education and training, sponsorship schemes for furthering education, learning credits.

Delivery

- booklet covering all the benefits and services
- self-study pack, finding out about all the services
- presentation.

Physical facilities

Objective

To familiarise new employees with the physical layout of the organisation. The length of time devoted to this part of the induction process will depend on the size of the organisation.

Content

Facilities which should be pointed out to new employees on their first day:

- toilets
- canteen
- own office/working area
- personnel department
- emergency exits/fire assembly points
- location of fire extinguishers and first-aid boxes
- vending machines if appropriate
- designated smoking areas if appropriate.

Other facilities:

- security
- location of specific departments/specific people
- telephone for employee use
- internal and external mail procedures if appropriate
- social facilities
- library
- wages and salaries department
- photocopiers/reprographics department.

The content will depend on who is being inducted, where they are going to work and the nature and size of the organisation.

Delivery

- tour around the organisation
- map.

Job role

Objective

To discuss in detail the specific role which new employees will play in the organisation, and to explain how their jobs fit into their departments and the whole organisation.

Content

- a breakdown of the key tasks and duties described in the job description
- a discussion of how the inductees will be making a contribution to the organisation; it may be appropriate at this stage to review the company mission statement and objectives
- setting objectives
- training required
- personal and professional development
- the process of reviewing performance
- a detailed look at the departments and where they will fit in, together with an organisational view of their roles.
- a chance to meet everyone in their department/section/team, including their mentors if appropriate.

Delivery

- informal one-to-one chat with immediate supervisor/manager
- if a group of new employees are being inducted, it may be more appropriate to conduct a presentation for some aspects of this section.

Note

Although the process of one-to-one delivery is time-consuming, there may be significant benefits in terms of proving to new employees just how valued they are by the company.

Rules and safety measures

Objective

To ensure new employees have a competent knowledge and understanding of the key rules and safety measures associated with their jobs, work areas and organisation. To ensure that they and their work colleagues operate in a safe environment.

Content
- detailed discussion of the health and safety policy, outlining both the employer's responsibilities and the employees' responsibilities
- discussion about emergency procedures, fire, evacuation procedure, assembly points, bomb threats, etc.
- introduction to first aiders
- location of first-aid boxes
- instruction on basic emergency first aid (this would probably depend on where the new recruit was working)
- protective clothing
- Control of Substances Hazardous to Health (COSHH) if appropriate
- safety training, e.g. employees must be over the age of 18 to use certain machinery
- manual handling
- safety rules, smoking and no smoking areas
- accident reporting procedures.

Delivery
- company handbook
- training videos
- training courses
- presentation by occupational health
- self-study pack
- on-the-job training, e.g. demonstrating the importance of goggles, ear defenders, safety guards on machinery, protective clothing and machine maintenance.

Note
Information regarding health and safety is a legal requirement. It is essential that new recruits receive information regarding health and safety as soon as possible. The policy may be issued on day one or prior to employment commencing.

Programme summary

The content of the above programme is comprehensive, but the reader must appreciate that not every organisation will deliver induction on such a scale. In some organisations, induction may be seen as an unnecessary luxury. What is essential, however, is that employers tailor their induction process to meet both the organisation's and the individual's needs, in terms of both content and timing.

Task

You are a recently recruited personnel officer working for a large manufacturing organisation which produces electronic typewriters. One of the reasons you have been brought in to work for the organisation is to try to reduce labour turnover. When you start to inspect the figures, you find that labour turnover is highest among new recruits, particularly at the operator level. You have read their exit interview notes and notice that a large number of leavers commented on the fact that they 'did not feel welcome at work' and felt that they had been 'thrown in at the deep end'. You also notice that this category of staff has the highest occurrence of first-stage disciplinary interviews in the factory. The majority of warnings seem to have been issued for failing to observe health and safety procedures or personnel policies and procedures. It comes as no surprise to you that there is not an induction programme set up for these staff.

You feel that in order to try to reduce labour turnover it is necessary to introduce an induction programme which would be suitable for operators. Your boss, the factory manager, has been with the company for 25 years and sees any training as a waste of time.

1 *Why do you think it is necessary to introduce an induction programme?*
2 *How would you structure the programme?*
3 *Who would be involved in designing, delivering and reviewing the programme?*
4 *How would you convince your boss that induction training would be beneficial to the organisation?*

Supervisor/mentor

The supervisor and mentor play critical roles in the induction process, ensuring that new employees settle into the organisation and feel motivated and committed to their jobs and to the organisation so that they are ready to make a valued contribution as early as possible. Their roles extend beyond the induction process **supporting** and **guiding** employees throughout their employment as required.

The two roles can be considered to be quite separate. The next section outlines their individual contributions.

The supervisor

The supervisor is the employee's immediate line manager. They are usually the first point of contact for sorting out work problems both on a departmental level and sometimes on a personal level. They issue instructions to their staff and deal with any potential disciplinary situations.

The mentor

Michael Meighan, in his book entitled *How to Design and Deliver Induction Training Programmes*, defines mentoring as:

> '*a support system wherein staff new to the organisation, new to a department, new to the job or involved in radical change are assisted in coping with the changes through the support of objective and independent third parties.*'

The role played by the mentor can range from being very informal to a more structured formal approach (see Figure 12.3). The role would tend to diminish as the new recruit settled into the organisation. An employee can benefit from having a mentor throughout the employment process, for example when changing departments, while studying, or after promotion (see Figure 12.4).

Figure 12.3 The different mentoring styles viewed as a continuum

Very formal approach, sounding board, advising

Structured formal approach, more directive, assessing and directing

Mentors must possess certain skills and ideally be supported and developed through training. They must be effective **listeners**. Careful consideration must be given when choosing which mentor will support a new employee. They must be compatible, otherwise the relationship will break down. Ideally, the mentor should be someone who is **objective**, an independent third party. Mentors do not have to be from the same functional area or background as the employee; in fact, there can be distinct advantages if they are not. They must, however, be experienced within the organisation.

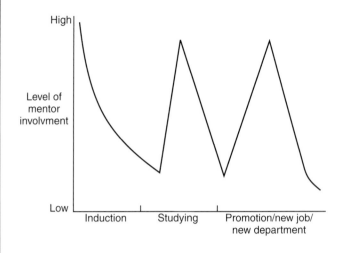

Figure 12.4 An employee's need for a mentor varies throughout the employment cycle

Task

1 *Discuss the skills that you think a mentor should possess.*
2 *Brainstorm the issues that a mentor may have to face when mentoring a graduate trainee.*
3 *Do you think the issues discussed with a mentor should be confidential? What would be the implications of your decision?*

Mentoring and cultural integration

New recruits face many challenges when they join an organisation. The mentor can therefore be a key figure in helping them to cope with these challenges. One important challenge will be trying to understand the culture of an organisation. Due to their experience and training, mentors can play a vital role in helping new recruits to adapt.

Johnson and Scholes talk about the 'cultural web' of organisations (see Figure 12.5), and it is really the key components of this web that new recruits need to become familiar with. The components of Johnson and Scholes' cultural web, given in *Exploring Corporate Strategy*, are identified below:

- The *routine* ways that members of the organisation behave towards each other, and that link different parts of the organisation, comprise 'the way we do things around here'.
- The *rituals* of organisational life, such as training programmes, promotion, and assessment, point to what is important in the organisation, reinforce 'the

Figure 12.5 Johnson and Scholes' cultural web

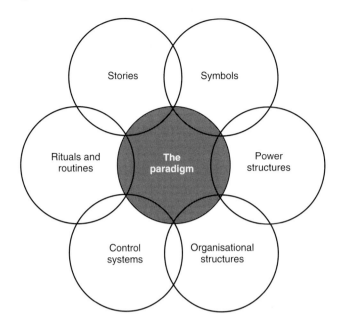

way we do things around here' and signal what is especially valued.

- The *stories* told by members of the organisation to each other, and to outsiders, to new recruits embed the present in its organisational history and flag up important events and personalities, as well as mavericks who 'deviate from the norm'.
- The more *symbolic* aspects of organisations, such as logos, offices, cars and titles, or the type of language and terminology commonly used, become a short-hand representation of the nature of the organisation.
- The *control systems*, measurements and reward systems emphasise what is important in the organisation and focus attention and activity.
- *Power structures* – the most powerful managerial groupings in the organisation are likely to be the ones most associated with core assumptions and beliefs about what is important.
- The *formal organisational structure,* or the more informal ways in which the organisations work, are likely to reflect power structures and, again, delineate important relationships and emphasise what is important in the organisation.

Communication systems

Communication systems, too, can be complex in organisations. It may take new recruits quite a while to identify who the key people are that they need to communicate with in order to assist them in their role. It is important that new employees understand their

organisation's communication systems to avoid upsetting key personnel. Take, for example, the distribution order for a memo. In some organisations there may be a strict sequence in which the names should appear, e.g. the most senior first, or alphabetically. If an employee fails to appreciate how important this is and randomly selects the order, he or she could cause considerable upset among certain members of staff. Other sensitive issues may include: consulting appropriate staff when making particular decisions and approaching appropriate staff to authorise particular instructions.

From an organisational point of view, the communication systems in place must allow new recruits to feel able to contribute their ideas early on and for these ideas to be taken seriously. One of the reasons for recruiting new staff, especially from external sources, is to bring 'new blood' into the organisation. If their ideas and initiatives are not welcomed, they may be less inclined to stay with the company.

New recruits will want to build up effective working relationships as soon as possible. The people who will be most important to them in the early days are their supervisor, mentor and work colleagues. They will also be anxious to impress their departmental manager. In addition to these pressures, new recruits will be trying to adapt to and absorb the culture of the new environment, as well as trying to bring their ideas, opinions and attitude to bear upon the organisation. The communication and cultural challenges facing new employees are summarised in Figure 12.6.

Figure 12.6 The communication and cultural challenges facing new employees

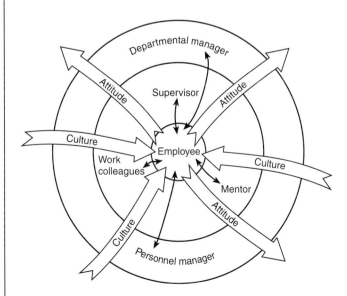

Task

1 *Discuss how each of the following should be involved in the induction process:*
   a *personnel manager*
   b *supervisor*
   c *departmental manager*
   d *managing director.*
2 *Discuss who you think should be responsible for the induction process*
3 *Discuss the consequences of a poorly organised induction programme on both the employer and the employee.*

Process of induction

The next part of the chapter focuses on the process of induction, discussing the factors which need to be addressed in order to ensure that the experience is a success for both the employer and the employee.

Duration

The duration of induction can vary greatly depending on the organisation and its perception of the value and worth of the process. The duration can also vary depending on the type, level and number of staff being inducted. What is most important, however, is that the personnel designing the induction process fully understand the needs of new employees in adjusting to their environment, and the needs of the employer in ensuring that they start making a positive contribution as early as possible.

The duration of the programme will be dependent upon who is being inducted. There are many different categories of employee, for example:

- employees starting work for the first time, e.g. school leavers or graduates
- employees re-entering after a career break
- employees retraining in a new department or a new job
- core workers
- periphery workers.

Each of these categories will have very different needs. It is essential that the employer recognises and meets these needs in order to ensure that the induction process is a positive and worthwhile experience. A poor induction programme can very often lead to demotivated employees.

Task

Discuss the contribution that you think each of the following motivational theories can make to the induction process:

- Maslow's hierarchy of needs
- Herzberg's hygiene factors
- Douglas McGregor's theory X and theory Y.

You will need to refer to Chapter 3 for information on these theories.

Staged induction

In order to ensure that the induction process is a success, the employer should consider the needs of the inductees in terms of both the **content** and the **timing** – when it is most appropriate for the new recruit to experience each part of the process. Paul Davis, in his book *Staff Induction: A Practical Guide*, comments on how important it is to give inductees information a little at a time:

> *'Learning and retention of information by inductees will be improved if induction is not crammed into the very early stages of the programme.'*

Michael Meighan believes the induction process starts before the new recruit even joins the organisation. In *How to Design and Deliver Induction Training Programmes*, he offers a model of how an induction programme may be split up into different stages. Figure 12.7 outlines this model.

Another approach offered by Michael Meighan is to split the induction process up into different levels of information that the new recruit needs. This process falls into three stages:

Figure 12.7 Model of an induction plan (schematic)

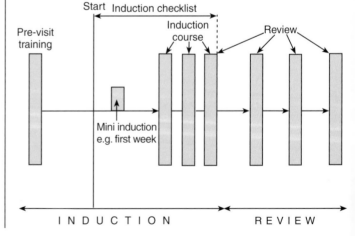

Figure 12.8 The must, should and could know approach to induction

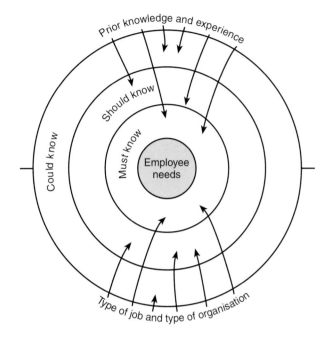

- what the new recruit must know
- what the new recruit should know
- what the new recruit could know.

The information given at each stage would be based on the type of job, the organisation and the new recruit's prior knowledge and experience. Figure 12.8 summarises this approach.

Facilities

Organisations have different training facilities, ranging from purpose-built, conference-style training rooms, fully equipped with televisions, videos, computer-based training facilities and interactive video, to just one room possibly equipped with a television and video. It should be possible for the first organisation to offer more variety due to the extended range of facilities available. However, it does not follow that the organisation using the most facilities will design the best induction course. The key factor is that the employees are at the centre of the learning process and the course is designed to meet their needs – their needs in the job and their organisational needs. The training facilities do not need to be elaborate to achieve this objective, just appropriate and effective.

In some organisations the induction process can be high profile and glossy. In some cases this is deliberate, for example when induction courses are all held at the company's head office. While not all employees attending

the course would necessarily work at the head office, the induction course gives them an opportunity to see what goes on in the head office environment and to meet some of the people who work there.

The focus, wherever the course is held, should be on the individual and not on the logistics of designing and implementing the course. The danger is that the induction will emphasise the process rather than the outcomes and not really address the needs of the new recruits. If this is the case, the induction process will have failed. The new recruits might have been impressed by the elaborate course setting, but could leave the course unclear about what they have actually achieved and whether they know any more about the organisation or their role within it.

As with any training course, the organisation must itself be receptive and supportive to enable the new recruits to put into practice what they have learned. The inductees must be able to transfer their learning to the workplace.

The induction course must honestly reflect how things are done in the workplace. New employees must not be given an unrealistic picture of what the organisation is. This not only would hamper their progress, but also could give them a poor impression of those who delivered the course and the organisation itself. The more realistic the process, the quicker the new employees will settle in, and the more motivated they will be to do a good job.

Evaluating the process

In order to assess how effective the induction process has been, time must be spent gaining feedback and reviewing the programme with the parties involved.

Feedback

The purpose of the feedback in this case would be to find out the new employees' impression of the induction process prior to their return to the workplace, in terms of:

- content
- delivery
- administration
- timing
- facilities
- appropriateness
- usefulness.

There are several methods of collecting feedback, including discussion and questionnaires. This information can be used to evaluate and improve the process.

Review

At the end of the process, or at the end of each stage where the induction is in stages, a review should be conducted. The review normally takes place at the workplace with the new employees' line manager. The purpose of the review is to look back on the induction process and to assess its success. The results of the review and the feedback should be used to evaluate the whole process of induction so that continuous improvements can be made.

The employees' role in the review is to:

- discuss what they have learned during the process
- discuss how they feel this will help them in their new role
- review how successfully their needs have been met
- discuss any improvements they feel could be made to the process.

The line manager's role in the review is to:

- discuss with the new employees how they will be able to transfer their learning to their job
- assess any outstanding development needs and identify further training needs
- discuss how these needs will be met and set a timescale for meeting them.

Planned training

Obtaining feedback, reviewing and evaluating the process form the starting point for improving the process for the next new recruits. The induction process can therefore be viewed as planned training. Kenney and Reid describe planned training as:

'a deliberate intervention aimed at achieving the learning necessary for improved job performance. Planned training can be defined as the process involved in:
– deciding whether training can help to resolve or prevent a problem, and if so determining whether training is the most cost effective approach;
– identifying what learning is needed and setting learning objectives;
– deciding which training strategy or strategies to adopt and planning appropriate training programmes and arrangements to meet this need.'

Figure 12.9 summarises the planned training process as outlined by Kenney and Reid in *Training Interventions.*

Cost

Finally, employers will be interested in the cost of induction, and in balancing this against the benefits.

Figure 12.9 Planned training

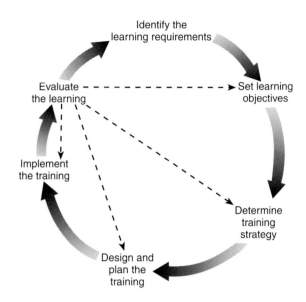

The key issue here is how to calculate the cost of the induction process. In a recent survey of 1003 managers, the Industrial Society found that 'more than one in four respondents were unable to give a cost. Of those that did, the average figure was £474 per employee.'

What should be included in the cost? The following lists detail some items which might be included:

Physical resources

- hiring training rooms if facilities are not available on site
- making company specific videos or buying training videos for generic parts of the induction process, e.g. health and safety
- designing and printing company handbooks and welcome/induction packs
- providing refreshments.

Human resources

- inviting guest speakers into the organisation, or from the organisation itself, to talk to new recruits about specific aspects of the induction process
- cost of employee's time spent away from the normal work station to attend the induction course
- cost of paying new employees a full salary when they are not contributing 100 per cent to the business.

Note

In some organisations, employees are put on to a training rate until they are fully competent in their role; when they are judged competent, they will be paid the full rate for the job.

Task

Refer back to the task on page 165. Construct a cost-benefit analysis of introducing an induction programme for operators at this manufacturing organisation.

Further reading

- *How to Design and Deliver Induction Training Programmes* by Michael Meighan. Kogan Page, 1995.
- *Staff Induction: A Practical Guide,* by Paul Davis. The Industrial Society, 1994.
- *Employee Induction: a Good Start,* 3rd edition, by Alan Fowler. Institute of Personnel and Development, 1996.
- *Exploring Corporate Strategy,* 3rd edition, by Gerry Johnson and Kevan Scholes. Prentice Hall, 1993.
- *Training Interventions,* 2nd edition, by John Kenney and Margaret Reid. Institute of Personnel Management, 1990.

13 Contracts of employment and contractual changes

On completion of this chapter, students should be able to:

- understand the rights and obligations of individuals in organisations
- understand the importance of the contract of employment and the contractual obligations of employers and employees
- know the information and procedures relating to dismissal
- understand and evaluate equal opportunities rules and laws
- understand and analyse how discrimination may take place, and the implications of discrimination in the workplace
- analyse different situations involving discrimination
- understand the rights of minority groups in the employment situation.

Rights and obligations of employees

Many people will spend a large proportion of their life at work. People work for a variety of reasons, but their main motive is usually economic, to obtain the resources to meet their physiological needs and to support a family. It is important that they know what is expected of them as an employee (their obligations) and, indeed, what they can expect in turn from their work organisations (their rights).

Obligations:

- punctuality
- good attendance
- safe working practices
- not to discriminate
- to produce conscientious work
- to produce work of a good standard
- to maintain skills

Rights:

- job security
- contract of employment
- safe working environment
- not to be discriminated against
- equality of opportunity
- reasonable pay

Many of these rights and obligations are laid down in law. It is therefore essential that those responsible for human resource management in an organisation are fully aware of their obligations to employees under the law.

The contract of employment

As soon as a person agrees to work for an employer and the employer agrees to pay wages, a contract exists. The Employment Protection (Consolidation) Act 1978 requires an employer to give all employees, working for 16 or more hours per week, written details of their main terms of service.

The written statement does not bring a contract of employment into being; once the employer makes an offer of employment to an individual and this is accepted, a contract is in existence. The details of the contract are known as the terms and conditions, and an employer must give each employee a written statement setting out the main particulars of the employment within 13 weeks of the date of engagement.

The object of the written statement is to give employees a clear understanding of their rights and obligations under their contract of employment and it must cover the following points:

- title and grade of job
- the date when employment began
- the minimum period of notice of termination of employment required by both parties
- the rate of pay and methods of calculating it
- the interval at which earnings are to be paid (i.e. weekly or monthly)
- hours of work and holiday entitlement
- details of payment when away from work through illness (sick pay)
- details of pension scheme provision
- details of the procedure if a grievance arises
- details of disciplinary rules
- arrangements for the termination of employment.

Many rights depend upon an employee's period of continuous employment with an employer. These include things like the minimum statutory notice, written particulars of employment, unfair dismissal, probation, redundancy pay and maternity rights. In order to qualify for rights in relation to these areas, an employee has to have worked for an employer for a minimum period of time.

Task

John Hill applied for the one-year post of Business Studies Lecturer at a college in the East Midlands. At the end of a day of interviews, he was informed that he was the successful candidate for the post and would shortly receive his contract of employment. He was supplied with details of his starting salary. However, the next day John was disappointed to receive a telephone call from the Principal. The Principal was highly apologetic, explaining that he had done his sums wrong and that it was now clear the college did not have enough money to employ John and therefore they could not offer him a contract of employment. Discuss what John's rights would have been in this case.

Unfair dismissal

In 1971, a new employment law gave employees the legal right not to be unfairly dismissed from their job. Prior to this, organisations had been able to hire and fire people as and when they needed to. This situation, of course, meant that individual employees had limited security in their jobs.

Under the Employment Protection (Consolidation) Act 1978, the law now states that employees have a right not to be unfairly dismissed and that those who think they have been may seek a remedy by taking a complaint to an industrial tribunal.

Dismissal: information and procedures

Employees are treated as dismissed if:

- their contract of employment is terminated with or without notice
- a fixed-term contract expires without being renewed
- they leave their employment due to their employer's conduct, such that they are justified in terminating their employment without notice (**constructive dismissal**).

Under the Employment Protection (Consolidation) Act 1978, only those employees who have been continuously employed for 16 or more hours per week for two years or more, or part-timers working between 8 and 16 hours per week for five years or more, can claim unfair dismissal. The extra limitation on part-timers' rights was amended by the Employment Protection (Part-time Employees) Regulations 1995. This was after a House of Lords ruling that the limitation on part-timers was not compatible with the European Union Equal Treatment Directive; as most part-timers are women, they suffered disproportionately from the limitation.

If an employee is entitled to make a claim for unfair dismissal, it must be lodged with an industrial tribunal within three months. The employer must then prove that the employee was dismissed for one of the potentially fair reasons laid down in law. These reasons are set out below:

1 *Capability or qualifications for the work which the employee must do.* This covers employee incompetence, short and long-term sickness, and lack of qualifications to do the job.
2 *Conduct.* A wide range of misconduct has been said to justify dismissal. If an offence entails gross misconduct, then dismissal can take place without notice.
3 *Redundancy.* Here the law is concerned with whether the employer acted reasonably in selecting employees for redundancy.

4 *Situations where continued employment of a worker would be illegal.* For example a driver who is disqualified from driving could be fairly dismissed.
5 *Some other substantial reason.* This covers justifiable reasons which do not come under the above categories.

As a guide to fairness in determining claims of unfair dismissal, the tribunal will use *Disciplinary Practices and Procedures in Employment* the code of practice issued by the Advisory, Conciliation and Arbitration Service (ACAS). The code of practice suggests that:

- individuals should be informed of the complaints against them
- the employee should be given the opportunity to state his or her case
- individuals should have the right to be accompanied by a trade union representative or a fellow employee when interviewed by management;
- for minor offences, an employee should be given a formal oral warning or a written warning, making it clear that the warning is the first formal stage of the procedure
- further misconduct warrants a final written warning, prior to suspension or dismissal; a written statement of the reasons for dismissal should also be given.

Failure to adhere to this code is likely to make it difficult for the employer to argue that he or she acted fairly.

Employees who successfully bring a claim of unfair dismissal against their employers are entitled to:

- *Reinstatement.* The employer must treat the employee as if the employment had not been terminated. Tribunals rarely order reinstatement because this would often result in difficult situations arising; they take into account the employee's wishes and the practicalities involved.
- *Re-engagement.* In this case the employee must be re-employed, but not necessarily in the same job.
- *Compensation.* This is awarded if an employer is not ordered to re-employ the dismissed employee or if such an order is ignored. The basic award is the equivalent of a redundancy payment award. A compensatory award is based on an assessment of the employee's loss arising out of dismissal, e.g. loss of earnings, loss of expected wage increases and increments, loss of pension rights, and the expense of looking for a new job.

If an employer has failed to comply with an order to re-employ an employee, an additional award may be given. Such awards may be reduced if the tribunal believes that the employee's conduct contributed to his or her dismissal.

Automatic unfair dismissals

In three situations, a tribunal will always find a dismissal unfair. These are:

- unfair selection for redundancy
- dismissal of a woman for pregnancy
- dismissal for union membership or activities or lack of union membership.

Equal opportunities

In its Code of Professional Conduct, the Institute of Personnel Management (IPM) lists equal opportunities as one of the principles of behaviour for personnel practitioners. The institute has produced statements and guidelines on discrimination and equal opportunities since 1969. It recognises that as well as being unlawful, discrimination in employment results in the misuse and/or waste of human resources.

Organisations should address the whole area of relationships between employees and employers and managers through their equal opportunities policy. Such a policy should state the organisation's commitment to give equal opportunities to all, irrespective of race, colour, sex, disability or marital status. There should also be an indication of how the organisation seeks to avoid discrimination in the various processes of recruitment, selection, progression and training etc.

The management team of an organisation has the responsibility to implement and publicise equal opportunities policies, to train and issue guidelines and to ensure that policies are being carried out.

Statutory provisions are designed to regulate discrimination in a number of areas (see Figure 13.1).

Discrimination

Under the Sex Discrimination Act 1975 and the Race Relations Act 1976, discrimination in employment is illegal. This affects the processes and procedures adopted in the recruitment process. These two Acts make it unlawful to discriminate against individuals on the grounds of an individual's sex, marital status, race, colour, or ethnic or national origin. Discrimination can occur either **directly** or **indirectly.**

Direct discrimination

This relates to how individuals are treated. No individual

Figure 13.1 Areas of discrimination covered by statutory legislation

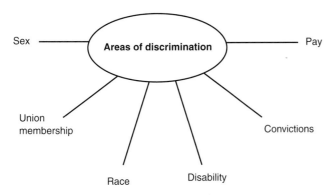

should be treated less favourably on the grounds of their race, sex or marital status. The following are clear examples of direct discrimination:

- not shortlisting or appointing applicants because of their sex, marital status or ethnic origin

  Whitehouse v Highland Regional Council (Industrial Tribunal)

  This was an example of unlawful refusal to employ a married woman, in the belief that it was wrong that both husband and wife should have jobs during a period of high unemployment.

- giving less favourable terms and conditions of employment because of a person's sex, marital status or ethnic origin

  McEvans and Others v Associated Biscuits (Industrial Tribunal)

  Temporary, part-time but qualified women were discriminated against when the employer recruited redundant men with less previous service for temporary, full-time work.

- recruiting to a post on the assumption that it is unsuitable for applicants of one particular sex or ethnic group

  Gordon and Murray v Fast Felin Ltd (Industrial Tribunal)

  The employer unlawfully refused men jobs on the assumption that they would not want to do 'boring' work.

Indirect discrimination

This takes place where a requirement or condition is specified with which few people in a particular group will be able to comply. The following are examples of indirect discrimination.

- asking questions relating to marital status, child care and family responsibilities, as such information may be used in a discriminatory way

  Elliott v Buttler (Industrial Tribunal)

  A candidate's domestic responsibilities were unlawfully assumed to be likely to conflict with the job requirement.

- having an organisational rule that female staff must wear dresses and skirts; this would have an adverse effect on some women due to their cultural or religious beliefs

- advertising a post, stating that there is a need for certain physical attributes (e.g. the ability to lift heavy weights) if this were not essential to the position and therefore present with the intention of discouraging female applicants.

Case Study

Discrimination in the workplace

In March 1995, the case of Wendy Underwood was presented to an industrial tribunal. Mrs Underwood claimed that she was forced out of her £17 000-a-year job after seven years upon becoming pregnant, and told it would not be a 'good idea to go back'.

The tribunal was told that the former flight lieutenant – who is claiming unfair dismissal on the grounds of sexual discrimination – was not told she could return to her post as an air traffic controller at RAF Cottesmore following the birth of her first daughter in June 1990.

In December 1989, Mrs Underwood discovered she was 12 weeks pregnant and immediately told her bosses. After talks with her commanding officer, it was agreed she could remain at her post until the twentieth week of her pregnancy.

Mrs Underwood said that all attemps to try to sort out her future in the RAF were met with a dismissive attitude which made her feel 'like a *persona non grata*'.

'Nobody wanted to tell me anything about what I should do or what I was entitled to. Nobody made it clear what my position was in the RAF".

At the time she had no idea she was entitled to re-enlist after the baby was born and was unaware of the RAF's policy actively to recruit women with children into the service. When she asked about coming back after having the baby, she was told by the station officer that it would not be a good idea.

Mrs Underwood contrasted her treatment with that of her husband who has been given unlimited time off to pursue his rugby career. Mr Underwood plays rugby for England.

Questions for discussion

1 *What do you consider to be the main issues of concern in this case?*
2 *Do you think that the case outlined involves discrimination? Explain your answer.*
3 *What do you think the judgement of the industrial tribunal would/should have been?*

Genuine occupational qualifications

In certain cases, where sex and race constitute a genuine occupational qualification, it is lawful specifically to recruit women, men or members of ethnic groups to a particular post.

Being of a particular racial group is a genuine occupational qualification where:

- the job involves participation in a dramatic performance or other group entertainment for which a person of a particular racial group is required for reasons of authenticity
- the job involves participation as an artist or photographic model in the production of a work of art, visual image or sequence of images for which a person of a particular racial group is required for reasons of authenticity
- the job involves working in a place where food and drink is provided and consumed by members of the public in a particular setting for which a person of a particular racial group is required for reasons of authenticity
- the holder of the job provides persons of a particular racial group personal services promoting their welfare and those services can most effectively be provided by a person of that racial group.

Being a man (or a woman, as the case may be) is a genuine occupational qualfication where:

- the nature of the job calls for a man for reasons of physiology (excluding physical strength or stamina) or in dramatic performances or other entertainment for reasons of authenticity
- the job needs to be held by a man to preserve decency or privacy because it involves physical contact, states of undress and use of sanitary facilities.
- the nature or location of the establishment makes it impractical for the holder of the post to live elsewhere than in the premises provided by the employer

- the work is concerned only with men and requires special care, supervision or attention (as in parts of hospitals and prisons)
- the job provides individuals with personal services in welfare and education and those services can most effectively be provided by a man
- the job needs to be held by a man because it is likely to involve the performance of duties outside the UK in a country whose laws and customs are such that the duties could not effectively be performed by a woman
- the job is one of two to be held by a married couple.

Task

In the following examples, state whether discrimination has taken place or not and whether this is direct or indirect discrimination. Some cases may involve a 'genuine occupational qualification'.

1 *The East London Players advertise for the cast of a Bengali play. They have advertised for 'actors of Bengali origin'.*
2 *The owners of a restaurant have put an advertisement in their window seeking 'young and attractive female students'.*
3 *The managers of a health farm are seeking a male sauna and changing room assistant.*
4 *An operative on a production line with the job of sewing a standard garment over and over again is sacked when a test indicates that she has poor written English skills.*
5 *A film producer advertises a part in a film requiring an 'attractive black female'.*
6 *A school insists on maintaining a policy that female staff are not allowed to wear trousers at work.*
7 *At an interview for a teaching job, a candidate is asked 'will your child-care arrangements enable you to be in school the same hours as the normal teaching staff?'.*

Recruitment and selection procedures

The responsibilities of human resource management mean that the issue of discrimination must be considered throughout many of the personnel procedures. Selection procedures for recruitment, promotion or transfers should be unbiased and objective.

An examination of these procedures will enable us to highlight good and bad practices at various stages.

The job description

As the document which defines a post in terms of major tasks, duties and responsibilities, it should be written in clear straightforward language, avoiding unnecessary jargon or complex terminology. In practice, job descriptions are often overstated, and this leads to the person specification setting unnecessarily high requirements for the characteristics of the post holder. For example, conditions of length of service or experience may have a disproportionate impact on women and thus indirectly discriminate.

The person specification

This should contain details of the attributes that applicants need to be suitable for a particular job. Care must be taken when writing a person specification to avoid bad practice such as using criteria of age, gender or physical ability to determine suitability. Where work is heavy, it is common to set physical standards which are higher than necessary and which exclude more women than men. Such a practice is indirectly discriminatory.

Obtaining candidates

Advertisements should not indicate any intention to discriminate. Care must also be taken with wording and illustrations. For example, the Sex Discrimination Act lays down that the use of single-sex words, e.g. waiter, postman, stewardess, shall be taken as an intention to discriminate unless there is a specific indication to the contrary.

Bias may occur if posts are advertised only in specific journals or papers intended primarily for one particular group. Care must also be taken when advertising internally where particular groups may not have access. Such limited advertising is potentially indirectly discriminatory.

Short-listing

The Equal Opportunities Commission and the Commission for Racial Equality strongly recommend that organisations adopt a procedure for recording reasons why applicants have been rejected at each stage of the selection process. The criteria used for short-listing must be job-related and applied consistently to all applicants.

Interviews

Appointments should be based on factors determined from the job description and person specification. A candidate's ethnic origin, gender, personal circumstances or disability must not be used in appointment decisions.

Oral or written fluency in English language should not be used as a selection factor unless it is a legitimate job requirement and identified on the person specification. The structure of the interview and the content should be applied consistently to all candidates for a particular post.

Monitoring

This is the process of checking whether unfair discrimination is happening and whether the organisation's equal opportunities policy is being carried out.

Monitoring which employees are in which grade in an organisation will enable the identification and investigation of under-representation by a particular group. For example, if women employees are heavily concentrated in the lower grades and men dominate the higher grades, further investigation will need to include consideration of whether factors such as age, marital status, child-related responsibilities and working arrangements are influencing recruitment and promotion decisions. An automatic refusal to consider requests for part-time working, for example, may result in unlawful discrimination.

Codes of practice to promote equal opportunities

The Commission for Racial Equality (CRE) and the Equal Opportunities Commission (EOC) have produced codes of practice in order to monitor and promote equal opportunities (see Figure 13.2).

Both codes require careful monitoring of employees. To comply with this, employers should check and record the

Figure 13.2 Promoting equal opportunities

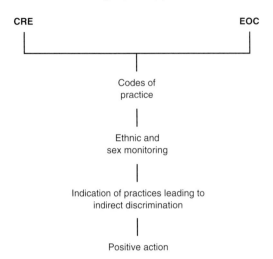

sex and marital status and ethnic origin of job applicants. This information should then feed into a review of selection criteria and personnel procedures. An organisation may find that women, married people or individuals from a particular ethnic group are not being promoted within the organisation. This may be due to practices which are indirectly discriminatory.

Although codes of practice are not law, failure to comply with them can be used against an employer in any proceedings taken against them, for example at an industrial tribunal.

Positive action

If an organisation's monitoring exercise shows that women or individuals from a particular ethnic group are not being promoted, the organisation cannot use 'positive discrimination' to promote them. Under the Race Relations Act and the Sex Discrimination Act, it is unlawful to use a quota system based on sex and racial origin. An organisation therefore could not allocate the next three promotion posts to women if they found women were under-represented, but it could make use of positive action to encourage women to apply. For example, it could set up a training scheme for women employees to encourage them into management posts.

Positive action provides a way of encouraging applicants of a particular racial group or sex to apply for specific posts if they have been under-represented in that area of work at any time during the previous twelve months. Applicants can be encouraged by including a statement in the advertisement and further particulars for a particular post, making it clear that applications from under-represented groups are particularly welcome. Appointments, however, must always be made on the

basis of merit. Other positive measures which may help under-represented groups to increase their representation in particular areas of employment include:

- job advertisements and outreach work to encourage applications from women, people from black and ethnic minority groups, people with disabilities, and lesbians and gay men
- encouraging women, people from black and ethnic minority communities and people with disabilities to apply for promotion and transfer opportunities, through career counselling or training schemes
- special training schemes for women, people from black and ethnic minority groups and people with disabilities who show potential for promotion or skills training but lack the necessary qualifications
- job advertisements designed to reach members of ethnic groups and to encourage their applications through the use of the ethnic minority press as well as other newspapers.

Equal pay

In addition to legislation covering discrimination in employment matters, the Equal Pay Act 1970 established the right of men and women to receive equal treatment with regard to the terms and conditions of employment when engaged in the same or broadly similar work or work of equal value. The act therefore requires employers to give equal pay to men and women if they are doing the same work or work regarded as equivalent, or if they are undertaking work of equal value. In order to claim equal pay an employee must meet one of these three conditions. A person making a claim for equal pay must compare him or herself with a person of the opposite sex. If a claim is successful, a tribunal can award up to two years' back pay and damages.

The law relating to the employment of disabled persons

The Disabled Persons (Employment) Acts 1944 and 1958 require employers of more than 20 people to employ a quota of disabled persons. At present the quota is set at 3 per cent of the workforce. It is not an offence for an employer to be below this figure, but an employer has a duty to engage suitable registered disabled people if anyone is available as and when vacancies arise.

Task

Study the employment record of an organisation that you are familiar with in terms of its employment of disabled people. What is the organisation's policy? How does this operate in practice? How are discrepancies between policy and practice justified?

The rehabilitation of offenders

The Rehabilitation of Offenders Act 1974 was designed to wipe clean the record of offences, so that people who have had a previous police conviction but have managed to keep out of trouble for a specified length of time should not be discriminated against due to their past conviction. The rehabilitation period runs from the time of the conviction and depends upon the sentence imposed. The idea is that for some offences the conviction could eventually be discounted. If, for example, an application form asks for disclosure of criminal offences, spent convictions can legitimately be left off the form. These rules do not apply to some offences and to some categories of job, including teachers, police officers and probation officers.

Union members rights

Until the 1970s, the law gave no rights to union members to protect them against victimisation by employers. Under the Trade Union and Labour Relations (Consolidation) Act 1992, it is unlawful to refuse employment because someone is, or is not, a member of a trade union.

Health and safety at work

The health and safety of people at work is governed by not only the Health and Safety at Work Act 1974, but also a range of other statutes and legislation covering working conditions and technical safety standards in particular areas of work.

The Health and Safety at Work Act establishes the **responsibility** of both employers and employees to provide safe conditions at work. The employer has a duty 'to ensure, so far as is reasonably practicable, the health, safety and welfare at work, of all his employees'. This duty includes:

- provision and maintenance of safe plant and systems of work
- ensuring safety in connection with the use, handling, storage and transport of articles and substances
- provision of instruction, training and supervision.

In addition, employers are required to issue a written health and safety policy. This should show that the organisation is committed to employees' health and safety and establish clear arrangements for putting that policy into effect. This includes appointing a safety officer and putting into operation a safety committee and safety representatives. It should also detail the training provision for employees in handling safety issues.

Enforcement

The Health and Safety Executive are responsible for enforcing the provisions of the Health and Safety at Work Act. They supervise the activities of the staffs of the various specialist inspectorates which deal with particular places of work.

Inspectors make routine visits of premises, both industrial and commercial, as well as being called in to investigate accidents. They have the authority to enter and examine premises, to examine records and to question employees.

The penalties for organisations that are found guilty of contravening the Health and Safety at Work Act can be severe. Penalties can be imposed against the organisation and or against individuals. In the case of serious breaches, an organisation can be fined an unlimited amount and any manager or employee who consented or whose neglect led to the offence may be fined an unlimited sum and or imprisoned for up to two years. For other breaches, organisations can be served with an **improvement notice,** where they must improve the practice within a time limit. **Prohibition notices** can also be served, where the practice must cease immediately.

Negligence

An employee can claim for damages resulting from an employer's negligence if the employer fails 'to abide by the duty of care to the employee so that the employee suffers injury or damage to health'. Employers have a duty of reasonable care for the health and safety of employees, and this responsibility extends to when they send employees to the premises of third parties.

Negligence occurs when there is a breach in the duty of care. This applies to:

- safe premises
- a safe system of work
- safe plant, equipment and tools
- safe fellow workers.

Further reading

- *A Handbook of Human Resource Management* by E. Towers. Blackwell, 1995.
- Race Relations and Equal Opportunities Commissions, *Codes of Practice* on Race Relations and Equal Opportunities.

Maintaining organisational performance

14 Systems for supporting corporate business objectives

On completion of this chapter, students should be able to:

- review and evaluate the process of control

- evaluate the contribution of work measurement to management

- review and evaluate the management by objectives approach

- identify key result areas and set objectives that meet MBO criteria

- apply SWOT analysis

- prepare an action plan

- review and evaluate the purposes and operation of staff appraisal

- review and evaluate total quality management and BS 5750 / IS 9000

- review the Investors in People Award

- review the contribution of information technology to personnel information systems.

The process of control

In a one-person business, the owner does all the functions: obtaining the orders, making the product or supplying the service, arranging delivery, keeping the records and collecting payment. Even where the owner employs a couple of staff, communication can be informal and face to face. Problems can be raised and resolved quickly. Control therefore is simple and direct.

Large organisations have all of the same functions, but communication and control become more complex. Functions such as marketing, production, finance and personnel are separated and put in charge of specialists. Informal face-to-face communication by itself is no longer adequate, reliable or even feasible. Information has to be stored and transmitted by means of paper procedures or computer systems, otherwise co-ordination and balance between the work of departments can be lost. For example, an export order to be delivered by a given date requires the activities of the separate departments to be co-ordinated so that the delivery date is met. If any of the individual departments, misunderstanding the arrangements or, experiencing difficulties, changes its priorities without consultation, the whole export order could be late.

Written plans express formally the contribution expected from each function and department. These cover all aspects of performance: the sales target, the quantity of items to be produced, the deadlines for their completion, the quality, and the cost levels not to be exceeded.

Management information systems provide the feedback for control. They report actual achievement, compare it with the target performance and analyse any shortfalls by causes, so that corrective action can be taken.

A business system consists of the procedures – that is the information flow, its processing and recording – the equipment and the staff. A good system supplies the required information accurately, economically and on time. Without good systems a business is unco-ordinated.

Standards of performance

Performance standards and control

Management seeks to control the following aspects of work performance:

- the rate of work and the meeting of deadlines
- the quality of work
- the costs incurred
- the utilisation of equipment
- behaviour standards: attendance and safety.

The emphasis given to each of them depends on the nature of the work and the philosophy of the management.

The basic steps in exercising control are:

1 set standards of performance
2 monitor actual performance and compare it to the standard
3 identify any shortfalls in performance and analyse the causes
4 take corrective action to restore performance to standard.

The general criteria for fixing standards of performance are discussed in detail in the later section on management by objectives. In general, standards should be **clear**, **unambiguous** and **realistic**.

Monitoring actual performance

Control systems intended to monitor performance need to be cost-effective, timely, obtain appropriate information and be easy to understand.

Cost-effective

Control systems cost money to design and operate. To give added value therefore, the benefits of such systems need to be greater than their costs. It is not too difficult to calculate the costs of operating a control system. The components are the salaries of the staff, the running costs, the depreciation of the equipment and the other overhead costs. However, it is more difficult to place a precise value on the increased control until it has been exercised.

Task

In order to improve the rate of work, a company decided to introduce a system of allocating work to staff and monitoring its completion. Discuss how the company could work out the cost/benefits of this approach.

Timely

Control systems signal that performance is deviating from standard. The longer the corrective action is delayed, the greater the loss to the company. If production machinery develops a fault, it is better to know this after it has produced ten items than after it has completed a thousand items.

Control information should be reliable, but sometimes it is better to get reasonably accurate feedback quickly than to have to wait for information that is absolutely correct but long delayed.

Task

The purchase department of a large retail organisation receives between 100 and 120 requisitions for replacement stock each morning. The performance standard for the department is that all purchase orders should be processed and mailed to the suppliers on the same day as the requisitions are received. What should be the frequency of the feedback to the supervisor responsible for processing the orders and why?

Appropriate detail and easy to understand

Control information should be appropriate to the needs of the recipient. Consider the following example of efficiency reporting. A general manager has five departmental heads reporting to her. Each department has between six and eight sections, each with a supervisor in charge. All the managers and supervisors need control information to meet their particular responsibilities.

If efficiency overall drops, the general manager needs to know which department has the problem and that corrective action is being taken. The particular departmental manager with the drop in efficiency needs to know which section has the problem and that the supervisor is handling it. The particular supervisor needs to know which of his or her staff are involved in the efficiency drop and why. It is superfluous to the needs of the supervisors to have the control information of the other departments and sections. The general manager does not need the details of the performance of all the staff.

Good control systems highlight the information that is significant to the particular users, helping them to direct their attention to where it is most needed. Poorly designed control information, particularly that produced by a computerised system, often gives excessive detail in a format not readily understood by the recipient.

Analysis of variations from standard performance

A good control system not only signals deviation from standard performance, it also analyses, where feasible, the deviations by cause and by responsibility. This principle can be illustrated by an example from standard costing. Where a company uses standard costing, it has a detailed specification for the manufacture of each of its products. Thus the manufacturing instructions specify:

- the type of materials
- the quantity of material for each unit of production
- the expected purchase price per unit of material
- the precise manufacturing operations
- the standard time which each manufacturing operation should take
- the grade of labour to be used for each operation
- the rate of pay per hour for each grade of labour
- the overhead rate per hour to cover costs such as heating, lighting, machinery, etc.

From this information, the expected or standard cost of each unit can be calculated in advance of production. When a batch of products has been manufactured, the actual costs might be higher than the standard, and appropriate action needs to be taken. Some possibilities are shown in Figure 14.1.

If the control system does not indicate the causes of substandard performance, management must investigate before it can take appropriate action.

Task

A company decides to set up a control system for staff absenteeism. After reviewing past rates of absence, it has set a target limit for the company as a whole. Each department will receive a monthly report comparing actual absence with the target limit. What analysis of the variance between target and actual would be useful to help the department managers to take appropriate actions, and why?

One of the justifications for delayering organisations – reducing the levels of managers and supervisors – is that computerised management information systems undertake much of the problem analysis formerly done by supervisors and managers. The system not only signals there is a problem, it analyses the causes and therefore points to the solution.

Corrective action

Corrective action is the end purpose of a control system. If no appropriate corrective actions occur, the system is an expensive ritual.

For example, a company had a system for following up the late delivery of goods that had been ordered. Each Monday the warehouses produced lists of out-of-stock items, showing the reference numbers of the overdue orders. Two staff in the buying office spent most of each Monday telephoning suppliers to chase delivery of overdue orders. In the majority of cases, it transpired that the goods were already on the company's receiving bay when the out-of-stock list had been prepared. The control system was regularly generating inappropriate action.

In other instances, managers and supervisors may be reluctant or too busy to act. Either way, the justification for the control system is undermined.

Control over the pace of work

The staff **establishment** for a department is the number that it is authorised to employ. Establishments are often fixed in practice by precedent, guesswork, financial

Figure 14.1 Possible reasons for excess costs

Reasons for excess costs	Responsibility
The price of the materials was higher than standard	Purchasing manager
Excess materials have been used because of operatives' errors	Manufacturing manager
Excess time was taken by operatives	Manufacturing manager
The wrong grade of labour was used	Manufacturing manager
The wage rate has increased beyond the budget	Industrial relations manager
Materials were not available when needed	Materials controller

pressures or haggling. A department has, say, 20 staff. No one currently employed knows how that figure was fixed. Suppose the workload increases. The department manager asks the establishment officer for more staff. The decision may be more staff, no extra staff or even a cut, depending on the case, the relative power of the two managers and the current finances of the company.

A more rational approach is **work measurement**. The number of staff needed to do a given job depends on the volume of work and the pace at which the staff do it.

Work measurement is a general term for a range of techniques that attempt to answer the following questions:

- How long *does* it take currently to complete given tasks?
- How long *should* it take under standard conditions?

The term **standard conditions** means:

- the staff have been properly selected and trained
- the correct working methods are used
- the appropriate equipment is available in good working order
- the physical working conditions are right
- the pace of work is such that it can be maintained over the day without undue fatigue
- the work is adequately serviced and supervised.

A **standard time** is the time taken to do a unit of work under the above conditions. The aim of work measurement is to fix time standards. Work measurement helps management to take rational decisions on:

- the expected pace of work
- staffing levels
- allocation and control of work
- costing
- comparison of alternative working methods
- financial incentive schemes.

Work measurement is easiest to apply where ten or more staff are doing routine, standardised, repetitive work. If there are fewer than this, the likely staff savings, or improved efficiency may not cover the costs of the work measurement survey. If the work is not routine, the techniques are more difficult to apply and the results may be less reliable.

The outcome of a work measurement survey should be a set of standard times for the main tasks in the department. These can be used for fixing staffing levels and for the other purposes listed previously.

The standards can also be used as a system of regular efficiency reporting. Figure 14.2 is a simplified example from a large accounts office checking incoming suppliers' invoices and certifying them for payment. The invoices were classified into five categories, each with different time

standards. The incoming work was logged and entered on to the monthly performance review sheet.

Task

1 Complete the calculations on Figure 14.2. Work out:
   - the standard hours for the month
   - the hours paid for in January
   - the hours paid for but not worked on measured work
   - the net hours worked on measured work
   - the variance and the percentage efficiency.
2 For what reasons might staff not achieve 100 per cent effectiveness?

All performance data needs careful interpretation. In the example given in Figure 14.2, some of the possible reasons for the low performance could be:

Figure 14.2 Monthly performance review sheet

PURCHASE RECORDS DEPARTMENT			
MONTH – JANUARY 199–			

A. STANDARD TIME FOR THE MONTH'S ACTUAL WORKLOAD

Unit of Measurement	column 1 Standard unit time per invoice (hours)	column 2 Actual units for the month	column 3 Standard hours for the month (col 1 × col 2)
Invoices – category A	0.0320	3900	
Invoices – category B	0.0395	6300	
Invoices – category C	0.0490	31600	
Invoices – category D	0.0525	14200	
Invoices – category E	0.0614	8100	

Total standard hours for the month's workload = hours

B. HOURS PAID FOR IN JANUARY

32 staff x 20 working days x 7.5 hours per day = hours

C. HOURS PAID FOR BUT NOT WORKED ON MEASURED WORK IN JANUARY

Illness	235 hours
Holidays	150 hours
Staff development	300 hours

Total hours paid for but not worked on = hours

D. NET HOURS SPENT ON MEASURED WORK (B – C) = hours

E. VARIANCE (A – D) = hours

F. EFFICIENCY $\left(\dfrac{A}{D}\times\dfrac{100}{1}\right)$ = %

- mistakes in fixing the standard times
- fluctuations in the work flow during the month; there may be little for the staff to do at certain times
- problems with the equipment used
- poor form design
- poorly selected and poorly trained staff
- poor allocation and supervision of work.

There would be little point in providing these reports each month, unless they lead to appropriate action to improve efficiency.

Provided the time standards have been correctly measured, they should not be adjusted. The company may recruit low calibre staff because it pays poorly, or it may choose not to train properly. The subsequent low performance against standard is the cost of these policies and should not be hidden by adjusting the standards.

Management by objectives (MBO)

Management by objectives is one method of focusing and co-ordinating the activities of departments and individuals. The approach was used as early as the 1920s. It was popularised by the writings of Peter Drucker in the 1940s and 1950s. In the 1960s and 1970s, consultants like Urwick Orr and partners advised companies on the use of MBO. The popularity as a consultancy technique has since diminished, although the approach has had a lasting influence on the use of objectives in management.

A common way of telling employees what is expected of them is to give them a job description – see Figure 14.3.

Personnel management uses job descriptions as a source of data for a number of purposes: selection, training and job evaluation. As a tool for organisation, however, they have the following limitations.

- It is time-consuming to revise them and, as the pace of change at work increases, job descriptions fall quickly out of date.
- They tell job holders what they have to do, but not what they have to achieve. In Figure 14.3, the first responsibility uses the phrase 'prompt completion'. What does that mean? Within two hours? The same day? Within a week?
- Job descriptions fail to give a guide to the relative priorities of the various duties. It happens in all jobs that under time pressure the job holder has to decide priorities. There is no guidance on this in the sample job description, apart from indirectly in the statement of the basic purpose of the job. Even if the job description had been arranged in the original order of

Figure 14.3 A job description

JOB TITLE:	Data Processing Supervisor
DEPARTMENT:	Management Services
RESPONSIBLE TO:	Data Processing Manager
SECTION:	Data Processing
TEAM:	Data Input Assistants
PURPOSE OF JOB:	To ensure that data is transferred to the computer accurately, efficiently and on time.

RESPONSIBILITIES:
1. To allocate the work and ensure its prompt completion.
2. To monitor the error rates and take corrective action to minimise errors.
3. To ensure the security of data in the data processing room.
4. To resolve queries with the departments supplying the data.
5. To resolve clients' complaints.
6. To complete monthly returns and submit them to the Data Processing Manager.
7. To train new staff.
8. To complete staff annual appraisal forms.
9. To maintain staff discipline: punctuality, attendance and work rate.
10. To report equipment failures promptly to the maintenance engineer.
11. To report heating, lighting and cleaning problems promptly to the building maintenance manager.

importance, it would not reflect the changes in priorities over time. For example, if the data processing section had a stable work force, fully trained, with no changes pending, then training new staff might be a low current priority. However, if five staff left in a short period, training would become a high priority.

The management by objectives approach addresses these problems: identifying the priorities, setting standards of performance, reviewing the results and taking appropriate corrective actions. A basic feature of the approach is the use of objectives.

Benefits of fixing objectives

Objectives give direction to effort and provide motivation. The argument is that people have more commitment to a purposeful activity and experience a sense of satisfaction when the target is achieved. The targets may provide a basis for other rewards like promotion and performance-related pay.

Objectives direct resources to where they are most needed. Focusing on the priority objectives diminishes the time spent on less important tasks. All resources are limited and can be put to alternative uses. Money allocated to be spent on one activity could be diverted to another activity, either within the section or in another department. For example, instead of spending money on training, management could improve the equipment in the data-processing centre. If money is limited – as it usually is – choosing to spend it in one way means giving up the opportunity to spend it on something else. Thus, the opportunity cost of the training is the value of the lost opportunity to improve the equipment. Setting clear objectives helps to crystallise the choices between alternatives.

Objectives provide a basis for evaluation of performance. They are set for a period of time, typically three months, six months or a year. At the end of the specified period, performance can be reviewed against the objectives. Provided the targets were unambiguously stated, it should be clear whether or not they were achieved.

Principles of setting objectives/targets

Objectives or targets should be relevant, attainable, agreed rather than imposed, and specific.

Relevant

Objectives should be relevant to the **needs** and **priorities** of the organisation. Setting objectives, and subsequently monitoring their achievement, absorbs time and resources. Therefore it needs to be done selectively. Not every activity is worth monitoring closely.

It is simpler to set targets for some activities than others, because some activities are easier to measure than others. For example, it might be easier to measure the costs of medical supplies used in a hospital ward than the quality of patient care. Priority should not be distorted by the

It'll definitely be finished by next week.

difficulty of setting a measurable target. The objectives should be relevant to the judged priorities. The method of measurement should follow the choice of priorities, not precede it.

Attainable

Objectives should be attainable. To try hard and still fail is demoralising. Whether or not objectives are attainable depends, in the first place, on the provision of adequate resources. If you have been asked at work, with the help of two staff, to complete a special project by a given date, it would not be surprising to fail should the two staff not be provided.

Agreed

Commitment is greater to objectives that have been agreed, than to those which have been imposed. It is better, therefore, to develop objectives for improvement through discussion between the job holder and the boss. Objective setting is then the logical consequence of an agreed need, rather than the exercise of arbitrary power. Unilateral imposition by the senior can cause resentment.

Specific

There should be no ambiguity in the expression of an objective. Vagueness in definition can cause different interpretations of what actions are needed and, at the review stage, disagreement over whether or not the objective was achieved. Wherever possible, objectives should be expressed in numbers and the time period specified. For example, 'to increase the sales of product X' is meaningless. Is the target increase 5 per cent, 10 per cent, or what? 'To increase sales of product X by 10 per cent' is still not clear. What is the base? Is it value or quantity of sales? By when is the increase to be achieved? Within a year; within two years?

A meaningful target might read: *'to increase the value of annual sales by 10 per cent on the value of the 1996 sales value by December 1997'.*

Management by objectives – stages

Organisational objectives

Setting objectives for the organisation as a whole starts from a review of current company performance, compared with that of its competitors. It includes market research, and a review of the availability and efficiency of resources. A SWOT analysis projects the review forwards. SWOT stands for:

- strengths
- weaknesses
- opportunities
- threats.

It is a technique for taking stock of an organisation's current state, and for deciding what needs to be done. The company assesses its strengths and weaknesses, in relation to the threats and opportunities posed by external changes. The assessment provides the basis for planning the organisation's responses.

Threats and opportunities might arise from changes in population, customer tastes, disposable income, competition, overseas markets, the law, and technology. All of these can present new opportunities, but also pose a threat to any organisation that fails to anticipate the external changes and adjust.

The organisation's current strengths and weaknesses might relate to the quality of the product or service, its response times, its equipment and technology, its marketing function, its location and transport, and the skills and versatility of its staff. Where these match the requirements of the anticipated external changes, they are strengths. Where they do not match, they are weaknesses that need to be addressed.

Task

A company manufactured high-quality bicycles with an international reputation. Its workforce was highly skilled and strongly unionised. Management succession was mainly by internal promotion. Most of the management had started work on a production bench.

From the 1950s onwards, people bought cycles increasingly for leisure and sport rather than for personal transport. This radically affected the design favoured by customers. New methods of manufacture, using powder metallurgy, were being introduced by overseas competitors. This allowed them to undercut prices. The main markets for the traditional sturdy bicycle at the time were Africa and the Middle East. A crisis in the economy of the main African market and a war in the Middle East meant the loss of both main export markets. Within a few years the size of the company diminished sharply.

Do a SWOT analysis on this company.

The review of the current business and forward projection leads to setting objectives for an organisation as a whole. In the example above, the objectives would have included the introduction of a new product range and the targeting of new markets.

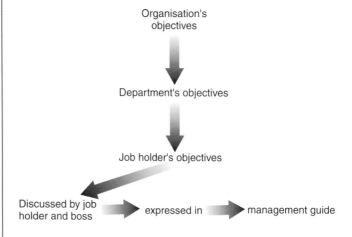

Figure 14.4   Management by objectives

The next stage is to agree objectives for each unit or department. These must integrate with, and contribute to, the overall organisational objectives. Thus in the above example, the objectives of the marketing department, the design department, the manufacturing department and the sales department would all need to be focused on an agreed launch date for the new products. The principles of objective setting, discussed earlier, apply in each case.

Once the unit or departmental objectives have been fixed, each manager within the unit must then know what contribution he or she is expected to make. This is detailed in a document called a **management guide.**

The sequence of events is shown in Figure 14.4.

Management guide

The management guide document is designed to record agreement reached on:

- *the key result areas:* the current priorities of the job
- *the performance standards:* what outcomes are expected in the key result areas
- *control information:* the feedback on performance that will be supplied routinely to the job holder
- *job improvement plans* to deal with identified problems.

Key result areas

All the activities of a job are not equally important. Some activities have a bigger impact on overall work results than others. For example, a salesperson who spends a disproportionate amount of his or her available time on administration, rather than selling, has wrong priorities. The Pareto principle suggests that 20 per cent of the activities of a job account for 80 per cent of the results. It makes sense therefore to concentrate control on that 20 per cent – the key result areas.

Task

Re-read the job description in Figure 14.3. Which are likely to be the top two or three key result areas and why?

Referring to the job description in Figure 14.3, it is likely that responsibilities 1, 2 and 3 would be the key result areas since they directly affect the basic purpose of the job. That is not to say that the other responsibilities have no consequence. For example poor staff discipline (responsibility 9) such as excessive absence would make it difficult to achieve responsibility 1 and failure in responsibility 7 would affect the quality in responsibility 2. However, they are contributory rather than central. The main contribution this section makes to the overall objectives of the company is processing data, not training staff.

Performance standards

The management guide should express the agreed performance standards for each key result area. The criteria for expressing these clearly were discussed in the section above on 'Principles of setting objectives'. A performance standard states the conditions that exist when the result is satisfactory. For example, the performance standard for responsibility 1 in Figure 14.3 might read:

> *'All incoming data is processed within 24 hours of its receipt in the department.'*

Task

A realistic performance standard for responsibility 2 might read:

> *'The keying-in error rate does not exceed 2 per cent.'*

How might performance standards be expressed for responsibilities 3, 4, 5, 6 and 7?

Control information for the job holder

The job holder needs to know if the standards for his or her area are being met so that any corrective action can be taken. The control information should be supplied direct to the job holder rather than to the job holder's boss. The first approach is focused on corrective action, the second on policing and discipline.

Job improvement plans

At the periodic reviews of the section's work, problems may be identified. These need to be prioritised and action plans drawn up to tackle them. An action plan has three components: what is to be done, by whom and by when. For example, a plan to improve the current training is shown in Figure 14.5.

Figure 14.5 Job improvement plan – retraining

Actions	By whom	By when
Analyse training needs of staff	Supervisor, Mr Akin	July 199-
Submit proposals for new on-the-job training programme	Training Officer, Ms Turner	Oct 199-
Approve / amend training proposals. Provide resources	Department Manager, Ms Jenkins	Dec 199-
Start to implement new training programme	Supervisor, Mr Akin	Jan 199-
Complete retraining of present staff	Supervisor, Mr Akin	March 199-

Task

Write an action plan for a project. It might be a course project or assignment, applying for jobs at the end of your course, or a leisure activity like planning a holiday. Work out what needs to be done in a logical order and assess the time needed for each stage. Fix your target completion date. Working backwards from that, fix the target completion dates of each of the other stages.

Performance reviews

Management guides and improvement plans cover an agreed future period: a year, six months or three months. At the end of the period: the job holder and senior meet to review progress. The possible reasons why a job holder has not met the target are:

- the original objectives may have been too optimistic
- the job holder did not perform well enough
- circumstances outside the control of the job holder may have changed
- promised support was not given. In Figure 14.5, for example, the manager had undertaken to provide resources for retraining, perhaps time free from

routine duties to implement the training programme. If this was not supplied, the supervisor could not be held responsible for the delay.

The issues raised by such reviews are discussed in more detail in a later section on staff appraisal.

Criticisms of management by objectives

The following are some common criticisms of the MBO approach:

- It is bureaucratic and expensive. The form filling, the meetings and the reporting systems take too much time.
- It shifts power, though this is not intended, from line managers doing the core business of making, selling or providing the services, to advisors and consultants.
- The sharp focus on results and personal responsibility can easily develop into a blame culture, where individuals are reluctant to innovate and take risks.
- Rapid change needs continuous interaction between managers and their teams, rather than ritualised reviews at periods of six months or a year.
- MBO is old fashioned. It is difficult for business consultants to sell management techniques unless they appear to offer something new. One solution is to give them new titles.

Despite these criticisms, the MBO approach has had a lasting influence on the setting of objectives, on performance standards, on performance reviews and on action plans.

Performance appraisal

To describe schemes of appraisal, alternative terms are used such as **staff appraisal, individual performance review,** and **staff development.** The various terms reflect different emphasis of purpose and of method. They also reflect the attempt to escape possible unpleasant associations with the term 'appraisal'. Staff development sounds more positive and less threatening than staff appraisal.

Why do organisations have appraisal schemes?

Appraisal schemes normally have a combination of some of the following purposes:

- *Problem-solving.* Current weaknesses in performance are identified. The causes are analysed and appropriate actions taken. These could be further

training, additional resources and changes in work procedures.
- *Development.* Particular staff may have potential beyond the demands of the present job. If this is identified, it can be developed through training, job shadowing and special projects.
- *Promotion.* Where potential has been successfully developed, staff may be included in a management succession programme.
- *Redirection.* Staff who are misfits in their present posts are transferred to other jobs or dismissed. These are likely to have been errors at the selection stage and identified during a probationary period of employment.
- *Financial reward.* The purpose is to reward good performance with money. This adds tension to the staff appraisal process, both for the employee and the manager. For this reason it is usually recommended that issues of pay, even though related, are dealt with separately from the performance review interview.

Common stages of staff appraisal

1 The boss meets with the job holder to discuss what is expected. The agreed expectations might be expressed in terms of targets, performance standards or required job behaviours – attributes, skills and attitudes.
2 The outcome of the meeting is recorded and usually signed by both parties
3 The job holder performs the job for a period of six months or a year.
4 At the end of the period, the job holder and boss meet again to review and discuss progress made. They draw up new action plans to deal with identified problems and agree targets and standards for the next period.

Basis of appraisal

There are three broad approaches to staff appraisal, based on personal attributes, skills or performance. They are not necessarily mutually exclusive. Company schemes may contain elements of each. A large organisation may use different schemes for different groups of employees.

Personal attributes

The designers of the scheme identify the personal attributes that affect job performance. These are used as the basis of appraisal. Some examples are:

- reliability
- judgement
- application
- initiative

Figure 14.6 Appraisal guidelines

Characteristic	Poor	Below average	Average	Above average	Excellent
Reliability	Makes many mistakes	Inclined to be careless	Reasonably careful	Few errors	Unusually high standard

- adaptability
- disposition.

There are several criticisms of this approach. For example, the attributes are open to wide interpretation by the many managers undertaking appraisal in different parts of the organisation. The system is also not consistent and therefore potentially unjust. To combat this, some appraisal forms provide guidelines, as shown in Figure 14.6.

Even so, the approach is highly subjective and can have the tone of an old fashioned school report. Where the forms are used for assessing merit payments, points may be allocated to each grade of each characteristic. Thus the points for reliability might range from 6 for 'poor' to 30 for 'excellent'.

Skills

Appraisal focuses on the employee's proficiency in the skills relevant to the particular job. Depending on the job, these might include technical competence, such as operating particular equipment; communication skills, such as report writing; and interpersonal skills needed to deal with customers. The person doing the appraisal, usually the manager, observes the employee over a period of time and records his or her judgement of the employee's competence. The standard could be the company's own, or it could be the performance standard of a relevant National Vocational Qualification.

Critics of this approach argue that it assesses potential rather than achievement. In assessing police officers, for instance, they might argue that it is more important to appraise by results – detection and arrest – rather than by acquisition of skills.

Performance

The basis of appraisal is the achievement of agreed performance standards or targets. Advocates of this approach point to its objectivity. However, it is difficult in some jobs to find a satisfactory measure of individual performance. The outcome of a nurse's performance is, for example, patient care. One way of assessing the success rate of patient care could be the discharge rate –

how soon the patients are fit to go home. However, there are many variables affecting this outcome: the quality of resources, the performance of the rest of the team; changes in policy and practice relating to discharge; the home conditions of the patients, and so on. To isolate the effects of an individual's performance may be difficult and expensive to achieve. Where close teamwork is desirable, assessment and grading of individual performance could be divisive.

Parties to staff appraisal

Typically appraisal involves the job holder and his or her boss. Inputs may be made also by the boss's assistant, the employee's supervisor or, exceptionally, by team colleagues, particularly in a group of professionals. The individual employee may be asked to do a self-assessment in preparation for the formal staff appraisal session. Appraisals are recorded and the employees normally sign a copy. They can register disagreement and there is usually an appeal procedure for staff who are aggrieved with their appraisal.

Records of appraisal may be vetted centrally by the personnel department to try to ensure uniformity of treatment and fairness.

Hazards to objective appraisal

In large organisations the many managers may interpret the appraisal criteria differently. To counter this, organisations need to define the criteria carefully and train the appraisers thoroughly. This is usually done when the scheme is launched. The problems arise when new managers are appointed.

Where appraisers have to rate employees on a scale for each criterion, there are a number of problems:

- The scale may ask for impossibly fine judgements. Most scales limit the choice to six or less.
- Assessors may play safe and award only middle grades. This avoids confrontations caused by low grades and jealousy caused by high grades. Schemes counter this by using a small even number of grades,

and by monitoring centrally the range of grades awarded by each manager.

- Individual assessors may have a tendency to either harsh or lenient grading. They may be reluctant to award deservedly low grades, thinking that they reflect badly on their own management. They may have strong feelings about one criterion which then colours their judgement on other criteria. Possible counter measures are training, comparison with a second independent assessor and central vetting of the grading. Assessments say something about the assessors as well as the assessed.
- The judgement of a manager with many staff to appraise may be affected by fatigue. It is difficult to maintain a consistent standard of judgement over a long period. This can be countered by sharing the load with another member of the management team and by careful scheduling.
- Managers of departments do not necessarily view staff appraisal in the same way as specialist personnel staff. Line managers may see it as a diversion from their other work priorities and as a possible source of friction between staff and themselves. If this is the case, they are likely to go through the motions of the staff appraisal system with no real commitment. Senior managers need to demonstrate their support by allocating adequate resources, particularly time, to the operation of the scheme. It should be possible to estimate the total time per annum needed by staff and managers to fill in the forms and complete the interviews. The cost of the scheme can then be calculated and budgeted. It seems that this is seldom done.

Staff appraisal is not scientific. Even with well-designed schemes there is bound to be a degree of subjectivity. The best that can be done is to make the approach systematic. In any organisation, people will be forming judgements of each other whether there is an appraisal system or not. The advantage of a formal system is that such judgements have to be expressed, justified and made subject to challenge.

Task

1 *Compare and contrast the different approaches to staff appraisal.*
2 *What might be the appropriate methods for appraising teachers? What would be the difficulties?*

Advice to managers conducting staff appraisals

- Give adequate notice to allow the employee to prepare. To give focus to the subsequent discussion, the employee might be asked to complete a self-development review form.
- Choose somewhere quiet for the meeting, away from the telephone and other interruptions. Allow enough time for each appraisal interview, including time to write down notes immediately afterwards.
- Prepare carefully. Review the record of this employee's previous appraisal and the reports of performance results since then. Consider your own contribution to his or her performance.
- The purpose is to improve future performance. No one can alter the past. The purpose of reviewing it should be to learn lessons, not to humiliate. It requires a joint problem solving approach, not an authoritarian, judgmental stance.
- Start the interview by recapping on the targets agreed previously. Ask the job holder what has gone well. Take the opportunity to praise good performance.
- Ask what the difficulties have been over the period and what the causes were. Self-criticism is usually more acceptable than external criticism. Draw out with questions where necessary. The manager needs to admit responsibility where appropriate, particularly for failures to support. Address the problems jointly. Ask for suggestions for improvement. Solutions could involve training, resources and revisions of targets, perhaps because of changed circumstances.
- Summarise what has been agreed. Complete the staff appraisal documentation. Allow the appraisee to read and register his or her agreement or dissension.

Advice to employees on appraisal

- Prepare yourself beforehand. Review your performance results and particularly any circumstances affecting them. Write these down, rather than relying on memory. Anticipate the issues and be ready with explanations. Know what you want out of the interview. It might be more resources, or personal objectives like career development.
- Beware of volunteering targets that are too ambitious. There will be more credit eventually for exceeding targets than for failing them.
- Do not be modest about your strengths. Your day-to-day contacts with the manager may be fleeting and much of your good work may go unnoticed. Unfortunately mistakes provide the drama that sometimes catches disproportionate attention.
- Do not be excessively frank about your weaknesses. Your boss is unlikely to be frank about his or hers.

- Make clear what support you need from the boss – training, resources, and time to correct weaknesses and achieve targets. Have promises of support recorded as well as your commitments, otherwise they may be conveniently forgotten. An appraisal agreement should be a mutual contract, not a one-sided pressure session.
- Make the most of the opportunity to obtain training and development to support your longer-term career aims. Despite the call for continuous development of staff, the line manager's focus is often shorter-term. Consequently, under budget restrictions he or she is more likely to give priority to immediate job-related training than to longer term career development. Appraisal sessions may provide opportunity for employees to negotiate on this.
- Do all this in a pleasant positive manner. The manager may find the encounter as stressful as you do. An organised positive approach will help both parties to achieve more of their objectives.

Total quality management (TQM)

In an economy of free markets, where organisations rely on repeat orders for their products or services, quality and price are crucial to the survival and success of a business. Historically, concern for quality focused on inspection to detect subquality work and to prevent it leaving the department or firm. Inspection as the final arbiter of quality was often seen, therefore, as responsible for quality.

Reflection will tell you that this is a false analysis. Inspection detects the absence of quality. Quality is determined not by inspection, but by the employees who make the product or provide the service in the first place. Heavy reliance on inspection is an admission of poor quality work.

Where a service is being supplied, it is not usually feasible to routinely inspect it, like a product, before delivering it. Within the constraints of resources, we expect the provider of services like medical care, nursing care and education to take personal responsibility for the quality of their services.

Total quality management adopts the same perspective – *that everyone in the organisation has responsibility for the quality of his or her own work and that this contributes to the quality of the company as a whole.* If successful, TQM pervades the whole of the organisation: its corporate objectives, its philosophy and its attitudes as well as its techniques and processes.

Basic assumptions of TQM

The operation of an organisation should be driven by the need to meet clients' or customers' **expectations**.

Task

Discuss what expectations a customer might have before, during and after the purchase of a video recorder from a departmental store.

Expectations

A customer will have a range of expectations. Some possibilities are:

- prompt courteous attention
- informative displays
- competitive prices
- a reliable product with the desired features
- good after-sales service
- a good guarantee
- knowledgeable assistants
- a range of choice
- credit facilities
- prompt delivery.

As far as the customer is concerned, quality is the required combination of these expectations.

Some departments in an organisation have no direct contact with the final customer. The clients of such departments may be other departments, which use their service, or which process the information they provide. For example, a payroll department provides a service to

employees, to the accounts department and to the Inland Revenue. The focus of quality is the same, i.e. what are the customers, the users of the service, entitled to expect?

Task

Discuss what expectations users of an in-company centralised reprographics service would have. What decides whether or not these expectations are realistic?

A customer's expectations may not be realistic. What is available to customers at a given price is determined by competition, costs, the efficiency of the supplying organisation and legal safeguards.

Entitlements

Customers' expectations become entitlements when they are expressed in the form of promises, contracts, or where rights exist under consumer legislation. Customer entitlements should inform and underpin the organisation's standards.

Quality performance standards

Quality standards express what each part of the organisation must do to meet consistently the customers' entitlements.

Basic essentials of TQM

To be successful, TQM needs the features discussed below.

Management commitment to quality

Successful quality management is not achieved simply by exhortation, quality posters or a few quick training courses. The commitment needs to extend to defining policy on quality, defining responsibilities for each aspect of quality, setting up quality systems and procedures, providing ongoing education and training, and allocating sufficient resources.

Clear quality performance standards

Standards should be expressed in ways that cannot be misinterpreted. Some examples are:

- Patients will be seen within half-an-hour of their appointed time.

- Letters will be answered on the same day as they are received.
- Incoming telephone calls will be answered within six rings.
- The error rate will not exceed X per cent.

The standards should be realistic in terms of the resources provided. It is not helpful, for example if your telephone call is answered within six rings but you are left listening to recorded music. Standards need to be met in spirit, not just to the letter.

Staff should understand the quality standards for their section or department and appreciate their necessity. Management is more likely to obtain commitment through education and consultation than through exhortation and threats, hence the use of quality circles, discussed in Chapter 18.

Case Study
Central services department – the reprographics section

The central services department (CSD) has two sections: the mail room with 11 staff and the reprographics section with 8 staff. The organisation structure is shown in Figure 14.7.

Figure 14.7 Organisation structure of the central services department

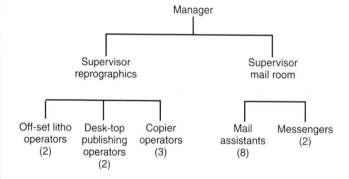

The CSD provides a service to all of the many departments in the head office of a large retail organisation. It occupies a converted property 500 metres from the main block of offices. The layout of the property is shown in Figure 14.8.

Some incoming work is received through the internal mail. However, the bulk is delivered by hand. Usually the staff from the requisitioning departments bring the rough draft or the prepared original, direct to the appropriate process. Clients collect the finished work.

Figure 14.8 Layout of the central services department

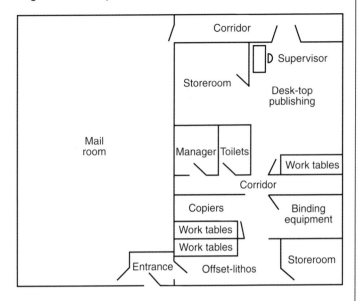

The operators of each process try to do the work in the same order as it was received, although the following factors frequently upset the sequence:

- incoming work is stacked on tables and gets out of order
- stronger personalities secure priority for their work
- some work has to be sent back to the requisitioning departments for proof checking before printing
- only two of the staff and the supervisor can use the desk-top publishing programme
- only two of the staff and the supervisor can use the off-set lithography equipment.

Most of the supervisor's time is spent dealing with telephone calls, desk-top publishing and operating the older off-set lithography machine. It is unreliable and often needs her attention.

Complaints about the service are frequent:

- finished work not ready for the time requested
- long searches in the reprographics room for completed work
- sheets badly printed, or printed in the wrong sequence.

Questions for discussion

1 *What defects do you see in the way the reprographics service operates?*
2 *Draft a job improvement plan for the section.*
3 *What performance standards might be set for the section?*

Organisation to prevent sub-quality work or service

Management creates the conditions in which quality performance by employees is possible. There must be reliable selection procedures to choose staff who are capable of absorbing the training. The training must give employees the skill, knowledge and attitudes to deliver a quality service or product.

A positive attitude to quality can be developed by:

- teaching the *why* as well as the *how* of each task
- giving more responsibility to employees for what they do
- consulting on how to maintain and improve quality.

With the staff, management needs to **diagnose** and **remedy** causes of poor quality. These may include poor physical working conditions, equipment problems, poor procedures, vague instructions, work overload, overlapping authority, monotonous tasks, and supply difficulties.

Effective systems and procedures

To ensure that the quality systems and procedures are effective, the organisation must:

- define the responsibilities for all aspects of quality and allocate the necessary authority to act on the problems
- document all aspects of the quality assurance procedure
- provide accurate information, correctly transmitted and recorded. For example, in a manufacturing company the design department might accept a modification, requested by a customer, to the normal basic design. Unless the manufacturing instructions to departments are carefully controlled, some departments may use the standard design rather than the revised version
- ensure traceability on quality problems. If a fault is discovered, it may be that the whole of that production batch is affected and should be recalled for examination. It is good practice, therefore, to mark production in such a way that faults can be traced to the date of manufacture, the production batch, and the particular machine or operator.

Positive attitude to quality problems

People seldom make mistakes deliberately. Quality faults should be regarded as problems to be solved rather than as an opportunity for scapegoating. Scapegoating encourages the concealment of mistakes. The prime concern becomes shifting the blame instead of dealing with the problem.

The customer has little interest in this process. He or she wants restitution and correction.

Measurement of the costs of poor quality

Ignorance of the true costs of poor quality encourages complacency. It is useful, therefore, to measure the costs of not conforming to quality standards. Non-conformance costs fall into two categories: the **immediate costs** of correcting the error and the **consequential costs.** Immediate costs cover rework, including associated administrative expenses. Consequential costs are expenses that are caused by the error but may not be identified with it.

Task

An error is made on an order for manufacturing components. Instead of 2400, the order sent was for 240. The error was discovered when the order was delivered. The immediate cost of the error was placing a new order for a further 2160. What are the possible consequential costs of the error?

Examples of consequential costs include:

- the cost of lost sales or lost production through supplies arriving too late
- the cost of business lost through giving inadequate or discourteous treatment to a customer
- the cost of returning excess stock ordered in error
- the cost of holding excess stock ordered in error
- the cost of recalling and inspecting batches of suspect items
- the cost of guarantee work
- settlement discounts lost through paying accounts too late
- bad debts through failure in credit control procedures.

The consequential costs of poor quality are more difficult to measure, but often more significant than the immediate costs of error.

British Standard 5750/International Standard 9000

Reliable quality is a prime concern when deciding which supplier of goods or service to use. Retail organisations like Marks and Spencer have, for many years, extended their quality control procedures into the suppliers' organisations to ensure reliability. Reputation for quality is important, but it can only be established over time. This presents problems for organisations tendering for orders from new customers. The British Standard (BS) 5750 certificate, and the equivalent International Standard (IS) 9000 certificate, indicate to potential customers that the quality procedures of the certificate holders are reliable and therefore capable of delivering consistently the promised quality product or service.

The BS 5750 certification process

- The organisation, usually with the help of a consultant, prepares a quality manual detailing its quality policy, organisation and procedures. This has to be detailed, comprehensive and conform to the BS 5750 standard for the quality control of all aspects of the business.
- An assessor visits the firm to check that the manual is comprehensive and that the procedures are being implemented correctly.
- The certificate is issued and the firm can quote the certificate on its stationery and documents. This helps when tendering for contracts.
- Regular visits, once or twice a year, are made by the certifying body to audit the correct implementation of the quality manual.

Criticisms of the BS 5750 system

- It certifies the reliability of the quality-assurance system. It does not certify directly the quality of the product or service itself. Two organisations could offer different levels of quality of the same product or service, but both could have a BS 5750 certificate.
- The certificate shows that organisations have reliable procedures to deliver the particular quality level they have promised. The industrial or commercial customer understands this and recognises that the level of quality is a matter of negotiation and contract. The more casual customer may assume wrongly that the BS 5750 assures an absolute quality standard, rather than a system capable of delivering the promised standard.
- It is expensive to obtain. Small organisations might think it is disproportionately so.
- The approach is bureaucratic, perhaps encouraging a procedure-centred rather than a people-centred approach to quality. In fairness, one of the requirements for certification is proper training.

Investors in People Award

The award signifies that the organisations holding it are implementing best training and development practices. The award was introduced by the then Department of Employment in 1991 when national targets for education and training were set. In England and Wales, the scheme is the responsibility of the Training and Enterprise Councils. In Scotland, Local Enterprise Companies are responsible.

The National Standard in training and development is defined in terms of 24 assessment indicators. Comprehensive detail is given in *Investors in People: A Guide to Achieving the Standard* by Don Mason. These are the criteria by which an organisation's application for the award is judged. The format and layout of the assessment indicators are similar to those of a National Vocational Qualification (NVQ).

Assessment indicators

The assessment indicators give precise expression to the standards in four sections.

The first section requires organisations to have a written but flexible business plan that specifies the contribution expected from employees. It needs to state how employees' development needs will be met. Organisations must demonstrate that this is communicated clearly to the workforce.

The second section requires organisations to review regularly and agree with each individual employee his/her development needs against the business plan. This includes the training of new staff and the continuing development of other staff. An effective staff appraisal scheme is needed to help individuals identify their training needs. In drawing up training plans, managers should agree targets, preferably in terms of NVQs. They should also agree time scales. All employees should have a written development plan. Adequate resources must be allocated for the implementation of training and development.

The third section is concerned with the implementation of all aspects of the training and development plan. Whether induction, basic job instruction, on-the-job, or off-the-job development, best practice is expected. There should be effective induction programmes for new staff, including an explanation of their contribution to the company plans and their entitlement to continuous development. Initial job training should equip starters to do their jobs efficiently. Managers and supervisors should be trained in coaching and instructional skills to deliver on-the-job training. Appropriate back-up should be provided, for example in the form of open-learning centres with text and computer learning packages. Financial support should be available to pay for fees for appropriate external training. Managers should hold pre-course briefings and agree targets for improved job performance to encourage transfer of learning from course to workplace.

The fourth section deals with the evaluation of training. The standards require organisations to assess the effectiveness of training against targets set out in terms of its contribution to the business plan, for example improved output and quality. Off-the-job training should be followed by a debriefing with the manager. This might include other members of the team who could share the benefits. Plans for the implementation of the new ideas should be agreed. These might take the form of assignments or projects. There should be a reliable system for identifying and recording training costs, not only external fees, but also the cost of time spent on internal training. Indirect benefits of continuous development, such as the effects on morale and motivation, could be assessed by employee surveys. The outcome of evaluation should be revised action plans and targets.

The certification process

- The organisation audits its current training and development practices against the assessment indicators to form a judgement of the implications, particularly on resources, of submitting to the accreditation process.
- Assuming the organisation decides to pursue its application, it sets about revising the organisation and practices of its training and staff development to conform to the standards. This is phased over time and may involve the use of consultants, depending on the expertise available within the company. Progress towards the standards is documented and, together with the business plan, forms a portfolio of evidence of that progress.
- When the organisation believes its training and development is operating to standard, it applies to the local Training and Enterprise Council (TEC) for recognition. An assessor, appointed by the TEC, studies the portfolio of evidence and visits the organisation. The assessment examines implementation as well as procedures. The assessor interviews a cross-section of managers and employees.
- If the standard is not yet being met, the assessor will make recommendations for improvement. Where the standard is being met, the assessor passes his or her recommendation for approval to the local TEC committee. If they approve, the award is given and the organisation is entitled to advertise its possession.

The award is for a period of three years, renewable by a further assessment.

Computerised personnel information systems

A computerised personnel information system should meet the different needs of staff operating the system, the managers and supervisors exercising day-to-day control, and senior management responsible for long-term planning. The general requirements of the system are:

- It must protect the confidentiality and security of the information held in the system. This means:
  - restricting access to areas where the information is stored or processed
  - restricting access to the system by user codes
  - restricting access to sensitive files by passwords
  - restricting access in files to 'read only' so that unauthorised changes cannot be made to entries
  - programming audit trails so that enquiries are recorded for later investigation.
- It should be accessible to authorised users, preferably on-line through a VDU.
- It should be user friendly, providing on-screen instruction. Descriptions are preferable to codes since they are self explanatory. When codes and abbreviations are used they should be interpreted on screen.
- Access to data should be referenced by commonly known information such as employee names or numbers.
- It should be able to generate reports of specified analysis of data, for example the number of women in a given occupational group due to retire in two years' time, or the names of all manufacturing staff who can speak French.

Personnel functions covered by computerised systems

Computerised systems may be used to assist the performance of the following personnel functions.

Staff establishments

The maximum staffing level for each grade of staff for each department is authorised and recorded. Variations such as part-time staff, staff on short-term contracts, temporary staff to cover long-term absence or peak workloads should also be authorised and recorded.

Replacement of staff who leave is not usually automatic nowadays. The department may have to justify the need for a replacement.

An accurate data bank of staff establishments and personnel records facilitates manpower planning and budgeting. The effects of alternative forecasts of increase or decrease in business activity, or of changes in technology, can be projected in detail on to manpower requirements, analysing it by grade, occupation, skills and age. The available working hours can be calculated by adjusting for absenteeism, labour turnover and staff development time. If changes are planned in any of these areas, the effects on the manpower budget can be calculated. This is particularly useful where the training of required staff takes two years or more.

Recruitment and selection

The system should be capable of producing all the support documents, including copies of job descriptions, acknowledgements of applications, and interview appointment letters.

Personnel records

These should hold employees' personal details, qualifications, training, previous experience and employment history, including dates of joining, transfer, promotion and leaving. The data will be obtained initially from application forms.

Salary administration

There is a case for combining personnel and salary records since most of the data are common to both systems. However, there are counter arguments. Payroll is usually seen as an accounting rather than a personnel function. Personnel may favour an on-line system. Payroll may prefer a batch processing system. Salary administration should include details and history of job grading and increments. It should be possible to update salaries and wages automatically to accommodate any authorised general increases. Likewise, when budgeting, it should be possible to calculate the costs of alternative forecasts of salary and wage increases.

Training and development

The individual personnel records should hold details of qualifications, skills and training. These need to be coded so that the information can be classified and summarised when the database is interrogated. Details of training on individual records should include titles of courses, dates attended, results, and evaluation of the course. The format, again, should facilitate summarising and reporting.

Absence and time-keeping

The system should record and accumulate absence by categories, for example annual leave, time-in-lieu for overtime, certified sick leave and self-certified sick leave. For each individual, the system may report annual leave outstanding, sick leave compared to entitlement, and an analysis of any pattern on sick leave such as Mondays and Fridays, or days before bank holidays. Similarly, monthly summary reports by departments may show trends and patterns of absence to be followed up by management.

Further reading

- *Business for Higher Awards* by D. Needham, R. Dransfield, R. Harris and M. Coles. Heinemann, 1995.
- *Computers and Human Resource Management* by M. L. Gallagher. Butterworth Heinemann, 1991.
- *Human Resource Management* by I. Beardwell and L. Holden. Pitman, 1994.
- *Investors in People: A Guide to Achieving the Award* by D. Mason. Technical Publications (Publishing) Ltd, 1995.
- *Personnel Management* by D. Torrington and L. Hall. Prentice Hall, 1991.
- *Quality Circles* by W. L. Mohr and H. Mohr. Addison Wesley, 1983.

15 Teams – managing diversity

O n completion of this chapter students should be able to:

- explain the value and importance of managing diversity in the workplace

- analyse the differences between HRM approaches based on diversity and those based on equal opportunities

- appreciate the value of cross-cultural teams

- identify ways of introducing and supporting diversity

- identify the leadership skills required for managing diversity

- analyse group behaviour and ways of developing high-performance teams

- evaluate the stages of development of teams, their objectives and composition.

Managing diversity in the workplace

In Chapter 4 we looked at teams in some depth from the point of view of managing and motivating people. In this chapter we will be building on these insights by looking at the ways in which teams and teamwork approaches can be used to maintain organisational performance.

We have already seen that many organisations favour the introduction of teamworking as a way of drawing on the wide range of skills and attributes of its employees. Team-building entails bringing together people with the right combination of specialist knowledge, role orientations and personal qualities.

Forward-thinking organisations have set out to nurture diversity as a means of moving organisations forward in times when it is essential to draw on the full capacity of the work team to gain competitive advantage.

The concept of managing diversity is about ensuring that all people within an organisation with their diverse skills and attributes, maximise their potential and their contribution to the organisation.

Task

Discuss the advantages and disadvantages for teamworking of having team members with (a) similar and (b) diverse skills, aptitudes and backgrounds.

Task

In his classic book, *The pursuit of WOW!*, Tom Peters asks the question: Which of the following companies (whether car producer, textile company, bank, etc.) is likely to create the most interesting products or services? The one where:

'The 17 members of the executive group of Company A file into the boardroom. All US born (whoops, sorry, one Canadian). Fifteen are white males, best guess at average age: 47. One

female. One Japanese-American. Dress: suits, suits, suits as far as the eye can see.'

Or this one:

'Company B's 16-person top team noisily straggles into the boardroom attired in everything from Brooks Brothers to Calvin Klein to Banana Republic to Venice Beach leftovers. Six of the sixteen are white males, four are women (two white, one African-American, one Hispanic), plus two Indian-born males, two African-American males, one Chilean-born male, and one British-born male. Average age: about 42, with two or three who are clearly on the side of 32.'

1 *Which of these two teams do you think Tom Peters sees as being more effective?*
2 *What arguments could be put forward to support this view?*

Diversity or equal opportunities?

Writers who examine the issue of managing diversity in organisations point to the way in which a management approach which recognises diversity differs from an equal opportunities approach. Kandola and Fullerton (1994) for example, suggest that diversity recognises the benefits to be gained from differences among employees, whereas equal opportunities has traditionally been a concept which sought to legislate against discrimination. The differences between managing diversity and equal oppportunities are summarised in Figure 15.1.

Liff (1996) suggests that equal opportunity approaches emphasise **equality** and are based on the idea that when people are in the same situation they should be treated in the same way. Managers should not make assumptions about employees on the basis of their gender but rather concentrate on an individual's specific capabilities. In contrast, a managing diversity approach sees gender **differentiation** as relevant. Currently, organisations are organised around the needs, values and approaches of a particular segment of the workforce – white males. If organisations are to maintain their success in the future, they will need to draw on a much wider range of talent. Arguably, they will only be able to do this if they create a culture in which differences are welcomed and accommodated.

Task

1 *Give an example of a situation in which an organisation might benefit from gender differentiation.*
2 *Give an example of a situation in which an organisation might benefit from another form of differentiation.*
3 *Do the examples that you have cited support the principle of encouraging diversity at work?*

Liff does, however, suggest that these two characterisations may provide an unfair representation of equal opportunities policies. For example, many organisations as part of their equal opportunities policies include measures to promote equality which recognise differences, e.g. child-care provision and flexible working hours. The provision of these recognises women's greater child-care responsibilities. Liff goes on to suggest that a move from equal opportunities to managing diversity would involve changes. First, an organisation would need to place greater emphasis on its need to adapt to 'non-standard' employees in contrast to an approach which expects employees to fit in to the existing operation of the organisation.

Although she highlights the differences, Liff also points to the inevitable overlap between the operation of equal opportunities policies and managing diversity:

'If one starts at the practitioner end and asks what is actually being done under the labels of equal opportunity

Figure 15.1 The differences between managing diversity and promoting equal opportunities

Managing diversity	Equal opportunities
■ Ensures all employees maximise their potential and their contribution to the organisation ■ Embraces a broad range of people; no one is excluded ■ Concentrates on movement within an organisation, the culture of the organisation and the meeting of business objectives ■ Is the concern of all employees, especially managers ■ Does not rely on positive action/affirmative action	■ Concentrates on discrimination ■ Is perceived as an issue for women, ethnic minorities and people with disabilities ■ Concentrates on the numbers of groups employed ■ Is seen as an issue to do with personnel and human resource practitioners ■ Relies on positive action

and managing diversity, the outcome is a model which is much less clear cut but which does reveal important strands within each approach. These may well coexist – that is the policies of any particular organisation may well spread over more than one category'.

Why the focus on diversity?

Organisations have tended traditionally to focus policies on a narrow range of groups. Typically, equal opportunities policies are seen as being for the benefit of women, ethnic minorities and the disabled. Managing diversity, in contrast, is not just about issues of discrimination against particular groups, but about enabling *all* individuals to maximise their potential and contribution to the organisation.

The basis of many equal opportunity initiatives has been that it would be disadvantageous to a particular group to emphasise difference. For example, questions about how women applicants will manage their child-care arrangements would be discriminatory, although it is recognised (and evidence supports the fact) that it is women who take the major responsibility for child care. Some would argue that gender equality is best promoted by minimising, rather than drawing attention to, these factors.

Critics of this standpoint would suggest that organisational stress on equal treatment and the apparent gender neutrality of organisational policies may lead many to believe that sexual equality already exists. The evidence suggests that many women and members of ethnic minorities still directly experience discrimination.

Salaman (1986) explored employees' reactions to the London Fire Brigade's equal opportunity policy, which had supported the recruitment of women and ethnic minority men. Many white firemen believed that under the new policy, standards had been lowered to let in inferior applicants. There is also evidence from other areas that, as a result of equality programmes, men feel *they* are now being unfairly treated.

Equal opportunities policies and programmes, then, have faced a number of difficulties: firstly, not actually achieving greater representation of under-represented groups in the workforce and, secondly, engendering opposition from those who see themselves as being excluded from such policies.

The managing diversity approach suggests that the importance of differences among employees or potential employees should be acknowledged and that this may overcome the problem of organisations whose structure still favours particular sections of the workforce.

Demographic changes

The very fact that population changes are taking place is one of the major reasons given by some writers for organisations needing to manage diversity. These demographic changes face the USA and Western Europe.

In the USA, for example, white men still dominate the workforce. In the immediate future, however, the biggest growth in entrants to the labour market will come from women, African-Americans and people of Hispanic or Asian origin. White men are retiring from the workforce in greater numbers, producing a more diverse workforce culturally. In addition, the USA has faced a drop in the numbers of 16-24-year-olds entering the labour market. Thus Cascio (1992) suggests that American organisations will find women and ethnic minorities indispensable and that the task of managing and motivating a culturally diverse workforce will be one of the biggest challenges facing management.

In the UK, demographic data indicates a number of major changes which are in the process of impacting on the labour force.

An ageing population

There are a falling number of young people entering the workforce. From 1987 to 2000 the number of 16–25-year-olds entering the labour market will fall by 1.5 million. School leavers will therefore represent a declining source of recruits for organisations.

Ethnic minorities form a larger proportion of the workforce

Members of ethnic minority groups are younger on average than the white population. Although 16 per cent of the total population is over 65 years of age, only 39 per cent are from ethnic minority groups. Therefore, the ageing population comprises a larger proportion of the white population. Although they will form an increasing part of the labour force, unemployment rates for people of ethnic minority origin are currently twice as high as the white population. This applies regardless of age, sex or level of qualifications.

Increasing participation of women

In 1993 women made up 44 per cent of the labour force and this is expected to increase to 45.8 per cent by 2006. Women are returning to work much sooner after pregnancy than previously and taking shorter breaks or remaining in the workforce.

Changes in the work environment

Given the ageing population and the increasing numbers of women and ethnic minorities entering the workforce, organisations are having to accommodate the needs and motivations of these different groups. This means changing working patterns and accepting more flexible ways of working.

If firms are employing more flexible forms of employment, it follows that the shape of people's working lives must be changing. Statistics show that 30 per cent of people in employment are in the flexible workforce (i.e. not permanent full-time employees). Some people may wish to be part of that flexible workforce and want to work part-time, but for others part-time work may be all that is available.

For many people the reduction in full-time, life long employment is a threat to their security and to that of their family. Given the position of many part-time jobs, it may seem that part-time and flexible employment is exploitative – after all, the relationship between part-time work and low pay is strong. It is often the case that full-time, core jobs are therefore preferred to flexible, 'peripheral' ones.

Patricia Hewitt (1993) argues that instead of resisting flexibility, employees should find ways of making it work for them. She suggests that flexible working patterns can allow employees the freedom to arrange their hours around their commitments outside work. In this way, both men and women may be able to contribute to the care of the family and family life.

> 'As employers compete to attract and retain educated, skilled, and experienced workers, then a choice of working hours will be added to pay, perks and attractive workplaces as inducements to employees. All this suggests some fundamental changes in the relationship between work and the rest of our lives. It is the hours spent at work which make non-work – leisure, family, retirement – possible.'

Hewitt argues that the male organisation of working time is incompatible with the care of children and other dependants. The time which men traditionally spend at work determines how much time they have for their families, whereas the time women spend in caring for their family tends to determine how much time they have for paid employment. As more women either remain in or rejoin the workforce after having children, the tensions between 'work' and 'family' become more severe. The growth of more flexible employment patterns therefore provides an opportunity for both men and women to make choices about the structure of their working time. It is, however, acknowledged that regulation of flexibility is needed in order to create justified limits on what some employers or employees may wish to do.

Case Study

Working women to death?

In June 1996, Market Assessment Publications produced a report on the place of women in Western Europe, indicating that women in the UK are getting a raw deal. Taking work, for example, the fact that 65 per cent of women work could be seen as a good thing. However, the statistics reveal that almost half of these women are working part-time, which is the highest proportion in Europe. Nor would it be true to say that those working full-time have taken over the breadwinning role. Instead, many part-time workers have partners who are either unemployed or also work part-time. Steve Cordingley of Market Assessment Publications reported that 'these women are probably the unsung heroes of the UK's population. They are having to work very hard to hold the whole thing together. The picture we have of women single-mindedly pursuing a career is not true. A large majority are slogging away and totally committed to their families.'

Questions for discussion

1 *To what extent do you see flexible working conditions as providing an appropriate opportunity for women to work?*
2 *Should we welcome or condemn flexible working?*

Cross-cultural teams

Cross-cultural teams are made up of people with different backgrounds and experiences. They are not made up of people who went to similar schools, have similar background, read the same newspaper and have similar value systems and approaches. Today we live in a diverse society, and organisations operate in markets which are global and multi-faceted. Organisations are increasingly realising the importance of creating this diversity as an internal strength. Shell UK, for example, has always benefited from being an Anglo-Dutch concern. However, in addition, Shell has divisions throughout the world. Increasingly the company is developing **synergies** by bringing together groups of people to work on projects to share their ideas and experiences. Significant benefits can be achieved by seeing things through a 'fresh pair of eyes'.

The benefits of accepting and managing diversity

Kandola and Fullerton (1994) examined evidence from a range of writers on the benefits of managing diversity. From this, they divided the benefits into three categories: proven, debatable and indirect.

Proven benefits

Access to talent:

- making it easier to recruit scarce labour
- reducing costs associated with excessive turnover and absenteeism.

Flexibility:

- enhancing organisational flexibility.

Organisations can benefit by being able to recruit, retain and promote from a more diverse potential workforce. They will have the opportunity to attract talent from a wider range of people and, if they are able to train, develop and retain those people, they should then benefit from reduced absenteeism and labour turnover costs. If, for example, women employees are offered child-care facilities and flexible working arrangements, organisations may retain talent which they might otherwise have lost.

Debatable benefits

Teams:

- promoting team creativity and innovation
- improving problem-solving
- better decision-making.

Customers:

- improving customer service
- increasing sales to members of minority culture groups.

Quality:

- improving quality.

A debatable benefit of managing diversity is that there will be greater team effectiveness. As we have already seen, many organisations are placing an emphasis on teamworking as part of their need to retain a competitive edge.

Some writers argue that the ideas, creativity and innovation which come with having diverse teams can be beneficial to an organisation. However, Kandola and Fullerton point out that the effectiveness of teams depends on a wide range of factors, not just whether the group is heterogeneous in terms of sex and ethnicity. Other factors which influence effectiveness include the role of the leader; the roles of the team members; the nature of the task involved; and the mix of skills and abilities of the team.

Indirect benefits

- satisfying work environments
- improving morale and job satisfaction
- improving relations between different groups of workers
- greater productivity
- competitive edge
- better public image.

The link between these benefits and a policy of managing diversity are difficult to prove and hence largely unsubstantiated.

Pursuing diversity-organisational initiatives

In a survey of 285 UK organisations, Kandola and Fullerton identified the ten most successful initiatives and the ten least successful initiatives (see Figure 15.2). Whereas the successful initiatives largely related to the individual needs of all employees, many of the least successful tended to focus on particular groups.

Liff (1996) suggests that the **individualistic** approach to managing diversity will appeal to many organisations.

> *'No longer should individuals wait for the organisation to deliver identical equality to all. Instead the organisation is a facilitator empowering able individuals to realise their full potential and then dedicate it to corporate goals! Such an emphasis can be seen as having links, in addition, to broader management ideas about the importance of decentralised organisations, teamwork and innovation. It is also a version of equality which can be "sold" to managers and employees at a time of scarce resources because it appears to support individuals without favouring members of particular groups.'*

Case Study
Addressing individual needs rather than group membership

A transport organisation was selecting staff for specialist and important positions. To do this it operated a procedure that involved interviews, psychometric tests and practical tests.

Figure 15.2   Organisational initiatives

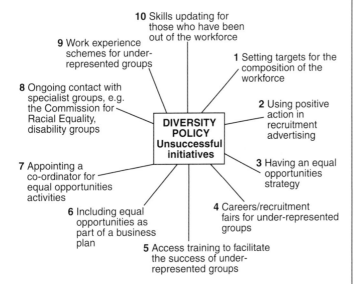

Most of the candidates were internal and there were significant numbers of ethnic minorities who applied. None of the ethnic minority applicants was successful. It appeared that the aptitude tests, in particular, presented a very considerable barrier. The organisation decided to investigate this further.

A session was arranged with some of the unsuccessful applicants where they were asked how they felt about taking the tests. Many of them had not taken such tests before and felt stressed beforehand. These feelings were not alleviated by the apparent coldness of the proceedings.

They were asked to take some tests while they were observed. It was discovered that their test-taking strategies were not very good. For example:

- some did not monitor how they were progressing against the clock
- others would continue working through the items in order even though they would have done far better to

have skipped difficult items and returned to them later
- many were confused by the instruction 'to work quickly and accurately without wild guessing'. They invariably chose to work accurately at the expense of speed.

To help overcome this problem, an open-learning booklet on test-taking skills was developed. Trials of the booklet showed that by improving test-taking strategies, test performance could be improved. So far, so good. The problem arose at the next stage. The organisation was approached by an equal opportunities group who maintained that this booklet should only be available to women as they were underrepresented in that particular type of work. However, another lobby felt that it should be made available only to ethnic minorities as they too were under-represented. In truth, the booklet would not have been distributed on gender grounds, as black men would have had access to it; nor would it have been distributed on ethnic grounds as white women would have had access to it. It would have been easier to say that if you were a white male applicant you could not have it!

The advice of the consultants was that the booklet should be made available to all candidates – the ones who would benefit the most would be those who lacked test-taking knowledge. It was the *need* that had to be addressed rather than *group membership* (Kandola and Fullerton, 1994).

Questions for discussion

1   *An organisation discovers through monitoring procedures that women and ethnic minorities are under-represented in senior posts within the organisation. What action could be taken to increase representation?*
2   *Which do you consider to be of most importance in addressing inequalities, individual needs or group membership?*

Groups and leadership

In Chapter 4 we examined ways in which teams can be built and the importance of leadership skills in developing effective teamwork. In many organisations, moving to a teamwork approach may involve changing the culture. A culture based on **consensus decision-making** is required, with employees at all levels coming together, discussing options and the way forward, not letting their judgements be clouded by preconceived views or historical differences.

Consensus decision-making can involve a huge culture change for management. Traditionally, in industries which were used to a hierarchical, command and control approach, managers were selected because of their tough autocratic, dictatorial style of getting things done through instruction and control. Today, however, managers are being asked not to control but to influence, to develop the team, to listen and to decide by consensus, even when the consensus decision is not one which they would have first chosen. In addition, managers are required to provide support, and counselling and to accept others' mistakes without having a 'witch hunt' followed by punishment and disciplinary procedures. All of this requires a sea change in leadership approaches.

Diversity and leadership skills

Loden and Rosener (1991) argue that effective leaders need to resist the urge to employ staff who look, sound or think just like themselves, if their organisations are to benefit from diversity. Effective leaders are those who empower diverse employees and are actively involved in promoting a culture of diversity. In particular, they argue, effective leaders exhibit six key qualities:

- vision and values that recognise and support diversity within the organisation
- ethical commitment to fairness and the elimination of all types of workplace discrimination
- broad knowledge and awareness regarding the primary and secondary dimensions of diversity and multicultural issues
- openness to change
- mentor and empowerer of diverse employees
- ongoing catalyst and model for individual and organisation.

These qualities emphasise the need for leaders/managers of organisations to be committed to the diversity which employees offer. Liff (1996), however, suggests that a great deal of evidence points to the fact that managers have a strong commitment to homogeneity in their workforce. Research on recruitment and promotion in organisations indicates that those making decisions tend to appoint and promote people who are like themselves.

The policy of managing diversity has the apparent advantage of responding to individual needs and wants. However, if used to replace an equal opportunities approach, it may disadvantage those groups for whom equality of opportunity is still questionable. Unless managing diversity is linked with existing equal opportunities approaches, the ways in which job structures and personnel practices disadvantage certain groups may override the benefits of managing diversity.

Case Study
Diversity in the police force

Despite the policy papers, the codes of good conduct, the training courses in equal opportunities and the benign pledges by senior officers, sexism in the police and armed forces remains rife, according to the women who work there and statistical evidence.

The spate of recent sex discrimination and harassment cases involving police officers is indicative that more women are willing to come forward with complaints. There have been cases of a policewoman denied promotion because she was pregnant, and a policeman sacked for harassing a female colleague weeks after winning a national award for curbing sexism in the workforce. There is also the case of a policewoman who in 1993 won damages against the Metropolitan Police for sexual and racial discrimination. She is taking Scotland Yard to an industrial tribunal alleging victimisation, because of the hostile treatment she has received since her return to work.

In 1992 Dr Jennifer Brown wrote the influential study *Sex Discrimination in the Police Force in England and Wales.* This showed that one in ten policewomen had given serious thought to leaving the police because of harassment and nine out of ten policewomen had been verbally sexually harassed.

The 150-year-old history of the police force offers the most telling story of how resistant men have been to the arrival of women. It let in the first policewoman in 1915, albeit grudgingly; the government was anxious to clear the streets outside soldiers' arsenals of prostitutes and decided that women were better equipped to do the job. Only during the Second World War did the role of women expand. But when the men returned they went back into retreat, and it was not until the Sex Discrimination Act 1975 that they became a serious threat to male domination of the forces.

Although all forces in Britain have actively sought to take up equal opportunities policies and codes of conduct in the past four years, and it is part of police training, there is a concern that the senior ranks are only paying lip service to the real problem.

According to academics who have researched women's status in the armed forces, nothing will change under the lip-service attempts to introduce equal opportunities policies. The only real impact will come when the critical

Figure 15.3 Women in uniform: the figures
Source: the Home Office and the MOD

POLICE (Regular force, England and Wales, excluding Metropolitan Police Service)

1995 Total: 125 222, Women: 17 891
(1 chief constable, 6 assistant chief constables, 43 superintendents, 55 chief inspectors, 251 inspectors, 1 198 sergeants and 16 337 constables)

1990 Total: 96 927, Women: 10 837
(1 assistant chief constable, 28 superintendents, 40 chief inspectors, 153 inspectors, 560 sergeants and 10 055 constables)

ROYAL NAVY/ROYAL MARINES
1996 Men: 44 676 (7 913 officers)
Women: 3 631 (457 officers)

1986 Men: 63 968 (9 650 officers)
Women: 3 405 (380 officers)

ARMY
1996 Men: 102 858 (12 733 officers)
Women: 6 529 (1 091 officers)

1986 Men: 154 393 (16 142 officers)
Women: 6 665 (964 officers)

ROYAL AIR FORCE
1996 Men: 59 126 (11 038 officers)
Women: 5 597 (941 officers)

1986 Men: 87 057 (14 543 officers)
Women: 6 181 (862 officers)

In 1986 there were no women above the rank of Brigadier in the army, and none above commodore in the RAF or the navy. In 1996, the same is true, while there are only two women of this rank on the air force (both air commodores); compared with six a decade ago.

FIRE SERVICE (Full-time staff)
1995 Men: 38 774, Women: 194

---

mass of women to men reaches a certain level that forces them to become accepted. As figure 15.3 shows, excluding the Metropolitan Police Service, about 14 per cent of police officers are women, but in the armed services and the fire service this is much lower.

Dr Jennifer Brown (Portsmouth University) carried out research among 1802 women police officers in 1993, finding that 40 per cent had experienced low-level harassment and unwanted touching. A further 6 per cent had experienced serious harassment including sexual assault at work, which was also significantly higher across the armed forces compared with other workplaces. Brown suggests that it is not until there is a critical mass of 20 to 25 percent of women that things will start to improve. When there is a small number of one group, in this case women, there isn't a critical mass to allow change. In the last 20 years, women have fought to be incorporated into all areas of police work, like traffic departments and CID squads, but it has been an inch-by-inch process.

Questions for discussion

1 *Examine the statistics of numbers of women in uniform for the police, navy, army and air force. Given the figures available, when do you think the critical mass of 25 per cent women might be present in those four services?*

2 *Given the cases cited above, why might the police force face difficulty in recruiting more women or ethnic minorities in order to reach the critical mass of 25 per cent?*

Group behaviour

In Chapter 4 we looked at roles and behaviours within teams. We will now look at this in more detail in terms of its impact on maintaining organisational performance.

The ability to create effective teams is an important element in the development of an organisation. When managers look for new staff, they do not just concentrate on those with the right qualifications, important though these are. In addition, and often more importantly, they look for people with the right personality for the job, who can cope with the work involved and also work with others.

In working together in groups, people's actions and attitudes will be determined by a range of factors such as their previous experience, their predisposition to work with others, their personality, the importance they attach to the task, and their views on other members of the group.

In building a team you need to move the group members forward from seeing themselves as disparate individuals into a clearly focused team. It is therefore essential to work on both the task and processes involved in interactions. Creating a task focus involves sharing objectives and creating a joint ownership of meeting those objectives. Creating an effective process involves aspects of team-building. Individuals need to appreciate the importance of supporting and helping each other in order to create a good working relationship based on high performance.

Composition/mix

The composition or mix of a working group is likely to be varied. Increasingly the emphasis today is on bringing together a range of individuals from across an organisation to work on particular projects. Because individuals are from different functional backgrounds, they are likely to have different attitudes and approaches. For example, we commonly hear statements in business that so-and-so has 'an accountant's mentality' or that somebody else 'is just concerned with selling'. Clearly, in bringing together a diverse team, the emphasis must be on a shared perception that individuals are not in competition with each other, and that the best results will be achieved by a **synergistic team approach**.

Choosing a team is all about matching the people you have with the roles that are required within the team. It is essential to build up a detailed understanding of potential team members and their characteristics in order to see what particular contributions they can make to a team. As we have emphasised above, it would be foolish to choose a team based purely on predictable conformists unless you want a very closed-ended and routine task to be performed. If you want to be bold and outrageous, you may need to take risks and build up a team of non-conformists. Miller and Form, in their book *Industrial Sociology,* suggest that in choosing a team you may need to develop a rating scale for team membership. For example, in evaluating the social skills required, they stress seven factors:

- scope of social contacts
- status range of contacts
- social demands of the job
- social leadership qualities
- skill intensity
- social participation
- personal responsibility for others.

Duration

Some teams are built for a specific purpose which may have a short duration, e.g. to identify the current strengths and weaknesses of an organisation, or to recommend changes in the health and safety policy. Other teams are far more long lasting. For example, it can be argued that

all members of an organisation are part of a large team – some of these individuals will stay with the organisation for many years. Traditionally, employees tended to work in a particular section of an organisation for a long period of time (although there was only a limited emphasis on team-building). Today, the emphasis is far more on bringing project teams together to complete whole projects. Some of these projects may last weeks, while others may go on for years. Individuals may be working in several different project teams at the same time.

Task

Individuals are increasingly involved in team-based projects. Discuss how this might enhance or detract from their commitment to these teams.

Objectives

The objectives established for a team will have an important impact on the way in which it is established and organised. We can see this, for example, in the creation of a sports team. Clubs like Newcastle United, Manchester United and Chelsea have in recent times set their sights on being more than just a success in the UK. These clubs want international success and to go beyond the boundaries of soccer to pursue a range of business, commercial and social interests. In order to achieve success they have drawn on a diverse array of talent from many countries, e.g. players from Colombia, the Netherlands, Russia, Belgium, Italy and France. These clubs have gone for the best from a diversity of footballing backgrounds in order to establish an ongoing team. To bring these players together into an effective working group, it is not sufficient simply to say 'here is a ball; go and show me what you can do with it'. Instead, the clubs have emphasised the importance of building a **team spirit** through shared social and cultural activities. These clubs have recognised that a 'team' strategy is not something you can establish overnight. It is an ongoing long-term process.

In establishing an effective team, it is essential to communicate your objectives to all team members. They should be invited to outline difficulties that already exist and might arise, as well as to take ownership for strategies to overcome these difficulties.

Formal and informal teams

Many teams develop through planned formal processes, others occur as a natural result of people working together.

It is important for managers to be just as aware of informal teams as of the formal structures which they create. The relationships that are created within an informal team can be just as powerful as for a formal team. Sensitive management recognises informal teams where they arise and, wherever possible, tries to build these teams so that they work to support organisational goals and objectives.

Task

Identify one formal and one informal work team that exists in the place where you currently work, or that operate in workplaces with which you are familiar. Which of these teams is more effective in helping the organisation to meet its stated objectives? What measures could enlightened managers take to develop more support from the informal work teams?

Stages of development

Jon Katzenbach and Doug Smith, in their book *The Wisdom of Teams* (Harvard Business School Press, 1993), argue that there is a threshold that a group must cross before it becomes a team. They define a team as:

> *'A small number of people with complementary skills who are committed to a common purpose, performance goals and an approach for which they hold themselves accountable.'*

Katzenbach and Smith argue that managers need to be able to understand the ingredients of a team if they are to operate a successful organisation. They set out a simple framework for the development of teams and show a team performance curve (see Figure 15.4).

Figure 15.4 Team performance curve

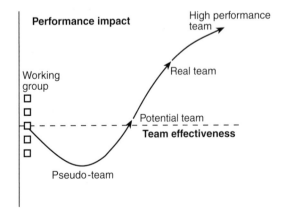

- *The working group.* This is a collection of individuals for whom there is no real opportunity or need to become a team. Each working group member produces something that helps the task to be completed without feeling a real part of the team. Being a part of the working group places no more demand on an individual than if he or she were working independently.
- *The pseudo-team.* In this situation there is no joint benefit of being a part of the team. Indeed, each member's performance is worse than if working alone. This is because there is no focus, no common sense of purpose and no set of goals. The group members are confused as to what they should be doing or how they should be working together. At some stage in your life you are almost certain to work in a pseudo-team. It is very frustrating. Team members are 'feeling their way in the dark'. This may generate antagonism between members, and the team will quickly crumble.
- *The potential team.* This is a collection of individuals with a clear performance need. They are seriously seeking to improve their impact on the group. In other words, they are aware that there is a need for something to be done in order to improve their performance and they want to do it. Unfortunately, however, they lack clarity about their aims as well as the discipline needed for a common working approach. Also, they will not have established the final criterion – **mutual accountability.** Many organisations are full of potential teams. This provides a real opportunity and a challenge for management.
- *The real team.* It is worth repeating that a real team is 'a small number of people with complementary skills who are committed to a common purpose, performance goals, and an approach for which they hold themselves mutually accountable'.
- *The high-performance team.* In addition to meeting the definition for a real team, this group will also be deeply committed – even beyond the team set-up – to the personal growth and success of its members. It will significantly out-perform other teams. Where such a team is based on diversity, the team will yield **premium performance.**

Task

Analyse the performance of a team that you have been a member of. Can you say what stage your team reached in the process of development outlined above? If it fell below that of the high-performance team, why was that?

Leadership theory and practice

In Chapter 2 we looked extensively at the importance of leadership. In particular, we stressed the importance of drawing a distinction between management and leadership. In this chapter we have emphasised the importance of developing a new model of leadership. Today we are looking for leaders who are able to bring out the best in others. More than that, it is essential that leaders are able to develop a clear understanding of employees with whom they work.

Case Study

Developing leadership

In his book *The pursuit of WOW!,* Tom Peters highlights a visit he made to Federal Express in Memphis which has developed a Leadership Institute for its employees. He quotes the example of a senior manager who had attended a Leadership Institute course. The manager explained that he worked in a plant where 75 per cent of the employees are Hispanic.

'After attending the course, my first goal was to learn as much Spanish as I could. If I'm going to work with Hispanics, I need to understand them and they need to understand me – and we all need to feel comfortable … Another thing that shocked me in the course was how naive and backward so many men are on women's issues. Men have got to treat women as equals, complete equals. Period. I went back and discussed all these issues with both my management team and my frontline folks.'

Questions for discussion

1   *What general lessons can you draw from the above extract?*
2   *To what extent do you think these lessons are applied in UK business practice?*

Theories of building, maintaining and evaluating effective teams

John Schermerhorn, James Hunt and Richard Osborn, in their book *Managing Organisational Behaviour,* argue that team-building 'is a sequence of planned activities designed to gather and analyse data of the functioning of a group and to initiate changes designed to improve teamwork and increase group effectiveness'. This involves a number of common steps:

1   someone in or outside a group notices that a problem exists or might develop
2   group members work together to gather data related to the problem
3   group members work together to analyse the data and plan for improvement
4   group members work together to implement the action plans
5   group members work together to monitor progress, evaluate results and take further action
6   group members work together to repeat this process as often as necessary.

In order to build an effective team, you need to engage in teamwork. This is why many organisations take their employees away together to do all sorts of crazy things such as outward bound or survival courses, where they live and work closely together for a period of time to build up a team ethos. In the same way, the England football team or a unit in the parachute regiment might live 'cheek by jowl' for periods of time in order to build up a team spirit. Team-building can therefore take place **on the job** or **off the job** (e.g. in a residential college).

Team-building requires an effective facilitational process. It needs to be carried out by people who are skilled team-builders and it needs to have clear objectives. Importantly all participants in the team-building process need to be able to share ownership of the project and need to be **willing participants**.

The important starting point is for participants to identify the sorts of barriers that will prevent effective team building and how these might be overcome. Clearly, there also needs to be some sort of 'payoff' in the form of better working relationships, conditions, status, mutual understanding, etc.

Team-building can be developed as an ongoing part of organisational development, supported by team leaders. Alternatively it can take place as part of a formal retreat or as an outward bound experience.

In creating a team atmosphere, it is particularly important to think through the early stages of development and how new recruits can be helped to feel part of the team in a sensitive way. Thankfully we are moving beyond the days in which new recruits to organisations were asked to undergo bizarre and often frightening rituals in order to win acceptability.

In building a team, it is important to think carefully through the sorts of norms and values which will characterise effective teamworking. Clearly there needs to be collective input in creating these norms and joint ownership of them once they are established. Positive reinforcement is far more likely to be effective than negative approaches.

A major influence on effective team performance will be the cohesiveness of a group, i.e. how well it works together. This depends on the skills of the leader, as well as on the teamwork skills of members. As we have emphasised in this chapter the leader needs to appreciate that typically he or she will be working with a group of people with different backgrounds, interests and motivations. A skilful leader will draw on this diversity to create an entrepreneurial, enjoyable and active team approach in which all suggestions are explored on their merits, and in which prejudgement is seen as a barrier to effective team development and growth. Good team members know how to have fun and to make things work.

They know how to value other people and to bring the best out of them. They know how to thrive on diversity. The organisation needs to create those structures and working practices to encourage such an approach.

Once a team is up and running, it is important to continually monitor its operation in order to evaluate its success. By identifying best practice and the high points and low points of group effectiveness, it becomes possible to build up models for future practice. *Success thrives on success.*

Further reading

- *Human Resource Development* by J. Stewart and J. McGoldrick. Pitman, 1996.
- *Managing Diversity: New Opportunities for Women?* by S. Liff. Warwick Papers in Industrial Relations, 1996.
- *Managing Human Resources: Productivity, Quality of Work Life and Profits* by F. Cascio. McGraw-Hill, 1992.
- *Managing the Mosaic: Diversity in Action* by R. Kandola and J. Fullerton. Institute of Personnel Development, 1994.
- 'New Approach Urged on Sexism in the Police' by C. Hodges, in *People Management,* 25 February 1995.
- *The Pursuit of Wow! Every Person's Guide to Topsy-turvy Times* by Tom Peters. Macmillan Press, 1995.
- 'When the Force is Against You' by P. Wynn Davies, in *The Independent,* 22 May 1996.
- *Workforce America: Managing Employee Diversity as a Vital Resource* by M. Loden and J. B. Rosener. Irwin Professional Publishing, 1991.
- *About Time: The Revolution in Work and Family Life* by P. Hewitt. IPPR/Rivers Oram, 1993.

16 Employer and employee organisations

On completion of this chapter, students should be able to:

- identify and explain the structure and objectives of employer and employee organisations

- explain how collective bargaining works and why it is important

- describe the nature and purpose of industrial tribunals

- outline and analyse procedural and substantive agreements

- identify negotiating rights

- outline the process of negotiation and critically examine negotiation skills

- describe and evaluate the role of the state in employee relations

- explain and critically analyse recent trends and developments in employee relations.

Employee organisations

Trade unions are made up of groups of employees who have joined together in an organisation to further their common interests. These employees may have in common a skill, a trade, an industry, an employer or an occupation. Trade unions are formed, financed and run by members, and a number of unions have existed for over a century.

Trade union density is a statistic showing actual trade union membership as a percentage of potential union membership. Since 1979 this figure has declined from over 50 per cent to about 35 per cent in late 1996.

Task

Study Figure 16.1 which indicates changes in union membership up to the mid 1990s with different governments in power. What explanations would you put forward to explain the changes in union numbers that are shown?

Figure 16.1 Changes in union membership

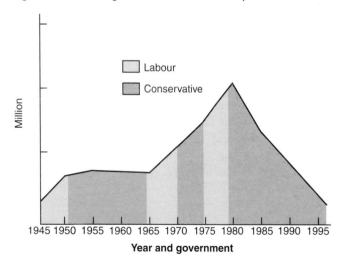

Figure 16.2 A typical union structure

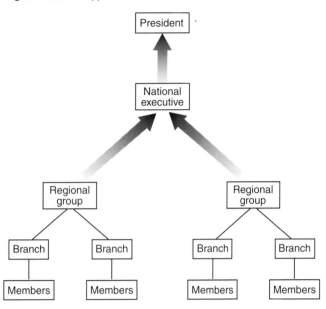

Trade union structure

Trade union structure varies in different industries, but a typical form is shown in Figure 16.2.

Groups of workers are members of a **branch**. They choose branch officials to represent them. The branches also choose members to represent them at a regional committee. **Regional groups** then choose representatives to go to an annual conference. The annual conference makes decisions relating to the industry and chooses a full-time body of officials known as the **national executive**. The top official in the union is the **president**.

A good example of union industrial structure is the National Union of Mineworkers (NUM). In this case the local branch is based on the colliery – the unit of operation in mining. The branch personnel deal with the day-to-day problems, disputes, grievances and many minor issues that can arise. Shop stewards as such are not found in the mining industry. The branch is based on the pit and includes in its membership all manual and craft grades. The branch officers undertake the duties allotted to shop stewards in other industries. (Factories in many trades are traditionally divided into **shops**, e.g. the cutting shop, the sewing shop. Each shop chooses at least one steward to represent it in the workplace. The leading shop steward is called the convenor and is responsible for calling together and organising meetings of stewards.) There is a single line of communication from the branch up through the area coal-field office to the national centre of the NUM, and similarly from centre to branch.

Unofficial trade union structure

While much trade union activity takes place on a day-to-day basis through the official union structure as described above, we should not ignore unofficial union activity. This takes place when members carry out actions not approved by the union, for example when local stewards call out workers in a lightning strike. In fact, in the United Kingdom most industrial action is unofficial but only short-lived. This was particularly true in the late 1970s in industries like car manufacture, in which shop stewards had a lot of local influence. Union funds cannot be used for unofficial action, because it is not officially approved.

Unofficial action generally takes place if local unionists feel that the national union is out of touch with their feelings or if they want to take prompt action.

Types of trade union

Trade unions are typically organised into four main categories:

- craft unions
- industrial unions
- general unions
- white-collar unions.

However, many unions do not fit easily into a particular class; often they have characteristics common to more than one class.

Craft unions

The earliest type of union in this country was the craft union. These unions were made up of highly skilled craft workers in a particular trade. Often these groups were mutual benefit societies before the welfare state came into being. Subscriptions could be quite high, and in return the union would provide sick pay, unemployment pay, a pension and other benefits. These unions are less important in the United Kingdom today. Their membership is relatively small.

Industrial unions

Industrial unionism is common in many European countries, notably Germany. The economy is divided up into industrial sectors, and employees in each sector belong to the industrial union for that sector. The NUM was at one time often quoted as an example of an industrial union. However, in the 1980s a rival union, the Union of Democratic Mineworkers (UDM) was formed, and on top of this there are smaller unions such as the pit deputies' union, NACODS. In many areas of industry today, there is a tendency for new 'super-unions' to take in groups of workers from several industries.

The advantage of an industrial union is that it caters for all workers in an industry whatever their job. Negotiation with employers is greatly simplified and all workers are united in their efforts.

General unions

These include some of the largest unions in the United Kingdom today. They recruit workers from several industries and include semi-skilled and unskilled workers. A particular advantage of this form of union is that it gives strength to workers who have a little power on their own and enables them to belong to a well-funded and organised body.

An example of the creation of a general union occurred in 1988 with the formation of what was then Britain's third largest union. The white-collar workers and supervisors' union, Association of Scientific, Technical and Managerial Staff (ASTMS), and the manufacturing union, Technical and Supervisory Staff (TASS), joined to form the Manufacturing, Science and Finance Union (MSF). The leaders of the two merging unions put forward their case in the following way:

> *'We can now tackle even more effectively the problems our members face … our objective is to work for a well-rewarded, well-trained, and highly skilled membership throughout the whole range of industries and services covered by MSF.'*

White-collar unions

White collar workers are those who carry out non-manual work. The term **white-collar** is used to distinguish them from **blue-collar** employees who carry out manual operations and would traditionally be associated with blue overalls. Examples of white-collar employees are office workers and bank clerks.

White-collar unions have seen the biggest increase in membership in the late twentieth century. As more people have become involved in office and administrative work, and as these groups have become more prepared to join unions, their ranks have swelled. Examples of white-collar unions include the teachers' unions such as the National Union of Teachers (NUT) and the civil servants union, the Civil and Public Servants Association (CPSA).

Professional associations

Many workers belong to a professional association. These organisations do many of the same things as trade unions but are not registered as trade unions. They tend to cover better paid, white-collar workers. An example is the British Medical Association (BMA) which is the body that negotiates on behalf of doctors. Professional associations also try to establish standards for members and to insist on a high level of competence for membership.

The Trades Union Congress (TUC)

This is the annual meeting of the trade union movement. All the major trade unions are members of the TUC and send a number of delegates to the conference depending on the size of their membership. The annual congress takes place in September every year at seaside resorts like Scarborough and Blackpool, where there is a lot of hotel space after the holiday season is finished and where large conference halls are available. The conference lasts for a week and during this time a number of motions and issues are debated. It is a false conception to assume that the TUC is concerned simply with wages. The congress discusses matters as far ranging as education, the health service, privatisation, AIDS and the environment.

The TUC appoints full-time officials, including a president and vice-president, and it has its own substantial headquarters. The TUC is an important organisation because it reflects the general feelings of the trade union movement. It is particularly active in the field of negotiation in industrial disputes. It offers advice and assistance to unions with problems and tries to iron out difficulties that arise between unions. It also acts as a pressure group, trying to influence the government and employers on a wide range of issues.

Despite its importance, the TUC is often regarded as having very little power. Individual unions are not bound by its decisions and the only threat it can use is to expel a union from membership.

Employer organisations

Like trade unions, employer organisations fulfil a wide range of functions, but the main one is **collective bargaining**. Faced by large and powerful trade unions, small employers would be at a disadvantage if they had to stand alone. An employer organisation may bargain on behalf of all firms in an industry. Other functions of employer organisations include:

- pooling ideas and funds for industrial research
- collectively setting up training centres
- discussing common interests such as the threat of foreign competition
- providing a collective voice to raise industry-wide problems with government and other bodies.

The Confederation of British Industry (CBI)

Britain's mouthpiece for the business community is the CBI. It exists primarily to voice the views of its members and ensure that the government and society as a whole understand both the needs of British business and the contribution it makes to the well-being of the nation. The CBI is acknowledged to be **Britain's business voice** and as such is widely consulted by the government, the civil service and the media. But it is not concerned solely with major national issues; an important part of its task is to represent business interest at local level. It is also directly involved in providing essential information and research services for its members.

CBI members come from every sector of UK business, including:

- more than 250 000 public and private companies – half of them small firms with fewer than 200 employees – and most of the nationalised industries
- more than 200 trade associations, employer organisations and commercial associations.

The organisation

The main elements of the organisation are:

- the CBI's ruling council, chaired by the CBI president, which sets policy
- 30 standing committees, 13 regional councils and a Smaller Firms Council contributing to policy-making
- the CBI permanent staff, headed by the director-general, based at Centrepoint in London, in the UK regions and at the CBI's own Brussels office

- the National Conference and the President's Committee, advising on major issues and overall CBI strategy.

The membership

Membership of the CBI is corporate – organisations and companies are members, not the individuals nominated to represent them. Well over 10 million people are employed by companies associated with the CBI, either directly or indirectly through trade organisations or chambers of commerce. CBI membership is extensive and almost exactly matches the profile of business in the United Kingdom: from manufacturing to retailing, from agriculture to construction, from computers to finance and from transport to consultancy.

The president

The president is the CBI's chief office bearer. Elected by the CBI membership, he or she normally serves for two years. The president chairs the monthly CBI council meeting and the annual National Conference. He or she also leads delegations to see government ministers.

The director-general

The director-general is the CBI's chief executive. He or she is appointed by the president of the day with the approval of the CBI council and regularly puts across the business view on radio and TV and in the press. The director-general heads the permanent staff who carry out the bulk of the day-to-day running of the CBI, preparing policy and negotiating with ministers and their civil servants.

Whom does the CBI seek to influence?

The short answer is anyone who, in turn, can influence how business performs – at Westminster and Whitehall, in the UK regions, around Europe and beyond, within the trade union movement and the general public.

Westminster and Whitehall

The well-publicised meetings that the CBI has with ministers and as a member of national development planning groups indicates the central role the CBI plays in national affairs, but they are only a small part of its work. The CBI seeks to influence government policy-making at an early stage in its development. It aims to be continually aware of the thinking of ministers, the research arms of political parties, backbench MPs and civil servants, in order to ensure that its views are put forward at the best possible opportunity. It is a lobbying process that continues as government policy is published and Bills pass through Parliament.

UK regions

The CBI has 13 regional offices which seek to influence local decision-making procedures.

Europe

The CBI has played a prominent part in influencing the process of completing the Single European Market. CBI experts have followed European Community developments for many years. The CBI is consulted by the European Commission as the voice of British industry. It is permanently represented in Brussels, where it opened an office even before Britain joined the European Community.

Trade unions

Although the CBI and TUC may put forward opposing views on a number of issues, a constructive working relationship is maintained both directly and through joint membership of such national bodies as the National Economic Development Council (NEDC), the Advisory, Conciliation and Arbitration Service (ACAS), and the Health and Safety Commission.

The public

As part of the process of explaining business needs and concerns, CBI policies and views need to be put to the public at large as well as to official bodies.

Who decides CBI policy?

CBI policy is decided by CBI members – firms large and small throughout the country. The policy work has two aspects. In the long-term, the aim is to make a constructive contribution to attitudes and forward thinking on issues affecting business, In the short-term, the CBI has to be equipped to react quickly and positively to any proposals by government or others that have a bearing on industry and commerce. More than 2500 people are involved in the CBI policy-making process.

The CBI's standing committees cover every aspect of business life and are responsible for most of the detailed work in policy-making.

The governing body

The CBI's governing body is its council, chaired by the president. Proposals must be approved by the council before they can become official CBI policy. Council

membership is made up of leading national officials, as well as representatives of employer, trade and commercial organisations, the public sector, the 13 CBI regional councils and people drawn from member-companies of all sizes and activities.

Collective bargaining

Collective bargaining, and hence industrial relations, is concerned with **communication** between the representatives of employers and the representatives of employees (see Figure 16.3).

Figure 16.3   Collective bargaining

Successful industrial relations involves striking a balance of interests. From the employer's point of view, industrial relations is about having the right to manage – the ability to plan for the future so that the company can continue to be a success, make profits for its shareholders, and keep its employees motivated. From the employee's point of view, industrial relations is about securing the best possible living standards for trade union members.

Collective bargaining takes place at several levels. It may involve a group of employers and employees making an agreement together (e.g. employers and employees in the car industry), or it may involve just one employer and a group of employees (e.g. employers and employees of a particular car manufacturer or a particular plant).

Collective bargaining may take place in a centralised or a decentralised way. With decentralisation, the critical question is the definition of the organisational level. In industrial relations terms this is known as the **bargaining unit**, but it means much more than that. The assumption is that decentralisation defines the boundary within which job grading, job-design issues, payment systems, contracts and promotion possibilities are fixed. In the past these matters were largely determined at national level and applied to all units in a more or less equal way. Today, collective bargaining decentralisation is almost commonplace.

Day-to-day industrial relations

On a daily basis, the main industrial relations bargaining usually takes place between the personnel department and a shop steward's committee. Normally they would meet regularly once a week and thrash out issues such as:

- pay
- bonuses
- the working environment
- disputes
- work schedules
- grievances
- health and safety at work
- hours
- production targets.

Major industrial relations issues

In addition to local bargaining, which is concerned with small-scale industrial relations, larger issues may be thrashed out on an industry-wide scale. Wages for state employees, for example, are usually agreed upon at an annual pay award. The parties involved will normally be the central executive of a union and employers' leaders.

Case Study

Moves to avert a national postal strike

In June 1996, Britain experienced its first major postal strike for eight years. This followed a period in which management had been seeking to implement new human resource developments, in particular involving the spread of teamworking in the Royal Mail service. For example, this would have seen groups of post men and women working as a team, sharing responsibility for a given area of work and working more flexibly in terms of responsibilities. However, many employees saw this as an initiative which might lead to falling employment and conditions.

On 2 June, leaders of the 138 000 postal workers announced a vote of more than two to one for a national strike. However, leaders of the Communication Workers' Union (CWU) and management agreed to meet the following week in an attempt to prevent industrial action. Richard Dykes, managing director of the Royal Mail, said that fresh proposals would meet concerns that the offer management had made in order to introduce new conditions left out more than 30 per cent of workers. Alan Johnson, joint general secretary of the CWU, warned that staff would not simply be bought off. Key

demands for greater efficiency would also have to be withdrawn.

In the union's ballot, 68 per cent of employees had voted for action to secure a reduction in the working week from six days to five. The union was also seeking enhanced job security, higher pay and assurances over the future of the second delivery. Growing distrust of management – which had led to 18 months of wildcat walkouts – had been fuelled by a series of proposals that postal workers believed were aimed at achieving higher productivity without reward.

Questions for discussion

1 *Why do you think that some employees felt they were being treated unfairly?*
2 *Why do you think that some employees were not prepared to support the union?*
3 *Why is it particularly important for management in cases like the one above to create a healthy industrial relations climate based on mutual trust?*

The above case study highlights the importance of creating an effective industrial relations climate. New employment policies require employee participation for success, since there is often a strong sense of loyalty and security attached to the old system. The aim is to get people to 'own' the new structure and ways of working, and this is where the use of joint working parties can pay off. We know that, at periods of organisational change, one of the most important activities is the management of expectations and the generation of realistic expectations that can be delivered over time.

Industrial tribunals

Collective bargaining is just one dimension of employee participation in the workplace (see Figure 16.4). At one level **direct communication** takes place between employees within the organisation as a regular part of day-to-day practice. In teamwork situations, for example, this will be the predominant mode of participation. In other situations, **consultation** will be the main form of participation, with key employees being consulted as part of the decision-making process. At another level we see the importance of **collective bargaining**, and this will typically be a high-level form of participation. At the top level, you may find **worker directors** in an organisation. For example, the Scott-Bader organisation in Northampton is based on a 'commonwealth' approach to

Figure 16.4 Level of employees participation

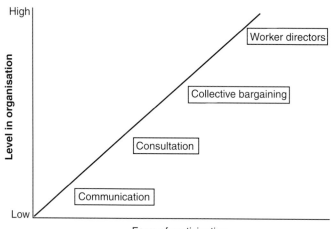

industrial democracy, with worker directors being elected by other employees and trained to take on an important direction role within the organisation.

Unfortunately, however, not all industrial relations issues can be resolved using the methods of participation illustrated above. Nearly every day the national and local press highlight cases which have had to be resolved outside of an organisation, using the forum of an industrial tribunal. An industrial tribunal is a relatively informal 'court' which will usually meet locally. It consists of a legally qualified chairperson and two ordinary members of the public with experience of industry and commerce.

Complainants can either present their own case to a tribunal or seek help from a more qualified expert. If the tribunal finds in the complainant's favour, it can do any or all of the following things:

- make an order declaring the complainant's rights
- order that the complainant is paid compensation, which could include lost earnings, expenses, damages for injury to his or her feelings, or damages for future loss of earnings
- recommend that the person or organisation that is complained against should take a particular course of action within a specified period, e.g. consider the complainant for promotion within a year.

Procedural and substantive agreements

In establishing industrial relations it is important to set out both the procedures governing relationships in the workplace, including bargaining and negotiation, and the substance, i.e. the specific details of agreements between employers and employees. For example, through collective bargaining the following **procedures** may be set out – that a works council will be established with six representatives of managers and six representatives of employees, and that this group will meet once a week to discuss work-related issues. During these meetings it may be established that a particular grade of employee will be entitled to a 5 per cent productivity bonus, and many other details which make up the **substance** of agreements.

In terms of employment:

- *substantive rules* set out the terms and conditions of employment, e.g. pay, hours and holidays
- *procedural rules* establish the way in which substantive rules are made and interpreted; they set out the means by which conflicts will be resolved.

Negotiation

Negotiation rights

Today countries like Denmark, Germany, The Netherlands and Belgium have much greater levels of employee participation than in the UK. Research carried out by Price Waterhouse and Cranfield in the early 1990s indicated that, while in other countries in Western Europe there was a marked increase in employer communications with the workforce, in the UK there was a decline in trade union influence and communications through staff representative bodies.

However, many large and small companies understand the importance of communications and participation in the workplace as a key route to competitive advantage alongside other human resource intitiatives. In the UK, employers and employees have the legal right to engage in free collective bargaining, and employees have statutory rights enabling them to be members of trade unions.

The UK government has, however, been opposed to measures under the EC Social Charter which would involve the creation of statutory rights for employees to increased participation in decision-making. The Social Charter set out provisions involving increased employee participation in organisational decision-making:

- in cases where the introduction of changes in technology have made major implications for the workforce in organisations
- in cases where restructuring operations or mergers have an impact on the employment of workers
- in cases of collective redundancy procedures
- in cases where transfrontier workers are affected by the

employment policies of organisations that they work for.

Negotiating procedures

It is in the interests of managers and employees to establish a clear set of workable negotiating procedures. A negotiating procedure sets out a framework in which parties can establish terms and conditions of employment. This framework will cover four main elements:

1 the area (geographical, occupational grouping, etc) in which the union representatives' role is acknowledged, e.g. 'This agreement covers industrial relations between Sunny Bakeries plc and the Bakery Union'
2 those issues that will be subject to negotiations, such as wages and salaries, conditions of work and union recognition.
3 the steps by which agreement will be sought, e.g. 'In the first instance a meeting will be organised between the personnel managers of individual plants and the divisional officer of the trade union'
4 the steps to be taken when there is a failure to agree; for example, the matter may be put before an outside negotiating body such as ACAS.

Preparation for negotiation will involve:

- drawing up detailed plans for negotiation which are approved by relevant managers prior to the negotiation, setting out short-term and long-term objectives
- carrying out an audit of all current grievances and issues to gain an understanding of the areas that are to be negotiated
- setting out a detailed analysis of what is being negotiated and what is involved; this will include, for example, examining the current collectively bargained agreements in your organisation and those in similar organisations
- carrying out a wage and benefit survey of competitors
- setting out a detailed analysis of the costs and implications of any offers that an organisation makes in an easy-to-understand format.

Task

Study a local or national negotiation which is presented in the press.

1 *What do you see as being the major objectives of the parties involved in the negotiations?*
2 *Set out an audit of the grievances and issues involved.*

3 *Set out a detailed analysis of what is being negotiated.*
4 *Set out a brief wage and benefit analysis of competitors (if possible; you may need to base it on estimates).*
5 *What do you see as being the major costs and implications of offers which employers are making and demands that employees set out?*

Negotiation skills

There are a number of possible outcomes to a negotiation (see Figure 16.5). An effective negotiation would be one in which both sides feel that they have won, i.e. a win–win situation. Situations in which either side, or both sides, see themselves as losers could result in a downward spiral in industrial relations.

In an American study of negotiation, skilled negotiators were defined in terms of three criteria:

1 being rated high by both sides in a negotiation
2 having a 'track record' of significant success
3 having a low record of 'implementation failures'.

The group of skilled negotiators (representatives of both unions and employers) were then compared with a group of 'average' negotiators. The results of comparing these two groups were as follows:

- *Planning time.* There were no major differences between the two groups.
- *Exploration of options.* Skilled negotiators examined a wider range of options.
- *Common ground.* Skilled negotiators gave over three times as much attention to finding common ground as did average negotiators.
- *Long-term versus short-term focus.* The skilled group made twice as many references to the long term as did the average group.
- *Setting limits.* Average negotiators tended to focus on a specific point, e.g. £20, whereas the skilled negotiators were far more likely to think in terms of a range, e.g. between £15 and £25.

Figure 16.5 Possible outcomes to a negotiation

	Outcomes	
Employers	Win	Lose
Employees	Win	Lose

- *Sequence and issue planning.* Average negotiators tended to link issues in sequence, e.g. A then B then C and finally D; skilled negotiators were far more flexible in their approach.

In negotiating, certain words and phrases can act as irritants, for example the term 'generous offer' used by a negotiator to describe his or her own proposal. Average negotiators use this term four times more often than skilled negotiators.

In negotiating, one party will put forward a proposal and then the other will put forward a counter offer. Skilled negotiators make immediate counter proposals significantly less frequently than do average negotiators.

Skilled negotiators tend to put forward fewer arguments for doing something than average negotiators. Skilled negotiators, therefore, will concentrate on why their arguments are important rather than diluting them by presenting lots of different arguments.

Over two-thirds of skilled negotiators claim they always set aside time after a negotiation to review it and consider what they have learned. This is only done by half of average negotiators. The implication is that the skilled negotiator is far more reflective and thoughtful.

In the following chapter we look in greater detail at the skills of collective bargaining negotiations. At this stage we will simply point out that win–win negotiators are most likely to be successful, and that such people tend to plan their strategies carefully and analyse and evaluate their negotiations on an ongoing basis.

Forms of union action

There are a number of types of action that trade unionists can use to put pressure on employers. A distinction needs to be made between individual and unorganised actions on the part of employees against management, and organised or group sanctions against them. In **unorganised conflict** employees will respond in individual ways, using strategies that seem right at the time, with little planning. **Organised conflict,** in contrast, is far more likely to form part of a conscious strategy to change the situation that is seen as the cause of discontent.

Unorganised industrial action can take the form of high labour turnover, bad time-keeping and high levels of absenteeism. It may also occur in the form of slackness by individuals, poor performance, deliberate time-wasting and similar practices. Other evidence of discontent will be revealed in complaints, friction, ignoring rules and apathy.

Trade unions can take a number of forms of organised industrial action, including the following:

- *Picketing.* Primary picketing is legal; this involves members of a union that is on strike standing outside a firm's entrance and trying to persuade other workers not to cross the picket line. Secondary picketing is not legal; this involves workers who are on strike from one firm trying to dissuade workers at a firm not involved with the strike from going to work. Secondary picketing is used by trade unions to spread the impact of their action.

- *Withdrawal of goodwill.* Workers become obstructive about things that require co-operation.
- *Go-slow.* Workers take their time over the work they are doing.
- *Work-to-rule.* Workers stick strictly to the book of rules relating to their particular job in order to reduce efficiency. For instance, railway workers may check that every carriage door is firmly closed at each station.
- *Ban on overtime.* Workers refuse to work more than the hours laid out in their contract of employment.
- *Official strike.* Workers cease work with the authority of the union.
- *Unofficial strike.* A group of workers ceases work without the official approval of the union.
- *Sit-in.* Occasionally workers may occupy a factory. Similarly, if a factory has been threatened with closure, the workers may remain at work operating a work-in, whereby they refuse to stop work.
- *Blacking.* Members of a firm refuse to handle particular materials or work with particular machinery.

Forms of employer action

Employers and management can use a number of sanctions against employees. These may take the form of unco-ordinated and individual actions, or organised and collective actions.

Unco-ordinated, individual actions include close supervision of working activity, tight works discipline, discriminatory employment practices against certain employees, lay-offs, demonstrations, and the unofficial speeding up of work processes or job tasks.

Organised, collective actions include the withdrawal of overtime, mass suspensions, changing of work standards without negotiation, lock-outs, the closing down of enterprises and the removal of workplace equipment.

Case Study

Employee representation in Germany

The German union structure has been shaped by the country's history. In the 1920s the German economy was racked by huge inflation and strikes. In reaction, a new concept know a *Mitbestimmung* (co-determination) grew up. This was based on the radical idea that workers and managers should have equal power in a company.

Under Hitler, unions were suppressed, but came back after the Second World War. Ironically, it was the British who were largely responsible for the shape of the post-war unions in Germany. As the occupying power, they saw the need for stable industrial relations and brought in experts to create the structure that still survives.

A small number of unions were created (there are now 16, headed by the engineers' *IG Metall,* the biggest union in the world) and a one-plant, one-union rule was established. With everyone from cook to toolmaker in the same union, there was never any possibility of demarcation (who does what) job disputes.

Mitbestimmung took on a definite legal form. It was introduced first in the steel industries and later spread to all large companies. Its basis was a two-level board system, with the workforce and employers equally represented on the supervisory board. If it came to the crunch, employers could always get their way, but the set-up did have a calming effect. Management was able to find out the wishes of labour early on in negotiations.

In addition, a works council – a non-union body that represents the workers' interests except on pay – has been in place since 1972. Conflict is illegal. The principle of co-determination sets the scene for the whole industrial relations atmosphere, which is remarkably free from confrontation (although this has risen lately).

But the other leg of the system – the legal framework – ensures that even if the unions do want to push wages up, their actions are strictly limited. Wage talks are carried out between unions and employer organisations. Some are countrywide, while *IG Metall* negotiates state by state. One state will be chosen by the union, the battle will be fought there, and other states will fall into line.

The idea is to thrash out collective deals which set basic pay levels for different grades of employee. These are binding and, as individual companies are not involved in the negotiations, there is no scope for one company to offer bigger wage increases than another.

The basic wage level is, however, rarely paid, because virtually every company adds a top-up that can boost basic pay by perhaps 25 per cent. These top-ups reflect local skill shortages and tend to be more generous in large companies. So the idea of the centralised co-ordinate pay settlement in Germany is really a myth.

Questions for discussion

1 *What are the main differences between the union structure in Germany and in the UK?*
2 *How and why did the differences develop?*
3 *Which do you think is the better system?*
4 *How does the Germany system incorporate the representation of employees in decision-making processes?*
5 *What are the advantages of employee representation?*

The government and industrial relations

Government has passed laws on a wide range of issues relating to industrial relations, which are dealt with in greater detail in other parts of the book. The main areas include the following:

- health and safety at work
- discrimination
- training
- employment of the disabled
- employment of young workers
- dismissal and redundancy
- pay
- industrial action
- restriction in the workplace.

The Advisory, Conciliation and Arbitration Service (ACAS)

This body was set up by the government in 1974 in order to improve industrial relations. ACAS is managed by a council of nine members: three chosen by the TUC; three chosen by the CBI; and three who are independent.

In an industrial dispute in which there is deadlock, the parties may ask ACAS to help. Sometimes they may allow ACAS to look at the issue and come up with a solution that is binding; at other times ACAS might simply be asked to make recommendations.

Conciliation takes the form of attempts to persuade the parties to reach, by negotiation, a settlement of their dispute.

Arbitration takes the form of an award made after the arbitrator has heard the cases of the parties involved in the dispute. In general, arbitration is more appropriate to disputes of rights (i.e. disputes over the interpretation of an existing agreement) than to disputes of interest (disputes over new terms and conditions of employment). In disputes of rights, the arbitrator can simply clarify existing rules; but with disputes of interest, the two sides may be reluctant to trust the proposal of new ideas or fundamental changes to an outsider.

The media and public tend to view ACAS as ambulance chasers and firefighters in situations of conflict. Although this sort of emergency repair work is a critical part of the work of ACAS, it is only a small part of the overall workload. ACAS deals with over 20 new collective disputes a week.

The greater part of the work of ACAS involves individual grievances. Each year in the 1990s ACAS has had to deal with over 50 000 cases of individual arbitration. Individual disputes involve a variety of cases including unfair dismissal and sex discrimination applications. ACAS has a legal obligation to try and resolve individual grievances before they reach industrial tribunals. Most individual cases will be resolved either through conciliation or because the complaint is dropped. Nine out of ten disputes involving ACAS are settled before industrial action is taken.

The rest of ACAS's resources are dedicated to **advisory** work involving both unions and employers, including surveys, projects, training activities and advisory visits.

Recent trends and developments in employee relations

Like other organisations in the business world, trade unions in the last decade of the twentieth century have had to adapt to a rapidly changing environment in order to survive. Some of the important changes in the external environment include:

- the development of new jobs and skills requiring greater flexibility of working practices and attitudes
- the growing importance of women in the working population
- the growth of part-time jobs
- the hiving off of non-core services and the contracting out by large businesses to smaller organisations (the development of the flexible firm)
- the growing affluence of many employees
- the growth of the service sector of the economy at the expense of manufacturing
- the development of new business practices related to human resource management.

These trends and others have demanded wide-scale changes. One noticeable change has been the decline in membership of trade unions. Rising employment in the 1980s was experienced mainly in service industry, where unions tend to be weak. The recession in the early 1990s made it difficult for unions to win back members as the numbers of people in employment fell. In the mid-1990s, the re-emergence of a 'feel-good factor' has again diminished the hold of trade unions. Many of the largest unions have continued to lose members and in the 1990s we have seen mergers of some of the very big unions. Unions in traditional manufacturing industries, such as the NUM, now have membership of less than 40 000. Public service unions, such as the National Union of Public Employees (NUPE) and the Confederation of Health Service Employees (COHSE) have declined in numbers with cut-backs in the public sector.

Responding to a changing environment

Today the trade union movement is facing the challenge of a rapidly changing world of work. Many of the old jobs are disappearing, to be replaced by jobs requiring new skills and working practices. Increasingly, employers are seeking **single-union deals,** with only one union operating in the industrial unit. The dominance of the blue-collar workers (manual operatives) has been whittled away by the decline of manufacturing and the rise of white-collar services (people who work with paper and pen). With 52 per cent of the total population now women, the percentage of male unionists is falling steadily. A growth in skilled jobs has led to more people being classed in the ABC1 social groups. Higher incomes have enabled more people to buy their own houses and to purchase shares in publicly listed companies. All these factors have helped to change people's attitudes towards trade unions and have let to changes in the relative size and importance of various trade union groups.

An indication of these dramatic changes was illustrated in a report from the Henley Centre for Forecasting, which cited the following example. The Centre predicted that by the year 2000 there will be over 700 000 electrical engineers in Britain. More than half of these will be women. Salaries for this group of workers will be on average 30 per cent higher than for similar workers in the late 1980s, for a maximum 35 hours a week. They will have the money to enjoy seven weeks' holiday a year, at least one of which will be spent abroad. When they are at home, each family will have the use of two cars. Unemployment will not be much of a worry and they are unlikely to want to become members of a traditional trade union. They will be attracted, not by ideas of solidarity and collective action, but by pensions, investment advice and fitness clubs.

Throughout the 1960s and 1970s, the numbers of employees who were members of trade unions continued to grow. During the 1980s, however, when the adoption of new technology in industry greatly increased, this trend was reversed.

Unions have not been seen as a natural part of some of the key growth industries and services. In response, a number of trade unions have become increasingly image conscious and have adopted new marketing techniques such as advertising and opinion research to influence public attitudes. For example, the General, Municipal, Boilermakers and Allied Trade Union spent £35 000 on hiring the Jenkins design group, which had worked for W.H. Smith and Next, to help improve its image. A number of changes were made, including shortening the initials of the unions to GMB and replacing its motto from 'Unity is Strength' to the softer 'Working Together'. Other unions, including the Transport and General Workers Union (TGWU), followed the GMB's lead. The TGWU launched a 'Link-Up' exercise to recruit part-timers, women and ethnic groups. The campaign started with a large rally at Wembley costing £500 000. Recruitment adverts were broadcast on the radio and co-ordinated literature and videos were produced to show the benefits of membership.

Unions are also realising that they have to provide better services. The Electrician's Union led the way with a range of services and benefits, including free legal advice and attractive insurance and pension schemes. Another way in which trade unions have responded to a changing environment is by merger. Most of the major trade unions have been involved in merger discussions during recent times. At the root of the merger talks was the loss of members and the resulting sharply lower incomes, coupled with what was regarded as changes in the law pertaining to trade unions in an anti-union way, all of which magnified the appeal of the economies of scale to be gained from the merger. The result of these mergers was to create at least five mega-unions with memberships of

over 750 000. Large unions have more resources, enabling them to offer more benefits and services.

Trade unions have also adapted to a rapidly changing economic environment by allowing and encouraging more flexible working practices. A number of recent reports have indicated that Britain now has a more flexible workforce and decades of demarcation between skilled and unskilled workers are being swept away. The reports paint a picture of rapid change in the way the country is working, particularly with respect to manufacturing companies, where there is a growing tendency for production workers to do routine maintenance, normally the preserve of skilled craft workers.

The increasing use of new technologies also means that the demarcation lines between manual, technical and clerical workers are fast disappearing. More people work flexi-time and part-time, and companies are increasingly turning to contract or temporary staff rather than hiring full-time employees. Increasingly employees are moving away from companies with big payrolls to those employing fewer people directly and relying on contractors or part-time employees to carry out peripheral work.

A further important development in trade union practice has been in the willingness to strike single-union deals with companies. Britain has tended to have a more complicated union structure than some of its major competitors at a plant level. It is not unknown for a UK car plant to have ten or more separate unions individually negotiating with management; deals regarding pay and conditions are struck at different times of the year and management has to negotiate with separate groups of employee representatives. This process can waste a lot of time and effort and lead to continual instability. Increasingly, unions are coming to accept the principle of having a single union operating within a plant.

Trade unions have also been active in creating better opportunities for women at work. Amid warnings of an increasing shortfall in teenage labour, market forces look set to bolster women's position at work as employers compete to retain their labour.

Possible strategies for trade unions

In recent years six possible strategies have been identified for the trade unions:

1 *Work for a Labour government and the legislation that it would create to support trade unions.* However, in 1992 the Labour Party was defeated for a fourth successive time. From 1993 the Labour Party in some measure distanced itself from the influence of the larger unions in order to encourage a more democratic membership structure. In turn, a number of influential unionists

have spoken in favour of constructive talks about such things as industrial strategy with the government 'of the day'. It seems likely that the Labour Party will have a stronger influence in the last few years of the twentieth century and may well be in government again.

2 *Merger of unions.* For example, in July 1993 NALGO, NUPE and COHSE formed UNISON, a union of 1.5 million members. Merger or absorption is often seen as a route to survival as well as to increased influence.

3 *Recruit new members in the fastest growing industries.* Women workers (who now represent one-third of all union members) are a popular target for many unions. The GMB, for example, has reserved 10 out of 40 places on its National Executive Committee for women.

4 *Improve services to members.* In recent years blue-collar unions have set the pace, with advisory and financial services in insurance, savings and share ownership, as well as private health insurance.

5 *Change trade union purposes.* There is debate among trade unions about their primary purpose. One view, put forward by the new realists, is that the primary purpose of trade unions is to further the needs and interests of their members in terms of pay and conditions, seeking to get the best deal for them. This view is supported by unions made up largely of core workers whose jobs are guaranteed. An alternative view is put forward by the new traditionalists, who tend to represent groupings of peripheral and part-time workers. These unions concentrate on wider social issues such as a community-based approach to women's issues, the needs of the disabled and other disadvantaged groups. The GMB talks about extending its membership to the new 'servant class', such as people on low incomes in low-status jobs.

6 *Develop firm links with the European Union.* A number of trade unionists see EU membership as providing a real opportunity for developing the strength and influence of unions through the Social Chapter of the Maastricht Treaty. Clearly a Labour government would be most likely to sign up to this Chapter.

High priority issues at the end of the twentieth century

In this book we have focused on the way in which human resource management has increasingly become the dominant discipline in people management as we move into the last few years of the century. In an increasingly competitive economic environment, management's top priority has been to control the growth of labour costs. Increasingly, therefore, managers are seeking greater flexibility in restrictive work rules. At the same time they are looking for closer links between payment schemes and company performance, and favour lump-sum bonuses that do not step up the wage base. Management is also looking for greater cost sharing of healthcare and other company-provided expenses. Increasingly, organisations are **delayering** and **restructuring** their operations to employ fewer people. In contrast, unions are seeking to resist cuts in company benefits and to create greater job security. The problem is always that one person's restructuring is another person's 'job loss'; one person's move to achieve 'competitive advantage' is another person's 'increasing stress and insecurity'.

Task

Identify a recent case where an organisation is restructuring. Find out the reasons why the restructuring is taking place. Explore the implications for management and employees. How effectively is management managing the transition? Are they retaining the confidence and support of employees?

Further reading

- *Handbook of Human Resource Management* by E. Towers. Blackwell, 1995.
- *Human Resource Management* by Karen Legge. Macmillan, 1996.
- *Industrial Relations* by G. Green. Pitman, 1994.
- *The New Industrial Relations* by N. Millward. Policy Studies Institute, 1995.

17 Employee relations

On completion of this chapter, students should be able to:

- distinguish between and evaluate the unitary and pluralist approaches to industrial relations

- review the types of collective agreements

- identify and analyse the influences on industrial relations

- analyse the sources of power at work

- review the concept of legitimacy

- distinguish between the ways in which organisations manage professionals and other employees

- review the sources of conflict in organisations

- evaluate the different approaches to resolving conflicts at work

- review the stages and organisation of negotiations

- analyse behaviour interactions

- review and evaluate team briefings; quality circles; profit sharing and employee share ownership; and joint consultation.

Task

Take stock of your present views on some industrial relations issues. Look at Figure 17.1 and decide who, in your opinion, should share the decision-taking in each case. If this is your own book, tick in the appropriate column. Otherwise use a separate sheet of paper.

Figure 17.1 Who should have a say in these decisions?

Issues	Employers	Employees	Trade Unions	Government
Maximum hours of work				
Minimum rates of pay				
Pay differentials				
Profit-sharing				
Holiday entitlements				
Selection of staff				
Promotion of staff				
Training opportunities				
Racial discrimination				
Sexual discrimination				
Health and safety				
Discipline				
Grievances				
Dismissal				
Redundancy pay				
Pace of work				
Quality of work				
Product range				
Investment decisions				
Contraction of the business				
Relocation of the business				
Right to be represented by a trade union				
Right to strike				

Come back to your answers when you have read the next section.

Perspectives on the employment relationship

Individual writers, theorists, employers and employees all have their own set of assumptions and values that they use, consciously or unconsciously, when making judgements. Their assumptions and values form the frame of reference that they employ when deciding something is good or bad, desirable or undesirable. This frame of reference is seldom stated. Consequently, the reader is invited to assume that the interpretation offered is the only one reasonable or even possible, whereas, given other values and assumptions, an alternative interpretation may be just as logical. It is useful, therefore, when making up your own mind, to examine the assumptions that underpin the arguments. This is particularly true when studying industrial relations. Inevitably the subject engages our personal values and political beliefs.

Consider the following phrases:

- 'the organisation's objectives'
- 'the survival of the organisation'.

What is **the organisation**? What does the word mean? It signifies a collection of people. An organisation does not have a single mind or a single set of interests. At any one time there is a measure of agreement. It is perhaps misleading, therefore, to speak of an organisation as if it is one person. Any collection of people has a diversity of personal interests and opinions.

Take the example of a company's product range. The inclination of the sales manager may be to maintain or increase the size of the product range. The larger the range, the better the chance of meeting a particular customer's wishes. The production manager is more likely to favour a reduction in product range. Small production runs mean frequent resetting of machines and more administration, thus pushing up production costs. The two specialisms bring different perspectives to the same problem.

Individuals, too, have their own personal objectives. For example they may want to:

- increase the importance of their jobs
- get promotion
- increase their salaries
- reduce the pressure on themselves
- make themselves secure.

Given the opportunity, they are likely to influence decisions in ways that favour their personal interests.

So, when we say that the organisation has fixed objectives, we mean that a number of people have reached agreement on those objectives. There has been a process of debate and negotiation, involving the use of logic, influence and power. Similarly, the phrase 'survival of the organisation' might be used to justify cost-cutting and redundancies. The reality might be that these actions serve the interests of some members of the organisation but not others.

People hold strongly opposing views on such issues as:

- How should the diversity of interests in an organisation be handled? How should they be represented and expressed?
- To what extent should employers recognise and accept trade unions?
- To what extent should trade unions be allowed to influence decisions, and on which issues?
- What are the sources of conflict in the employment relationship?
- Do trade unions generate conflict, or do they provide a channel for expressing and resolving it?

There are two broad, opposing frames of reference on the role of trade unions: the unitary perspective and the pluralist perspective. It is, however, an oversimplification to suggest that individuals have one of these perspectives on all issues, all of the time.

The unitary perspective

- To achieve success, members of an organisation must share common goals. This finds expression in the belief in mission statements and techniques like management by objectives. Organisations measure their success by their achievement of those objectives. Trade unions may weaken or subvert the organisation's unity of purpose.
- There is one source of authority in an organisation: the appointed management hierarchy. They have the expertise. Management should be the one focus of loyalty. Trade unions may undermine management authority and divide loyalties.
- The development of factions in an organisation is bad. Employees should accept their place in the hierarchy, work to the best of their ability and support the appointed leader. The notion of employees, through their representatives, sharing the management of the business is a romantic ideal. They do not have the necessary expertise.
- Appointed leaders should win respect and loyalty. There needs to be an emphasis on team-building in management training.

- Conflict is disruptive and destructive. It should be prevented.

Critics of this perspective say that it is an idealised view of organisations. It is removed from the reality of everyday life in an organisation, as experienced by ordinary members.

The pluralist perspective

- The individuals and sub-groups that make up organisations inevitably have related but different interests and expectations. For example, they might all want a prosperous organisation, but have different views on how that prosperity should be achieved and shared.
- Where there is diversity of interests, it is natural that there should be rival sources of leadership. The existence of informal leaders or trade union leaders is not subversive, it is normal.
- Rival interests cannot be successfully ignored. They need to be acknowledged and negotiated into a working arrangement.
- Conflict is normal. It is therefore important to have channels and procedures for handling it constructively.

Some views on pluralism

- It is sometimes assumed that there is a rough balance of power between trade unions and employers. This is questionable. The balance varies over time, in different organisations and in different situations.
- Some radical trade unionists believe that collective bargaining strengthens management. By being party to agreements, unions legitimise management decisions and actions. That is, they accept that management is entitled to do what they are doing. Some trade unions

Figure 17.2   Summary of unitary and pluralist views on industrial relations

Unitary	Pluralist
Role of trade unions	
■ Rejects role of trade unions	■ Fully accepts role of trade unions
■ They undermine loyalty and authority	■ Incorporates them into the system
■ They introduce conflict	■ Normal for employees to have their own leaders
■ They cause workers to make unreasonable demands	■ Need to harness the union structure, rather than fight it off
■ They block change and inhibit efficiency	
■ They are irrelevant. Unlike the past, workers are safe in the hands of enlightened employers	■ They bring order into collective bargaining, disputes, discipline and grievances
Trade union recognition	
■ Resists trade union recognition	■ Encourages union membership
	■ Quickly recognises moderate unions
	■ Agrees closed shop to facilitate orderly negotiation
	■ Provides facilities for unions: training, clerical support and time off
Management decisions	
■ Employees should trust management to be objective and impartial	■ Managers should have to justify their decisions, particularly on major changes
	■ The act of consultation is often as important as the decision itself. The actual decisions are often the same as if management had not been consulted
	■ Certain issues such as investment policy are technical. They are not suited to consultation
Conflict	
■ Conflict should not arise. If it does, it is caused by troublemakers, rumour, incompatible personalities or misguided employees. The solutions are: get rid of agitators, improve communication, educate employees	■ Conflict is an indicator of morale, but absence can indicate stagnation
	■ A degree of conflict is normal and inevitable
	■ Unions do not cause conflict. They express conflict that is already latent
	■ Procedures are needed to handle conflict constructively. Conflict need not destroy relationships

oppose the appointment of worker directors. They argue that their involvement could inhibit trade unions from protecting the interests of their members.

- Negotiation contains and limits desire for more radical change. It is better, the argument goes, for workers' attentions to be focused on issues of pay and working conditions than on ownership of the business. Much of the energy of trade unions is spent on procedures.
- Employers' acceptance of trade unions increases union power. It helps unions to increase their membership and strengthen their bargaining power.

The unitary and pluralist perspectives are summarised in Figure 17.2.

Refer to the exercise at the beginning of this chapter. Do the views expressed by your list tend towards a unitary or pluralist viewpoint?

Task

1 *Discuss the view that the pluralist approach to industrial relations is weak.*
2 *Discuss the view that the pluralist approach to industrial relations is based on the mistaken notion that business can be run as a democracy.*
3 *Discuss the view that conflict is the outcome of poor management.*

Employment relations

The study of industrial relations is concerned with the **influences** on the employment relationship. Before the 1980s, the subject was dominated by the study of trade unionism. The substitution of the word 'employment' for 'industrial' perhaps reflects the reduced role of manufacturing in the economy and the diminished influence of trade unions as the intermediary between employer and employees. Later parts of this chapter examine approaches such as team briefing, quality circles and joint consultation as the links to employees instead of union representatives.

Relationships and agreements

Methods of reaching agreements include the following.

Joint consultation

Employers or their management representatives meet employee representatives to discuss matters of mutual interest. The employer is not bound by the views expressed. A later part of this chapter discusses joint consultation in more detail.

Joint negotiation (collective bargaining)

Representatives of employers and employees bargain until they reach terms acceptable to both sides. The outcome is usually the signing of a collective agreement.

Agreements are of three types:

- *Procedural agreements (how)*. These define the rules and procedures specifying how both parties will behave in situations such as negotiations, discipline and grievances.
- *Substantive agreements (what)*. These define what each of the two sides gets from an agreement. The main issues are pay, working conditions, terms of employment and productivity.
- *Mixed agreements (what and how)*. These cover both procedure and content. For example, a redundancy agreement might specify compensation and also the procedures for selecting those to be made redundant.

Agreements may be reached at different levels: national, district, local, company or individual workplace.

Influence of employers and employees in their relationship

Employer dominance is common in small businesses and in industries that have low union membership, a majority of women workers, a high proportion of casual or part-time workers and no wage bargaining procedures.

Employee influence is more pronounced where trade union organisation is stronger. However, trade unions are generally weaker than they were in the 1960s and the 1970s. The reasons for this are discussed later.

Influence of the state on employment relations

This takes the form of Acts of Parliament and Codes of Practice. Statutory regulation covers such areas as terms of employment, dismissal, redundancy, equal pay and opportunity, health and safety at work and trade union procedures.

The government sets the climate for industrial relations with its policies on:

- economic growth
- location of industry
- health service
- capital investment
- social security
- incomes
- fiscal policy
- pensions.

Other influences

There are many interacting influences on employment relations (see Figure 17.3). The interplay of these influences can be illustrated by a brief review of the changes in industrial relations over the past 20 years.

Figure 17.3 Influences on industrial relations

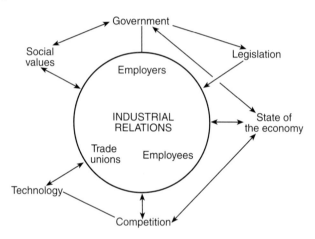

Prior to the 1980s, the main features of British industrial relations were as follows:

- Collective agreements were written but not legally binding. The courts and government were not involved in their enforcement. This approach is sometimes referred to as **voluntarism.**
- The government intervened with minimum wage orders in industries where trade unions were weak or non-existent.

A high rate of strikes and disputes in the 1960s created pressure to reform industrial relations. The Industrial Relations Act 1971 made collective agreements legally binding. Trade unions lost their general immunity from legal action. They had to register under the act to get any legal rights. Unions could be prosecuted for unfair industrial practices. The employers were reluctant to use the law and the act was largely ignored. It was repealed under the Labour government of 1974–9.

The Conservative Party returned to power in 1979. In its 1981 consultative document, it described trade unions as irresponsible, undemocratic, intimidating and the fundamental cause of weakness in the British economy. It went on to describe closed shops as destroying the rights of the individual. Between 1980 and 1993 the government passed a series of acts to reform, in its view, industrial relations. The main provisions are described in the next section.

Changes in the legal framework of industrial relations

The main changes introduced by the Conservative government were as follows:

- A ballot of affected members is required before industrial action is taken.
- Trade unions can be sued for unlawful industrial action. This includes unofficial action, unless a senior union official repudiates it in writing. Thus union funds are in jeopardy.
- Secondary industrial action, including secondary picketing, is illegal. Pressure cannot be brought to bear indirectly through industrial action against suppliers and customers.
- The pre-entry closed shop is prohibited. An employer cannot make union membership a condition of engagement.
- Union members cannot be disciplined by unions for failing to take industrial action.
- Industrial action to enforce union membership is illegal.

From the point of view of the Conservative government, the legislation has worked. The balance of power has shifted from the trade unions to the employers. However, amendments to the law were not the sole causes of the changes.

Changes in the economy

There has been a long-term decline in British large-scale heavy manufacturing. The consequent restructuring has seen a rise in service industries. Recession brought levels of unemployment not experienced since before the Second World War. International competition in declining markets made the reduction of costs a management priority.

Changes within business organisations

In the response to competition, organisations sought ways of improving productivity and cutting costs. Firms decentralised and made each division accountable, closing or selling off loss-making units. They stripped out layers of management. They reduced the workforce to a core of permanent employees. The remaining staff were expected to learn a wider range of skills and to be more flexible in their attendance patterns. Temporary upsurges in business were covered by part-time staff, casual labour or subcontracting. Firms made greater use of short-term contracts.

In the public sector, privatisation was seen as a way of removing perceived blockages to improved productivity. The proceeds from the sale of these enterprises improved government finances.

In some of the remaining public-sector organisations, services were opened up to competitive tendering. Services like catering, and cleaning and refuse disposal were open to tender. The contract for a given period went to the supplier prepared to offer the defined service at the lowest cost.

New technology, particularly information technology, instigated and accelerated some of these changes.

Outcomes

Membership of trade unions has declined from 13 million in 1979 to 8 million in 1992.

Whereas 53 per cent of employees were members of unions in 1979, this had dropped to 37 per cent by 1990. In 1983, 50 per cent of workers had their pay and conditions covered by collective agreements. By 1992 this had fallen to 35 per cent of the workforce.

A 1990 survey of workplace industrial relations was reported by Millward in 1992. The main findings were as follows:

- Collective bargaining was no longer characteristic of the British economy as a whole.
- Collective bargaining had not been replaced to any significant extent by alternative methods of communication and consultation. A quarter of workplaces had no grievance procedures. A fifth of employers had no disciplinary procedures.
- In non-union firms compulsory redundancies were more common. The rate of dismissal was twice as high as unionised firms.
- Strikes were rare.
- Pay levels were set by management rather than by negotiation.
- The range of pay differentials had increased. Low pay was more common.
- There were more performance-related pay schemes.

Critics of the review's findings suggest that the increase in the number of small firms is partly responsible for the changes identified.

Cause and effect?

It is difficult to separate the cause-and-effect relationship between the influences on industrial relations. Have social values on unemployment, social security and the distribution of income changed radically? Did the government shape public opinion, or respond to it when passing legislation to reduce the power of the unions? Was it solely the legislation that weakened the power of the unions? Were the structural changes mainly responsible: smaller firms, more female and part-time employees, and the loss of heavy manufacturing? How did the recession shape the responses of employers and unions? Our social values and political opinions are bound to affect our judgements on these issues.

Task

1 *Discuss the view that trade unions are no longer needed.*
2 *Review and evaluate the various influences on industrial relations in this country.*

Power and control

Power is the capacity to influence the actions of others. Most people have some degree of power over someone.

Members of organisations depend on each other's actions to achieve their own objectives: owners want their profits; managers want to achieve their targets; and employees want security, financial and non-financial rewards. They depend on each other for the achievement of their goals. In that sense, each of them has power. The nature and extent of the power is different in each case.

Task

Discuss the following questions:

1 *Which of the following have power over you:*
   - *your employer*
   - *your college tutor*

- *your colleagues*
- *the police?*

2 *Why do you do obey them in each case?*
3 *In each case, what aspects of your behaviour are they entitled to control?*
4 *In each case, what aspects of your behaviour are they not entitled to control?*
5 *What power, if any, do you have over them in each case?*

Power has three dimensions: weight, domain and scope.

Weight is the amount of effect the power has. A shop steward who can persuade his or her workers to stop work immediately has greater weight of power than another steward who takes a week to achieve the same action.

Domain is the range of persons affected by the power. The domain of the official power of a supervisor is the group of employees reporting to that supervisor. In your discussion, the domains of the police, the employer and the tutor are different. Some of them overlap.

Scope is the range of responses affected by the power. You may accept that the police have the right to tell you where not to park, but not how to vote. In your discussion, you probably made distinctions in the aspects of behaviour that each of the parties is entitled to influence. This raises the issue of legitimacy of power.

Legitimacy

We legitimate others' powers over us by accepting them. In your discussion, there was probably agreement over some aspects of behaviour that each of the parties was entitled to control. You regard those powers as legitimate. Provided those powers are exercised properly, we obey. Conflict arises when we do not accept that the power is legitimate.

Power holders seek to legitimate their powers. It makes them feel more secure and saves expending energy and resources in conflict. Organisations do it by:

- *Recruitment.* Assessment of applicants' attitudes is usually an important consideration in selection. Employers assess candidates' job-related abilities. They also assess if recruits will accept and comply with the values of the organisation.
- *Induction and training.* Through these processes, newcomers learn to conform to the way the organisation wants them to behave. If observance of rules, regulations, procedures and practices become second nature, less direct control is needed.
- *Appraisal and career control.* Able and ambitious workers have a greater incentive to conform. Their potential rewards and losses are greater.

- *Ideology.* Ideology is the process of promoting a view of society that supports or justifies the existing distribution of power. This might include using methods of participation that have the appearance of democracy, but actually share very little of the power.

Mission statements and organisational objectives assume unity of purpose. They exclude the possibility of differing individual interests and objectives. People are less likely to challenge the existing order if they see it as natural and permanent.

Changes are particularly uncomfortable where, like the health service, they bring in new ideologies to support a new style of management.

Sources of power

Power can derive from many different sources. The following factors influence the power of an individual or group in an organisation.

Substitutability

The easier it is to replace a service or function, the weaker the power of the group or individual supplying it. People with scarce, valued skills and experience that take a long time to acquire have a potentially strong bargaining position. This explains, in part, why some crafts and professions have tried to control and restrict entry. It also explains why employers and government have wanted to weaken or remove such controls. A combination of changes in technology and industrial relations law has weakened the power of the printing unions, for example.

Heavy reliance on a few particular people, or a few particular functions, makes the organisation vulnerable to stoppages in those areas. Employers may seek to reduce their vulnerability by rewarding such people highly, thus ensuring their loyalty. Alternatively, the employer may seek to improve substitutability by the use of technology, by multi-skilling or by decentralising, so that if one unit closes, another can take over.

Pervasiveness

Failure in some functions affects mainly their own area. Failure in other functions pervades the whole organisation. For example, unless there are effective contingency plans, a strike in a centralised computer service could paralyse most of the other functions of the business. A company might think it important to either discourage unionisation of the computer staff or weaken their solidarity with the rest of the members. The employers might choose a location for the computers away from union influence, or they may reward the computer staff well and cultivate an image that identifies their interests with management.

Immediacy

The quicker the impact of an action by a group, the greater its power. A firm running production lines on a 'just-in-time' basis, for example, is vulnerable to strikes in the suppliers of components. An employer may be able to manipulate the timing of an unavoidable strike and prepare for it, so that the impact is diminished. The firm is less vulnerable if it has reliable alternative suppliers or has managed to build up stocks in anticipation of the stoppage.

Coping with uncertainty

Organisations try to reduce uncertainty by anticipation and planning. They use techniques like market research, SWOT analysis, forecasting and operations research. Any function that can reduce uncertainty is therefore likely to wield power. It need not necessarily be particularly sophisticated. A maintenance department reduces uncertainty by quickly repairing breakdowns. A strike by maintenance staff could therefore cause disruption disproportionate to the number of staff involved. However, an effective preventative maintenance programme decreases the probability of breakdown and therefore reduces the likely immediate impact of the withdrawal of maintenance services.

Application of power

A group of people may have power but not use it effectively in their own interests.

- They may be unwilling to act because their values inhibit industrial action. Some professionals, such as doctors, midwives and teachers have codes of behaviour that place the interests of clients first. They may be reluctant to strike, even when badly treated, because of the impact on clients or other workers.
- They may be unaware of their potential power because they have no tradition of militancy and have no sense of unity.
- They may lack effective leadership.

An employer will take all of these factors into account when negotiating.

Successful use of power in disputes

A union requires good timing to achieve maximum impact. Low demand for the product or service, large stocks and alternative supplies all reduce the power of the union. It also requires a choice of methods (e.g. go-slow, overtime ban, selective strikes) that are cost-effective. To maintain power in the future, the outcome has to be favourable. Each failure reduces the union's credibility in the eyes of its members and the employer.

Task

Discuss how organisations control their members. What limits an organisation's power? What decides the degree of power available to employees in an organisation?

Professional staff

This is a broad term and can be used to cover such staff as doctors, engineers, architects, solicitors, accountants, managers, pharmacists and senior technical staff. Historically, professional staff working in organisations have been treated differently from manual workers. Whereas manual workers were paid hourly, professional staff were salaried. The professional's conditions of service, holiday entitlement, sick pay, pension rights, and even canteens, were superior. Training and development were also different. Manual workers had jobs; professionals had careers. Manual workers were recruited locally; professionals were recruited nationally, often with different qualification requirements for different levels of the hierarchy.

A professional job usually carries more personal discretion in judgements. The effects of mistakes are longer-term. For these reasons, it is more difficult to assess professionals' performance and work measurement has seldom been applied to their tasks. The application of performance-related pay has therefore caused difficulties with groups like probation officers and teachers.

Professionals, such as doctors, solicitors and accountants have obligations to their profession's ethics and standards of behaviour. They are expected to have the clients' interests as their central concern. They tend to guard their autonomy. This can cause tensions between the objectives of their employing organisation and the standards of their professional body.

Professionals control entry to their profession by qualification and by forms of apprenticeship. They tend to resist appraisal other than by their profession. In the past, professionals were well rewarded and found it unnecessary to use their power openly in negotiating their rewards. There have been signs recently that this situation is changing, particularly in the public sector.

The loss of markets for primary manufacture, together with developments in technology, have reduced the demand for unskilled labour. The proportion of staff with technical and professional qualifications will increase. This will have implications for recruitment, development, motivation, appraisal and styles of management.

Task

Discuss the problems of controlling professionals in an organisation.

Conflict

Potential conflict

Conflict in organisations derives from three principal sources.

The first is **competition for scarce resources.** All resources are limited and the demand for them is variable. The greater the demand, the more intense is the competition. Examples of this are everywhere, including competition for jobs, promotion, training places, pay increments, budget allocation, office space, equipment, and a share of the profits. Such competition may be between individuals, between departments or between employers and employees.

The second source of conflict is the **power relationship.** Individuals or groups may seek to gain control over others or to weaken others' dominance over themselves.

The third source of conflict is **disagreement over goals and the methods of achieving them.** An executive team may disagree on whether the company should be consolidating or expanding. If it agrees on expansion, it may disagree on the means of achieving it. A trade union committee may agree or disagree on whether the time is right to press for an increase in members' pay. If it agrees to press, it may disagree whether the drive should be for a flat rate or a percentage increase.

The potential for conflict is always there, but it may not necessarily be recognised or expressed.

Perceived conflict

This is when groups or individuals can recognise and analyse the causes of conflict. However, individuals and groups may suppress such recognition for a variety of reasons. They may dislike handling any resulting confrontation and thus prefer to avoid it. They may lack the confidence and skills. Their upbringing and values may inhibit assertive behaviour. They may have an exaggerated deference to authority. All of these reasons may cause people to suppress recognition of a latent conflict of interests and goals.

It is also possible for parties to perceive a conflict of interests where none exists. This will occur when there is insufficient information to form a correct judgement. This can easily happen when changes are introduced or during negotiations. However, communication will not necessarily reduce conflict. Sometimes the truth may reveal an even bigger divide in interests than had previously been perceived.

Emotional conflict

Conflict can be at the intellectual level of differences in ideas and opinions. Logic and reason are the means of resolving such differences. Perhaps more typically, conflict engages people's feelings. Emotions have the positive effects of increasing motivation and determination, and of securing group solidarity. They can also cloud judgement and make a rational solution more difficult.

Expressed conflict

Conflict can be expressed in the form of aggression, disruption, non-cooperation and apathy, directed at damaging the interests of the other party in the conflict. A relationship is a continuing series of interactions. Conflict is one event in that series. Damage to the relationship depends on how the conflict was resolved or suppressed.

If badly handled, it sets the seeds for further potential conflict.

Managing conflict

There are some common areas of conflict in organisations. Examples are pay, application of discipline and working conditions. Most companies have standard procedures that provide a channel for handling and resolving such conflict.

Individuals or groups in conflict are often unclear about the issues that separate them. An important first stage in resolving a conflict is to agree and define the central issues, otherwise negotiation will be confused. It is difficult to identify the central issues if emotions are high. At least one of the parties needs to be patient and calm. Sometimes a neutral third party can help.

Where one side in a dispute dominates the other, superior power can be used to impose a settlement. This method is quick and commonly used in organisations. The drawback is that the goodwill of the loser may be forfeited.

Alternatively the two sides can negotiate. There are different approaches to negotiation. One approach emphasises the **competition** between the two parties. The assumption is that one side can win only at the expense of the other. Tactics include negotiating ploys and even 'dirty tricks'. Relative power, tactics and assertive skills determine the outcome. Another approach emphasises **co-operation.** The assumption here is that both sides can win, since they may have different but related goals. For example, the employees might want a wage increase and the employer might want increased flexibility and increased productivity. The two sets of objectives are different but not incompatible. The conflict is treated as a problem to be solved rationally. Success depends on trust, openness and straight talking. They are all useful qualities in a long-term relationship.

Task

1   *Discuss the following proposition in relation to settling conflicts at work: 'Nice guys lose; smart guys win.'*
2   *Evaluate the different approaches to resolving conflict at work.*

Negotiation

Negotiation is the process of adjusting positions and making concessions to reach an agreement. In industrial relations, management and trade unions negotiate to resolve differences and to advance the interests of either or both parties. Their relationship is long-term. Therefore negotiations, if successful, do not leave the losers resentful.

On each side in a negotiation there may be several parties to satisfy. On the union side there are the interests of the full-time officials, the part-time officials and the different occupational groups to reconcile. On the management side the interests of the personnel department, the line departments and the owners will not necessarily be identical in all respects. Before and during negotiations, each side has to resolve differences between their own constituents. When negotiations are complete, each side has to sell the outcome to its own members. A good settlement will allow both sides to save face with their constituents.

Preparations for negotiation

Before negotiations can begin, the parties must be clear about their objectives and the roles of different members of their teams.

Bargaining objectives

Each party defines the objectives it wants to achieve. Suppose, for example, a union wants a four and half per cent increase on the basic rate of pay, a reduction of one hour in the working week and two extra days' annual holiday. It will decide its priorities and classify each objective as **essential, desirable** or **optimistic.** To help fix their objectives and build their case, the negotiators will assemble and process relevant information. Examples are changes in wage rates, profits, markets and technology. They will calculate the costs and benefits of their proposals.

In fixing their targets, the negotiators are influenced by their assessment of their own and their opponents' bargaining power. Bargaining power is the ability to make the other side give concessions. The elements of power were discussed earlier in this chapter. The elements are not constant. For example, a threatened strike has less leverage when stocks are high and sales are low. Therefore the timing of negotiations can affect power.

Negotiators seldom get all they want. They express their target as a range. This is illustrated in Figure 17.4.

Figure 17.4 Bargaining positions

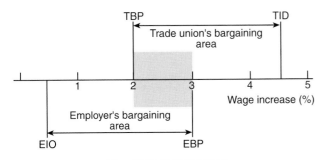

KEY EIO = Employer's initial offer
     EBP = Employer's break-off point
     TID = Trade union's initial demand
     TBP = Trade union's break-off point

Source: Adapted from Towers (1992) *Handbook of Industrial Relations*

In this example the trade union's most optimistic target wage increase is four and a half per cent, and that is its initial demand (TID). The lowest offer it will accept is two per cent. If it cannot get that, it will break off negotiations (TBP).

Separately, the employers have decided their bargaining range. The employers' initial offer (EIO) will be half a per cent. They will not be pushed beyond three per cent. At that point they will break off negotiations (EBP).

Beyond the break point, the costs of giving way are greater than the costs of refusing. The employer thinks that the cost of a higher settlement will be greater than the costs of a stoppage. The trade union thinks that above its break point, the value of an increase is greater than the cost to the members of industrial action. Bargaining takes place between the two break points. Neither side knows the other's break point. Part of the preparation, using all available information, is to predict it.

In practice, information is incomplete and both sides may miscalculate.

Negotiating teams

Negotiation is usually done by a team, with each member assigned to a particular role. Typical roles are:

- *the chief negotiator* who leads and does most of the talking
- *the secretary* who takes notes
- *the analyst* who watches carefully for any clues that might help to interpret the other side's intentions. He or she will ask for clarification of any ambiguous positions; this helps to check his or her side's understanding of the other's case.

Pattern of negotiation

The following pattern can be seen in most negotiations.

Opening

The initial assumptions are that both parties will:

- keep existing agreements
- use sanctions only as a last resort
- be prepared to move from their initial positions.

The union explains its proposals, including the benefits to the employer. It justifies the claim and clarifies any ambiguities. The employers explain their proposals.

Analysis

The parties adjourn to evaluate each other's proposals and link them to their own. They form an opinion of the other's negotiating range and therefore gauge a possible settlement. They identify issues that need clarifying. They decide negotiating tactics for the next stage.

Seeking agreement

Both parties return with their proposals for a settlement and seek agreement through linked adjustments and concessions.

Closure

The negotiation is usually completed by one of the following:

- *Concession closure.* If agreement is near and the difference is small, a further minor concession may be offered, provided the other party is prepared to make a deal immediately.
- *Summary closure.* One side summarises the state of the negotiation, emphasises the concessions made by themselves and the benefits to the other side. They conclude by making it clear that this is the final offer.
- *All or nothing closure.* This might be used where a valued package deal is being negotiated and one or two additional concessions are being sought. The negotiator declines to deal with these separately. He or she states that the whole package is at risk if agreement is not reached on the remaining items.

After closure

Once the negotiations are finished, the parties should record and sign the agreement. Otherwise second thoughts may lead to different interpretations later.

In a complex negotiation, it is not easy to anticipate all the problems that might arise during implementation. The agreement should include procedures for resolving such problems.

Sanctions

As a last resort, the parties may decide to use sanctions to try to get the others to shift their position. The unions might use go-slow, work-to-rule, overtime bans and strikes. The employers might resort to lock-outs or litigation. Both will be looking for the most cost-effective choice. Each party might canvas public support through their public relations officers.

Third-party help

If the dispute is deadlocked, the parties may agree to use the Advisory, Arbitration and Conciliation Service (ACAS).

The provision of conciliators helps the opposing parties to find new common ground for a negotiated settlement. Arbitration binds both parties beforehand to accept the decision reached by an arbitration panel.

Task

Explain the stages in the negotiation process.

Negotiation skills

There are different opinions on the nature of the skills used. One school of thought emphasises the **tactics** used. A second school of thought describes such tactics as 'dirty tricks'; it views them as destructive and ultimately, self-defeating when both sides use them. This school emphasises **interactive skills.**

Tactics

The following are some examples of tactics used in negotiation:

- displaying aggression and impatience to pressurise the opposition
- focusing attention on the least experienced member of the other team
- emphasising differences and contradictions in statements made by different members of the other team

- role-playing the 'hard' and 'soft' approach. The 'hard' member, who is awkward, unpleasant and aggressive, starts the negotiation. The 'soft' member, who is polite and pleasant, takes over. The hope is that the other party will react to the contrast and respond to the second approach
- prolonging sessions to exhaust and weaken the opposition. The team using this tactic pre-arranges their own schedule to allow their members to take rests
- opening with exaggerated demands so that the real demands look reasonable by comparison
- making the others feel guilty by suggesting that they are breaking some code or accepted practice
- adding further demands, a little at a time, to see how far the opposition can be pushed
- making concessions hypothetical and provisional: 'If we were to ... would you ...?"
- making it easier for the others to concede, by allowing them to save face: 'The situation has changed ...'; 'New information ...'.

Interactive skills

There are three basic assumptions to the interactive skills approach.

- *Personal behaviour affects the results of face-to-face encounters.* It is not just the content of our message that affects the outcome; it is also the way we express it and the way we behave.
- *Personal behaviour needs to vary in different situations.* It is not sufficient simply to do what comes naturally. There may be times when a placid person needs to simulate anger; there may be situations where irascible people need to control their natural inclinations.
- *Business conversations are purposeful.* We talk in order to get something done. Personal behaviour needs to be in step with our objectives.

Behaviour categories and likely reactions

Through direct observations and video, Peter Honey and colleagues have closely studied contributions in conversations at work and the reactions to them. They recorded the most frequent responses to each behaviour category, as shown in Figure 17.5.

We plan an encounter by deciding what outcome we want and therefore what responses we want from the other person. From the information in Figure 17.5, we know what contributions are most likely to provoke the required responses. For example, if we want a calm rational discussion with minimum misunderstanding, we should avoid:

Figure 17.5 Behaviour categories and likely reactions

Contribution	Reaction
Seeking proposals/suggestions (inviting others' contributions)	Proposals Suggestions Seeking information
Proposing (Stating a course of action in a 'take it or leave it' style)	Supporting/difficulty stating Seeking information Disagreeing Building
Suggesting (A proposal that invites free comment, e.g., 'Suppose we ...')	Supporting Difficulty stating Building Seeking information Disagreeing
Building (Acknowledging the value of a previous suggestion or proposal and adding a further suggestion to it)	Support Seeking information/building
Supporting (Agreeing, backing others without contributing any new ideas)	Increases others' contributions – relevant or not
Disagreeing (Direct declaration of difference of opinion)	Reaction depends on how it is stated. If a non-hostile intention is signalled, it can stimulate discussion. Otherwise it can lead to a negative spiral.
Defending/attacking (Usually involves value judgements and emotional overtones)	Likely to provoke defending or attacking in return
Blocking/difficulty stating (States difficulties without reasoned arguments and without alternatives, e.g. 'It won't work', 'We couldn't possibly accept that'	Seeking information Disagreeing Attacking
Seeking information (Asking for facts, opinions or clarification)	Giving information
Giving information (Offering facts, opinions or clarification)	Seeking information Supporting Building Disagreeing

- defending
- attacking
- blocking/difficulty stating.

We should be doing the following:

- seeking information
- giving information
- disagreeing (positively signalled)
- proposing
- building.

It is inappropriate to classify the categories as good or bad. What matters is whether or not you are using those categories that are consistent with your objectives. If your aim is to upset the other person and frustrate a possible settlement, it could be entirely logical to attack, defend and block. Socially skilled people are aware of what they are doing and use the different categories appropriately.

Using behaviour categories for training

- The trainer chooses a negotiation exercise.
- The opposing teams negotiate for shares of each other's scarce resources needed for the exercise.
- Each team sets its objectives for the negotiation. It plans which categories of statements to use and which to avoid.

- Analysis of the negotiations can be handled in two ways.
    - The trainer records the negotiations on cassette or video. At the review the trainer plays the statements back one at time. The teams categorise each statement and assess its appropriateness.
    - Alternatively, the teams are separated and negotiate through the trainer. They send one written statement at a time. Each team classifies its own statements and the responses of the other group. At the review, the teams compare their classification of the interchanges and the effects the statements had on them.

Task

If you are working with a group of students, set up a negotiating situation and role-play it as described above. You will probably find the second method of analysis easier to manage.

Employee participation

An employer may want employees to participate in the business beyond the contractual duties of attending and working. The purposes of introducing a scheme of employee participation may be:

- to increase motivation.
- to increase loyalty
- to increase commitment to the corporate goals, particularly quality, productivity and competitiveness.
- to benefit from employees' ideas
- to provide a degree of business democracy
- to follow current management or political dogma.

There is a wide range of staff participation schemes currently in use. They can be classified into two groups:

- *Direct participation.* These engage individual staff directly. Examples are team briefings, quality circles and financial schemes like profit sharing and share ownership. Following job enrichment principles, some so-called delegatory schemes hand responsibility and authority to individual working teams
- *Indirect participation.* Employees participate indirectly (if at all) through representatives. Examples are joint consultation and workers' representatives on the board of directors.

A company's choice of participation scheme is influenced by its views on industrial relations, as discussed in the previous sections; legal requirements (there are none in this country, but some firms may be influenced by EU directives on worker representation); and its experience of previous schemes.

The Employment Act 1982 requires companies covered by the Companies Act and employing more than 250 people to report annually on action taken to introduce, monitor and develop employee involvement. It does not, however, require companies to do anything other than report; no action is necessary under the act.

Team briefings

Employers encourage and train supervisors to hold regular meetings of their teams.

The aim is to improve job satisfaction and efficiency. The Industrial Society's guidelines on team briefings are:

- They should be held regularly, at least monthly, on a pre-arranged basis. Otherwise they are likely to be shelved.
- Each meeting should last no longer than 30 minutes. Most people have a low toleration of lengthy meetings and time is money.
- Teams should have no more than 15 members. Above that number it becomes difficult to get staff actively involved.
- The composition of teams should be decided by area of work rather than by occupation. Thus, in a college, a team might include the lecturers, technicians and administrative assistants serving a particular set of courses.
- Ideas for the central message at a meeting should come from senior management. The message should not have to pass through more than four levels. The same message should reach all employees within 48 hours. The central message should take up no more than 30 per cent of the meeting's time.
- There should be time for questions at the end of the meeting. General discussion should be discouraged, presumably because it extends the meeting and it may develop into a moan session.
- The meeting should be led by the immediate manager or supervisor.

Task

Discuss the following questions:

1 *How do the above principles match your own experience of attending briefing meetings?*

2 *What do you think are the benefits of regular team meetings?*

Possible problems

- Shift workers, part-time staff and dispersed workers such as community staff in the NHS, may find it difficult to get to meetings.
- After the initial enthusiasm, new information may not be provided regularly. Consequently, the discussion will degenerate into trivia or a moan session.
- The team leaders may not have the skills or personality to run effective meetings. They need to be trained for the role.
- First line supervisors may have more in common with their team, than with their manager. This may affect the way they present the management message.

Claimed benefits

- It reinforces the role of the supervisor as the leader of a team, accountable for results.
- It provides a sense of purpose.
- It reduces misunderstanding and rumour.
- It reduces resistance to change.
- Some observers suggest that team meetings reduce the opportunity for shop stewards to put a union interpretation on management information.

Quality circles

Total quality management is discussed in Chapter 14. According to this approach one of the basic requirements for success is to engage all staff in meeting quality standards. Quality circles provide a way of securing that involvement.

A team of up to about 12 volunteers, typically led by a supervisor, meet for an hour every week or fortnight. Members of a circle are drawn from the same area since the focus is quality problems in their work. In this country, the meetings are usually held in working hours.

Facilitators provide a link to the senior executive responsible for quality management. The facilitators provide resources and information to the circles. They ease the problems of implementing the quality circles' recommendations. They organise training for the team members.

The training is crucial. Members need problem-solving skills and meeting skills. Some quality circles have been very successful; other companies have dropped them within three years of setting them up. Failure has usually been attributed to lack of senior management support in the form of resources, training and implementation.

Profit sharing and employee share ownership

Supporters of this form of participation argue that it helps employees to link their interests to the success of the company. It educates them in the need for efficiency and competitiveness.

The employer sets aside a proportion of the profits to be shared between the employees according to an agreed formula. This might take into account basic pay and, in some cases, length of service. Alternatively, the bonus may be in the form of shares in the company. They can be held or sold. There are tax advantages in this form of payment.

Critics of these schemes suggest that there is no direct link between employees' efforts and the bonus payments or shares. The values of both are affected by factors outside the control of the employees: their own executives' decisions, the competition, and the state of the markets products and for the shares. The schemes were designed in rising markets. Some unions warn that in falling markets employees could lose both their jobs and their savings.

Joint consultation

Joint consultation is an indirect form of participation. It has been around for many years. Its popularity has waxed and waned with changes in political and management philosophies.

Management representatives meet regularly with elected representatives of the employees to hear their views and thus inform the organisation's decision-taking. A central problem is how this fits in with collective bargaining. Trade unions sometimes see joint consultation as a method of undermining their function of representing the workers. It is usual, therefore, to exclude issues of pay, working hours and other substantive issues from the agendas of joint consultative committees (JCCs). This avoids friction with the unions. However, it can result in a one-way flow of management information or in agendas of minor complaints. Cynics have dubbed JCCs' agendas as the three T's: tea, toilets and trivia.

For JCCs to succeed, the following conditions are important:

- Elections for representatives are best arranged on a rolling basis so that there is always a proportion of experienced representatives at the meetings.
- Constituencies should be compact to allow regular contact between representatives and their members.
- Meetings should be held regularly and at convenient times.
- Senior management representatives should attend. Failure to attend is a comment on the perceived

importance of the function. Managers can undermine joint consultation by:

- not convening meetings
- sending junior management representatives
- using the meetings only for downward flow of information
- restricting discussion to trivial items
- neglecting to keep official detailed minutes so that unfavourable discussion can be re-interpreted afterwards
- failing to implement agreed action.

These acts may be accidental or deliberate.

- The meetings should be efficient.
- The secretary should issue agendas well ahead of the meetings. The agendas should present the items for discussion in a logical order and describe the business clearly. Supporting papers should be attached to give members time to study them.
- The chairperson should keep discussion to the agenda and to the time schedule. The discussion should be fairly distributed between members. The chairperson should summarise regularly, call for a vote when appropriate, and crystallise remaining areas of differences for further discussion. A vote indicates the weight of opinion. It does not bind management. JCCs are advisory, not executive committees. Where management has agreed to do something, it should draw up an action plan, specifying what is to be done, by whom and by when.
- Committees can agree to delegate to sub-committees any items requiring lengthy detailed investigation and discussion. They report back at later meetings. This saves time in the main committee.
- Rotating the chairperson's job can emphasise the consultative nature of the committee. Whoever holds the chair needs to be trained, and supported by a good administrative service.
- After the meeting, the secretary should produce the minutes promptly. Once approved, the minutes should be published, distributed and displayed prominently.

Worker directors and works councils

The notion is that representation at board level brings employees closer to where the important strategic decisions are taken. In Europe, representatives of employees of firms with more than 1000 workers can request the formation of a works council. The United Kingdom is exempt from this EU directive.

Experiences of two public sector organisations that have used worker directors suggest that the idea is not popular in this country for the following reasons.

- Worker directors have difficulty in handling the information provided. They are disadvantaged by not being present at prior discussions in management committees before the board meeting. They lack the training and background to interpret the disclosed information.
- Management is opposed to trade union representation at board level.
- Trade unions have reservations. Some feel that it would inhibit their freedom to act in the workers' interests.
- Workers in general are indifferent to the proposal.

Task

Compare trade union representation with other methods of employee participation.

Further reading

- *Face to Face* by Peter Honey. IMP, 1976.
- *Handbook of Industrial Relations Practice* by Brian Towers. Kogan Page, 1992.
- *Improve Your People Skills* by P. Honey. IPM, 1992.
- *Managing Industrial Relations* by Mike Marchington. McGraw Hill, 1982.
- *Personnel Management* by D. Torrington and L. Hall. Prentice Hall, 1991.
- *Personnel Management in Practice* by M. Armstrong. Kogan Page, 1995.
- *The Challenge to Management Control* by J. Storey. Kogan Page, 1980.
- *The Skills of Negotiating* by Bill Scott. Gower, 1982.
- *Understanding Industrial Relations* by D. Farnham and J. Pimlott. Holt Rinehart and Winston, 1983.

Maintaining individual performance

18 Enhancing performance

On completion of this chapter, students should be able to:

- distinguish between different approaches to the study of human behaviour
- review the functions and formation of attitudes
- evaluate the influences on attitude change
- apply the principles of attitude change
- review the short-term and long-term effects of stress
- evaluate the causes of stress
- use a stress-reduction plan
- review the features of effective teams
- evaluate methods of improving team performance
- distinguish between education, training and development
- evaluate learning theories
- analyse barriers to learning
- review the trends in learning methods
- review the government role in training and development

The study of human behaviour

Psychology is the study of human and animal behaviour. Organisations are interested in psychology because it offers them answers to two basic related questions about human behaviour at work. The first is 'why do people behave as they do?' The second is 'what can organisations do to get people to behave as organisations want them to?'

Psychological research can offer insights into many work-related issues, such as:

- low or high levels of effort
- absenteeism
- aggressive behaviour
- errors
- design of workplace and equipment
- accidents
- stress
- resistance to change
- breaking rules
- learning skills slowly or quickly
- customers' reactions to sales promotion.

The choice of research method determines what aspects of behaviour are studied; it also determines the sort of explanation produced. The main psychological approaches include psychoanalysis, behaviourism, cognitive psychology, the phenomenological approach, and social psychology. We look at these in more detail below.

Psychoanalysis

This is a method of treating abnormal anxieties and mental disorders. Freud initiated it and others developed it. It involves investigating the interaction of conscious and unconscious elements in the mind.

A theory of personality known as **transactional analysis** is in the same tradition as psychoanalysis, although it is concerned with everyday conversations rather than neurotic disorders. It shares the view that adult personality is subject to three sources of influences:

1 'The parent'
   Our personal values are acquired during our formative years from the family and other influential figures. These values are the basis of the many instant

judgements we make each day. They affect our relationship with others and act as a conscience for our own actions.

Such values, whilst necessary, may also be irrational, too sweeping and out of date, leading to inappropriate actions. We need, as part of our development, to expose and re-examine the hidden values which shape our attitudes.

When we are under the control of our parent component, our speech expresses approval or disapproval. We use words like 'should', 'ought', 'must', 'will', 'want you to'. The words, tone of voice, gestures and facial expressions express prejudice, criticism, caring or nurturing.

2 'The child'
As human beings we are all subject to a range of feelings: anger, joy, affection, amusement, anxiety, curiosity and grief. Such feelings may be triggered by current events or by associations with past events.

When our statements are under the control of our child component, we are likely to express towards others either stubborn or illogical behaviour, or playful, spontaneous acts and statements. It is not just the words that reflect this, but also the tone of voice and behaviour.

3 'The adult'
The adult component of personality is our rational, unemotional side. It is directed at objective gathering and processing of information. It tests both 'parent' and 'child' influences to see whether they are true and appropriate.

The theory suggests that we need all three components of our personality. Each, when predominant, gives a distinct tone to our statements and behaviour and will produce a different response from those we are talking to. We use all three components in our conversations with others, but each of us has a tendency to use one of the three more frequently. A socially skilled person consciously chooses the mode suitable to the situation and to the person he or she is dealing with. Some organisations use transactional analysis as a method of improving employees' sensitivity and conversational skills in activities such as selling and management.

Critics of the psychoanalytical approach to human behaviour believe that it lacks scientific rigour. In their view, the concepts cannot be proved by scientific methods.

Behaviourism

Researchers dissatisfied with the intuitive approach of psychoanalysis thought that reliable advances in psychology would come only through the use of **scientific methods**. This means that the researchers study the available data on a problem. They form a hypothesis – a provisional explanation of cause and effect – and design experiments to test it. The design of the experiment must follow scientific rules. The purpose is to show that controlled changes in the independent variable (the cause) are responsible for the changes in the dependent variable (the effect). Other variables need to be held constant to rule out the possibility that one of them is responsible for the effect. This scientific discipline excludes conjecture about mental processes such as thoughts, beliefs, and attitudes that cannot be isolated, observed and measured in this way.

The behaviourist approach to psychology suggests that the main influence on people's behaviour is their environment. Experience from infancy onwards shapes our behaviour. The events that provide the experience start with a **stimulus** and end with a **response.** For example, if subjects sit in front of equipment that puffs air into their eyes, they will blink. The stimulus is the puff of air; the blink is the response. The theory is that we can be **conditioned** to respond in particular ways to a stimulus by the rewards or punishments associated with that stimulus.

The early behavioural experiments were done with animals. For example, pigeons learned to operate controls with their beaks. The pigeons' random pecking was conditioned – shaped – by rewarding with food those peckings that approximated to the required movements. The required peckings at the controls were **reinforced** by the rewards.

Possible reinforcements to shape behaviour are:

- *Positive reinforcement, where something pleasant follows the behaviour.* Simple examples are praise given to someone learning a task and money paid for extra output.
- *Negative reinforcement, where the removal of something*

unpleasant follows the behaviour. An example is rewarding diligence on a necessary but unpleasant task with a transfer to other tasks.

- *Punishment, where something unpleasant follows the behaviour.* Examples are disapproval, criticism, unpleasant assignments and reprimands.

Both negative and positive reinforcement increase the probability of the behaviour preceding them.

Punishment suppresses rather than extinguishes the behaviour it follows. It is only effective where it follows every incident immediately it occurs; otherwise the behaviour will re-emerge.

Later behaviourists suggested that learning takes place through **imitation.** We are conditioned through observing others' experiences and reinforcement as well as by our own direct personal experience. Social roles, some would say stereotypes, such as mother, father, male and female, are learned in this way.

Criticisms of behaviourism

- It limits the problems studied by psychologists. It concentrates on simple learning and leaves untouched perception, problem-solving, language and thinking.
- It implies a distorted or degraded view of human beings. A rat learning to run through a maze to find food, for example, is not a suitable model for explaining human behaviour.
- The concepts of stimulus, response and reinforcement become difficult to apply meaningfully away from a laboratory setting.
- Its rejection of reports by human beings of their experiences and feelings means that important areas of human behaviour are excluded.

Cognitive psychology

Cognitive psychology is concerned with the mental processes – which behaviourism excluded. Human behaviour is not a simple response to external stimuli. Human beings receive information (stimuli) through their senses. The processes of perception and interpretation of the messages coming into the brain through the nervous system are active and complex. The processes are affected by:

- the individual's personality, itself a product of genetic and social influences.
- the individual's intelligence, memory and other mental skills.

Before responding, the individual may make conscious choices related to his or her goals.

The study of cognitive processes and individual cognitive

differences has practical implications for organisations. Intelligence, memory, verbal ability, numerical ability, spatial ability, perceptual speed, reaction times and motor co-ordination are relevant to job design and personnel selection.

The phenomenological approach

The emphasis of this approach is on human **experience** rather than behaviour. The argument is that behaviour is the outcome of an interaction between an individual's beliefs, attitudes, needs, expectations, perception and personal strategies and the environment. Behaviour is not simply the result of passive reaction to the environment.

Consider behaviour in a meeting of staff at a college. The meeting is discussing a proposed contentious change. The behaviour of the individuals may be affected by many factors:

- They will have different personal agendas in terms of serving personal interests, such as increasing the size of their budget, increasing the size of their departments or getting promotion.
- They will have different relationships with the senior person and with others in the group; they will have alliances and emnities.
- They will interpret differently the motives of the other people present.
- They will have different values and attitudes to the topics under discussion. For example, they may have different attitudes to current changes in learning methods and practices.
- They will have personal strategies for trying to get what they want from the meeting.

The phenomenological approach accepts self-reporting as a necessary part of studying human behaviour. The researcher can obtain some information only by asking the person who is the subject of the study.

Social psychology

This approach has been described by Gordon Allport as:

'an attempt to understand how the thoughts, feelings or behaviour of individuals are influenced by the actual, imaginery or implied presence of others.'

This is relevant at the different levels of grouping we have: society, class, family, organisation, working groups and pairs. Each of them has an impact on individual behaviour. We learn and apply patterns of behaviour for different social situations. We may not even recognise that we have been programmed by society to behave in certain ways. Smooth skilled interaction with other people in particular social situations requires that individuals know how to play their role.

Potential embarrassment in a medical examination, for example, particularly when one person is male and the other is female, is managed by a series of social conventions or norms of behaviour. They include dressing and undressing behind a screen. Although the patient may be asked to expose intimate parts of the anatomy, the rest of the body may be covered. The language will be formal, rather than familiar, to maintain a professional distance. For a smooth interaction, both parties have to act the appropriate role.

If you find this difficult to credit, reflect on behaviour in a job selection interview. What would be your chances as an applicant, if you played the role of the interviewer rather than your assigned role as an applicant? Suppose you turned up in casual dress. After the introductions, you sat down uninvited in the more imposing chair. You dictated the pattern of the conversation. You started by asking what salary and holidays you would get. How would you be viewed?

There are many regular patterns of behaviour for different situations which we act out on a daily basis.

Task

1   *What are the normal patterns of behaviour when socialising in a public house?*
2   *What are the normal patterns of behaviour in a work meeting?*

Since interaction between people is a significant feature of their operation, organisations have shown interest in many of the applications of social psychology. The following are some examples:

■   the influence of the immediate work group or team on the individual's behaviour
■   the effects of different leadership and management styles on team members' behaviour
■   behaviour in negotiations and their effects
■   responses to conflict: passive, aggressive and assertive behaviour
■   causes of stress and reactions to it
■   the significance of non-verbal communication in face-to-face conversations.

Task

1   *Examine critically the different learning theories.*
2   *Review your present learning. Which aspects of learning theory fit your experience?*

Attitudes

There are many occasions at work where we are concerned about people's reactions. If we are selling a product or a service, we like to think that we can obtain a positive reaction from the customer. A manager explaining changes at work, plans to get the co-operation of the staff. An employee asking for some concession, hopes the boss's reaction will be favourable. In all of these situations, the outcome depends on the strength of the case and how well it is presented. It also depends on the attitude of the person receiving the information.

In the first example, the manager presents the same information to all the staff attending the meeting. However, each employee will register, or miss, different parts of the message. Each employee's understanding of the message will be different, since each perceives it differently. Their reactions will depend on their attitudes to the speaker and to the subject matter. Some will accept the truth of the manager's assurances. Others may interpret them as manipulative and untrustworthy. *Attitudes are the personal filters through which we interpret information* (see Figure 18.1).

Figure 18.1   Processing incoming information

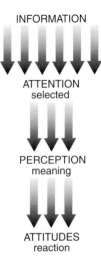

An attitude is a predisposition to act or react in a given way to certain stimuli: people, situations and opinions. The reactions of people we know well are less likely to surprise us than those of strangers. We know the attitudes of people close to us and we can therefore predict their reactions more accurately.

Task

The following is a random list of topics:

- middle-class people
- promotion
- university graduates
- working-class people
- unpaid overtime
- taking time off work
- trade unions
- punctuality
- older people
- bosses
- money
- safety.

It is likely that you and your colleagues have an attitude to most of them. See if you can predict your colleagues' attitudes to each of them.

Functions of attitudes

Our attitudes have several functions in helping us to get through problems and take advantage of opportunities.

Frame of reference

Every day our senses are bombarded by a mass of stimuli, sights and sounds, words and behaviour. We need to process them mentally and react appropriately. We reduce the chaos of this mass of stimuli by two processes. First, our senses select only some of the stimuli for conscious attention. Second, our attitudes provide a basis for snap judgements on situations and people. We do not need to think out our responses from first principles.

Attitudes give us a feeling of stability and continuity. Attitudes shared with other people make it easier to relate to and commuicate with them.

Instrumental

Negative attitudes may originate from past unpleasant experiences of people and situations. They reduce the chance of being involved again with the same situations or people. Positive attitudes would have the opposite effect.

Ego defensive

Attitudes can be a way of protecting self-image. People with deep feelings of inferiority may bolster their own self-image by negative attitudes towards some minority group. Denigration of the other group allows the attitude holder to experience feelings of superiority.

Value expressive

Attitudes are a way of expressing values which are important to us. For example, the attitude of a teenager, exhibited by opinions, dress and speech, may be expressing a central value of independence from adults. Workers who respond better to requests rather than orders may be expressing, by their attitudes, central values of autonomy and personal dignity.

Formation of attitudes

- Does it bother you if you are late for work or for an appointment? How do you feel if other people are late and keep you waiting?
- Would you stay off work with a bad cold or would you struggle to keep going? How do you feel when other members of your team take a day off work because of a cold?

Irrespective of your attitudes to punctuality and absence, you can probably justify your views rationally in terms of 'not letting others down', 'spreading the infection' and 'getting better more quickly'. It is also possible that you are really responding with attitudes to punctuality and minor illness that you acquired from your family upbringing or from some later training.

We may have been taught values directly or we may have learned them through the example of influential others. Such attitudes may be internalised and resistant to change. Even when rationally we behave in contravention of the earlier attitudes, we may still experience guilt feelings. The person who has rationally stayed at home with a heavy cold may still feel guilty about his or her action.

Our attitudes are developed or shaped by subsequent life experience. Joining an organisation is likely to mould our attitudes, not necessarily uniformly for all members. In the book *Psychology in Business,* Eugene McKenna cites examples of attitudes common to chartered accountants and attributed to their training and job experience.

Significant life events, such as unemployment, ill health and death in the family, can cause changes in attitudes.

However, two individuals undergoing the same experiences will not necessarily form the same attitudes. There is the question of how new attitudes fit the web of existing attitudes. There is the variable of the individual's personality. Some people are more resistant to attitude changes than others. For example, army training and discipline secures obedience. In a few cases it may be compliance rather than a true conversion of values.

Sources of attitude change

Kelman suggested three possible reasons for attitude changes:

- *Compliance.* This is where a person adopts the attitudes of another for anticipated extrinsic rewards. The other person might be, for example, a boss or a client. The rewards might be a sale, promotion or a pay increment. The attitude is supported by no genuine belief. It is held solely for instrumental reasons. For illustration of these attitudes, listen to the views expressed by subordinates in the presence of an opinionated, authoritarian boss; then listen to their views when the boss is not present.
- *Identification.* These are attitudes adopted to maintain a relationship, valued for its own sake rather than for extrinsic rewards. In a work context, people may have positive attitudes to their job to please a person they respect and admire.
- *Internalisation.* This is where an individual adopts an attitude because it fits his or her own personal set of values. A racist's attitudes to any new issues on ethnic minorities are likely to fit the pattern of his or her other racist attitudes.

Kelman's work is explained in more detail in Chapter 6 of *Psychology in Business* by E. F. McKenna.

Influences on attitude change

Employers want to influence employees' attitudes since they affect work performance. Initiatives such as customer care and total quality management typically require revised employee attitudes to the customer and to the product or service. Campaigns to reduce accidents at work are also directed at changing the attitudes of the workers. In both cases, there are many other things management has to attend to, such as resources, procedures and practices. Such planning can be undermined by negative employee attitudes. There will be accidents despite safeguards and safety clothing if employees' attitudes to safety is poor. Sophisticated total quality management will fail if the attitudes of the staff to the customer are negative.

Membership of a group

In most jobs, people work as a member of a team or group. Employers set standards of behaviour for the group in terms of quality and pace of work, attendance, safety and discipline. Management implements and enforces the standards by induction of new staff, training, appraisal, procedures, rules and direct supervision. These express the official or **formal norms** of behaviour.

Each group also has **informal norms** of behaviour. Custom and practice might cover attitudes towards the pace of work, the degree of compliance with rules, working unpaid overtime, changes in working practices, use of company property and so on. None of these is written down, but regular members of the group know what they are. Members of the group experience pressure to conform to the informal norms. Failure to conform may mean forfeiting the acceptance, support and friendship of the other members. Without the support of other employees, individuals feel vulnerable. They may adopt the attitudes of the group for reasons of both compliance and identification.

Individual reaction to group pressure depends on three variables:

- *The importance of the group to the individual.* Temporary members are less likely to respond to group pressure than permanent members. For example, graduate management trainees are more likely to use their graduate intake as their reference group rather than the group to which they are temporarily assigned.
- *The group structure.* The cohesion of a group affects the influence it exercises on its members. Small groups (ten people or less), doing work that requires co-operation and frequent face-to-face interaction, are more likely to be cohesive than nominal groups on an organisation chart whose members rarely interact.
- *The personality of the individual member.* Some individuals, as a feature of their personality, are more resistant to group pressure than others.

Exposure to new information

Studies have been done on the effects of exposure to mass media. The findings suggest that the initial effect on attitudes is generally small. The effects are greater afterwards when the information is discussed with others. It may be that a formal presentation on quality is more effective if followed by meetings of small working groups.

Forced contact

An attitude may be a severe distortion of reality. Being

forced to confront the contradiction between the attitude and the reality may be a first step to revising the attitude. At work, secondment to a department or section may cure negative attitudes to that group if the prejudice is unfounded. The setting of new goals that require the co-operation of the two groups instead of competition, may have the same effect.

Festinger believed that we try to maintain harmony between our beliefs, attitudes and behaviour. If this balance is disturbed, we feel uncomfortable. He called this state of imbalance **cognitive dissonance.** According to the theory, if individuals are forced by circumstances to behave contrary to their attitudes, they may alter their attitudes to fit their behaviour. This could explain why forced contact sometimes modifies behaviour.

Read Chapter 6 of *Psychology in Business* by E. F. McKenna for a more detailed account of Festinger's views.

Rewards

People may change their attitudes for social approval and for tangible rewards. Both have been used in influencing employee attitudes to quality.

Persuasion

The effectiveness of persuasion depends on the credibility of the persuader. People judge credibility firstly on the speaker's **trustworthiness.** This rests on the history of past dealings. Secondly they judge it on the speaker's personal **status.** This might be assessed in terms of rank, qualifications or appearance. Self-presentation is particularly important where we have very little knowledge about the person as an individual. We are more likely to be persuaded by someone who appears confident. Trust and status do not necessarily go together. A high status manager may be distrusted because of past broken promises.

We are less likely to go back on an attitude change once we have committed ourselves to it publicly. This emphasises the role of discussions and meetings in the process of bringing about lasting attitude changes. In most groups there are opinion leaders. Persuaders will direct their primary attention at the opinion leaders. Once converted, the opinion leaders make the task of convincing the rest easier.

Attitudes and behaviour

There is no agreement between psychologists about a simple cause-and-effect relationship between attitudes and behaviour. Eugene McKenna points out that safe driving, for example, is not dependent solely on personal attitudes to

road safety; it will be influenced by other factors such as the state of the vehicles, the state of the roads and driving skills.

At work, a drive for improved quality is likely to be unsuccessful without positive attitudes from the staff. However, management would also need to attend to the design of the product, the materials, and the operating processes and procedures. Positive attitudes make quality possible, but not inevitable. They are a necessary precondition, but not sufficient by themselves.

Task

A company wishes to improve employee attitudes to safety at work. How should it conduct its campaign?

Stress

People are living under increased pressure. Their jobs are less secure, thus increasing financial worries. The pace of change is greater, increasing uncertainty and insecurity. Those in work are having to work longer and harder. The resulting stress causes unhappiness and illness. It should cause employers concern, not only on humanitarian grounds but also on grounds of efficiency. Many hours of work are lost through stress-related illnesses.

The causes of stress are complex. The degree of stress we experience at work depends on the sort of person we are, our job, how well we are trained, and our current personal circumstances. There are no simple answers.

Arousal and stress

Pressure does not necessarily produce stress. It is normal and helpful to be keyed up for an important event. This state of increased arousal helps us to perform better. There are many situations where we need to be alert. The following are some examples:

- interviews
- doing any kind of presentation
- driving tests
- examinations
- driving through a strange city
- crossing a busy road with small children.

An appropriate level of arousal heightens our senses and improves our performance of the task. However, if the state of arousal becomes excessive, we experience tension and stress. This degree of arousal interferes with our performance and, if prolonged, can make us ill.

Take the example of doing a presentation. You have prepared thoroughly, but on the day your nerves get the better of you. Your memory lets you down; you can't think straight. You handle your notes and your visual aids clumsily. The audience shows its embarrassment You could write that off as a negative but not abnormal first experience. However, if you underwent the same experience day after day for a prolonged period, it would very likely affect your health. We all experience anxiety and stress sometimes, but our experiences differ in degree and duration.

Task

Discuss the following questions:

1 *What aspects of jobs cause stress at work?*
2 *What causes stress in life outside work?*
3 *How does the one affect the other?*

Effects of stress

Imagine that candidates are waiting to go into an important interview. What will be happening to their bodies: their hearts, their stomachs, their lungs, their mouths, and their bladders?

In response to a perceived severe threat, our body undergoes autonomic changes. Our ancestors' bodies evolved these responses to deal with the physical threats in the environment. They are described as 'flight or fight' responses. In either case the body needs maximum energy and efficiency during the period of the threat. The body

meets the need for increased energy by the following responses:

- The heart beats faster to increase the flow of blood. The blood flow is increased to the major organs, the lungs, the brain and the larger muscles. The reduced flow to the hands and feet may leave them feeling cold.
- The rate of breathing increases to augment the oxygen supply and the chest may feel tight.
- Physical effort produces body heat that needs to be dispelled. The body anticipates this by opening the sweat glands and typically, the hands feel clammy.
- The muscles become tense, ready for action.
- The digestive system shuts down for the period of the threat. Appetite is lost; saliva in the mouth dries up.
- The body discharges its food: we may be sick or our bowels go loose; we need to urinate more frequently.
- Our sense of awareness is sharpened; we feel on edge.

All of these physiological changes are unconscious and, for an animal under short-term physical threat, functional. There is explosive action. The energy is dispelled and, for the survivor, there is a period of rest and recuperation.

The threats that give us anxiety today, however, are seldom physical or short-term. We worry about job security, finances, being able to cope with job demands, and relationships. We are unable to solve them by running away or by a burst of physical aggression.

The short-term physiological changes may therefore become longer-term and harmful.

Task

Discuss what kinds of disorders and illnesses are suffered by people under long-term stress.

There is a wide range of stress-related illnesses. (We should emphasise that stress is not the sole cause of any of the following conditions.) Prolonged stress can contribute to high blood pressure and heart disease. Appetite loss, indigestion and stomach ulcers are also common reactions. Stress may trigger migraine, asthma, dizziness and skin conditions. The individual may be unable to sleep. The tension in the muscles can become permanent rather than short-term, causing the head, neck, shoulders, back and legs to ache. The long-term effects of stress are exhaustion, depression and mental illness.

Causes of stress

The causes of stress are multiple and complex. Two people in the same job will not experience the same stress, and one person will experience different stress levels in the same job at different times. This is because work stress results from an interaction between personality characteristics and job factors (see Figure 18.2).

Figure 18.2   Stress at work

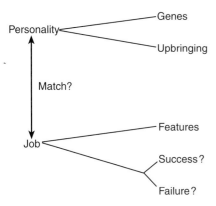

Personality

Friedman and Rosenman conducted long-term research into the correlation between certain behavioural characteristics and the incidence of heart disease. This study discovered that people with particular personality characteristics were more prone to develop heart disease in later life. The study used two categories of personality characteristics.

For more details of the study read Chapter 1 of *Anxiety and Stress Management* by T. J. Powell and S. J. Enright.

Type A

Such people are achievement orientated. They are involved in and committed to their jobs. They are competitive, aggressive, impatient, tense and restless. They are always in a hurry. They speak quickly and finish other people's sentences for them. They have little time for social interchange and may be seen by others as unfriendly and even hostile. They display these characteristics in their everyday lives as well as their jobs. Queues and traffic jams infuriate them. They welcome responsibility. They are prone to take on several tasks at once and find it difficult to delegate. They always seem to be working to tight deadlines. They are likely to work late and take work home regularly. They feel guilty if they are not occupied, and find it difficult to relax. Not surprisingly, they are likely to be valued by their employers and promoted. According to Friedman and Rosenman's

research, they are also likely candidates for a heart attack.

Type B

Type B personalities have the opposite behaviour characteristics to those listed above. They do not display the same urgency and are not constantly setting themselves targets and time limits. When finished, they can switch off from work and relax. They seldom voluntarily take work home or work late. According to this study, Type B are much less likely to get heart disease.

The above description presents a two-type explanation. It could be presented better as a continuum, with A and B at the opposite extremes, and the bulk of the population distributed between the two extremes.

Type A personalities generate stress for themselves and others. Their behaviour may be the result of their genes or their upbringing, or a combination of the two. A mismatch between the personality characteristics of the job holder and the demands of the job can also cause stress. Someone who is quiet and withdrawn by nature might find it stressful to do a job that requires meeting and socialising with strangers. Because of personality differences, one person may find a job stressful, whereas another person may find the same job challenging and rewarding.

Job features

Job features which commonly result in high stress levels include:

- an excessive workload and having to work at a fast pace
- tight deadlines
- too many diverse decisions needed in a short time
- severe consequences if an error occurs
- long hours
- too little to do
- highly repetitive or boring work
- poor work relationships – lack of mutual support
- a weak, incompetent, or unpleasant boss
- multiple, conflicting bosses
- reprimands, humiliation
- a highly competitive atmosphere where problems cannot be admitted and shared
- insecurity, threatened redundancy
- career frustration and inability to move
- erosion of salary differentials
- inability to cope: overpromotion or lack of training and support
- conflicting role demands, such as a supervisor with loyalties to the team and to management
- work difficulties through others' incompetence or carelessness.

Doing a difficult job and succeeding is exhilarating and rewarding. Doing the same job and failing can be stressful. Management contributes to success by the way it selects and trains the employees and organises the work. Competent management can eradicate many of the above causes of stress.

Social causes of stress

Stress at work can cause problems in relationships at home; equally, stress in people's private lives can cause problems at work.

Events in our private lives, such as marriage, separation, divorce, moving house, changing jobs, redundancy, unemployment, debts, and coping with illness or death in the family, are all stressful. Research by Holmes and Rahe in America suggested a link between major life changes and illness. We may be resilient enough to cope with some of these pressures. It is often a combination of them that brings a person to breaking point.

For details of the research by Holmes and Rahe read Chapter 1 of *Anxiety and Stress Management* by T. J. Powell and S. J. Enright.

Approaches by the individual to reducing stress

There are four approaches you can try.

- *Where you have the choice, reduce the demands that create the stress.* Consider new commitments carefully before taking them on. Assess the impact on your total load. Know your limits and learn to say no politely but firmly. Seek training and preparation for tasks you will find difficult. Running meetings, giving presentations, instructing staff and other high-profile tasks are all stressful if you have not had the opportunity to learn the skills beforehand.
- *Improve your coping skills.* Make the most of any opportunity to improve your coping skills, such as time management, assertiveness and interpersonal skills. They all contribute to reducing the day-to-day stress in jobs.
- *Change your attitudes.* Be prepared to talk about your problems to someone you trust. If you share any of the extreme Type A characteristics, train yourself to modify them. You may owe it to your partner and children. Check your perspective on work problems. Compare your work problem with an event like a death in the family or debilitating illness. The work anxiety may be out of proportion.
- *Reduce the stress reaction.* A common relief from stress is alcohol; the drawback is that it may lead to further problems. Physical activity can relieve tension built up by stress. Relaxation techniques can break the cycle of

mental and muscular tension. They are not difficult to learn and they do not need a lot of time. A hobby or an interest are also useful antidotes to work stress.

Task

Draft a stress-reduction plan for yourself.

Performing as a team member

Efforts to improve performance can be concentrated on the working group rather than the individual. There is a range of techniques for improving team performance. The choice depends on what aspect of team performance requires attention. We will review the characteristics of effective team performance and then explain the techniques for addressing specific weaknesses.

Effective teams

Indicators of team effectiveness include:

- high work standards: quality and pace of work
- success in handling change and innovation
- willingness to cover and support other team members
- few grievance and discipline problems
- low leaving rate for negative reasons
- low absenteeism and lateness.

Effective teams have the following features:

- They have clear shared goals. Each member knows what contribution he or she is expected to make to the team's overall goal.
- The team works in an atmosphere of support and trust. The team members have respect for each other. They have empathy for other members' feelings. They feel comfortable asking for and giving each other support.
- Their dealings are open and frank. They accept that occasional conflict is natural and can be constructive in bringing about necessary changes. People will contribute their ideas and express them assertively. All are open to persuasion by reason.
- Problems are seen as normal. The focus is on solutions rather than blame.
- Members are skilled at face-to-face communication, both the words and the non-verbal behaviour. They transmit their own messages and feelings clearly. They interpret others' communication accurately.

- The team has leadership appropriate to the needs of the members and therefore willingly accepted by them.
- The team has clear procedures for making decisions and delegating responsibility. It meets regularly and reviews its progress.

Task

Review a team you are working with or have worked with in the past. How would you rate its effectiveness? If you think it was an effective team, list four reasons for its effectiveness. If you think it was an ineffective team, list four reasons for its ineffectiveness.

Diagnosing team problems

Weaknesses in team performance can be caused by factors outside the team, such as inadequate resources, poor selection, and poor communication with other groups. A good starting point is for the team to examine its perception of the way the team is currently working and the nature of any problems. In his book *Team Development Manual*, Mike Woodcock provides a 'Building Blocks Questionnaire'. Team members complete it individually and the answers are summarised into blocks. Each block refers to one aspect of the features of effective teams listed above, such as support and trust, regular review or leadership. The scores indicate the aspects of team activity that, in the view of the members, need developing.

Ways of improving team performance

Suggested ways of improving the peformance of teams are discussed below.

Increasing mutual trust

Trust is influenced by past record and therefore built over time. It is also influenced by the manner of the parties. We tend to trust open frank people and distrust secretive manipulative people. (Our judgements are not always correct. Some smooth confidence tricksters succeed in projecting an open manner.)

In any relationship, there is information that is disclosed to the other party and there is undisclosed information. Even in the closest relationship, few people disclose everything. The closer the relationship, the more the two parties know how the other thinks. The more we know about other people – their values, perceptions, feelings and their interests – the less likely we are to make mistakes in the relationship.

As a relationship develops, people are prepared to open up and share more about themselves, particularly in respect of contrary views, misgivings and weaknesses. In short, the relationship becomes more honest. However, there are risks in opening up. Others may take offence or use your weaknesses against you. Therefore the initiative for more openness has to come from the more senior person before the other team members will respond.

Training in this area is designed to develop sensitivity to the effect of an individual's behaviour on others. In normal conversation we do not tell other people how their comments have made us feel and we may go to some lengths to avoid disclosing our reaction. In training, we are encouraged to disclose these feelings.

Improving interaction skills

In Chapter 17 there is a section on interactive skills (see page 238). It explains that the content and style of other people's comments to us are determined partly by the manner and content of our comments to them. Studies by Bales, Honey and Rackham suggest that socially skilled people can reduce the chance of unanticipated and undesired reactions by the way they shape their own contributions to a conversation. For a fuller account read *Improve Your People Skills* by Peter Honey. Thus in a meeting, a good positive atmosphere is more likely to result when the parties are using 'suggesting' and

Figure 18.3 Team roles

Type	Typical features	Positive qualities	Allowable weaknesses
Company worker	Conservative, dutiful, predictable	Organising ability, practical common sense, hard-working, self-discipline	Lack of flexibility, unresponsive to unproven ideas
Chairman	Calm, self-confident, controlled	A capacity for treating and welcoming all potential contributors on their merits and without prejudice. A strong sense of objectives	No more than ordinary in terms of intellect or creative ability

Source: Belbin (1981) *Management Teams*

''building' categories. Suggesting means phrasing proposals in a way which leaves options to the other person, for example 'How would you feel about?' Building means acknowledging and valuing another's suggestion and adding further value, for example 'I think that was an excellent idea of Joan's. Could I add to it the suggestion that...?' Practice in planning and using the categories is a useful way of improving interactive skills.

Examining and restructuring team roles

R.M. Belbin undertook research into the effectiveness of teams. Initially his subjects were teams on management courses at the Administrative Staff College at Henley, but the study was then extended to teams in industry. Belbin identified different roles filled by members of the teams. Each role was associated with a particular personality type. Successful teams were not necessarily those with the highest average intelligence, but they had the right blend of roles. In his book *Management Teams,* Belbin lists what he views as the key roles in teams. An extract is given in Figure 18.3.

There are eight different roles identified in the analysis. The book provides a self-perception inventory which helps individuals to identify which team roles are likely to suit them best and which team roles they would find most difficult. It also helps teams to analyse their composition and decide which roles need strengthening. For example, a team which generates good ideas, few of which come to fruition, may be short of someone to fill the 'Completer-Finisher' role.

Improving team leadership

There are techniques which help to analyse leadership functions and styles. For example, John Adair's 'action-centred leadership' analyses three interrelated functions: task needs, individual needs and team needs. Development is directed at strengthening the weaker functions. Blake and Mouton's 'managerial grid' (see page 22) provides a framework for analysing current management style. It indicates what behaviour patterns need to be adopted to change to alternative styles.

Role negotiation

The techniques described so far assume a concern for good personal relationships in working teams. This does not fit the culture of all organisations. Where power is the central issue in an organisation, team contributions may be decided or changed on a negotiated basis. Agreement is conditional. Thus team members may agree to something like: 'I will do more of . . .', or 'I will do . . . better, if you

do less of . . .', or 'stop doing . . .'. The approach sidesteps the issues of feelings and relationships and concentrates exclusively on the behaviour.

Quality circles

The purpose of quality circles is to improve quality performance. Small groups of employees, usually from the same work area, meet regularly to identify, investigate and solve quality problems in their area. The groups are linked to each other and to senior management by facilitators. They provide training for the circle members, arrange resources and progress their recommendations.

Quality circles work best as part of a **total quality management** approach, where all aspects of performance, including product design, supplies and marketing, are considered. Success also depends on support from senior management, acceptance by trade union representatives, and the service of able facilitators.

Quality circles are also discussed in chapter seventeen.

Training and development

Three terms are used in relation to learning: education, training, and development.

- *Education* is the long-term learning process directed at the perceived needs of both the individual and the society. There is general agreement on some of those needs: literacy, numeracy, communication skills, social skills and computer skills. More contentious are the values and roles to be acquired.
- *Training* is learning directed at the acquisition of knowledge, skills and attitudes for an occupation or task. The ability to absorb and benefit from training is influenced by education. As the technology of work becomes more sophisticated, organisations need better-educated recruits. This is why even governments with non-interventionist creeds are concerned about educational standards.
- *Development* is a term used by organisations for learning activities directed at future rather than present needs.

From the individual's point of view, development means acquiring skills to meet personal career needs. Changes in technology, global competition, employee and industrial relations, and social values have all eroded the prospects of predictable life long careers. Career needs are likely to emphasise a sound educational base and transferable core skills such as the ability to communicate, to analyse and solve problems and to learn new skills quickly. From the organisation's point of view, development means exercising foresight where extended learning is needed. For example, the organisation may introduce training for relevant workers, anticipating the need to replace senior and other skilled staff.

Learning theories

Learning is defined as a relatively permanent change in behaviour as a result of previous practice or experience. Learning sets the potential limit on performance. Motivation determines whether the learning is applied to that limit.

Operant conditioning

In animal experiments, behaviourists discovered that behaviour occuring naturally could be shaped to new forms by application of rewards and punishments. For example, if a disc is placed in a pigeon's cage, sooner or later the pigeon will peck near the disc. If this action is then rewarded by the release of corn into the cage, the pigeon will peck more frequently near the disc. The reward can be modified so that only pecks on the disk release the corn; the pigeon will then peck only on the disc. The experimenter has shaped or conditioned the pigeon's behaviour by a system of rewards.

A simplified summary of these findings is that rewards (or the removal of something unpleasant), reinforce the behaviour that they follow. Punishment suppresses the behaviour that it follows. In both cases the animal learns a new behaviour pattern.

In shaping people's behaviour, we use attention, praise, approval and rewards as positive reinforcement. The learner decides whether or not a reinforcement is effective. If I do not value you as a person, for example, your approval may not matter much to me. Human reaction to reinforcement is more complex than a pigeon's.

The application of the theory of operant conditioning can be seen most clearly in **programmed learning.** The programmer arranges the material in short, simple, logical steps. The learner reads one step at a time and has to respond to a question testing the understanding of that step. A correct answer is reinforced with praise and the right to move to the next step. Failure is not reinforced and the learner returns to either an earlier step or to a remedial learning loop in the programme.

Organisational behaviour modification

The operant conditioning model is implicit in financial incentive schemes. Required productive behaviour is reinforced by extra financial rewards. However, there are a number of problems. The reward must be perceived as significant by the employees. The rewards for not working too hard may be more attractive. The reward must also be closely associated with the individual's effort – contiguous, in the behaviourist's terms. The reward must be given promptly. Many financial incentives schemes, like annual bonuses, do not meet this condition. The incentive payment may actually reward undesired behaviour. High pressure selling may damage the longer-term interests of the organisation, but incentive payments tend to encourage this behaviour in the sales force.

Two theorists have advocated the operant conditioning approach to improving organisational performance. Hamner advocated the approach described in Chapter 14 as 'management by objectives'. In this approach, supervisors set quantified performance standards for their staff. They keep a continuous record comparing actual performance with the target performance. Supervisors praise particular examples of good performance (positive reinforcement). No comment is offered on poor performance.

Luthan's approach was similar.

He maintained that:

- the crucial behaviours causing good or poor performance in a job should be identified through observation and discussion
- the frequency and strength of the behaviours should be verified by observation and recording
- the causes of the behaviours should be established.

McKenna gives the example of sales representatives wasting time returning to the head office. The main cause was the satisfaction of chatting to colleagues. When the functionally desirable and undesirable behaviours have been identified, an appropriate system of rewards should be instituted to shape employees' behaviour patterns to those consistent with high performance. The approach categorises a wide range of rewards which organisations could use. Details are given in Chapter 4 of McKenna's book *Psychology in Business*.

The organisational behaviour approach has been criticised on the following grounds:

- the research was done on single behaviours like absenteeism; generalisation to all behaviours is therefore dubious
- the model is simplistic; it ignores the different perceptions and thinking of individuals
- the approach is manipulative and demeaning.

Cognitive learning

This approach focuses on the mental processes of **attention, perception** and **memory**. It emphasises that

Figure 18.4 The memory system

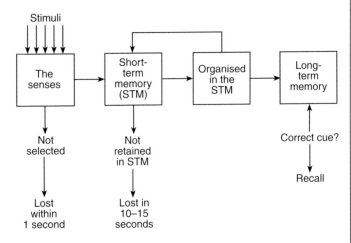

the individual learns by processing information from the environment rather than simply responding to stimuli. The overall model is shown in Figure 18.4.

We take in information through the senses. A trainee cook, for example, learning how to prepare a dish, takes in information through seeing, hearing, touching and smelling. In a busy kitchen, there are more sights, sounds and smells at any one time than the trainee's senses can cope with. The learner therefore selects some of the stimuli for attention. The rest are disregarded. The stimuli selected are likely to be:

- relevant to the learner's interests and purposes – not necessarily the instructor's
- unusual for the context.

Each of the senses holds incoming stimuli for a very short time. Selected stimuli are transferred to the short-term memory; the rest quickly fade so that the senses are open to further new stimuli.

Task

What implications do the properties of the senses, described above, have for instructional techniques?

Selected stimuli are transferred to the short-term memory (STM). Its function is to organise incoming stimuli for transfer to the long-term memory. The STM has a limited capacity. It can cope with about seven units of information in a period of approximately fifteen seconds. For example, you will have no difficulty in memorising a telephone number – probably three or four pairs of digits – providing no one interrupts you. If you are disturbed, your STM's capacity is taken up with the new information and the

telephone number is forgotten. The capacity of the STM restricts the rate at which you can process new information.

Task

What implications do the properties of the short-term memory have for instructional techniques?

Information which has structure is more easily stored and recalled when required. If the incoming information lacks a structure, an active learner will impose his or her own structure on it. The structure may be hierarchical. Subsidiary concepts are held under higher-order concepts. For example, people can remember lists of animals better if the names are arranged in generic groups. Some people find it easier to recall material from branching diagrams they have drawn themselves rather than from conventional notes. The diagrams illustrate the structure of the ideas.

Mnemonics are imposed structures. The first letters of the key concepts form a word which is easily remembered. The word provides a cue for the recall of the key concepts from the memory. The key concepts provide the key to the recall of the subsidiary concepts. For example, the word MASTER is a mnemonic for the headings of an approach to selling:

Make ready
Approach with benefits
Stimulate interest
Tell the facts
Eliminate retardents
Request action

The problem with some memory techniques used for rote learning is that they provide only one route for recall. If you have forgotten the mnemonic or the rhyme, you have lost the means of recall. New information that has been integrated into an individual's long-term memory through thinking, talking and discussing is less likely to be forgotten. It is like a filing system with cross-references – there is more than one route to access the stored information. There is no evidence of a limit to long-term memory. The more we know, the better the framework for assimilating new information.

It is important to make the distinction that memory does not necessarily foster understanding and reasoning. Increasingly jobs require understanding and reasoning rather than rote learning.

Task

What implications do the properties of the long-term memory have for instructional techniques?

Instructional implications

- Choose the time and place carefully to minimise distractions.
- Find out what the learners know already and how they perceive their learning needs in relation to the work they are preparing to do. Try to arouse their interest and motivation to learn. Provide encouragement.
- Use a multi-sense approach. Each of the senses has a limited capacity. Their combined capacity is greater. Let the learners hear, see, do, discuss and, where appropriate, smell and taste.
- Organise material in a logical sequence. Link it to existing knowledge.
- Avoid rote learning – involve the learners. Recognise the limitations of the short term-memory. Provide a structure that allows time for consolidation, practice, review and consideration.

Barriers to learning

Lack of motivation is the first barrier. At work, the knowledge that the learners will have to do the job themselves usually provides the motivation. An understanding of the significance of the work can also intensify interest.

As we have seen, anything that interferes with the operation of the learners' senses diminishes learning. This requires attention to practical issues like the distance and angle of viewing, volume and clarity, and distractions.

There are also personal factors. As discussed in Chapter 9, individuals prefer different styles of learning. Where it is possible to accommodate this, individuals are likely to make better progress. Learners may lack confidence because of past unpleasant learning experiences or because of breaks in service caused by unemployment or child-rearing. In such cases, the learning needs to be graded and structured so that they can experience success. Some may require help in acquiring learning skills so they can benefit fully from the training offered.

Learning can, however, be too tightly structured. According to research done by Sylvia Downs, trainees benefit from freedom to use their initiative. Their mistakes are a useful source of further learning. Details of Sylvia Down's findings are in the *Handbook of Training and Development* listed in the further reading section.

Lack of time and too much information at once are common problems. The learning programme needs to include time for consolidation through practice and time for review.

Practice needs to be accompanied by honest constructive criticism from the trainer and colleagues, otherwise the learners may simply be consolidating their faults.

Progress in practical skills can be uneven. Trainees' upward learning curve can level out into a plateau where, for a while, no further progress is made. The instructor's support is particularly needed at this stage to give encouragement and maintain motivation.

Task

List the learning barriers you experience. Compare them with the experiences of other people in your group. Work out strategies for dealing with each of the barriers.

Favoured approaches to learning

Current trends in learning methods are as follows:

- The emphasis has shifted from instruction to learning. The approach is centred more on the trainees and their learning processes.
- Experiential learning is favoured. This approach might be described as trial and error, but with the consequences of errors limited. It is an active form of learning, encouraging initiative, planning and problem-solving.
- Participative learning is used. Trainees are encouraged to have their say. Their views are the starting point for an exploration of the issues.
- Self-criticism and self-evaluation are encouraged. This may be extended to the peer group.
- Flexibility is encouraged. Ideally learners should be able to move at their own pace. This is feasible where there are individual learning packages available.
- Work in pairs or small groups is encouraged to increase involvement and active learning.

Government role in education and training

The government is concerned with the standards of both education and training. Apart from other important social and cultural reasons, education and training affect the efficiency of industry and commerce. They directly influence the country's ability to compete with other countries for world trade. As technology advances there will be fewer jobs for the unskilled workers.

The government sets National Education and Training Targets (NETTs), which give specific targets for achievement in education and training. **Foundation learning targets** focus on young people and aim to raise attainment at school and the start of working life. **Lifetime targets** state that *all* employers should be involved in training and development activities. They aim to raise attainment in the whole workforce and improve investment in people by employers. Details of the NETTs are given in Chapter 5.

Identification of training needs

Organisations identify their training needs at different levels and by a range of techniques. They may start with the company's business plan and trace its implications for the training and development of the staff. They may devolve the responsibility for analysing training needs to the individual departments. At workforce level, the aim is that each employee should have his or her own training plan negotiated with management. There is a range of techniques for analysing training needs: job analysis, functional analysis, flexibility analysis, skills analysis, and training benefits analysis. These are discussed in Chapters 5, 9 and 10.

Task

Review the different methods of training needs analysis. Explain the circumstances under which each method is suitable.

Approaches to the delivery of training and development

Approaches are influenced by learning theory, by government initiatives through the Training and Enterprise Councils and by economic circumstances. We should not assume that the present approaches are necessarily the optimum ones. In state education there has been an ebb and flow of the influence of **traditionalists** and **progressives** on teaching methods. To a lesser degree, there has been a debate about the standards achieved through the National Vocational Qualifications route and the traditional academic, professional route. No doubt each approach will continue to modify and refine its position.

When planning delivery of training and development, organisations face a number of issues. They need to decide whether it will be done on the job, off the job, in house or by external providers. They will decide the extent of integration with the job. The continuous development approach implies wider use of assignments, projects, secondments and coaching. The implications are discussed in Chapters 5 and 9.

Target setting and performance appraisal

Training and development increase the potential of individual employees. Motivation and organisational planning translate potential into high performance and achievement. Target setting, performance appraisal, and training and development should therefore be seen as related and integrated techniques. Target setting and performance appraisal are discussed in detail in Chapter 14.

Further reading

- *Effective Team Building* by John Adair. Gower, 1992.
- *Handbook of Training and Development* edited by S. Truelove. Blackwell Business, 1992.
- *Management Teams* by R.M. Belbin. Heinemann, 1981.
- *Managing People at Work* by P. J. Makin, C. L. Cooper and C. Cox. BPS Books and Routledge Ltd, 1994.
- *Psychology in Business* by E.F. McKenna. Lawrence Erlbaum Associates Publishers, 1987.
- *Team Development Manual* by M. Woodcock. Gower, 1989.
- *Training and Development* by R. Harrison. Institute of Personnel Management, 1988.
- *Anxiety and Stress Management* by T. J. Powell and S. J. Enright. Routledge, 1990.
- *Improve Your People Skills* by Peter Honey. IPM, 1990.

On completion of this chapter, students should be able to:

- review the causes of alienation and the measures to counteract it
- review the causes of frustration at work
- review and evaluate theories of motivation
- review the historical influences on job design
- evaluate and apply job enrichment
- review and evaluate techniques of reward management:
  - job evaluation
  - merit rating
  - performance-related pay
  - financial incentive schemes
  - profit sharing
- review the provisions of the Employment Protection Act and its impact on job evaluation
- review the current trends in reward systems.

Alienation

Large organisations, sometimes called bureaucracies, are designed to ensure continuity. Roles are defined by job descriptions. If an individual leaves, a replacement picks up the same role and the function continues. Rules and procedures govern the conduct of employees, so that consistency and continuity prevail.

The major decisions, affecting the lives of employees, are taken by senior management who are never seen by the majority of staff and, for the most part, are totally unknown. Consequently, members of the organisation may feel alienated. In a state of alienation, people feel powerless to influence their conditions. Their work is seen as meaningless, apart from generating income. They do not share, in any real sense, the values and objectives of the organisation. Mission statements and charters are viewed cynically and seen as so much management rhetoric. The result is apathy and a level of effort just sufficient to avoid sanctions.

Various approaches are used to try to combat alienation:

- dividing organisations into smaller units with separate identities and accountabilities
- delegation and empowerment to take decisions at lower levels
- consultation and participation in decision-taking
- team-building
- redesigning jobs to apply motivational theories.

Motivation

The word **work** has two meanings: place of work and effort. The two are not the same and should not be confused. Organisations want employees to attend regularly, but they also want them to give their best efforts when they are there. Hence management's interest in motivation.

Task

Take a few minutes to answer the following three questions:

1 If you had a choice of alternative jobs, which three of the following list would be the most important influences on your choice?

List A – choice of alternative jobs
- good rate of pay
- interesting work
- pleasant colleagues
- opportunity for further training
- a regular routine to the job
- good work surroundings
- convenient hours of work
- promotion prospects
- secure employment
- pleasant bosses
- good pension
- opportunity to use your present skills
- opportunity to use your own ideas.

2 If you quit a job, which three of the following list would be the most likely reasons for your leaving?

List B – quitting a job
- poor work surroundings
- boring work
- no chance to use your own ideas
- unpleasant work colleagues
- poor pension
- unpleasant boss
- risk of redundancy
- inconvenient hours of work
- poor pay increases
- constant changes in work routines
- no chance to use your skills
- no chance of further training.

3 Which three of the following list would exert the greatest influence on your efforts at work, on a day-to-day basis:

List C – day-to-day effort
- knowing you are doing a good job
- good basic salary
- a regular work routine
- knowing your job is secure
- pleasant work colleagues
- good promotion prospects
- pleasant bosses
- good work surroundings
- opportunity to use your own ideas
- seeing good results from your efforts

- finding the work interesting
- opportunity to use your skills
- opportunity for further training.

Questions for discussion

1 *Are your answers for the three lists the same or different?*
2 *Compare your answers with those of your colleagues. Are there common patterns for each of the three lists?*
3 *Are the reasons for taking a job (list A) and working hard (list C) the same or different?*
4 *What have been your experiences of work so far? Have you enjoyed it, tolerated it or hated it? Which aspects of the job in each case?*

The people who control organisations manage according to their assumptions about behaviour at work . This can be illustrated by reference to McGregor's **Theory X and Theory Y** (see Chapter 3). They represent two opposed sets of assumptions about behaviour at work.

Theory X assumptions are that:

- people dislike work and will avoid it if they can
- most people must therefore be threatened or bribed to work hard enough
- the average person prefers to be directed, dislikes responsibility, is unambitious and, above all, seeks security.

Organisations that operate with these assumptions will tend to have authoritarian management, using direct financial schemes and tight controls where conditions allow it.

Theory Y assumptions are that:

- the expenditure of physical and mental effort in work is as natural to human beings as play or rest; people need to be engaged in activity
- control and punishment are not the only ways of getting people to work
- under proper conditions, people will work hard, be committed and take responsibility
- many workers have abilities that are under-used.

Under Theory X, lack of motivation is a human condition. Under Theory Y, lack of motivation is seen as a problem caused by the way work is organised and people are treated. The solutions to lack of motivation under Theory Y are the reorganisation of work and changes in management style.

Many practising managers would deny they subscribe to any theory of motivation, but they act out, each day, their own assumptions about behaviour at work. There are several motivation theories. Their interpretations are different, but they share some common ideas:

- Employees work in order to satisfy needs, e.g. for income, for security, to develop, and so on.
- Needs are many. They are not all equally important to the individual. The consequences of both the satisfaction and the denial of different needs are different.
- The denial of the opportunity to satisfy needs causes frustration. Employees' frustration is bad for them and for the organisation.

Frustration

If our efforts to achieve something are blocked in some way, we will attempt to remove or overcome the obstacle. How hard we try depends on the importance of the objectives to us, how strongly we feel entitled to them, and the probability of achieving them.

Task

1 *What are your attitudes to promotion at work? What would you be prepared to do, and not do, to achieve promotion?*
2 *How would you react if you were persuaded to do extensive part-time study to prepare yourself for promotion and then were not promoted?*
3 *How do people expect to be treated on an everyday basis at work? Which of those expectations, when they are denied, upset people the most?*

We would, perhaps, like to win the national lottery or the football pools, but we experience little sense of frustration when the winning ticket or coupon is not ours. Realistically, our expectation is low. We experience stronger feelings over, say, humiliation in front of others or mistreatment of our property. We do not expect to be treated in that way. The more strongly we feel we are entitled to something, the greater the feeling of frustration when it is denied. The way an individual reacts to frustration depends on that person's temperament and cumulative experience of frustration.

Reaction to frustration commonly takes one of the following forms:

- *Renewed effort.* We might respond with renewed effort, in the hope that this will win the next promotion.
- *Aggression.* Anger takes over. The body becomes charged with adrenalin and ready for physical action. At

work we are unlikely to become physically violent, but we may transfer this anger into verbal abuse or towards physical objects, such as slamming doors. We may also redirect the anger away from the boss, the source of our frustration, to a safer target – to a scapegoat like junior staff or the next customer. If we continue to experience severe frustration over a long period of time, our feelings will become pent up and we may suffer stress illnesses.
- *Resignation.* To protect ourselves from continuing stress, we may quit a job. However, this may not be possible when we have family commitments and no alternative employment. In this case, we may remain in the job but, to protect ourselves from further stress, we may reduce both our expectations and our effort. In effect we resign *in the job.* This may be healthy for us, but not for the organisation.
- *Fixation.* Fixation is when we persist with a form of behaviour long after it is obvious that it will not achieve our objective. For an ambitious person to continue accumulating qualifications, when it is quite clear that qualifications are not that employer's main criteria for promotion, would be fixated behaviour. The individual, rationally, would do better looking for another employer or changing his or her tactics for gaining promotion with the present employer.
- *Regression.* Regression is reverting to childish emotional behaviour in the face of frustration. Fortunately it is rare at work, but embarrassing when it occurs.

Common sources of frustration at work include:

- faulty equipment, late information and conflicting orders
- no recognition for work well done
- broken promises on promotion or pay increments
- affronts to intelligence, dignity and status
- unfair workloads
- unnecessarily unpleasant working conditions
- discrepancy between the desire and the ability to do a task
- boredom.

Frustration can also result from a person choosing incompatible goals. For example, wanting both a supervisor's job and a hassle-free existence is bound to lead to frustration, since the goals are incompatible.

Good management will attempt to prevent or minimise these sources of frustration; otherwise the likely outcomes are increased labour turnover when other jobs are available, increased absenteeism, reduced effort and aggressive behaviour towards colleagues and others.

Theories of motivation

Theories are formulated by individuals who are subject to the influences of their own backgrounds and the values of the society in which they live. Theories of motivation and their popularity therefore change over time. Industrialists and managers will tend to choose the theories that fit their current set of values and with which they feel comfortable.

Maslow's hierarchy of needs

Maslow's theory, as discussed in chapter 3, deals with motivation in general, not just at work. He suggested that there is a natural hierarchy of needs. The hierarchy is as follows:

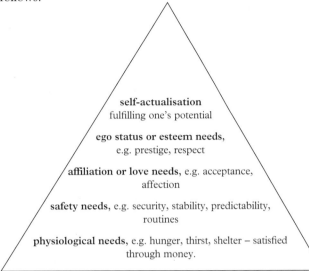

self-actualisation
fulfilling one's potential

ego status or esteem needs,
e.g. prestige, respect

affiliation or love needs, e.g. acceptance, affection

safety needs, e.g. security, stability, predictability, routines

physiological needs, e.g. hunger, thirst, shelter – satisfied through money.

The lower-level needs are more insistent and need to be satisfied first. The higher-level needs come into action only when the lower-level needs have been met. If people are desperate for money to meet physiological needs, they have little concern for relationships and personal prestige.

The typical sequence might be represented as follows. People's first concern in taking work is to earn enough to support themselves and their family. Once in employment, the next concern is to keep the job, or to get another that is secure, and have a predictable, reliable income. Once secure, individuals want to be accepted and liked. They want to feel at ease with the group. Then they want to be valued, to earn the respect of others. Finally they want the opportunity to develop and fulfil their natural potential.

Satiated needs no longer motivate. For example, a young adult might be prepared to work extensive paid overtime, whereas an older person with an established home, the mortgage paid, might prefer leisure time to overtime. Maslow's view was that the higher-order needs are less easily satiated than lower-order needs and therefore offer more persistent motivation. However, this does not mean that the lower-order needs are unimportant. They need to be met first, before the higher-order needs can operate.

Task

1   Can you think of examples where people have placed higher-order needs before their lower-order needs?
2   Review the items you ticked on lists A, B and C earlier in the chapter. To which levels do they belong? How do they fit Maslow's theory?
3   What kinds of jobs, and what levels of jobs, offer the opportunity to fulfil the higher-level needs of ego status and self-actualisation? What kinds of jobs do not?

Herzberg's motivator-hygiene theory motivation

As discussed in Chapter 3, Herzberg's view was that things which *prevent dissatisfaction* at work are not the same things which *create satisfaction* at work. He calls those which prevent dissatisfaction **hygiene factors** and those which create satisfaction **motivators.**

The word 'hygiene' is not used in its literal sense. The analogy or example is this: if a community has poor hygiene, health will suffer; to improve health you bring hygiene up to a satisfactory standard; to improve health further, you switch to actions other than hygiene, such as housing, diet and exercise. Hygiene prevents disease; it does not cause good health. Herzberg's theory of motivation follows the same logic. Thus 'hygiene' factors prevent dissatisfaction at work, but the 'motivators' lead to greater effort and better performance.

Hygiene factors
- good salary
- satisfactory work relationships
- job security
- good physical working conditions
- adequate status.

None of these is connected *directly* with the performance of tasks. A stranger could give you information about each of these and you would still not know, necessarily, the nature of the person's work. All of these factors are the **context** within which the actual work is done.

'Good', 'satisfactory' and 'adequate', are comparative terms. A person deciding if the salary is good might compare it with that earned by others doing similar work, or he or she might compare it with earnings of people from similar social backgrounds. If the 'hygiene' factors are less than satisfactory, the negative consequences of frustration will result. Effort and commitment will drop. The prediction of the theory is that, if the 'hygiene' factors are higher than average, employees will be satisfied with the job, but they will not necessarily work harder. Job satisfaction and motivation, it is suggested, are two different things.

Motivators

- *interesting, stimulating work* – having the opportunity to develop one's abilities.
- *a sense of achievement* – being able to see and understand the results of the work
- *responsibility and authority* – having some discretion to decide and act
- *recognition for work well done* – being appreciated.

Well done! You've really produced a good report here.

All of these relate to the **content** of the work. They are concerned with what you are allowed to *do* at work, rather than the rewards you get for coming to work. Jobs that are high on motivators cannot be learned in a short time. They require training and they provide the opportunity to use the skills learned.

Herzberg stressed that 'hygiene' factors should not be seen as secondary to 'motivators'. Both are necessary and important, but their effects are different.

Not all theorists believe that the nature of the work is the sole determinant of motivation. McClelland suggested that cultural and parental values influence our motivation. Even within the same jobs, some people will be more highly motivated because of the personal attitudes they bring to work.

Task

1 *Compare Maslow's and Herzberg's theories. In what respects are they the same and in what respects are they different?*

2 *Refer to the lists at the beginning of this chapter. Are the items you ticked in lists A and B hygiene factors? Are the items you ticked in list C motivators?*
3 *Compare people you know in terms of their motivation towards their jobs. Is their level of motivation a feature of the particular jobs they do, or of their personality?*

The process theory of motivation

A major criticism of the theories of Maslow and Herzberg is that they assume one model applies to all employees and that there is, therefore, one best way to motivate. Vroom, Porter and Lawler argue that individuals' needs and goals differ, since they are influenced by many variables such as age, experience, personal values and culture. There is therefore, in their view, no one best way of motivating all employees.

To find the effective way of motivating an individual, management needs to:

- establish what the individual employee wants most, for example extrinsic rewards like pay and a company car, or intrinsic rewards like autonomy and job interest
- define the standards of performance expected of the employee
- link what the employee wants to the achievement of the required standards of performance
- make sure there are no negative consequences of the reward system, for example neglecting existing customers because new customers win the best rewards
- ensure the rewards are sufficiently attractive to encourage effort.

Task

1 *What problems do you see in implementing the process theory of motivation?*
2 *What problems do you see in implementing Herzberg's theory of motivation?*

Job design

Industrialisation led to radical changes in the way work was organised. Planning was separated from performance. The choice of working methods, the selection and training of workers, the selection and supply of materials, and the scheduling of work became specialist functions. The worker's role was to follow the planner's instructions.

The trend was intensified by the pioneers of scientific management and work study pioneered by Taylor and Gilbreth. They brought the skills and attitudes of engineers to the organisation of work. The benefits were significant increases in productivity. They underestimated, perhaps, the negative effects of boredom on commitment, caused by overspecialisation and repetitive tasks.

Later, the social science disciplines brought a different perspective. Workers are not just resources. They have values and feelings. They develop relationships and they react to the way they are treated. Productivity is not simply a matter of planning work methods and financial incentives. Management also needs to develop and maintain good working relationships.

Boredom in a job can be reduced by job rotation or job enlargement. **Job rotation** introduces variety by changing, periodically, the duties an employee does. In job enlargement, the employee takes on, permanently, an extended range of duties. It does not mean necessarily that the tasks have changed qualitatively; each may still be boring.

Herzberg's theory of motivation has implications for job design. **Job enrichment** is a deliberate attempt to increase the 'motivators' in a job by restructuring its content. The main principles of job enrichment are to:

- organise jobs so that employees deal with whole units of work that are meaningful to them
- increase the authority and accountability of employees; judge on results rather than on apparent activity
- lessen traditional controls such as short-term task allocation; avoid piece work payment
- arrange direct feedback to employees on the results of their work, rather than a supervisor telling them
- provide progression, growth and advancement for employees in their jobs.

Case Study

New starters

An office employing 35 staff was organised into five sections, each with a supervisor in charge. The office was part of a large organisation.

Most years this department recruited four school leavers. A supervisor allocated duties to them on a daily basis. Typically they were asked to help the filing assistants, sort documents, deal with outgoing mail and take documents to other departments. At the end of a year, those new starters who had not left, joined one of the sections where there was a vacancy. Occasionally they might apply for a job in another department. The personnel department advertised these vacancies on company notice boards.

In line with company policy, employees under the age of 19 were released from work, for one day a week, to attend a local college. The four junior staff in this department attended on different days and were studying for GNVQ's. Occasionally, when a keyboard was free, they practised the word-processing they were learning at the college. The company training officer organised all the day-release details; departmental involvement was minimal.

Mistakes by the junior staff were commonplace. Their absenteeism and staff turnover were high. They complained of boredom.

Question for discussion

As manager of the department, what actions would you take?

Homan's theory of distributive justice

When discussing Herzberg's theory, we suggested that terms like 'good', 'adequate' and 'satisfactory', when applied to rewards, are judged by social comparison. Homan's theory addresses the same issues.

According to Homan, a job holder incurs **costs** and receives **rewards**. The costs are effort, stress, the hours of work and, sometimes, coping with difficult physical working conditions. The rewards are pay, security, fringe benefits, status and job interest. **Profit** is the difference between rewards and costs:

$$\text{Profit} = \text{Rewards} - \text{Costs}$$

A further element in the equation is **investment**. In this context, investment is a long-term commitment that cannot be reversed easily or at all. The principal investments are education, training and experience. The longer the training and education, and the more difficult it is, the greater the investment.

Profit needs to be judged in relation to investment. Fairness, or distributive justice, exists between employees A and B when:

$$\frac{\text{Employee A's profits}}{\text{Employee A's investment}} = \frac{\text{Employee B's profits}}{\text{Employee B's investment}}$$

Put simply, people expect time spent in extensive education, training, and experience to be reflected in their comparative 'profits'. In many pay scales, required qualifications and experience are indeed elements in deciding the comparative rates of pay.

However, there will be situations where distributive justice is not done. For example, the profits of A and B might be the same, but A spent many years gaining the qualifications and experience required for his or her job, whereas B did not.

A has no control over the rewards, nor can he or she reverse the investment decisions taken years ago. Homan predicts that the equation can only be brought closer to balance by A reducing his or her costs – reducing effort. The closer A and B work together, for example a chef and a waiter, the greater the opportunity for continuous comparison.

Companies making individual pay awards that cannot be defended on distributive justice grounds are usually very keen that such awards should be kept confidential.

Task

Discuss how extensive unemployment affects the operation of Homan's theory.

Pay and reward systems

Objectives
- attract and keep staff of a suitable calibre
- motivate good work performance
- control costs.

Considerations and techniques
- encourage achievement through:
  - performance-related pay
  - financial incentive schemes
  - bonus payments
  - profit sharing
  - merit rating
- ensure fairness through job evaluation
- monitor recruitment and retention of staff through annual reviews
- control costs through salaries and wages surveys.

Job evaluation

In companies without formal pay scales, increments may be awarded by individual managers. Apart from budget constraints, there may be no overall strategy and no agreed criteria for awarding individual increments. Over the years, anomalies in pay develop. Within the same department, more demanding jobs may be paid less than easier jobs. Staff doing similar jobs, but in other departments, may be paid significantly different rates of pay. The result is that there is no logic to the pay differentials.

This is usually concealed by throwing a cloak of secrecy over salaries. Managers tell individuals not to reveal their pay and increments to other employees in case it upsets them. Payroll administration is unnecessarily complicated since there is a multitude of pay rates, some with insignificant differences between them. Job evaluation is a technique to design pay structures with logical differentials.

Job evaluation is the process of assessing, in an organisation, the value of one job in relation to another, without regard to the abilities or personality of the individuals currently holding the jobs. It is a method of deciding the differentials in the **basic** pay or salary of jobs. Job evaluation results in a pay **range** for each job. An individual's personal worth is recognised by awarding increments within the fixed range for that job.

Task

Discuss what factors an employer should take into account when fixing the pay differentials between jobs.

Stages of job evaluation

The introduction of a job-evaluation scheme may go through the following stages.

Consult with employees
The aim of job evaluation is to devise a structure of pay differentials that is accepted by the employees as fair and reasonable. It makes sense therefore to consult employees, through their representatives, at an early stage.

Form a job-evaluation team
A team is formed to select, or design, and then implement a job-evaluation scheme. A team can share the workload and bring a spread of different perspectives to neutralise, hopefully, individual bias in judgement. The team might include management services staff, members of line management and trade union representatives. Management services staff, such as work study or organisation and methods, have the time and the necessary analytical skills. Members of line management,

collectively, have direct knowledge of the implications of the jobs studied. Trade union representatives know the implications for their members and their likely reactions.

Choose the job-evaluation scheme

There is a range of job-evaluation schemes. These are discussed in detail in a later section of this chapter. The considerations influencing choice are:

- the number and complexity of the jobs
- the nature of the jobs
- the views of the employees and their representatives.

A large organisation may use different schemes for different staff.

Train the evaluators

It is important that evaluators interpret and apply the scheme consistently. Members of the team should therefore have a thorough training in the use of the scheme.

Obtain job descriptions

Members of the team grade jobs according to the relative demands made on the employees. In a large company, the evaluators cannot be personally familiar with the detail of all the jobs under review. They therefore need access to detailed job descriptions. (For an example of a job description, see Figure 14.3, page 187.) Job descriptions may be readily available, since they are basic to the organisation of duties and to selection and training. If they are not available, they need to be written.

Select and evaluate key jobs

The number of jobs in a big company is too large to grade simultaneously. The approach is to start by selecting 15 to 20 jobs, giving a spread across the whole range of jobs to be evaluated eventually. The word 'key' does not indicate intrinsic worth. It means that these jobs provide initial examples of jobs at different levels. The evaluators grade the key jobs and report their findings to the evaluation committee. The proposals are discussed, possibly amended, and finalised.

Evaluate the remaining jobs

Once the team has graded the initial sample, they evaluate the rest of the jobs and gain acceptance of the gradings. There is usually an appeals procedure for employees who believe their job has been graded too low.

So far the committee has a list of jobs arranged in order of their relative value to the company. At this stage no monetary value has been attributed to the grades.

Survey the salary market

It would be unrealistic to assign pay scales that are below the market rates to these jobs; there could be industrial disputes and staff might leave. At the same time, an organisation would not want to pay more than is necessary. The company, therefore, surveys the rates paid by competitors for the same types of jobs. There are many sources of information on pay: professional institutes, trade associations, government surveys, consultants, and analysis of job advertisements.

Calculate the costs

The next step is to calculate the costs of introducing the proposed job-evaluated rates. The evaluation committee takes the arranged list of jobs and divides it into groups. On the basis of its salary survey, the committee decides a salary band for each group. The bands usually overlap as illustrated in Figure 19.1.

Figure 19.1 Salary bands in a job-evaluated structure

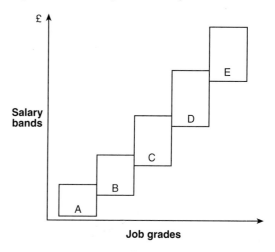

Companies tend to favour a few broad bands, rather than many finely graded bands. This gives them the flexibility they want on pay decisions, particularly in times of rapid changes. A large company, where there is a wide diversity and range of jobs, may have more than one job-evaluation scheme.

The committee compares the proposed new pay rates with the existing rates. Where the current rate is higher than the proposed revised rate, one of the following options is adopted:

- The present job holder continues to draw the present salary. This employee would be expected to transfer to a job that merits the higher pay when a suitable vacancy occurs. The replacement in the overrated job would join at the new lower job-evaluated rate.

- The present job holder is paid the new lower job-evaluated rate immediately and receives a one-off lump payment as compensation.

The cost of the proposed pay structure is compared with that of the existing structure and the executive decides whether or not to implement the proposals. It has been known for companies to abandon or postpone the project at this stage. Initially, job evaluation usually incurs additional costs: previously underrated jobs receive more; overrated jobs do not immediately receive less.

Install the new structure

Assuming the scheme goes ahead, management needs to arrange briefing meetings and information packages to make certain that all employees understand the changes. The payroll and personnel departments have a heavy workload revising their records.

Maintain the system

As responsibilities and duties change, so should the grading of the jobs affected. There should be regular reviews. However, if resources are short, it is likely that the onus for an upgrading will rest with the jobholder or the jobholder's boss. They may need to use the appeals procedure to get the upgrading.

Methods of job evaluation

There are several methods of evaluating jobs, including the following.

Ranking

Each job is considered as a whole and ranked in order of its importance to the company. Usually members of the committee independently arrange the jobs in rank order. Then they compare their gradings and resolve the differences. They group the jobs into grades and allocate a salary band to each. The method is simple and therefore cheap. Each committee member needs to understand the overall importance of each job. The method is only suitable for small companies with a limited range of jobs. The method arranges the jobs in order of value; it does not measure the extent of the differences in value *between* jobs.

Paired comparison

This is a modification of ranking. Each of the jobs is compared, in turn, with one other of the remaining jobs. Thus the comparison is more sharply focused than in ranking. The evaluator awards points as follows:

- two points if the job is more valuable.
- one point if it is of equal value
- no points if it is less valuable.

The number of points accumulated by each job in this series of comparisons is totalled. Finally the committee arranges the jobs in rank order of their total points. The method is more systematic than ranking. New jobs can be slotted in easily. It has the same disadvantages as ranking.

Task

Assume you have the responsibility for deciding the relative rates of pay for the following jobs:

- police officer
- nurse
- refuse collector
- postman/woman
- doctor
- teacher
- bus driver
- park attendant.

Choose the job you would pay the highest, and list the rest of the jobs below it in rank order. Ask your colleagues to do the same independently, with no consultation.

1 *Compare your rankings with those of your colleagues.*
2 *Justify your ranking by explaining specifically what aspects of each job caused you to rank it where you did.*
3 *Did different colleagues focus on different aspects?*
4 *Does your ranking place any of the more highly paid jobs lower down the list? Would that cause any difficulties in recruiting suitable people for those particular jobs?*

Classification or grading

A system of classification is determined before the individual jobs are examined. The characteristics of each classification are defined. These might include, for example, the level of decisions, the types of skill required, and the level of responsibility. The evaluators then examine the individual jobs against these criteria and slot them into the appropriate grade of the classification system.

This system is more objective than ranking since it has fixed criteria. It tends to be used by large dispersed organisations. In these circumstances, its simplicity is helpful in achieving consistency of judgement.

Points rating

This is the most popular method in the UK. The evaluating committee decides which factors will be taken into account when grading the jobs. The factors might be in terms of requirements such as physical effort, mental effort, skills, experience, responsibility, qualifications, coping with adverse working conditions, for example the heat of a foundry or the cold of a refrigerated plant.

Task

List the above factors in order of importance to you when deciding the level of pay for a job. Compare the order of your list with that of your colleagues.

The evaluation committee then **weights** the selected factors according to their judged relative importance. The effects of weighting can be demonstrated by the following simplified example. Assume that there are five factors in the scheme, and that the maximum possible point to be awarded is 100. A straight average would give a maximum of 20 points to each factor. Applying weighting, the most important factor might have a maximum of 30 points and the least important a maximum of 10 points. Care must be taken not to overweight the importance of physical requirements since this has the effect of discriminating against women.

The committee defines the criteria for awarding the available points in each factor. For example, in the case of experience it might be in terms of months or years. In the case of skills it might be in terms of levels of qualifications. The tighter the specifications, the fewer anomalies there are likely to be.

Once the framework of a points rating scheme has been agreed with the employees, its application appears to have the advantages over the other schemes of greater objectivity and finer judgement. The weighting is likely to be the biggest area of contention, as perhaps illustrated by your own discussions. Weighting decisions might reflect market rates of pay or personal value judgements.

The use of computers in job evaluation

Computers can be used to store and process the data created by a job-evaluation system. They can also be used to both generate the data and evaluate the jobs. This can be achieved by programming a questionnaire that elicits from the respondent the relevant information for evaluating the job. The computer uses the same criteria and logic as a conventional job-evaluation scheme but applies it faster and more consistently. It is not necessary to write job descriptions since the questionnaire obtains the required data. Examples of proprietary and computer-assisted schemes of job evaluation are given in *Reward Management* by M. Armstrong and H. Murlis.

Criticisms of job evaluation

- Job evaluation is not as objective as its supporters claim it to be. Evaluators, when interpreting data about jobs, are influenced by their own values and backgrounds. Like any other system it can be manipulated. Those employees who are skilled in the presentation of information about their tasks can secure higher gradings for their jobs.
- Job evaluation is expensive. The initial costs of designing or buying a scheme, setting up the procedures and training the evaluators are all high. So are the continuing costs of maintenance: introducing new jobs, revising job descriptions and re-evaluations following changes to existing jobs.
- Job evaluation introduces rigidity into pay structures, making it difficult to respond to market forces or to individual performance. The declared purpose of job evaluation is to introduce and maintain fairness and order into pay structures, but one person's 'order' is another person's 'rigidity' .

  Where there is a shortage of a particular skill, the market rate may rise above the job-evaluated rate. In the past this has happened particularly with transferable skills, like management services and accountants. The usual solution has been to pay a 'temporary' premium above the job-evaluated rate. This is a less expensive solution than revising all other scales upwards. The dilemma is in deciding the extent to which market forces should determine not only the general level of pay, but also the differentials between jobs in the same organisation.

  Individual performance can be rewarded, within a job-evaluated structure, by increments within the scale or by promotion.
- The technique of job evaluation was introduced when organisations had stable structures and unchanging job descriptions. Increased teamworking, flexibility, multi-skilling and delayering have undermined those assumptions.

Equal Pay Act 1970

Women have the right to equal pay with men under three circumstances:

- *When performing work of the same or broadly similar nature to men's work.*

- *When employed on a job which is different from a man's job, but which is graded equally with men's work under a job-evaluation scheme.* If the organisation attempts to justify unequal pay on the grounds that it has been decided by job evaluation, the employer must demonstrate that the scheme is analytical (not ranking) and free from sexual bias in design and application.
- *When performing work of equal value.* For example in 1988 a cook, employed by Cammell Laird, claimed that her job had value equal to that of a painter, a joiner and a thermal insulation engineer, irrespective of the fact that they were not covered by the same job-evaluation scheme. The House of Lords, applying the EEC's directive on equal pay, ruled in her favour.

In making a claim for equal pay, a woman can only compare her pay to a man working for the same (or associated) employer as herself. All employees in the same job do not have to be paid the same. The employer can still pay more to any individual who has longer service, is more efficient or produces more. Complaints on equal pay can be referred, via conciliation, to an industrial tribunal. It may award the applicant the difference between her pay and men's pay for an arrear's period of up to two years.

Men have the same rights in respect of discrimination against them.

Merit rating

Merit rating is a system where the individual employee is awarded increments or bonuses based on a systematic appraisal of his or her performance. It is effectively a staff appraisal system (see Chapter 14) with monetary awards. It usually operates within a job-evaluated pay structure. Job evaluation sets the pay bands, while merit rating determines the position of the individual within the pay band. A typical pattern is shown in Figure 19.2.

The merit-rating scheme defines and weights the factors against which the manager assesses each employee annually. Typical factors are job performance (volume and quality of output), initiative, adaptability, attendance and punctuality. Managers need to be trained to use the system.

Merit rating has the same weaknesses and problems as staff-appraisal schemes. It has been used mainly with junior management, administrative staff and indirect workers such as maintenance staff. The schemes are unpopular with unions. They see merit rating as subjective and open to favouritism. From a management point of view, a weakness in most schemes is that the

Figure 19.2 Merit rating

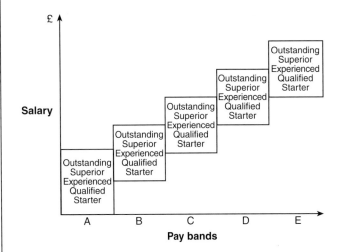

Starter:	Degree of efficiency expected from a learner
Qualified:	Able to perform normal aspects of the job
Experienced:	Able to deal with all circumstances of the job
Superior:	Ready for promotion; equivalent to starter of the next grade
Outstanding:	Equivalent to qualified of the next grade

award is permanent, even if performance drops to a previous level.

Performance-related pay

The automatic increases of a fixed pay scale have largely disappeared from the private sector and are under pressure in the public sector.

Performance-related pay (PRP) has largely replaced merit rating as the method of deciding non-manual workers' progress through their salary band. Merit-rating schemes, in the past, often relied on managers' subjective assessment of employees' personal characteristics. The increments, if awarded, were usually stepped and fixed. Performance-related pay schemes use performance and/or competence as the criteria for deciding the size of increments and therefore also the rate of progress through the salary band.

The PRP approach is based on a management by objectives philosophy of agreeing:

- the key result areas of the job
- clear standards of performance and target levels of competence
- regular, objective reviews of performance and competence.

Task

1 *What are the characteristics of well-defined standards of performance?*
2 *What is meant by the term 'key result areas' and why is it an important concept?*
3 *What are the claimed advantages of the management by objectives approach?*
4 *What are the possible dysfunctional effects of the management by objectives approach?*

Check your answers by re-reading the sections in Chapter 14 on performance standards and management by objectives.

As a result of a PRP review, the manager might, for example, assess an employee as outstanding, superior, standard or developing. The percentage pay increase awarded would be influenced by:

- *Market forces in the labour market for that particular occupational group.*
- *The financial state of the company.*
- *The present position of the particular employee in the salary band.* The percentage increase, if awarded, is usually greater for those at the bottom of the salary range than those at the top. The reward for those already at the top of the salary band should be promotion. If this is not possible, they may be awarded a lump sum that, unlike other increments, is not consolidated into the salary.
- *Company policy on speed of progress through the salary band.* Guidance to managers might be expressed thus:

Review grade awarded	Pay increase
Outstanding	12%
Superior	8%
Standard	5%
Learning	2%

The scale of percentage increases might be different according to the employees' current position in the pay scale: larger for those at the bottom end of the scale; smaller for those near the top.

Comments on performance-related pay

Like any other new or revived approach to management, PRP has its advocates and detractors. Here are some of the views expressed:

- There is no clear evidence, either way, in the argument over whether or not the financial incentives offered in PRP increase motivation.

- For the majority of staff, the increments offered under PRP are too small to be significant. However, they communicate the importance management attaches to performance.
- There are important aspects of performance in some jobs that cannot be measured conveniently or satisfactorily. Advocates respond that competencies can be assessed instead.
- A narrow focus on annual or bi-annual targets can cause neglect of long-term results, quality and risk-taking innovation. The counter view is that there is no reason why these cannot be included in targets.
- Emphasis on *individual* review is divisive and harmful to teamwork.
- The need for control requires expensive bureaucracy.
- PRP is likely to fail if it does not fit the culture, that is the values, of the organisation. There needs to be acceptance of the view that these important values can be quantified and assessed.

Financial incentive schemes

Most employees are paid a salary or a weekly wage that is fixed. It may be calculated as an hourly rate. Fixed rates are easily understood by employees and cause few industrial disputes. They are simple and therefore cheap to administer. They are widely used for management, administrative and service jobs, where conditions may make it difficult to apply incentive payments even if the organisation wished to do so.

Why use financial incentives?

The aim of financial incentive schemes is to **improve productivity.** On average, production workers who are paid financial incentives produce between 25 and 30 per cent more than workers paid a flat rate. The workers' earnings are higher, but the employer benefits. A higher volume of output from the same facilities means that the cost per unit is reduced, even though the employees earn more.

However, it is worth emphasising that productivity can be increased or reduced by factors outside the control of the workers' efforts. Positive examples are improved technology, better equipment and improved working methods. Negative examples are interruptions in supplies, faults in materials, delayed instructions, and equipment breakdowns. Since none of these is the fault of the worker, employees expect their earnings to be protected from the effects of these contingencies. Agreements commonly include provisions for average earnings or other forms of fall-back pay when these contingencies occur.

The introduction of financial incentives has an impact on the role of supervision. More time has to be spent on ensuring a smooth work flow and attending to the common side-effects of incentive schemes: unsafe working practices and a fall-off in quality.

Incentive schemes – general principles

- The scheme must be acceptable to those it covers. This depends both on the features of the particular scheme and on management/employee relationships.
- The employees must perceive the rewards as attractive. Marginal payments are unlikely to generate significant extra effort.
- There should be a clear link between effort and reward. The link can be weakened: by complicated calculation of bonus, delayed payments and use of a group rather than an individual bonus.
- When introducing the scheme, the agreement with the staff should cover:
  - the method of setting the incentive rate of work
  - the method of measuring output
  - safeguards on fall-back pay
  - procedures for introducing changes and for handling complaints.
- The value of the increased productivity should be significantly greater than the costs of administering the incentive scheme. Incentive schemes often generate extensive clerical records and procedures. The connection between these costs and the productivity benefits is not always clearly made.

Incentive schemes – pre-conditions

For the scheme to work smoothly, the following conditions should exist:

- It should be possible to measure the output and attribute it to individual staff. There are many jobs where this cannot be done easily or at reasonable cost.
- The pace of the work should be controlled by the worker. There is no point in paying incentives on a job where the machinery determines the pace of the work.
- There should be a steady flow of work, otherwise the employer will have to pay for the idle time spent by the workers waiting for the next batch of work.
- There should not be frequent changes in working methods. Workers earning a good bonus have a vested interest in the existing methods. Learning new methods reduces their earning potential, at least in the short-term. Financial incentive schemes tend to increase resistance to change.

Setting standards

Incentive payment is given for reaching a standard of performance: that is, completing a unit of work within a given time. If the standard is set too high, the incentive is lost since it is impossible to earn a reasonable bonus. If it is set too low the scheme becomes too expensive to the employer. Unless the workers have confidence in the way the standards are set, there are likely to be frequent disputes.

It is normal practice, therefore, for trained work study officers to set the standards, using work measurement techniques.

Methods of incentive payments

Methods by which incentive payments may be calculated and awarded include the following.

Individual payment by results (PBR)

The payment can be calculated on the number of acceptable units of work completed – piecework. Alternatively it can be calculated on the time saved by working faster than the standard. For example, assume the standard time for a unit of work is four minutes, and a worker completes 150 units in an 8-hour day. The worker has done the equivalent of 600 minutes work (150×4) in 480 minutes (8×60). The time saved is 120 minutes ($600 - 480$). Depending on the scheme, the worker may be paid, as a bonus, the full value of the time saved at his or her rate of pay or an agreed proportion of it.

Group payment by results

A bonus can be calculated for a team of workers and then shared either equally or in proportion to their basic pay. Employers may use this approach where it is difficult or too expensive to identify and record the output of individual workers. This can cause friction between team members and lead to demotivation if they believe that their contributions are unequal.

Measured day work

Work measurement is used to establish the number of staff needed to complete a given volume of work at standard performance. If the staff agree to work consistently at a higher pace of work – a bonus pace – they move on to a higher rate of pay, the measured day rate. This system has been used in the health service for services like catering and gardens maintenance. If, as in these examples, the volume of work is fairly constant, the unit will operate on a lower staff level than at the normal standard pace of work. The employer benefits from lower staffing levels; the employees benefit from higher earnings.

Figure 19.3 Measured daywork is sometimes used to set rates of pay in health service catering

The claimed advantages are:

- wage costs are predictable since they do not fluctuate as in individual PBR
- once the system is agreed, there are fewer disputes over bonus times and rates
- employees have a more flexible attitude to changes than under individual PBR.

The potential problems are:

- the better workers are not motivated to give their best
- the overall level of performance suffers if drops in individual performance are not picked up and dealt with quickly.

Plant and enterprise schemes

Traditionally, payment by results has been applied to production work where performance can be reliably and conveniently measured. Consequently some employees earn a bonus while others do not. This can cause dissatisfaction.

Plant and enterprise schemes share the bonus benefits with all employees.

There are different bases used for calculating the bonus, according to the nature of the work. Some examples of the different bases are:

- increase in the value of sales over the period, excluding price increases
- increase in the ratio of sales value, excluding price increases, to total wage costs over the period
- increase in the volume of production, where a single product is made
- increase in added value over the period, excluding price increases. Added value is sales revenue minus expenditure on bought-in materials and services.

The aim in each case is to find a way of measuring the effects of improved performance by all the employees, not just the production workers. Critics of such schemes suggest:

- the incentive effect is low, since the link between individual effort and eventual payment is weak
- the bases for calculating the bonus are affected by influences, such as inflation and market forces, outside the control of the employees.

Profit sharing

The bonus is a proportion of the profits earned by the company in the previous accounting period. Different companies divide the bonus between employees on different bases:

- in proportion to basic salary
- weighted by service.

The bonus may be paid in the form of the company's shares. The employer hopes that this will increase commitment and loyalty. There is a tax advantage for the employee. It also improves the company's cash flow, since no payment is made. The bonus is welcome, but the incentive to increased effort over the year is doubtful. Most employees do not make the daily connection between today's efforts and next year's bonus. Trade unions would prefer that the profit payments were consolidated into basic pay. Share prices can go down, so members could lose their savings as well as their jobs.

National trends in pay and reward systems

The current trends are:

- a closer alignment of human resources management and pay systems with organisational objectives; the traditional caring, welfare image of personnel, valuing loyalty and long service, does not fit the current climate in most organisations
- a move away from fixed pay increments related to service or cost of living
- increased emphasis on performance awards, with more one-off bonuses rather than permanent pay increases
- the development of simpler, more flexible, computer-assisted job-evaluation schemes
- more flexible pay structures with broad salary bands, accommodating different individual rates of progression through them
- increased use of rewards for the acquisition and application of new competencies.

Further reading

- *Human Relations* by A. DuBrin. Prentice Hall, 1988.
- *Introduction to Payment Systems* by ACAS.
- *Job Evaluation* by ACAS.
- *Kluwer's Effective Remuneration* by Kluwer Publishing, 1993.
- *Managing People at Work* by P. J. Makin, C. L. Cooper and C. Cox. BPS Books and Routledge Ltd, 1994.
- *Pay Systems* by R.H.S. Beacham. Heinemann, 1979.
- *Personnel Management* by D. Torrington and L. Hall. Prentice Hall, 1991.
- *Reward Management* by M. Armstrong and H. Murlis. Kogan Page, 1994.

On completion of this chapter, students should be able to:

- evaluate the purposes of rules and disciplinary procedures
- review the reasons for both observing and breaching rules
- apply problem-solving techniques to breaches of discipline
- use counselling interview techniques
- use disciplinary interview techniques
- review the ACAS code of practice on discipline
- review the legal framework for handling discipline problems
- review practices for preventing grievances occurring
- review grievance procedures
- use grievance interview techniques.

Discipline

Discipline depends on an agreed set of rules. Rules provide guidance to managers, supervisors and employees on the expected standard of behaviour. Rules also depersonalise power: we are obeying a set of regulations common to all of us, rather than submitting to the direct personal power of an individual supervisor or manager.

Disciplinary rules

The nature and the range of disciplinary rules vary according to the size and nature of the business. Hygiene regulations, for example, are paramount in catering and food processing factories, but not in engineering plants. However, there are some common areas. Company rules generally cover:

- *Absence:* when a medical self-certificate is sufficient; when a doctor's certificate is needed; who to notify at work and by when; who approves holiday dates; and when holidays may be taken.
- *Time-keeping:* required practices on clocking-in or signing-in; flexitime arrangements; and time-in-lieu for unpaid overtime.
- *Health and safety:* prohibited practices such as smoking, operating machinery without guards, and other hazardous practices.
- *Use of company property and facilities:* authorised use of company vehicles, telephones and copiers.
- *Gross misconduct:* some rules are so important that a breach is grounds for dismissal without notice. Examples are fraud, assault, deliberate damage to property, serious negligence, and serious insubordination. The company should make clear which rules, when broken, classify as gross misconduct.
- *Discrimination:* racial and sexual abuse, and harassment by employees are specifically prohibited. The company must take care that its own rules are not discriminatory. For example, it must not require forms of hair style and dress that discriminate against a racial group and have no functional justification.

Task

1 *What are your personal reactions to rules and regulations? Why?*
2 *Can you think of examples of rules which are consistently disregarded and ones which are consistently observed? What accounts for the difference?*

Characteristics of rules

Rules should be:

- kept to a minimum
- clearly relevant to current needs
- capable of being implemented
- clearly expressed
- consistently implemented.

Some rules clearly do not fulfil these criteria. They may be incomplete, impossible to obey or dysfunctional. Sometimes unofficial rules become established practice to the detriment of the company.

Incomplete
Some rules need interpretation. For example, when is an employee 'under the influence of alcohol'?

Impossible to obey
Transport drivers are expected to obey traffic regulations, but they may be given delivery schedules that can only be met by breaking speed limits.

Dysfunctional
Rules on time-keeping are designed to maximise available working time. In one organisation, staff regularly worked unpaid overtime at the end of the day to complete unfinished tasks. The unofficial practice was a relaxed attitude to starting on time the following day. A new manager took a strong line on punctuality. The staff responded by leaving promptly in the evening. In total, the company lost more time than it gained. It is difficult to frame rules to cover goodwill. The issue here was not so much punctuality as the way the problem was handled.

'Working to rule' is interpreting rules literally rather than intelligently. The observance of the rules operates against the interests of the organisation, rather than for it.

Unofficial
Employees may conform to the expectations of their work colleagues. Behaviour, sometimes in contravention of official rules, may become custom and practice, like using company vehicles for private journeys, exaggerating expense claims, making personal telephone calls, or leaving the company premises to fetch food.

Why do people conform to rules?

Fear of punishment
This works only if people think their breach of the rules will be noticed. If the risk of detection is low, or the probability of sanctions is low, they may be prepared to gamble on being caught. This is illustrated by drivers' attitude to traffic regulations. Similarly, in places of work there are frequent breaches of minor regulations. Where punishment is applied, particularly if perceived as unfair, it may cause resentment and a desire for revenge.

Self-interest
We are more likely to obey rules that have a direct bearing on our self-interest. For example, although drivers will commonly exceed the 30 miles an hour limit, they are less likely to drive on the right-hand side of the road since this would put themselves and their vehicle at risk. Employees need to understand why rules exist and how they affect their interests. Understanding the risks of serious injury is an important element in learning safety rules.

Conforming is normal
We are less likely to break rules when we see that most others are regularly complying. Consistent application of rules is needed. Personal compliance is an indication of the value a manager or supervisor places on a rule. For example, it is difficult to take punctuality seriously if senior staff regularly flout the rules.

Task

Make a list of the main rules you are expected to follow in the institution (university, college, place of work) you attend. Do you have a copy of the rules? If so, check to see if you have remembered them accurately.

Why do people break rules?

Ignorance of the rules
In large organisations rules may be numerous and detailed. New employees should be given a copy of the rules when they join an organisation. They are unlikely to find it riveting reading, however, so induction procedures should also include coverage of disciplinary rules. Even

then, new employees may be so overloaded with information that reminders may be necessary at later stages of employment. These could be in the form of prominent notices in the workplace and oral reminders from supervisors. Failure to do so may undermine an employer's case for dismissal for a breach of discipline.

Unable to conform

An employee who has not been given adequate training could not be expected to conform to rules of performance on quality and pace of work. An employee also cannot be expected, reasonably, to conform to contradictory rules, as cited in the case of the transport drivers.

Particular rules are considered pointless

Rules should be reviewed regularly and, when they serve no current useful purpose, they should be scrapped. Some rules on dress code at work, active 15 years ago, would appear ludicrous to present employees. Where the purpose of a currently disregarded rule is valid, it should be justified to the staff and consistently implemented.

Selfishness / carelessness

Employees may do damage to the business, property, themselves and others by careless acts. They may also knowingly break rules for selfish gain. For example, IT technicians in an organisation were running their own small electronics repair business, using the employer's time, facilities and equipment. Quite clearly they knew they were doing wrong, but were tempted by the money.

Handling disciplinary problems

For the purpose of analysis and explanation, we divide approaches to staff problems into categories: fact-finding, counselling, reprimand, and grievances. In practice, the supervisor or manager may be faced with a staff problem that is messy and confused. A methodical approach is needed to handle the problem rationally. The five stages in problem-solving are as follows:

1 Define the problem and fix the objectives for its solution
  – What am I trying to achieve?

Case Study

Reducing lost time

A long-stay hospital was situated seven or eight miles from the nearest city. For staff without cars, the hospital arranged for bus companies to run special buses along various set routes through the city to bring staff to and from work. Staff missing the special transport had to catch the country route buses which did not arrive until half an hour after the start of the shift.

A newly appointed nursing manager was appalled at the time lost through lateness. She decided to interview personally all staff arriving late. The effect was immediate. Lateness dropped dramatically, but one-day absences increased. Over a six-month period total lost time increased. The action had converted lateness into one day absences.

The ultimate objective in the problem was patient care. Absent staff cannot provide patient care. This is not to advocate a soft approach on punctuality. However, if the manager had focused on an objective of reducing lost time in total, she might have made a deeper and more constructive analysis of the problem.

2 Analyse the problem in light of the objectives
  – What do I need to know about the problem and where can I obtain the information? The sources are other people, records and direct observation.
  – What are my limitations in handling this problem? They could be resources, time, authority, rules and procedure.

Task

What information would have been useful to the nursing manager in the previous case study? How might she have collected it?

3 Consider the possible alternative solutions and choose the most appropriate one
  – What are the alternatives?
  – How do they compare in respect of achieving the objectives?
  – What problems might be created by the alternative solutions?

4 Implement the decision
  – Who do I need to tell?
  – How and when should I tell them?
  – What progress reports do I want?

5 Follow up the decision
  – Was the decision effective?
  – What have I learned from the experience?

Case Study

The time-keeping problem

Joan Morgan is the recently appointed office manager of the bought-out goods department. Office hours are 8.30-12.30 and 1.30-5.00. Joan's predecessor used to arrive at 8.45 a.m. Most of the staff arrived between 8.30 and 8.45 a.m. Some of the staff used to slip out before 5 p.m. by a rear exit. Soon after taking up her appointment, Joan wrote a memo in polite terms asking that staff should be punctual and not leave before time. It had the desired effect.

Six months later, the staff were reverting to their old habits. Joan noticed two of the staff leaving before 5 p.m. They admitted they were leaving early but said they were not the only ones. The next day Joan wrote another memo, in similar terms to the previous one.

A week later, Joan returns at 4.50 p.m. from a meeting and sees a section supervisor leaving by the rear exit. She is wearing outdoor clothes and she is carrying her handbag and shopping basket. A couple of paces behind her is a word-processing operator from another section, similarly attired. As Joan approaches, both of them avoid looking at her and show every intention of passing without saying anything.

Notes
- The section supervisor has got two years to go to retirement. She has 21 years' service, interrupted by marriage, in this one office. She frequently works unpaid overtime to assemble information at short notice for the head buyer, Joan's immediate boss. The head buyer rates the supervisor highly.

- There are several exits in the office block. All must remain open during the day. All exits are used legitimately to shorten journeys about the large site. Only the main entrance has a doorman.
- There is no clocking-in procedure or official flexitime. Introduction of these would require agreement by central personnel. This is unlikely.

Question for discussion

Take the problem from the point where the two staff are approaching Joan Morgan. If you were her, what would you do at that point and subsequently? Use the framework of the problem solving approach, discussed above, to tackle the case.

Interview techniques

At some stage in handling disciplinary problems, managers need to talk to staff. Their approach should be dictated by their purpose at the time. For fact-finding the approach needs to be non-accusatory, neutral and objective. For counselling the approach needs to be encouraging, analytical and supportive. Where the facts have been established and a reprimand is warranted, the approach should be direct, explicit and formal.

Advice is given below on interview techniques. Take any opportunity offered in your studies to practise with role play. To minimise the pressure of performing in public, break into groups of three or four. Two should play the roles of the manager and the member of staff involved; the other one or two members should act as observers and give structured feedback, using the observer checklists at the end of this chapter.

Counselling

The counselling approach is particularly suitable when the work problem is rooted in the personal circumstances of the employee. In this approach the manager helps the employee to analyse the problem and reach his or her own solution. The counselling interview is concerned with the following issues:

- What is the employee's problem?
- What does it mean to the employee?
- How does it make the employee feel and act?
- What can the employer do about it? What are the alternatives?
- What will the employee do about it? How can he or she do it?

The manager acts as a **sympathetic listener** and catalyst, while setting acceptable limits for the solution of the problem. The interviewer should always:

- allow plenty of time for the interview
- choose somewhere private and free from interruption
- prepare for the interview by collecting information about the work problem, the interviewee's work record and personal background.

There are three stages of a counselling interview: attending, responding, and guiding.

Attending

State the work problem in a quiet, non-accusatory manner. Explain that you want to help to find a solution. Encourage the employee to explain his or her view of the problem. The initial task is to establish rapport and trust. The interviewee will read your attitude from both your comments and your behaviour.

Show your attentiveness by your non-verbal behaviour. Turn your body to the speaker. Lean forward. Maintain eye-contact. Give small nods of the head to register comprehension. Show appropriate facial expression.

Repress the temptation to correct or interpret the speaker's statements at this stage. Check you have understood his or her point of view by reflecting statements back:

'As I understand it you . . . '
'You feel that . . . '
'Let me just recap . . . '

The aim is to make it acceptable for the interviewee to give you an honest view of his or her thoughts and feelings.

Responding

Once rapport is established and the employee is speaking freely, you can make a more positive contribution. There are four common types of response:

- *A supportive response.* These express understanding and sympathy for the interviewee's feelings, e.g. – 'That must be difficult for you'. It helps to create an encouraging climate for someone who is agitated, anxious or depressed.
- *A probing response.* A stressed employee is unlikely to give a coherent account first time. As the interview progresses you can start to fill in the gaps by following up leads:
  'Did you say that . . . ?'
  'How long have you . . . ?'
  'Why . . . ?'
  It is important to avoid an accusatory tone. It should be apparent that your purpose is to get a clear picture rather than conduct a cross-examination.
- *An interpretive response.* As you come to understand the problem more clearly, you should start to look for causes and ways of explaining the situation. You need

to check these to confirm with the interviewee that you are on the right lines and that you are not simply imposing your own interpretation. The kinds of questions are:
  'The problem appears to be . . . ?'
  'Is it fair to say that . . . ?'
  'It seems that . . . ?'
- *An advising response.* In some situations, it may be appropriate for you to give more direct advice, not to impose a solution but to give the employee a steer in the direction where he or she may find a solution:
  'Have you thought about . . . ?'
  'Would you like me to make arrangements for you to . . . ?'
  'Why don't you go and have a look at . . . ?'

Guiding

The guiding phase must come at the end. Guidance should not be attempted until the problem has been fully explained. Quite often, this phase will be brief. By the time the interviewee has thought through the problem and has been helped to analyse it, he or she should be able to see the way ahead. Use questions like:

'How can you avoid that in the future . . . ?'
'What do you think your options are . . . ?'

Guiding has two objectives:

- formulating clear goals for the solution of the problem
- agreeing and summarising action to attain those goals.

You have the responsibility for seeing that the company's legitimate goals – attendance and work performance – are met. These are the limits within which you are trying to help the employee to solve any personal problems that are frustrating those goals. There are two cautions to make. Firstly, you need to be aware of your limitations, and know when to refer to professionals such as marriage guidance counsellors, or legal experts. Secondly, in the unlikely event of counselling developing into a disciplinary situation, the interview should be concluded, otherwise the employee's rights of representation are being frustrated.

Task

Practise your counselling skills by role-playing the following situation. Get two of your colleagues to help. One can play the role of the trainee. A brief is given in Appendix 1 at the end of this chapter. The other can act as an observer and give you feedback, using the checklist in Appendix 2.

The trainee technician problem

You are a manager about to interview one of your trainee technicians. He/she attends one day a week at a local college on a three-year course, and will sit the second year's examinations in three months' time. In the first year the trainee had excellent reports. However, you have heard from the college that recently his/her standard has slipped and there are two assignments overdue.

As part of his/her internal training, the trainee spends three months at a time in different departments and has to write a report on the work of each of them. During the past two months there have been adverse reports from the departments about his/her work. He/she is apparently often tired, unenthusiastic and has not completed the report from the previous department.

The trainee is getting married in six months' time and it is rumoured that he/she has taken a part-time job. There are no explicit rules on part-time work, but the practice is frowned upon for trainees. Trainees get a £1500 per annum increase on qualification.

Prepare yourself and then conduct the interview.

Disciplinary interviews

If the following procedure is adhered to, disciplinary interviews are more likely to be successful.

Before the interview

- Fix an appointment with the employee. Tell the employee what the complaint is and that he or she has a right to be accompanied by a friend or union representative.
- Make sure that you have all the facts about the alleged incident and other relevant information such as written statements of witnesses, and the employee's personal details and disciplinary record.
- Check what actions have been taken in similar incidents in the past.
- If possible, arrange for another member of the management team to be present to take notes and act as a witness.

During the interview

- Introduce all present to the employee.
- Explain the purpose of the interview and the procedure.
- State the complaint and the supporting evidence.
- Listen attentively to the employee's case. Question as necessary. The aim is to establish the truth.
- Be formal but polite. Do not get involved in argument. Do not make threats or personal remarks.
- Summarise the main points, including those made by the employee, and matters still to be decided.
- Adjourn to consider the case.

After the interview

- Check any unresolved issues.
- Take into account the employee's disciplinary record, general work record and the relevant circumstances such as provocation, health, or domestic problems.
- Decide the penalty. The normal procedure is a formal oral warning for a minor offence. A formal written warning is given for a more serious offence or for a succession of minor offences. The employee may be dismissed without notice for gross misconduct or for breaches of discipline after a final warning.
- Tell the employee the decision face to face. Explain the reasons. Following a warning, it should be made clear what improvement is required and by when.
- Details of the incident, the decision and the date should be recorded in a confidential file. Assuming no further offence is committed within a specified period, usually six months to a year, the record should be disregarded.
- After the hearing, the employee's behaviour should be monitored to see that any agreement is met.
- If dismissed, employees with more than two years' service have the right to a written statement of the reasons for their dismissal.

Advisory, Conciliation and Arbitration Service (ACAS)

This independent body was established under the Employment Protection Act 1975 to help improve industrial relations. The main work of ACAS is to provide:

- *Advice.* ACAS regional staff are available to offer advice to trade unions, employers and individuals.
- *Conciliation.* Conciliation officers are available to help management and trade unions to settle disputes, whether groups or individuals.
- *Arbitration.* ACAS can make arrangements for arbitration in a dispute, provided both parties want it.
- *Codes of practice.* Under the terms of the Employment Protection Act, ACAS is required to provide guidance for improving industrial relations. Their advice is published in the form of codes of practice. Action cannot be taken against an employer for not following

a code's provisions but, in cases of unfair dismissal, industrial tribunals may take into account whether or not an employer complied with the code's recommendations.

Code of practice – disciplinary practice and procedures

The following is a summary of the main recommendations:

- A copy of the organisation's rules and disciplinary procedure should be given to all employees.
- The procedures should not be prolonged.
- Employees should be told what the complaint is and given the opportunity to defend themselves.
- They should have the right at any meeting to be accompanied by a representative of their choice.
- Incidents should be thoroughly investigated before disciplinary action is taken.
- Immediate supervisors should not have the right to dismiss without reference to senior management.
- No one should be dismissed for a first offence except for gross misconduct.
- Any disciplinary penalty should be explained and employees should know their right of appeal.
- Minor offences warrant an oral warning. More serious offences carry a written warning.
- Special procedures should be made for night-shift workers and those in isolated situations.
- No action should be taken, other than an oral warning, against a trade union official until a senior trade union representative or full-time official has been consulted.

Industrial tribunals

Industrial tribunals were first set up under the Industrial Training Act 1964. They operate now under the Employment Protection Act. They hear cases for unfair dismissal, racial and sexual discrimination, failure to provide written terms of employment, claims for equal pay and redundancy pay. Claims for unfair dismissal account for more than half of their case load.

An industrial tribunal consists of a legally qualified chairman and lay representatives chosen from lists submitted by employer and employee organisations. The person bringing a complaint to the tribunal is known as the **applicant.** The person resisting the complaint is the **respondent.** Both the applicant and the respondent may represent themselves, thus avoiding legal costs. They may choose to be represented by another suitable person or legal counsel.

Tribunal proceedings

Proceedings at tribunals are relatively informal. The chairperson may guide and lead those who are uncertain how to proceed. Witnesses can be called to give evidence under oath. They may be questioned by either side and by the tribunal. Applicants and respondents may be questioned by each other and by the tribunal. The burden of proof is on the applicant. Decision is by majority vote, but most judgements are unanimous.

Tribunal's powers

Where an employee is found to have been wrongfully dismissed, the tribunal may order:

- *reinstatement* of the employee into his or her original job.
- *re-engagement* into an equivalent job
- *compensation* paid to the applicant by the respondent. Such awards may have two elements:
  - basic award based, like redundancy payments, on length of service, age and earnings
  - compensation based on estimated net losses.

Compensation is more common than re-engagement or reinstatement. It is difficult to re-establish a damaged relationship, and in some cases the employee may have got another job in the meantime.

Taking a claim to an industrial tribunal

All formal complaints of unfair dismissal are automatically passed to ACAS for consideration. The function is separate from the industrial tribunal. A conciliation officer from ACAS attempts to approach both the employer and the individual.

There is no compulsion on either party to take part or to settle the claim. Assuming the company's internal procedure has been exhausted, the conciliation officer will explore whether the employer is prepared to re-employ the member of staff or, otherwise, what voluntary compensation the employer is prepared to pay. With the employee, the conciliation officer will explore whether the preferred settlement is re-employment or compensation and whether he or she is prepared to settle without proceeding to an industrial tribunal.

In recent years the proportion of cases proceeding to tribunal has dropped from one-third to one-sixth. For the employer, this avoids adverse publicity and voluntary settlements are lower, on average, than tribunal awards.

Grievances

A grievance is a real or imagined cause for complaint. It usually involves issues of comparative justice. The employees feel that they have been treated less well than others or less well than their entitlement. Strong feelings can be roused over issues that, to an outsider, may appear trivial. It is not only junior people who behave in this way. Managers' feelings can be aroused by the allocation of status symbols, such as car-parking spaces and the standard of furnishing in private offices.

Preventing grievances

Managers and supervisors should be sensitive to issues of comparative justice. Some examples are:

- assignment to unpopular shifts
- assignment to unpopular tasks
- allocation of preferred equipment, vehicles, space and furniture
- allocation of preferred holiday dates
- appraisal ratings
- job gradings
- pay increments
- promotions
- inconsistent application of rules
- different personal manner to different employees.

Grievances arise from a perceived denial of rights, for example sexual or racial harassment, abusive personal manner, unpleasant working conditions and excessive overtime. Even if a grievance is objectively untrue, it will continue to affect the employees' behaviour as long as they *believe* it to be true. The way a manager operates affects the probability of grievances occurring.

Handle changes sensitively

A manager should tell employees face to face, and early, the reasons for any changes or unavoidable problems.

- Explain why the change is necessary. Most people resent arbitrary change.
- Make clear the expected benefits since these justify the change. Wherever possible, try to connect the benefits to the staff's interests. For example, increased efficiency may make the company more viable and the employees' jobs more secure.
- Anticipate the staff's anxieties about the change and explain what management plans to do about them. Give any authorised assurances.
- Explain what you want the staff to do and when. These are the 'mechanics' of the change and are often the

primary focus of management – to the neglect of the benefits and anxieties which are the staff's primary concern.
- Encourage questions. It is better for issues to be raised openly, so the manager can deal with them, than for complaints to fester in sub-group gossip.

Listen carefully and act promptly

Unresolved grievances sour relationships and diminish commitment to work. It is generally in the interest of the manager to have grievances expressed openly as there is then a better chance of either resolving the perceived grievance or helping the complainant to accept the situation. Many managers dislike handling grievances because they take time and may require the managers to tackle their own seniors or other departments. Consequently, many managers develop defence mechanisms: they are unapproachable; they belittle or dismiss complaints without investigation. To a manager sitting in a warm private office, employees complaining about their cold room may seem an unwelcome interruption to his or her other urgent tasks. The employees' perspective is quite different.

Be fair and be seen to be fair

Enforce rules realistically, consistently and fairly. Do not lay yourself open to a charge of favouritism. Assign unpopular shifts and unpleasant tasks with careful thought and explain the basis of your decisions so that the fairness is apparent. Sometimes such decisions are more acceptable if they can be reached through team consultation. The supervisor or manager remains responsible for the outcome and must therefore approve the final decision.

Case Study
Bought-out goods department – holiday arrangements

Joan Morgan is the manager of the bought-out goods department. The department's organisational structure is shown in Figure 20.1. It is October and she has just completed her first five months in the post.

For a fortnight in summer, Joan had to work until 7.30 p.m. because the assistant manager and the tax section supervisor were on holiday at the same time. Joan was often harassed to provide cover for the personal assistants and pricing assistants on holiday.

Figure 20.1 Organisational structure of the bought-out goods department

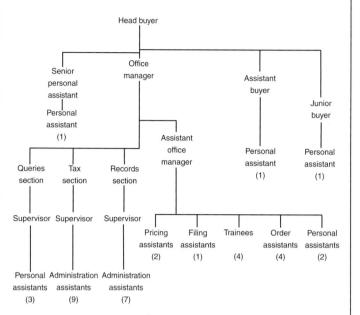

Considering the situation, Joan has noted the following points on her pad:

- Holiday entitlement per person is three weeks.
- Company policy:
  - Holidays may be taken at any time convenient to the departmental manager. Employees are told in the leaflet issued by the personnel department that one week may have to be taken out of the holiday season, between October and May.
- Present practice in the bought-out goods department:
  - Personal assistants clear their proposed dates with the person from whom they normally take dictation.
  - The administrative assistants on the records and tax sections clear their dates with their respective supervisors.
  - The office manager, assistant manager and section supervisors all decide their dates independently.
  - All others come to what arrangements they can between themselves.
  Dates, once fixed, are notified to the assistant manager who keeps the holiday list in his drawer. At the appropriate time he notifies the salaries department of the absences.
- Most of the staff take their holidays in late July, August and early September. Some of the staff have children of school age. Some have spouses whose holiday dates are fixed by their firms closing for annual holiday. Two or three of the personal assistants go away on holiday together.

- The work cycle on each section is different:
  - *Tax section:* all work must be completed by the quarter end.
  - *Queries section:* no query should be held for more than three days.
  - *Records section:* no deadline as such; the records are always out of date – a source of exasperation for the buyers.
  - *Order processing:* all orders must be processed and mailed on the same day as the requisition is received.
  - *Filing:* no deadline, but backlogs of filing cause considerable inconvenience in tracing orders.
  - *Correspondence:* policy is to reply to all letters on the day of receipt.
- Only five of the nine personal assistants are considered sufficiently skilled and experienced to handle the correspondence of the buyers. The nine include the head buyer's personal assistant.

Questions for discussion

Assume you are the office manager.
1 *What policy will you adopt for the following year's holidays? Define it in detail (priorities over dates, etc).*
2 *Draft your announcement to the staff. Will you give it orally or in writing? Why?*
3 *Prepare any charts you think would be useful.*
4 *What problems do you think your arrangements will solve?*
5 *What problems might they raise? How will you deal with them?*

Grievance procedures

Organisations should have a written grievance procedure. All employees should have a copy. The aim of a grievance procedure is the prompt resolution of complaints about employment issues. The formal procedure usually consists of three stages:

- The aggrieved employee approaches his or her immediate boss and may choose to be accompanied by a colleague or union representative. The boss should give a decision within a specified time – usually a matter of days.
- If the employee is still dissatisfied he or she has the right to put the complaint to the next level of management, again accompanied if desired. There is a time limit for management to respond – usually a week.
- The final stage of the internal procedure for a dissatisfied employee is an appeal against the decision outside line management – to, for example, the group

personnel manager, a director, or an outside body as defined in the procedure.

Organisations' procedures vary in detail, but the principles are the same: prompt hearings, fair treatment and the right of appeal. The purpose is to resolve problems internally and quickly before they escalate. Failure may result in an industrial dispute or an industrial tribunal hearing.

Handling a grievance

- Know and follow the company's grievance procedure. Talk somewhere private and free from interruption. An audience adds to the tension and may make the manager unduly anxious about his or her dignity.
- Ask what the complaint is and let the employee speak freely. If an employee thinks that those in authority will interpret the situation in the same way as the complainant, the complaint will be expressed openly and directly. This is seldom the case. Opposition is expected. Frustration builds up and the employee may open the encounter aggressively, determined not to be brushed aside. An immature manager will respond aggressively to the apparent insubordination and thus make the matter worse. It is better to let the employee discharge his or her emotion. Keep calm. Listen carefully and signal attention with appropriate non-verbal communication. Do not interrupt at this stage, even though you may recognise incorrect statements. Do not offer instant solutions. Hear out the whole complaint.
- Make certain that you understand what the complaint is and how the employee feels about it. You may need to piece it together. An emotionally charged person is unlikely to give a coherent account. Use summaries to check your understanding and to give opportunity for clarification:
    'Can I just check . . . ?'
    'As I understand it . . . ?'
    'Am I right in saying that you feel . . . ?'
  This formula allows you to check without committing yourself to the other person's point of view. Once the complainant has had a chance to calm down, he or she may begin to amend any extreme statements.
- When you understand the employee's version of the complaint, use questions to probe for facts. If the story is involved, ask for permission to take notes. This can signal that you are taking the complaint seriously and is useful if the grievance goes beyond the first stage. Check your notes back with the complainant.
- Avoid hurried decisions. You may need time to consider any wider implications and check on policy and rules. You may regret snap decisions that placate the complainant, but create an awkward precedent.

For example, an unpopular shift or rota may be difficult for members of staff with heavy domestic commitments. However, allowing them to opt out may cause resentment from other staff similarly placed. It may make it difficult to meet the work deadlines. Tell the employee when to expect a decision.

- Recall the employee. Give the decision and explain carefully why it was reached. If the person is still dissatisfied, explain the rights of appeal under the procedure. Brief your senior if an appeal is likely, so that all the information and the background is available at the outset.
- Take any promised action promptly. Goodwill can soon be dissipated by delay.

Task

Practise your interview skills by role-playing the following grievance interview. There should be three or four people in each practice group: the manager, J. Richards, and one or two, observers. There is a brief for J. Richards in Appendix 3 at the end of this chapter, and an observer's checklist in Appendix 4. After role-playing, discuss how the interview developed and what the next step might be.

Grievance 1 – the scenario

You are the manager of an office. In your department there is a small partition room on the north side of the building. Ten of your staff work in it. Although the office block is new, you have had three complaints already that it is cold in this small room. The company heating engineer has been twice at your request to take readings, and has assured you on both occasions that the temperature was adequate.

It is Monday morning and J. Richards, an administrative assistant who works in the small room, knocks on your door and enters your private office. You know this employee to be someone who stands up for his or her rights. Take the grievance interview from there.

Task

After discussion of the above exercise, try handling the following more complicated grievance. You will need a group of four or five: the manager, J. Johnson (brief in

Appendix 5), G. Green (brief in Appendix 6), and one or two observers (check list in Appendix 4).

Grievance 2 – the scenario
You are the recently appointed manager of a large open-plan office. There are 30 staff, organised into four sections with a supervisor in charge of each. *You are about to hear a complaint from the supervisor of the records section, G. Green. It will involve another of your supervisors, J. Johnson of the tax section. The two sections occupy adjacent areas of the open office.*

G. Green, who is 50, has worked in the department for 18 years, the last six years as the supervisor of the records section.

He/she is conscientious and hard-working but, you suspect, a poor supervisor. You think the work rate of the section is low, but you have no proof at this stage. When you have had more time to settle into your post, you are going to have to do something to improve the work rate of this section. G. Green is quick tempered.

J. Johnson is 38. He/she has worked for the organisation for 15 years. A year ago, a personnel department notice advertised a vacancy for the supervisor of the tax section. J. Johnson applied for the post and was successful. Previously he/she worked in the audit department. J. Johnson is keen. From what you have seen so far he/she is a good supervisor. The staff seem to work well and deadlines are met.

Consultants have been surveying the work of another department. This has unsettled some of your staff. You do not know yet if your department will also be surveyed.

Further reading

- *Croner's Reference Book for Employers* edited by P. Tover. Croner Publications Ltd, 1996.
- *Discipline at Work* by ACAS, 1990.
- *Handbook of Industrial Relations Practice* edited by Brian Towers. Kogan Page, 1992.
- *Handbook of Personnel Management Practice* by M. Armstrong. Kogan Page, 1995.
- *Personnel Management* by G. A. Cole. DP Publications, 1993.

Appendix 1: The trainee technician problem
Brief for the trainee

The allegations in the interviewer's brief are true. You and your partner are converting an old cottage outside the city. You are doing much of the work yourselves. You want it ready by the time you marry in six months' time. Unfortunately, however, you have underestimated the costs of the conversion. To raise money you and a friend buy seconds in bulk from local textile firms and sell them at a Saturday market. Most weeks your profit is more than your trainee technician's salary. Most of your friends earn more than you do, without having to study. You like your work, but you are becoming disillusioned with the prospects. With the work on the cottage, and the market work, you have got behind with two college assignments and one work report.

Tactics during the interview
Start off nervous and defensive. Stress your previous good record. Don't volunteer much information initially. Respond to the way you are treated. If it is sympathetic, be more co-operative. If it is authoritarian, hint that you were thinking of leaving. Be prepared to compromise, but get the best deal you can. Try to get excused from the overdue report because of the pressure you are under.

Appendix 2: Counselling

Observer's check list

Attending
- Did the interviewer listen carefully?
- How did the interviewer signal attentiveness?
- What attitude did the interviewer's manner convey?
- How did the interviewer show understanding of the employee's problems?

Responding
Which of the following responses did the interviewer use?

- supportive
- probing
- interpretive
- advising

Quote examples.

Guiding
- What guidance was given? Was it appropriate?
- What action was agreed?
- Was it clearly summarised?

Appendix 3: Grievance role play 1

Brief for J. Richards

You and the other nine staff *know* the room is cold. The other nine complain between themselves, but are not prepared to tackle the manager. The room is cold in the mornings and you have complained twice before. Each time the heating engineer has waited until late afternoon, when the temperature has risen, before coming to take the readings. You regard this as a confidence trick.

Tactics during the interview
Start off aggressively – 'You'll have to do something about the heating.' Be sarcastic about the manager's nice warm office. Respond to the way you are treated. If the manager tries to fob you off, maintain the aggression and ask to speak to someone more senior.

Appendix 4: Grievance interviews

Observer's check list

- Did the interviewer make the employee comfortable?
- Did the interviewer listen carefully? How was this signalled?
- Did the interviewer avoid interrupting in the early stages?
- Did the interviewer avoid being drawn into argument?
- Did the interviewer interpret and summarise the complainant's case accurately?
- Did the interviewer avoid rash promises?
- Did the interviewer make clear what the next step would be?

Appendix 5: Grievance role play 2

Brief for J. Johnson

The incident

Mrs Jenkins was shouting across the office to a colleague. She has a piercing voice and was disturbing your section which was busy with the quarter end figures. After a few minutes you stood up. Noticing that G. Green was not about – as usual – you walked over and politely asked her to be quiet. At that moment, G. Green bobbed up from behind a cupboard and stormed across to you. You started to apologise and explain, but G. Green became so enraged that you walked away to avoid a scene in front of the staff.

Background

On several occasions before, in G. Green's frequent absences, you have had to speak to members of the records section about the noise they were making. You think G. Green is a hopeless supervisor. You dislike having the records section next to your section. Your staff can see a marked contrast between the work pace of the two sections and you think it makes it unnecessarily difficult for you to run your section properly. You had thought about speaking to the manager earlier, but you do not like complaining about a fellow supervisor, although you dislike G. Green. Now is the chance to expose him/her. You have tried talking to G. Green, but he/she will not discuss the problem of the noise rationally.

Appendix 6: Grievance role play 2

Brief for G. Green

The incident

You were bending at the cupboard getting some documents (omit this in your account of the incident). J. Johnson, supervisor of the tax section, came over and reprimanded, in your presence, one of your staff, Mrs Jenkins, for being noisy and not getting on with her work. You are furious. You told J. Johnson to mind his/her own business (omit reference to this in your account). You have come straight into the boss's office to complain. You expect the boss to reprimand J. Johnson.

Background

Mrs Jenkins was chatting to someone two desks away. Mrs Jenkins, who is a good worker, had completed a batch of work and was waiting for you to allocate the next batch from the cupboard.

On two previous occasions J. Johnson has reprimanded a member of your section in your absence. You do not like J. Johnson. You think he/she is an officious creep. You have heard a rumour that consultants are being brought in. You suspect that the records and tax sections will be combined. You think J. Johnson is jockeying for the position of supervisor of the combined sections. You do not approve of J. Johnson's methods of supervision. You think that to motivate staff you have to keep them happy – not breathe down their necks like "big brother".

If there is any hint in the interview that you are not doing your job properly, make the point that in six years you have never had any criticism of the way you supervise.

Action

Complain bitterly to the office manager about the incident, bringing up the following points:

- interference
- in your presence
- undermining your authority: J. Johnson should have complained to you
- upsetting your staff
- after your job.

7

Conclusion

There are always dangers associated with trying to predict figure changes. Not least of these difficulties is the fact that people in the future will want to make a break with the past. Today's good ideas, such as human resource management, will be modified or replaced by new models of working. We have a constant wish to reinvent patterns of working relationships and ways of doing things. Hopefully we will be able to welcome these changes.

The growing influence of human resource management

In recent times, human resource management has become an established way of running many organisations. And it is not just the large organisations that have taken on board this approach. For example, recent research by a team at Loughborough University has shown that increasing numbers of small firms are using new initiatives such as culture change programmes, devolved management, teamworking, performance appraisal, the use of mission statements, team briefings, quality circles, harmonised terms and conditions, psychometric testing, delayering, and increased flexibility. If we accept David Guest's definition of human resource management (*Journal of Management Studies*, September 1987) – a set of policies designed to maximise organisational integration, employee commitment, flexibility and quality of work – then we find such patterns emerging in many (although not all) organisations.

A way of thinking

However, as we have seen in this book, HRM goes beyond a set of policies. More importantly it is expressed as a mission which establishes the need for an alternative form of management. The appropriate management style is one which is proactive rather than reactive. It treats the labour force as the key resource rather than a cost and is goal-orientated rather than depending on relationships. Above all, it is based on **commitment** by employees rather than compliance.

An environment of change

Enhanced communication, globalisation and improved technology have put the pressure on organisations to find ways of winning business. This has made it necessary for organisations to rely increasingly on the intelligence of their workforces. Many employees today have been given the scope to think for themselves and to identify improvements in working practices. Tapping these abilities provides employees with a route to increasing productivity and effectiveness. Managers need to find ways of supporting employees in a process of continual development which aids the employees and the organisation. From the employees' point of view it makes sound sense to look after the firm they are working for, to enhance its success and thus to improve their own job security and opportunities for job development. Commitment is a two-way process. Learning faster may be the only sustainable competitive advantage.

The importance of flexibility

In today's market it is important to be a flexible organisation which is able to adjust to change. By gaining the support and commitment of the workforce, it is easier to introduce and carry out change, and then follow this up with sustained competitive advantage.

The importance of diversity

Tom Peters, in his recent book *The Pursuit of WOW!*, has argued that the successful organisation of the future will be the one that makes the best use of the diversity of its human resource. If your Board of Directors is made up of 15 white males in grey suits, they may all have very similar experiences to draw on. However, if you employ a team with diverse backgrounds and experiences, they will be able to draw on this range of knowledge to tackle problems. The diverse team is the one which is most likely to come up with the creative ideas in 'topsy-turvy' times. The benefits obtained through teamworking are easy to understand; the harnessing of diversity leads to better decisions, reduced friction and a more satisfied workforce. Similarly, the productivity gains that teamwork and flexibility can provide support the claim that 'the whole is greater than the sum of the parts'.

The importance of trust

Empowerment is a way of thinking and working designed to enable everyone who has a good idea for improvement to carry the idea through, taking ownership of the idea themselves or in a team. It is part of a larger organisational structure which must have a supporting culture at its foundation. Empowerment therefore needs to be built on a solid foundation of existing practices such as teamworking, trained facilitators and quality circles. In *The Pursuit of WOW!*, Tom Peters argues that

> *'Hierarchies are going, going, gone. The average Mary or Mike is being asked to take on extraordinary responsibility. He or she may be on the payroll or, at least as likely, an independent contractor. In any event, the hyperfast-moving, wired-up, re-engineered, quality-obsessed organisation – virtual or not – will succeed or fail on the strength of the trust that the remaining, tiny cadre of managers places in the folks working on the front line.'*

The importance of the 'people company'

In this book we have made a distinction between the **people company** and the **machine company**, arguing that the old type of machine organisation has been replaced by a people-centred focus through human resource management. A family business is the most obvious example of a people company. What counts is the family who runs it.

For their continuing success, family companies require a succession of talented sons and daughters, followed by talented grandsons and granddaughters and so on. However, in the course of time these companies tend to be taken over by talented outsiders. Nonetheless, the ideal of the family company, with staff treated as **members**, lives on, even if the levels of qualifications for continued membership are constantly rising. Such a company will be more likely to enjoy employee loyalty.

Loyalty in a sense can be bought. The machine company that pays the best wages and salaries can expect its employees to continue working for its best interests. But in times of difficulty when the wages and salaries fall, so does the loyalty, and the company suffers. The people company is better placed. Even in prosperity, it will tend to do better than the machine company. People are people, they are not machines. They will generally prefer to work in a people company.

Seeing beyond the three Cs

Across Europe, many organisations have been engaged in large-scale restructuring as they have slimmed down their management hierarchies to speed up decision-making. At the same time we have seen the delayering of other parts of the organisation as more and more jobs are shed. The driving force behind many of these changes has been the 'three Cs of business' – namely **costs, competitors** and **customers.**

Increasingly, aggressive international competition, the impact of new technologies, and existing overcapacity on many organisations have forced a slimming-down process. On the downside this means that organisations have had to reduce their workforces and break away from existing relationships with people who may have come to expect 'a job for life'. On the positive side, however, in the drive to improve performance, organisations have started to employ approaches which involve placing the development of employees at the top of their agenda. Increasingly organisations are developing new cultures in which empowerment is the driving force. Organisations are adopting human resource approaches in which individual and team development is given a priority rating. This has become the focus for success.

Today, individuals need to understand that the world of work has changed. They no longer have the guarantee of a job. Instead, they need to engage in a process of lifelong learning and to prepare themselves for a portfolio of careers. Increasingly they will need to sell their experience, knowledge, approaches and skills to buying organisations. For many this will be a challenge with substantial rewards which, of course, will be accompanied by periods of anxiety and insecurity. For others, those with the fewest qualifications and skills, the future appears bleak and this is a Europe-wide picture. It is essential for these individuals to be placed on a learning and development ladder which provides them with a means of achieving success. No society can afford to ignore those who are least well equipped to cope with a changing world of work. A commitment model of organisation-wide and economic development requires a commitment to *all* members of society. Without this commitment the future will be bleak.

Further reading

- *The Empty Raincoat: Making Sense of the Future* by Charles Handy. Hutchinson, 1994.
- *The Pursuit of WOW!: Every Person's Guide to Topsy-turvy Times* by Tom Peters. Macmillan Press, 1995.
- *If You Mean Business!* by Bryan Oakes and Rob Dransfield. Shell Education, 1996.

Index